At the Margins of the Global Market

Contemporary scholars debate the factors driving despotic labor conditions across the world economy. Some emphasize the dominance of global market imperatives; others highlight the market's reliance on extra-economic coercion and state violence. *At the Margins of the Global Market* engages in this debate through a comparative and world-historical analysis of the labor regimes of three global commodity-producing sub-regions of rural Colombia: the coffee region of Viejo Caldas, the banana region of Urabá, and the coca/cocaine region of the Caguán. Drawing on insights from labor regimes, global commodity chains, and world historical sociology, this book offers a novel understanding of the broad range of factors – local, national, global, and interregional – that shape labor conditions on the ground in Colombia. In doing so, it offers a critical new framework for analyzing labor and development dynamics that exist at the margins of the global market.

Phillip A. Hough is a Colombian-American sociologist who specializes in political economy, labor and agrarian movements, global commodity studies, comparative and world historical sociology, and Latin American development. His current research focuses on labor/agrarian struggles, state and paramilitary violence, class and state formations, forced displacement, and surplus populations.

Development Trajectories in Global Value Chains

A feature of the current phase of globalization is the outsourcing of production tasks and services across borders, and the increasing organization of production and trade through global value chains (GVCs), global commodity chains (GCCs), and global production networks (GPNs). With a large and growing literature on GVCs, GCCs, and GPNs, this series is distinguished by its focus on the implications of these new production systems for economic, social, and regional development.

This series publishes a wide range of theoretical, methodological, and empirical works, both research monographs and edited volumes, dealing with crucial issues of transformation in the global economy. How do GVCs change the ways in which lead and supplier firms shape regional and international economies? How do they affect local and regional development trajectories, and what implications do they have for workers and their communities? How is the organization of value chains changing and how are these emerging forms contested as more traditional structures of North–South trade complemented and transformed by emerging South–South lead firms, investments, and trading links? How does the large- scale entry of women into value- chain production impact on gender relations? What opportunities and limits do GVCs create for economic and social upgrading and innovation? In what ways are GVCs changing the nature of work and the role of labor in the global economy? And how might the increasing focus on logistics management, financialization, or social standards and compliance portend important developments in the structure of regional economies?

This series includes contributions from all disciplines and interdisciplinary fields and approaches related to GVC analysis, including GCCs and GPNs, and is particularly focused on theoretically innovative and informed works that are grounded in the empirics of development related to these approaches. Through their focus on changing organizational forms, governance systems, and production relations, volumes in this series contribute to on- going conversations about theories of development and development policy in the contemporary era of globalization.

Series editors

Stephanie Barrientos is Professor of Global Development at the Global Development Institute, University of Manchester.

Gary Gereffi is Professor of Sociology and Director of the Global Value Chains Center, Duke University.

Dev Nathan is Visiting Professor at the Institute for Human Development, New Delhi, and Visiting Research Fellow at the Global Value Chains Center, Duke University.

John Pickles is Earl N. Phillips Distinguished Professor of International Studies at the University of North Carolina, Chapel Hill.

At the Margins of the Global Market
Making Commodities, Workers, and Crisis in Rural Colombia

Phillip A. Hough

Florida Atlantic University

CAMBRIDGE
UNIVERSITY PRESS

CAMBRIDGE
UNIVERSITY PRESS

Shaftesbury Road, Cambridge CB2 8EA, United Kingdom

One Liberty Plaza, 20th Floor, New York, NY 10006, USA

477 Williamstown Road, Port Melbourne, VIC 3207, Australia

314–321, 3rd Floor, Plot 3, Splendor Forum, Jasola District Centre, New Delhi – 110025, India

103 Penang Road, #05–06/07, Visioncrest Commercial, Singapore 238467

Cambridge University Press is part of Cambridge University Press & Assessment, a department of the University of Cambridge.

We share the University's mission to contribute to society through the pursuit of education, learning and research at the highest international levels of excellence.

www.cambridge.org
Information on this title: www.cambridge.org/9781009005760

DOI: 10.1017/9781009036757

First published 2022
First paperback edition 2023

A catalogue record for this publication is available from the British Library

Library of Congress Cataloging-in-Publication data
Names: Hough, Phillip A., author.
Title: At the margins of the global market : making commodities, workers, and crisis in rural Colombia / Phillip A. Hough, Florida Atlantic University.
Description: Cambridge, United Kingdom ; New York, NY : Cambridge University Press, 2021. | Series: Development trajectories in global value chains | Includes bibliographical references and index.
Identifiers: LCCN 2021026745 (print) | LCCN 2021026746 (ebook) | ISBN 9781316517109 (hardback) | ISBN 9781009005760 (paperback) | ISBN 9781009036757 (epub)
Subjects: LCSH: Coffee industry–Colombia. | Banana trade–Colombia. | Coca industry–Colombia. | Labor–Colombia. | Agricultural industries–Colombia. | Economic development–Colombia. | Colombia–Economic conditions. | Colombia–Social conditions. | BISAC: BUSINESS & ECONOMICS / International / General
Classification: LCC HD9014.C72 H68 2021 (print) | LCC HD9014.C72 (ebook) | DDC 338.109861–dc23
LC record available at https://lccn.loc.gov/2021026745
LC ebook record available at https://lccn.loc.gov/2021026746

ISBN   978-1-316-51710-9   Hardback
ISBN   978-1-009-00576-0   Paperback

Contents

Figures and Tables

Tables

Maps

Acknowledgments

The initial premises of this book were first explored in my doctoral dissertation at Johns Hopkins University, where I worked under the guidance of Beverly Silver and the late Giovanni Arrighi (1937–2009). Since my arrival at Florida Atlantic University in 2007, I pushed its conceptual framework in new directions, conducted new rounds of fieldwork, regularly updated and reanalyzed my longitudinal datasets on Colombian social protests and political violence, and tried my desperate best to keep up with the flood of secondary literature on the country's coffee, bananas, cattle, and cocaine industries. Until now, my research publications have only reflected small fragments of this work. It was through the writing of this book, however, that I have been able to pull the various strands of my research on Colombian labor regimes into one thread.

Like all books whose preparation spans such a long period of time, it would not have been possible without the help of numerous individuals and institutions. Funding for my fieldwork and data was made possible by a Fulbright scholarship (2003–4) and multiple FAU Morrow Fund Research Grants (2009, 2013, 2015). A fellowship from the American Council of Learned Societies (ACLS) in addition to a full-year sabbatical in (2018–19) gave me the time I needed to write a full first draft of the manuscript. Special thanks to Lesley Gill and Roberto Patricio Korzeniewicz for supporting my ACLS fellowship and to Ann Branaman, Cathy King, and Aimee Kanner Arias for working out the logistics of my sabbatical. I would also like to thank Beverly Silver, Marta Petrusewicsz, and Fortunata Piselli for organizing the "Capitalist Development in Hostile Environments" conference at the University of Calabria, Italy, in 2017, as well as Liam Campling and the editors of the *Journal of Agrarian Change* (JAC), who published a special issue on Arrighian agrarian political economy in 2019. The Calabria conference gave me an opportunity to test out some of the central claims of this book with some of the sharpest scholars of historical capitalism. The special issue of JAC (coedited with Jennifer Bair and Kevan Harris), which developed from conversations in Calabria, in turn, helped connect my ideas to contemporary debates in the field of agrarian political economy.

While conducting fieldwork in Colombia, I incurred countless debts to individuals who graciously offered hours of their time for interviews, field visits, and explanations of local institutions and practices. A full list of the activists, journalists, independent researchers, academics, government officials, industry representatives, and others who assisted me during this project would be exceedingly long. A few, however, went above and beyond and deserve special thanks. Jorge Enrique Robledo, Oscar Gutierrez Reyes, and Aurelio Suarez of Colombia's Movimiento Obrero Independiente Revolucionario (MOIR) and Dignidad Agropecuaria movement were eager to inform me of the latest news regarding agrarian issues and politics, supply me with hard data on trends, introduce me to fellow militants, and even set up meetings with their adversaries so that I could develop an informed perspective of Colombian agrarian politics. Conversations with Gilma Benitez of the Peasant Users Association (ANUC), Fabio Arias Giraldo of the Colombian Labor Federation (CUT), and labor-activist Enrique Daza were also helpful in providing national context to my interviews with Colombian workers and farmers. Angela Inés Villa Cardona, Alberto Rendón Ríos, Juan Guillermo Alba, and Juan Pablo Estupiñan, then students at the Universidad de los Andes where I was based, helped construct the original foundations of my longitudinal datasets. Angela also assisted me with a first round of field visits to Viejo Caldas in 2004.

My research on Colombia's coffee industry would not have been possible without the help of Christopher London, Oscar Gutierrez Reyes, Luis Fernando Samper, Carlos Andres Marín, Hernando Duque Duque, and Diana Pardo. I am also humbled by the hospitality of Jairo Rodriguez and Eduard Aníbal Ramírez Ocampo, who opened their homes to me during a bout of fieldwork in June 2015. In Urabá, Paul Wolf provided me with countless documents and legal memos, in addition to valuable contacts in Apartadó. Michael Evans also provided important legal details on the Chiquita Brands scandal. Alonzo Orozco, Carlos Mayorca, and Pedro Umaña helped establish my early footing in Caquetá. Estafania Ciro, Óscar Neira, Isabel Peñaranda, Rigoberto Rodriguez, and Alex Diamond, in turn, helped keep me up-to-date with the latest developments in the Caguán since the peace negotiations of 2016. Alejandro Cadena was always eager to provide me with the latest data from the Popular Education Research Center (CINEP) and Adriaan Anselma of *Colombia Reports* was quick to clarify any questions I had about late breaking news.

Outside Colombia, I have benefited immensely from a community of globe-trotting colleagues and friends whose own research around the globe has been a continual source of inspiration: Joel Andreas, Nicole Aschoff, Jennifer Bair, Ben Brewer, Alex Diamond, Yige Dong, Tim Gill, Kevan Harris, Amy Holmes, Ho-fung Hung, Ricado Jacobs, Sahan Savas Karatasli, Sefika Kumral, Michael Levien, Zach Levinson, Jason Moore, Manjusha Nair, Dan Pasciuti, Corey Patterson, Kristen Plys, Ben Scully, Beverly Silver, Shaohua Zhan, and Lu Zhang. I am also indebted to numerous colleagues and graduate students at Florida Atlantic University. Lynn Appleton, Farshad Araghi, Laura Backstrom, Ann Branaman, Mark Harvey, Carter Koppelman, Phil Lewin, Will McConnell, Sharon Placide, and Lotus Seeley have always kept their doors open to my queries and musings. I would also like to thank Alberto Gomez DaBoin, Jai Tumulo, Mayra Girasol, Paul Clements, Michael Suarez, Claudia Giribaldi, Rob MacPherson, Karthik Balaji Ramanujam, Jordanne Kessel, and David Sanchez for helping me update my longitudinal datasets and references; Lina Henao, Jackie Carassa, and Andrea Ruiz for helping transcribe some of my interviews; and Matthew Menendez and Ka-Kei Ng for their help in making this book's maps. Special thanks to the sociology students who enrolled in my Labor and Globalization (Spring 2018) and Economic Sociology (Spring 2020) seminars: Javier Acuña, Deborah Ford, Mayra Girasol, Alberto Gomez-DaBoin, Davyd Heasley, Jordanne Kessel, Ricky Konsavage, Christine Matragrano, David Sanchez, Amanda Sherrill, Nicola Spence-Burrell, Rand Sutton, Jai Tumulo, Lucas Lopez-Arrastia, Cassio Marques, Lisa Noel, Karthik Balaji Ramanujam, Adrian Rebegal, Frank Schioppa, Jessica Shoemaker, and Ernes Sifran. The labor seminar's focus on commodity chains helped me reconnect with some of the core secondary research on the global coffee, bananas, and cocaine industries. The economic sociology seminar's focus on twenty-first-century experiences of precarity and surplus populations, in turn, introduced me to contemporary writings on social reproduction that informed this book's conceptual framework. Perhaps without knowing it, these students' observations, comments, and critiques helped sharpen some of the key arguments of this book.

I received comments on drafts of this book that helped me clarify and strengthen my core arguments and empirical claims, sharpen my prose, and smooth out its rough edges. Jennifer Bair, Ben Brewer, Alex Diamond, Kevan Harris, Sefika Kumral, Manjusha Nair, Nancy Peluso, Kristen Plys, Aaron Tauss, and Frances Lynne Thomson provided detailed comments on various chapters of the book.

Of course, I am also indebted to Stephanie Barrientos, Gary Gereffi, Dev Nathan, John Pickles, and Jennifer Bair for enthusiastically including this book in their book series: Development Trajectories in Global Value Chains. Also special thanks to Valerie Appleby, Dhivyabharathi Elavazhagan, and Tobias Ginsberg for assistance with the backend of the publication process. Finally, thanks to Gour Sundar Saha for helping me with the book's index and to Alex Diamond for providing me with the cover image.

In addition to this scholarly and professional support, I have also been incredibly lucky to have a vast social support system of family in Bogotá, who have gone out of their way to make Colombia a home. *Un agradecimiento especial a* Sara

Gallardo, Gonzalo y Maria Constanza Sánchez, Gisella Sánchez, Alejandro y Maria Clara Sánchez, Henry Mauricio Gallardo. My parents, Charles and Maria Cristina Hough, have been enduring supporters of my work and constant travels, even if and when they feared that these pursuits were putting me in harm's way. Finally, I could not have written this book without the love and boundless support from my wife, Carrie. It is to Carrie and my kids, Olivia, Daniela, and Phillip Jr., that I dedicate this book.

Introduction

The Contradictions of Colombian Development

[Latin America's] crucial problem has been a lack of conventional means to render our lives believable ... It is only natural that they insist on measuring us with the yardstick that they use for themselves, forgetting that the ravages of life are not the same for all, and that the quest of our own identity is just as arduous and bloody for us as it was for them. The interpretation of our reality through patterns not our own, serves only to make us ever more unknown, ever less free, ever more solitary.

(Gabriel García Márquez, Nobel Address (1982))

Drugs, violence, mafias, death squads, guerrilla armies, authoritarianism, corruption, crisis, death. These are the images conjured when I tell people about my research on labor regime dynamics in rural Colombia. Sensationalized in popular films and mass media, Colombian society is often likened to its most valued export, cocaine, its politics a dysfunctional banana republic, and its population poor and powerless victims. To many consumers of these media images, people living predominantly in core centers of global capitalism, these depictions of Colombian everyday life might appear chaotic and surreal in comparison to the routinized, orderly, and lawful realities of their own social and economic livelihoods. Indeed, the juxtaposition of stereotypes of violent oppression and chaos in Colombia, and Latin America more generally, to the democratic orderliness and stability of the countries in the global north, sparked the ire of Colombia's Nobel prizewinner author, Gabriel García Márquez. In his 1982 Nobel address, García Márquez lambasted the hypocrisy of such sensationalized depictions and made an impassioned plea to international observers to critically reexamine the capitalist West's own arduous and bloody history and to analyze Latin American development using its own conceptual yardstick. This book is, in large part, an attempt to create such a yardstick.

Unfortunately, these sensational, albeit stereotypical, accounts of the violence and crisis of everyday life in Colombia are rooted in actual historical realities. Rural Colombians have experienced endemic low-intensity warfare from the country's early experiences with laissez-faire liberalism at the turn to the twentieth century, through the years of state-directed developmentalism in the decades following World War II, and into the present era of twenty-first-century neoliberal globalization. During the nineteenth century, partisan conflict between Conservative and Liberal parties resulted in at least nine full-scale civil wars. These hostilities climaxed at the turn of the century with the deadly "Thousand Day War" (1899–1902), which led to nearly three decades of uneasy Conservative party domination marked by labor-repressive state measures meant to open the economy to foreign investment. Another wave of political violence resurfaced in the late 1940s following the assassination of populist Liberal candidate, Jorge Eliécer Gaitán, on the streets of Bogotá in 1948. A period of violent urban unrest known as *El Bogotazo* spread to the countryside, where it morphed into a decade of intense rural partisan warfare known simply as *La Violencia* (1948–57) that pitted dissident Liberal and Communist insurgency groups against Conservative security forces and paramilitaries. This spiral of violence was initially constrained by a 1953 military coup headed by General Gustavo Rojas Pinilla, an independent initially backed by Liberal and Conservative party leaders. But Pinilla's incipient populism soon threatened the established class order, pressuring Colombia's political elites to put their squabbles aside and join forces to oust Rojas Pinilla. In the wake of Pinilla's ouster, they formed what became known as the National Front government (1958–74), a bipartisan power-sharing "gentleman's agreement" that rotated executive positions between parties, suppressed antiestablishment political participation by outlawing third-party candidates, and instituted "state of siege" measures to quell social unrest. The authoritarianism of the National Front regime, combined with its promotion of disruptive state-directed industrial development measures, fanned the flames of Colombian political violence again as a number of Marxist and left-populist armed insurgency groups including the National Liberation Army (ELN), Revolutionary Armed Forces of Colombia (FARC), Popular Liberation Army (EPL), and April 19th Movement (M-19) established bases of support among disaffected peasant communities, agricultural workers, urban proletarians, and radicalized students.

By the 1980s, hopes for a lasting solution to Colombia's endemic violence arose once again with the election of Belisario Betancur (1982–86), a liberal reformer who entered into peace negotiations with guerrilla groups and instituted a series of political democratization measures that dismantled the National Front system. His successors, Virgilio Barco (1986–90) and César Gaviria (1991–94), continued the democratization process that culminated in the writing of a new, more inclusive constitution in 1991 and the demobilization of some guerrilla groups. Despite these efforts, Colombian society became embroiled in ever deeper and more complex forms of violence. Narco-trafficking mafia groups like the Medellín and Cali Cartels and heavily armed right wing paramilitary groups like the Self-Defense Forces of Colombia (AUC) engaged in terrorist actions that undermined peace negotiations and democratization efforts, while extant guerrilla groups bolstered their war-making activities through engagement in the illegal drug trade, extortion, and kidnapping for ransom. After a failed peace negotiation with the FARC (1998–99), the Colombian government revamped its militarization response through "Plan Colombia." Ostensibly an institution-building initiative, the Plan became in essence a US-financed military effort that attacked guerrilla strongholds and facilitated the expansion of paramilitarism throughout the countryside. The election of hardline right wing President Álvaro Uribe (2002–10) escalated the militarization process by aligning the Colombian government's efforts with US President Bush's "War on Terror" initiatives, giving an implicit greenlight to paramilitaries to terrorize inhabitants of guerrilla strongholds and anyone else presumed to be complicit with them. By 2006, the balance of power shifted so far to the right that the Uribe government was able to oversee the demobilization and social reintegration of the AUC with impunity, offering little in the way of compensation to their victims. Soon thereafter, with guerrilla forces radically diminished, Uribe's predecessor, Juan Manuel Santos (2010–18) implemented peace talks with the country's largest group, the FARC, and began negotiations with the ELN. Despite the demobilization of armed groups on the right and left, incidents of rural violence continue into the present, as new, smaller paramilitary groups, drug trafficking cartels (*cartelitos*), and active splinter guerrilla factions now jockey for control of rural territories, resources, and populations.

The impact of this endemic violence in Colombia's countryside bears out in the numbers. According to Human Rights Watch's *World Report* 2019 (2019:151), violence associated with Colombia's armed conflict has led to the forced displacement of 8.1 million people since 1985, a shocking number of people in a country of just over 49 million in total.[1] Worse still, over 200,000 more rural residents have been displaced amid ongoing armed conflict since the signing of the Santos peace agreement in 2016, as new armed actors have struggled to fill the "power vacuum" left from the disarmament of the FARC. Predictably, this massive exodus from the countryside has itself compounded systemic problems of over-urbanization, crime, unemployment, and rural poverty. With guerrilla groups like the FARC pushed aside, Colombia has experienced an unprecedented wave of "narco land grabs" driven in large part by elaborate and often illegal land-

---

[1] The UN Refugee Agency (UNHCHR 2018:85) notes that Colombia's overall number of internally displaced persons since 1985 makes it the country with the largest number of IDPs in the world.

laundering schemes developed by Colombian elites that have concentrated a shocking 81% of the country's total productive land into the hands of 1% of the population.[2] And while rural Colombians have borne the brunt of this political violence, the primary targets of directed acts of repression and terror are leftist social activists, including community organizers, human rights workers, journalists, and especially labor leaders and union members. The International Trade Union Confederation's *Global Rights Index* reports (2016, 2018) find Colombia to be "the country with the highest number of [trade unionist] murders of any country. Over 2,500 unionists have been murdered in the past 20 years, more than in the rest of the world combined."

Colombia's protracted and seemingly exceptional tendency for social and political violence has spawned a vast body of scholarly literature that has focused on local conditions that have given rise to armed insurgency groups, drug trafficking mafias, and social unrest. Indeed, much ink has been spilt explaining Colombia's troublesome and endemic history of social and political violence over the past half century. In fact, there is even an informal group of Colombian scholars known as *violentólogos*, or specialists in the study of Colombian violence.[3]

This focus on violence, however, often overshadows a different, and in comparison paradoxical, side of Colombian social and political history. Most striking here is the fact that Colombia remains Latin America's most long-standing and stable electoral democracy. The country has held regular competitive elections with peaceful transfers of power consistently since the last century with few exceptions.[4] Of course, party politics in Colombia remains the exclusive affair of elites, corruption continues to permeate the country's political institutions, and voter turnout remains low.[5] Yet, much to the chagrin of the Colombian left, it is also true that the traditional parties and their recent offshoots continue to retain the loyalty of the vast majority of the country's voters.[6] Indeed, the hegemony of Colombia's traditional political establishment runs surprisingly deep. Explaining the country's political conservatism, Charles Bergquist (2001:203) argued that the

---

[2] Oxfam (2017:11, 14); see also Ballvé (2012); McSweeney et al. (2017).

[3] See Bergquist et al. (1992, 2001) for an overview of the work of Colombia's *violentólogos*.

[4] The 1953 coup of Gustavo Rojas Pinilla as well as the likely electoral fraud of the 1970 presidential election are two notable exceptions.

[5] Martz (1997); Pérez-Liñán (2001); Fornos et al. (2004); Palacios (2006). For contemporary trends in voter turnout, see IDEA (n.d., accessed December 12, 2020 at www.idea.int/data-tools/question-countries-view/521/82/ctr).

[6] The exception of Colombia's political landscape are mayoral elections in Bogotá and Medellín, which has recently elected leftist and center-left candidates.

leftist politics espoused by Colombia's guerrilla groups "[have] had limited appeal for the vast majority of the people. Throughout the twentieth century, in fact, Colombia has had the weakest left of all the major Latin American countries." And while most of Latin America shifted leftward during the years of the "pink tide" in the early twenty-first century, the Colombian government locked step with the United States and became a stalwart of neoliberal policy initiatives pushed by global multilateral agencies.[7] It is this enduring political conservatism that twice elected hardliner Álvaro Uribe (2002–10), then his former Minister of Defense and hand-picked successor, Juan Manual Santos (2010), and most recently another Uribe successor, Iván Duque Márquez (2018–22), to the presidency.

The country's historically vibrant national economy and stable economic growth also contrast sharply with its endemic violence. In comparison to the development histories of other Latin American countries, wherein capitalist transformation triggered powerful anticapitalist movements that led to experiments in populism, economic nationalism, and socialism, Colombian politicians and economic policymakers have been described as predominantly "risk-averse" and "pragmatic technocrats," shielded from mass politics by the hegemony of the traditional political establishment.[8] Moreover, this pragmatic economic liberalism actually delivered on its promise of sustained economic growth over the course of the 20th century, making Colombia a developmental lodestar showcased by the United States and the global multilateral agencies as a progressive alternative to economic nationalism and communism. For example, in 1949 Colombia became the first site of the World Bank's new "economic missions" meant to extend Franklin Roosevelt's "Fair Deal" developmental vision to the Third World. New Deal economist, Lauchlin Currie, headed the mission and came to view Colombia as a beacon of "accelerated economic development."[9] Three years later, eminent economist Albert Hirschman also moved to Bogotá, becoming a founding member of Colombia's new National Planning Board and an economic counselor to Colombian President, Carlos Lleras Restrepo, to whom he later dedicated his classic *Journeys toward Progress: Studies of Economy Policy-Making in Latin America* (1963).[10] Both Currie and Hirschman saw in Colombia's exceptional growth a universal template of national development and modernization for the Third World. In the aftermath of the Cuban Revolution, when guerrilla insurgencies

---

[7] Hershberg and Rosen (2006); Prashad and Ballvé (2006).
[8] Urrutia (1991).
[9] Brittain (2005).
[10] Sandilands (2017).

were spreading across the countryside of Latin America, Africa, and Asia, Colombia became a key testing ground of the Kennedy Administration's "Alliance for Progress" and the World Bank's rural development initiatives, both designed to thwart rural radicalism by bolstering economic productivity and social stability in the countryside. In the 1970s, the vibrancy of Colombia's economy granted its policymakers the privilege of sidestepping the debt incurred by many developing countries to finance large-scale development projects and promote domestic industrialization. Combined with the influx of capital from illegal drug trafficking in the 1980s, this allowed Colombia to essentially elude the crushing debt crisis of the 1980s and therefore sidestep the imposition of virulent structural-adjustment loans and austerity measures advocated by the International Monetary Fund and the World Bank in the 1990s.[11]

To be clear, contemporary scholars have challenged "the developmentalist illusion" linking economic growth and industrialization to social welfare in the global south, showing it to be only loosely correlated at best and antithetical at worst.[12] In Colombia, economic growth brought with it fabulous wealth for a small segment of the population and some of the worst levels of economic inequality in the region. A 2018 World Bank report on economic mobility in Latin American middle class, for example, describes Colombian inequality as "stubbornly high," with 10% of income earners garnering 40% of the country's wealth and its Gini co-efficient (50.8) the second worst in Latin America (only Brazil scored higher).[13] Rural Colombians have been particularly affected by this inequality, as Colombia ranks highest in Latin America for its extreme concentration of land ownership and sizable population of precarious rural migrants.[14] This said, Colombia's economic growth has also produced a sizable and durable middle economic strata that stands out in the region.[15] And this middle class is not only urban. Colombia's countryside has also been the home of one of Latin America's few "middle class peasant" populations – coffee-producing, or cafetero, farmers – who have been largely impervious to the revolutionary politics of Marxist guerrilla insurgency groups, the pull of the illegal narcotics economy, and the social and political violence that has taken root in other rural regions of the country.

---

[11] Urrutia (1991).

[12] Arrighi and Piselli (1987); Arrighi et al. (2003); Arrighi et al. (2010); Ferguson (2015); Harris (2017); Bair et al. (2019).

[13] World Bank (2012); Ferreira et al. (2013).

[14] Oxfam (2017); Ballvé (2012).

[15] This is adjusted for purchasing power parity at constant 2005 prices (Ferreira et al. 2013; World Bank 2012).

How can we explain the coexistence of these complex and contradictory dynamics of Colombian development? Why has capitalist development in Colombia produced both bastions of support for an entrenched class of elites and endemic social crises and violence? And what does an analysis of development in Colombia teach us about the broader prospects for social well-being and stability for those living at the margins of the world market?

This book answers these questions through a comparative and world historical analysis of the labor regime dynamics of rural Colombia's most important global commodity-producing regions: the coffee region of Viejo Caldas, the banana region of Urabá, and the coca (base ingredient of cocaine) region of the Caguán. Analyzing development trajectories through the lens of labor regimes is uncommon. Indeed, since its origins in the 1940s and 1950s when development economists likened national economic growth and industrialization with the high mass consumption culture associated with North American and European livelihoods, the concept of national development has undergone significant definitional reiterations and major conceptual unlearning. In this book, I use the term "development" in its most generic formulation as the set of policy initiatives and practices implemented by states to promote economic growth through the production of commodities for the global market. Such initiatives are "capitalist" because the production of these commodities becomes ensconced in a market logic that gives priority to the ceaseless accumulation of capital above all else. Analyzing development from the perspective of labor regimes analysis thus reorients the discussion away from abstract thinking about the relationship between economic growth and social welfare toward concrete analysis of the social contradictions, unintended social consequences, and labor control strategies that arise when developmental processes seek to transform marginalized regions into sites of capitalist growth and production.

Focusing on the labor and development dynamics of Colombia's coffee, banana, and coca regimes is especially useful because each of these commodities has played a central role linking rural land, labor, and capital to the world market while also expressing the broad diversity of development dynamics that have taken root in the country.[16] In different ways and to varying degrees, coffee, banana, and coca production have both absorbed rural labor and expelled it through violent processes

---

[16] Colombia's economy is the fourth largest in Latin America as measured by gross domestic product. It also specializes in the production of numerous export commodities and industrial products, including coal and petroleum, gold and other precious minerals, electronics and appliances, shipbuilding, automobiles, natural gases, cut flowers, in addition to having vibrant tourism, financial services, and construction industries.

of rural land dispossession. They have generated foreign exchange, regional economic growth and development as well as highly exploitative and dangerous working conditions, underdevelopment, labor repression, and economic marginalization.[17] They have expanded the territorial presence of the state to frontier regions of the country, producing both bulwarks of conservative electoral support and state legitimacy as well as radical political opposition that has challenged the interests of capital and brought the state to the brink of collapse.

Taken collectively, the dynamics of these three commodities paint a picture of Colombia's highly varied and contentious development trajectory from the country's early experiences with laissez-faire liberalism at the turn of the twentieth century, through the years of state-directed developmentalism in the decades following World War II, and into the present era of twenty-first-century neoliberal globalization. Coffee and bananas, for instance, were the main commodities (along with oil) that first propelled Colombia's insertion into the world economy. As such, they helped transform the largely stagnant and "inward-looking" economy inherited from the era of Spanish colonialism in the nineteenth century into a liberal growth economy by the early decades of the twentieth century. Both generated the foreign investment and foreign exchange needed to finance the developmental goals of rapid industrialization, urbanization, and "high mass consumption" that had become Colombia's national growth model throughout the postwar decades. Yet, they differed significantly in terms of their ability to generate local social and economic stability.

Colombia's coffee sector was bolstered by what has been called the "Pacto cafetero," a developmentalist social compact instituted by the parastatal National Federation of Coffee Growers of Colombia (Fedecafé) that regulated the domestic coffee market and generated what I describe as a *hegemonic labor regime* characterized by the active participation of cafetero farmers in the expansion of the sector. Under this social compact, Colombia's coffee farms transformed into highly rationalized "factories in the fields" while its producers transformed from coffee-producing campesino peasants into market-dependent cafetero farmers. And while Colombia continues to churn out some of the world's most highly valued mild Arabica coffee beans, the economic and social viability of the *Pacto cafetero* has been crushed by the weight of macro-structural transformations in the world coffee economy. Since the early 1990s, Colombia's coffee regime has erupted in

---

[17] In 2013, the total value of unroasted coffee and banana exports was over US$19 billion and US$9.7 billion, respectively (FAOSTAT n.d., accessed July 26, 2019 at www.fao.org/faostat/en/#home). Cocaine exports were estimated to be some US$84 billion (UNODC 2011:5).

waves of cafetero militancy that have thrown Fedecafé's hegemonic control into deep crisis. The continued vibrancy of the coffee sector has become, in many ways, a gauge of Colombia's ability to continue its developmental successes of the past into an uncertain future of twenty-first-century global market turbulence.

Bananas, in contrast, have a more controversial significance in Colombia's developmental history. Banana production first arose as an export enclave in the Santa Marta region of Colombia's Caribbean coast, where it remained under the dominion of the US-based United Fruit Company (UFC). When banana workers organized a strike for better wages and working conditions in 1928, Colombian military forces were called in, leading to a massacre that tarnished the reputation of the UFC and led to the company's divestment from the region over the ensuing years. In the early 1960s, banana production arose once again, this time through the establishment of domestically owned plantations and exporting firms located in the coastal region of Urabá. Unlike coffee, which incorporated land-owning cafetero farmers into a hegemonic social compact, the banana regime of Urabá developed through the dispossession of local populations from the land and the full-proletarianization of their labor, leading to the consolidation of a wage-dependent and polarized class structure in the region. This modality of commodity production – proletarianized workers in state-backed agro-export centers – became the developmental model promoted by the Colombian state during the postwar decades and a barometer of its economic success. But rather than facilitate local development, Urabá quickly deteriorated into a *despotic labor regime* marked by state and (later) paramilitary violence used to quell labor militancy and avert redistributive demands that threatened the continued economic vibrancy of the sector. While Colombia's banana plantation owner association (*Asociación de Bananeros de Colombia*, Augura) was able to rely upon labor repression to contain worker militancy during Urabá's early decades of production, this strategy itself unraveled in the 1980s and into the 1990s when the region experienced its own deep crisis of labor control.

The cocaine industry is the latest iteration of rural commodity production and development in Colombia, one that is best contextualized historically within the present era of neoliberal globalization. Emerging in the 1980s when the postwar developmental model was becoming exhausted, and consolidating in the 1990s when the Colombian state began to adopt neoliberal policies meant to dismantle its erstwhile developmental institutions, coca and the cocaine economy arose as one of the few commodities capable of absorbing rural surplus labor and providing a relatively stable livelihood for landless migrants. The Caguán region emerged as a key site of coca production in the 1980s, only after its rural inhabitants experienced decades of despotism driven by local landed elites and large-scale cattle ranchers. The region's transformation into a coca-producing regime occurred through the actions of the revolutionary FARC guerrillas, who instituted their own protective social compact that regulated the domestic coca market, protected coca farmers from land dispossession, and generated what I describe as a *counter-hegemonic labor regime*. By the turn of the twenty-first century, however, FARC counter-hegemony ran up against the US' "War on Drugs" and "War on Terror" initiatives, eventually forcing the FARC to give up its territorial control of the region under the 2016 peace negotiations.

Analyzing these diverse experiences of capitalist development that have arisen across Colombia's coffee, banana, and coca regimes raises two sets of questions that guide this book. First, *why do we see such starkly differently local labor regimes in rural Colombia at the same period in time, that is, during the postwar developmental decades? Why did hegemony prevail in the coffee regime and despotism in the banana and cattle-turned-coca regimes?* And second, *why did these stable, albeit contrasting, labor regimes of the postwar developmental decades converge toward crises of labor control and counter-hegemonic social formations in the 1980s and 1990s?*

Conceptual Approach: Labor Regimes, Commodity Chains, and World Hegemonies

To explain the diverse experiences of global commodity production across rural Colombia, I extend insights from three bodies of scholarly literature: labor regimes analysis, global commodity chains, and world historical sociology.

Extending Insights from Labor Regimes

Scholarship on labor regimes arose in the 1970s and 1980s to analyze the social contradictions and production politics that arise from capitalist labor processes. At the core of labor regime scholarship is what might be described as Antonio Gramsci's questions, that is, under what conditions do workers and commodity producers acquiesce to capitalist labor processes and consent to the logic of market imperatives and under what conditions must labor control be obtained through overt expressions of coercion and labor repression? Over the past decades, labor regime scholars have traversed the globe, engaging in rich ethnographic and historical analyses of the varied strategies of labor control deployed by capital and states across distinct industries and national contexts.[18] In their efforts to analyze

---

[18] See Burawoy (1985, 2003, 2013); Burawoy et al. (2000); Lee (2007); Webster et al. (2008); Anner (2015); Baglioni (2018).

the diverse ways that local labor regimes have adapted to the structures of global capitalism, contemporary labor regimes scholars have provided important insights into the ways that contemporary processes of economic globalization have generated new forms of capitalist labor control that are highly coercive in form but that have not relied explicitly upon direct expressions of the types of state and capitalist violence that characterized the early despotic labor regimes described by Karl Marx and other early critics of capitalist labor processes. Market despotism, they argue, is the emergent form of labor control in a globalized economy that promotes capital mobility and flexible production systems, while forcing local workers to accept increasingly precarious working conditions or lose their jobs.

Indeed, the core focus of this book analyzes the ways that Colombian workers have been harnessed by capital and state agencies to meet the demands of global markets and the social struggles that this process has engendered. However, it also challenges some of the core assumptions of labor regime scholarship regarding the link between contemporary processes of globalization and market despotism. And instead, it develops a novel, more nuanced conceptual framework that is sensitive to the specific sets of social contradictions and labor control dynamics that arise in highly marginalized spaces of world capitalism. It does this in two ways. First, I reconceptualize labor regimes as *hegemonic class projects* in which ongoing and profitable processes of global commodity production and labor control are a social accomplishment rather assumed *a priori*. Far from institutions of capitalist class domination, labor regimes are constituted by efforts, actions, and strategies created and acted upon by specific groups of capital and state agencies and actively contested by local workers, families, and communities. As this book demonstrates, in the remote regions of rural Colombia that produce coffee, bananas, and coca, labor is not always effectively controlled, market institutions are highly unstable, and capitalist development is a risky enterprise and rare achievement rather than an immutable feature of progress and modernity. Efforts to harness labor to meet the demands of commodity production for the world market can just as readily swing between consensual and coercive mechanisms of labor control to endemic crises of labor control and even the establishment of counter-hegemonic regimes that exist outside of the dominion of capital and state. Broadening the labor regime framework beyond the consent–coercion dichotomy to include the endemic crises, frequent use of extra-market violence, and the breakdown of capitalist production altogether are thus essential to an understanding of capitalism in rural Colombia and other marginalized regions of the world economy.

Second, I demonstrate how capitalist firms and state agencies that operate at the margins of the global market – that is, where the very institutions of the market are perennially challenged, subverted, and reconstructed – are tasked with a broader set of social and economic imperatives than their counterparts in advanced centers of world capitalism. As a consequence, they must adopt a broader range of institutional and extra-institutional strategies to control labor and stabilize market transactions. While the interventions of their capitalist counterparts in core centers of the world economy typically engage in market-regulatory efforts in order to mediate class conflicts and cultivate worker acquiescence, the capitalist firms and state agencies driving the establishment of labor regimes in rural Colombia are often "developmental organizations" that must *create the structural and institutional conditions of the market itself.* As we shall see, state developmentalist interventions in rural Colombia have played a critical role in the clearing of forests, the migration of workers through state-backed settlement and land colonization practices, the establishment of land titles and property rights institutions, and the construction of transport and other vital infrastructure to connect production sites to global markets. Importantly, however, these interventions do not merely extend the market to new geographies and new commodity frontiers. In rural Colombia, state development interventions must also actively engage in practices meant to create and reproduce pools of landless and market-dependent working-class populations, or what might simply be described as *proletarianized working-class formations.*

Moreover, the developmental strategies, institutional practices, and organizations deployed to reproduce market-dependent livelihoods have varied significantly. Some regimes have relied heavily on the use of state and paramilitary violence to dispossess rural inhabitants from the land and repress labor unrest and militancy. Others have created hegemonic discourses and institutional rationales that connect systems of commodity production to ideological constructs intended to imbue greater meaning and legitimacy to what would otherwise be viewed as mere commodity production, raw profit, or simply a job. As this book points out, far from structures of the global market generating the labor control required for global commodity production across rural Colombia, developmentalist state, parastatal, and indeed quasi-state organizations have played a critical role.

The organizations that I study – the National Federation of Coffee Growers (Fedecafé), the Association of Banana Growers (Augura), the National Federation of Cattle Ranchers (Fedegán), and the Revolutionary Armed Forces of Colombia (FARC) – vary radically in terms of their organizational origins and imperatives. They are therefore unlikely comparative units. Fedecafé, Augura, and Fedegán are all Colombian industrial trade associations, or interest groups, that were created to lobby the state and advocate for the commercial expansion of their respective sectors. However, Fedecafé also developed into a parastatal organization that was granted state-like authority to tax coffee exports, regulate domestic market transactions, and institute developmental projects related to the coffee sector. The FARC, in turn, is a revolutionary Marxist insurgency group that has taken on state-like functions in the areas under its territorial control, including the taxation and regulation of the coca sector. Despite these differences, I demonstrate that each organization has struggled with the same structural problem of how to harness local land, labor, and livelihoods to meet the demands of commodity production for the global market and in doing so, they have developed surprisingly comparable, albeit distinct, hegemonic projects with varied labor regime outcomes.

Extending Insights from Global Chain Studies

Like most labor regimes analyses, this book explores the complex social dynamics and historical processes that have made the production of global commodities across rural Colombia possible. However, unique to this book is an equally compelling analysis of the global markets in coffee, bananas, and cocaine and an elaboration of how the local labor regime dynamics of each is shaped by, and indeed shapes, the global markets in which they are embedded.

To understand this connection between global markets and local labor dynamics, I draw from and extend insights from the scholarly literature on what sociologist Jennifer Bair (2009:1) has aptly described as "the field of global chain studies." Since its early origins in world-systems analysis, scholars have used the commodity chain metaphor to map out and analyze the networks of labor and production processes that transform natures, raw materials, and human labor into finished products sold in capitalist markets. World-systems scholars like Immanuel Wallerstein and Terence Hopkins developed the commodity chain construct as a heuristic tool to demonstrate how systems of commodity production have historically cut across national territorial boundaries and, through processes of unequal exchange, reproduced core–periphery spatial inequalities in the world economy.[19] Since this early formulation, the chain metaphor has undergone significant reformulations as new bodies of scholarship have further unpacked the social and institutional workings of global industries and reappropriated its heuristic power to analyze a broad range of world market dynamics. Indeed, recent iterations in the literatures on global commodity chains (GCC) and global value chains (GVC) have developed a robust conceptual toolkit to analyze how global industries and markets differ significantly in terms of their governance structures, institutional norms and practices, and the opportunities for economic and social

---

[19] Hopkins and Wallerstein (1977, 1986); Wallerstein (2004).

upgrading they provide to local populations, firms, and governments across the world economy.[20]

This book draws from two tools in the commodity chain toolkit. First, it revisits the early world-systems emphasis on commodity chains as mechanisms that reproduce global inequalities by analyzing how local labor and development dynamics in rural Colombia are impacted by the relative profitability of their nodal location within the sequence of production processes that transform raw materials and human labor into value-added finished products. Following the work of Giovanni Arrighi and Jessica Drangel (1986), it distinguishes the core–periphery nodal location of Colombia's coffee, banana, and coca regimes by their access to the unequal distribution of wealth produced along each commodity chain. Core locations are those that occupy the most profitable niches, with "core-like wealth" accruing to firms that are able to externalize competition in the market down the chain to peripheral actors. Peripheral positions, in contrast, are characterized by greater market competition and therefore less access to the overall wealth generated by the totality of production processes that constitute the chain.

As we shall see, accessing the wealth associated with *core positions* in the commodity chain does not only open opportunities for local economic growth and development. It also makes available additional resources that can be used to generate and finance new, albeit costly, hegemonic labor systems. As highly competitive market niches marked by lower profits and greater economic instability, *peripheral positions* narrow the range of strategies that can be used to effectively contain labor, thereby increasing the propensity for despotism and crises of labor control. Situating Colombia's coffee, banana, and coca regimes *spatially within the core–periphery structures* of their respective commodity chains therefore provides crucial insights into the opportunities and obstacles that each market presents to local regime actors, with some providing local regime actors in Colombia access to core-like profits and others remaining stubbornly structured by deep core–periphery divisions that throw up significant barriers to local growth, development, and worker well-being.

If the first insight from the field of global chain studies comes from this book's use of core–periphery nodal locations to identify the structural obstacles experienced by local regime actors, the second insight comes from an analysis of the actions deployed by local regime actors that challenge these core–periphery structures. As Gary Gereffi (2018) points out, global industries are composed of distinct governance structures, institutional practices, and market norms that have important bearing on the capacity of local firms and states to "upgrade" to more

---

[20] See Gereffi and Korzeniewicz (1994); Bair (2009); Gereffi (2018); Ponte et al. (2019).

profitable market niches along the chain. Put simply, core-peripheral nodal locations are not overdetermined by the uneven spatial geography of world capitalism. Rather, they are dynamic locations that vary over time within any given commodity chain and that vary starkly across distinct global markets.[21] Indeed, the institutional mechanisms and practices that reproduce core-peripheral positions are themselves key sites of contestation within any given market or global industry, the outcome of which has important ramifications for a regime's prospects for upgrading to more profitable market niches.

This book contributes to our understanding of industrial upgrading in two ways. First, it draws attention to how processes of upgrading do not only result from the actions of firms or industry groups that move into new product lines, transform production processes, increase skills, or shift investments to new industries.[22] Instead, upgrading processes can arise through changes in the geopolitical and institutional contexts of a chain itself, which can open opportunities to access core-like profits without substantially changing existing labor processes or production strategies. Second, it clarifies the social implications of upgrading processes by drawing attention to how processes of upgrading, and indeed downgrading, impact the range of strategies available for local labor control. In this sense, we are better able to identify the sociological mechanisms that link processes of economic upgrading, or the shift to higher-value-added activities, to the "social upgrading" that is associated with improvements in the rights and entitlements of workers and to favorable local development outcomes.[23]

As we shall see, the hegemony of Colombia's coffee regime of Viejo Caldas was premised upon developmental and parastatal strategies that upgraded the regime's location in the world coffee market from a peripheral niche to a core-like niche. It was access to core-like wealth that permitted Colombia's parastatal coffee organization, Fedecafé, the means to institute a protective social compact that proved essential to the construction of hegemony on the ground in Viejo Caldas. Likewise, albeit by vastly different means, the FARC's ability to generate a counter-hegemonic labor regime in the Caguán region of Colombia has been premised upon its capacity to access core-like wealth through the illegal cocaine

---

[21] The field of global chain studies has developed an extensive set of conceptual tools to analyze how value chains dynamics operate across distinct global industries. For an overview of this literature, see Gereffi and Korzeniewicz (1994); Bair (2009); Gereffi (2018); and Ponte et al. (2019). See also Ciccantell and Smith (2009), Bair and Werner (2011); Taylor et al. (2013); Dunaway (2014); and Suwandi (2019) for reformulations and critiques of the GVC and GCC perspective.

[22] Humphrey and Schmitz (2002); Gereffi (2019).

[23] Gereffi (2005, 2018); Barrientos et al. (2011); Selwyn (2013).

market. Despite the vast differences in the global market dynamics of coffee and cocaine, local regime actors in rural Colombia were able to take advantage of the opportunities to upgrade in each respective market to access core-like wealth, and this upgrading process has been critical to their ability to control labor locally. The establishment of hegemonic and counter-hegemonic regimes in Caldas and the Caguán stand in stark contrast to the despotism of Colombia's banana regime, which has been anchored firmly within the most peripheral niche of the international banana market. Unable to upgrade to avoid the hyper-competitiveness of the banana market, Colombia's banana-producer association, Augura, has been forced to rely upon more repressive measures to contain labor unrest and avert redistributive demands from below.

Extending Insights from World Historical Sociology

Situating Colombia's rural labor regimes within the core-peripheral dynamics of their respective commodity markets provides a more nuanced and useful understanding of how the spatiality of regimes within their respective markets provides local regime actors with the resources needed to control labor through consensual rather than coercive means. Yet, one should be cautious about developing unidirectional explanations of the impact of global market structures on local labor regime outcomes. Indeed, as this book demonstrates, the strategies of labor control deployed break down over time, giving way to deep crises of labor control and even to the establishment of alternative social formations that operate outside of the effective control of the state. The global markets in coffee, bananas, and cocaine themselves have been subjected to systemic bouts of labor militancy and geopolitical contestation that have seriously threatened the continued profitability of core market actors and forced significant restructuring of the markets themselves. And as we shall see, these periods of systemic upheaval have transformed the core–periphery structures of global markets in ways that have opened opportunities to upgrade and thereby avert the social and economic ramifications of peripheralization.

To understand the geopolitical contestation and historical dynamism of global markets, I situate Colombia's labor regimes temporally within the arc of rising and falling world hegemonies. Following the work of Giovanni Arrighi (1994, 2009; Arrighi and Silver 1999), I argue that *periods of world hegemony* arise through the systemic reorganization of the institutions of world capitalism and the emulation of the dominant state by other states, both of which foster the stabilization of the world market and the systemic expansion of world production and trade. *World hegemonic unraveling* occurs when interstate rivalries and inter-capitalist competition intensify in ways that challenge rather than bolster the geopolitical power of the world hegemon. As capital accumulation shifts from production and trade to finance, the global governance institutions deployed by world hegemons unravel, system-wide social conflicts arise, and are eventually abandoned altogether, giving rise to periods of *world-systemic chaos*. These world hegemonic transitions occurred at various periods of global capitalism, including through the rise of Dutch hegemony in the seventeenth century, British hegemony in the nineteenth century, and US hegemony in the twentieth century.

In this book, I demonstrate how the emergence of local labor regimes in rural Colombia have been shaped by, and indeed shaped, the historic rise and contemporary decline of US world hegemony. Situating Colombia's labor regimes world historically is useful for three reasons. First, it illuminates the economic and political impetus driving the production of global commodities in rural Colombia and the adoption of various upgrading strategies. As we shall see, US efforts to stabilize and expand the workings of the global market through governance institutions and foreign aid gave credence to the idea, shared by Colombian state and parastatal agencies, that global commodity production for export could become a viable strategy of development and economic growth.

Second, the fact that Colombia's developmentalist ventures indeed produced results on the ground further intensified the state's efforts to maintain its developmental efforts even when these efforts generated deep social contradictions and crises rather than sustained growth and development. By situating Colombia's labor regimes world historically within the arc of US world hegemony, we see that the violence and despotism of Colombia's labor regimes has not only been rooted in the efforts of capitalist firms and agencies to adapt to competitive and peripheral niches of global markets. Rather, the pervasive use of violence and terror to contain labor unrest and instill capitalist control of the labor process has been deeply implicated in the developmentalist logic of the Colombia state, which has prioritized economic growth above the interests of rural workers and commodity-producing farmers.

Third, situating Colombia's labor regimes temporally within the arc of rising and falling world hegemonies draws attention to the critical role of US hegemonic institutions themselves in facilitating local efforts to contain, repress, and mediate the social contradictions of the country's labor regimes. Like other studies of US imperial interventions in Colombia, this focus on US world hegemony draws attention to the ways that US foreign policy, development aid, and militarization strategies have propped up the power of domestic elites, promoted capitalist expansion into the countryside, and contained popular struggles that have arisen to democratize the country's political and economic institutions. Unique to the world hegemonies perspective, however, is its attention to the fragility, variability, and unintended consequences of these efforts to control, stabilize, and expand the workings of capitalism into marginalized regions of the world economy. During the heyday of US hegemony in the postwar decades, US hegemonic actions were critical factors influencing the Colombian government's efforts to ensure social stability in the countryside through market-based forms of development. In Viejo Caldas and Urabá, US hegemony manifests in its support of the geopolitical restructuring of the international coffee and banana markets that were designed to open opportunities for local growth and development. In the Caguán, the United States helped finance rural development initiatives that were critical to the frontier colonization of the region. By the 1980s and 1990s, each of these interventions backfired and the United States responded by abandoning its support of local development in favor of neoliberal policies backed by military interventions under the aegis of the US wars on drugs and terror. As we shall see, the most significant impact of the unraveling of US world hegemony on Colombia's rural labor regimes has been a general shift, not from hegemony to despotism but from hegemony and despotism to deep crises of control across each region.

Overall, conjoining the insights of labor regimes, global commodity chains, and world historical sociology draws attention to a critical, albeit overlooked, factor that has been especially destabilizing of Colombia's rural labor regimes: the socially toxic convergence of local processes of full-proletarianization with global processes of market peripheralization. I describe the convergence of these two processes within a given labor regime as *peripheral proletarianization*. Whereas market peripheralization indeed restricts the options made available to capital and state agencies in their efforts to harness labor to the whims of the world market, the social contradictions of proletarianization alone can be partly ameliorated when workers and farmers retain access to nonmarket strategies of economic survival. When these nonmarket-based avenues are closed off and livelihoods are made dependent upon the vicissitudes of the world market, the mechanisms of labor control tilt toward despotism and crisis. Understanding the forces driving peripheral proletarianization and the consequences of it on local labor regimes, I argue, provides valuable insights into the contradictory impulses of Colombian national development during the heyday of US world hegemony in the mid-twentieth century and the increasing precarity of social and economic life in rural Colombia as US hegemony has unraveled.

Methodological Approach: Comparative and World Historical

The questions at the center of this book ask why we see such stark variation across Colombia's rural labor regimes during the heyday of US world hegemony in the postwar developmental decades and why these distinct, albeit varied, labor regimes broke down into crises of labor control in the 1980s and 1990s as US world hegemony unraveled. Given the nature of these questions, the methodological approach used is comparative and historical. As a variation-finding strategy, the *comparative methodological approach* is uniquely situated to understand both the vast differences and common patterns that have arisen across Colombia's rural labor regimes and the markets for their respective commodities.

As the primary object of analysis, much of the empirical focus of this book utilizes the comparative-historical case method to understand the varied and complex ways that rural frontier regions in Colombia were transformed into sites of global commodity production and the varied strategies of labor control that were deployed to make these systems of commodity production viable. Given the historical timing of the formation of each labor regime, the comparative method offers novel insights into how each labor regime was affected by the developmental opportunities and strategies that have arisen across three distinct periods of time: the period of laissez-faire liberalism from the late nineteenth century to the period of the Great Depression in the 1930s, the heyday period of developmentalism ushered in through the rise of US world hegemony in the postwar decades, and the rise of neoliberal globalization that has been associated with the unraveling of US world hegemony since the 1980s.

My use of the comparative-historical method is not limited to an analysis of labor regime dynamics on the ground in rural Colombia. Importantly, I also use it to analyze continuities and differences in the global commodity chain dynamics for coffee, bananas, and coca, thus pointing out the varied ways that the core–periphery structures and governance institutions of each commodity market have provided opportunities and obstacles to labor regime actors in each region. Using the comparative-historical method in this double way offers insights into both the significant *historical ruptures* and surprising *historical continuities* that have arisen across each labor regime and global market over time. Understanding these spatial and temporal dynamics provides a robust set of comparisons of nine comparative units: three rural labor regimes (coffee, bananas, and coca) across three periods of world historical time (laissez-faire liberalism from the mid-nineteenth century to the 1930s, developmentalism from the close of World War II until the 1970s, and neoliberalism from 1980s until the present). Understanding the continuities and differences that have arisen across these comparable units forms the backbone of the empirical analysis of this book.

However, I also draw from the methodological insights of world historical sociology to add an additional layer of complexity to the analysis. As world historical sociologists point out, one should be skeptical of the comparativist notion that individual cases can be analyzed as self-contained units.[24] As we shall see, the dynamics of Colombia's labor regimes are not simply produced by the actions of local actors, be they capitalist firms, state agencies and institutions, or local populations. Nor are they unidirectionally shaped by outside forces that act upon these actors, whether these forces emanate from national state offices in Bogotá, the boardrooms of transnational corporations, or the halls of the US Pentagon, Capitol Hill, and the White House. As this book highlights, the regime dynamics of each is impacted directly and indirectly by the dynamics of the other regimes.

Analyzing *interregional dynamics* provides insights into the complex ways that Colombia's coffee, bananas, and coca labor regimes have direct and indirect bearing on one another. As we shall see, the early successes of Colombia's coffee regime in generating regional growth and social stability provided Colombian policymakers with a model that guided national development endeavors and promoted the marketization of other rural export zones of the country, including the banana region of Urabá and what became the coca region of Caquetá. And importantly, the state continued to support these developmental initiatives in Urabá and Caquetá, even when the regions degenerated into sites of labor militancy, guerrilla activity, and heightened political violence. This complex interplay of interregional dynamics across rural Colombia also acted in more direct ways. As we shall see, the successes and failures of each regime in absorbing labor and generating stable livelihoods pushed and pulled migratory flows of rural labor and settlement that impacted the strategies of labor control and labor politics of each. Understanding the indirect and unintentional ways that rural Colombia's commodity regimes co-constitute one another and shape larger national development trends is a major finding of this book.

Measurement and Data

Analyzing the divergent spatial and temporal patterning of Colombia's rural labor regimes from a comparative and world historical perspective requires extensive research on the complexities and particularities of each local regime, on Colombian state developmental policy and national political trends, on the core–periphery structures and governance institutions of the global coffee, banana, and cocaine markets, on US foreign policy, and more. Due to the breadth of the study,

---

[24] McMichael (1990); Arrighi (1994); Arrighi and Silver (1999); Bair and Hough (2012).

the research design naturally rests chiefly upon secondary sources, including the vast academic literature amassed by Colombian and North American social scientists and historians, governmental documents, publications issued by nongovernmental organizations and Colombian think tanks, as well as pamphlets and other documents issued by activist groups and organizations. These secondary texts were the central sources of empirical data used to construct the historical narratives for each of the three regional case studies.[25] While each of these secondary sources was written according to its own particular theoretical agenda, all of them use in-depth ethnographic and/or historical methods that were instrumental in either tracing the class dynamics of each local labor regime over time or in honing in on macro-structural transformations of the market for each commodity. The "value added" comes from bringing these different sources into dialogue with each other.

One of the most critical elements of the research design, however, is the capacity to identify and measure what may be considered the "dependent variable" of the study, namely, the spatial and temporal patterning of Colombia's labor regimes across what I conceptualize as four distinct labor regime types: hegemony, despotism, counter-hegemony, and crises of control. This required longitudinal data that could distinguish the *key mechanisms of labor control deployed* and identify periods *when these mechanisms were effective* in maintaining capitalist control of the labor process.

Critical to my measurement of the *key mechanisms of labor control deployed* was the extent to which capital used violent labor repression. To operationalize "labor repression," I spent a substantial amount of time amassing, recoding, and analyzing a longitudinal dataset that measures the number of incidents of state, paramilitary and other forms of political violence that occurred within each region over time. This data was originally compiled by a Bogotá-based Jesuit peace institute, the Popular Education Research Center (CINEP), which collected newspaper and human rights reports of all incidents of political violence that occurred in the country and published their findings in the journal *Justicia y Paz* (1987–96) and later in the journal *Noche y Niebla* (1996–present). This data was particularly useful

---

[25] I rely heavily upon the work of Charles Bergquist (1986); Marco Palacios (1980); John Talbot, Christopher London (1995, 1997, 1999); Jorge Enrique Robledo (1998, 1999); Jaime Vallecilla Gordillo (2001); and Jaime Vallecilla Gordillo et al. (2005) for the case study of the coffee regime, Hernando Botero Herrera and Diego Sierra Botero (1981); Hernando Botero Herrera (1990); Steve Striffler and Mark Moberg (2003); Marcelo Bucheli (2003, 2005); and Leah Carroll (2011) for the banana regime, and Robin Ruth Marsh (1983), Leon Zamosc (1986), Álvaro Delgado (1987); Nazih Richani (2002); Leah Carroll (2011); and Winifred Tate (2015) for the frontier-coca regime of Caquetá.

because it specified the type of violent act perpetrated, which I then recoded to distinguish *acts of labor repression* such as death threats, kidnappings, killings, massacres, and other acts of violence that are meant to repress a regional population of commodity producers, workers, and peasants already under its effective control from *acts of warfare* such as combat activity, raids, territorial skirmishes between armed groups (state forces, paramilitaries, guerrillas, etc.) that arise from territorial struggles to control a region. The dataset also specified the group or individuals who allegedly perpetrated the act (including paramilitary groups, all branches and divisions of the Colombian armed forces, police forces, private individuals or groups, and guerrilla groups), the exact location and time in which the incident took place, the occupation of the victim, and a brief description of the context and circumstances in which the act of violence took place. Because this CINEP data only dates back to 1987, during the period when the developmental state was being dismantled and before the adoption of the neoliberal model, I assembled a research team that searched the archives of the largest Colombian newspaper, *El Tiempo,* and compiled all of the incidents of violence that occurred within the territorial demarcations of the regional cases from 1975 until the CINEP data began in 1987. This broader longitudinal dataset, which I call the "coercion dataset," therefore covers the period from 1975 to 1987 and 1987 to 2017. This broad temporal sweep, from 1975 to 2017, was essential to capturing the general increases and decreases in the incidents of labor repression occurring within each region over the transition from the developmental to neoliberal eras.

Critical to my measurement of effective labor control was the extent to which workers and commodity producing farmers engaged in protest activities and political actions that challenged capitalist efforts to control their labor and land. In order to measure this contestation and labor unrest from below, I used three other key data sources in addition to the secondary texts. The first, also the product of CINEP investigators scanning domestic media sources and NGO reports, documented all known incidents of social protest activity that occurred across the country between 1975 and 2016. These protest incidents were coded according to the specific location in which the protest activity took place (including municipality and department), the time and date of its occurrence, the groups and actors involved, the target of the protest (state, local government, private business), and the type of protest activity that occurred (labor, peasant and indigenous, student, urban, and other actors).[26] In addition to the social protest

---

[26] This CINEP "social movements team" consists of Mauricio Archila N., Alvaro Delgado G., Martha Cecilia Garcia V., and Esmeralda Prada M. See Archila Neira et al. (2002) for a description of this research program.

data that captured the extra-institutional politics of each regime, I also analyzed electoral data compiled by the Colombian National Registry Office (RNEC). This data was critical to understand the institutional politics of each regime's workers and commodity-producing farmers and to measure the extent to which local political positions remained dominated by traditional elite-led parties rather than falling into the hands of populist and leftist political parties. Finally, neither the social protest data nor the electoral data captured forms of labor unrest and class politics that arose through armed struggle. Since politics in Colombia is often militarized, and class struggles engulfed by guerrilla insurgency activity, I used the "coercion dataset" to trace the patterns of guerrilla activity in each region.

I spent a great deal of time and effort constructing and analyzing the datasets and the secondary literature. However, I also conducted multiple bouts of field-work in Colombia. The first period of fieldwork was in the summer of 2001, when I established initial contact with various organizations and individuals in Bogotá to ascertain whether the project was feasible or not. These initial contacts were essential in paving the way for a second round of fieldwork that I conducted over a twenty-month period between 2003 and 2004.[27] During this period, I was kindly afforded an office in Universidad de los Andes' *Centro de Investigaciones Socio-culturales e Internacionales* (CESO) in Bogotá, which became my base of operations. During this time, I worked together with a group of research assistants to compile and code the data that became the coercion dataset.[28] I later updated this data in 2009–10, 2015–16, and 2018 with the assistance of numerous MA students at Florida Atlantic University.[29]

Between 2003 and 2004, I conducted over forty structured and semi-structured interviews with key informants, including local, departmental and national governmental representatives, local and national military leaders and police officials, social and political activists, union leaders and rank-and-file militants, peasants and large landowners, workers and business leaders, and ex-guerrilla leaders, in

---

[27] I received a "pre-dissertation research grant" from the Program in Comparative Sociology and International Development from Johns Hopkins University for the summer of 2002, a Fulbright Student Research Grant from September 2003 to September 2004, and an additional Fulbright Research Grant Extension that lasted until December of 2004.

[28] My research team at the Universidad de los Andes included four political and social science students: Angela Ines Villa Cardona, Juan Guillermo Alba, Albert Rendón Ríos, and Juan Pablo Estupiñan.

[29] The FAU MA students who assisted me with the compilation and analysis of this data include: Robert MacPherson, Claudia Giribaldi, Mayra Girasol, Alberto Gomez-DaBoin, and Karthik Balaji Ramanujam.

addition to academics, specialists and experts, in addition to countless nonstructured interviews and conversations. It is worth noting that the feasibility of conducting qualitative research in Colombia has been severely limited by the widespread use of violence by public and private actors on both the left and the right of the political spectrum. Many academics have fallen victim to this violence, including the shooting of a leading political scientist at the National University in Bogotá. This "climate of fear" against academics, and particularly those who speak openly about human rights issues, was made painfully clear in a report that showed no fewer than twelve incidents of violence perpetuated against academics in 2006 alone![30] For this reason, it was too risky for me to enter the Caguán region of Caquetá, which was considered to be a "hot spot" of political violence between 2003 and 2004. And while I was indeed successful in establishing rapport with many key informants who lived and worked in Urabá, a trip to this region was also avoided due to an unexpected incident in Bogotá in May of 2004, when I was drugged, beaten, robbed, and kidnapped for a short period. Despite these limitations, I was able to interview key actors from Urabá from the relative safety of Medellín, where both Augura's and Urabá's banana worker union offices reside. Even operating with these precautions, I had to become accustomed to groups of armed men "testing my politics" before a scheduled interview, bouts of phone tag and scheduled meeting spaces that mysteriously took me from safe public spaces into dark corridors and remote fields, interviews with politicians and elites who appeared to maintain a strange inability to critique leftist guerrillas and interviews with labor activists who seemed unwilling to critique paramilitaries or local elites, situations that allow you to gain the loyalty of one group while simultaneously losing the capacity to enter sites occupied by antagonistic groups, the occasional provision of armed body guards and attack dogs when walking to and from interviews, and of course the pistol set strategically next to your microphone on the interview desk. Such is the nature of field research in Colombia, and is itself a reflection of the degree to which contemporary Colombian society has become characterized by coercive forms of domination and crisis.

Since these initial periods of fieldwork in 2001 and 2003–4, rural territorial contestation in Colombia has calmed, making it easier to enter field sites that were off limits at the time. To be sure, this relative calming of incidents of political violence is itself the product of a period of intense militarization and repression that began under the Uribe Administration (2002–10). Nonetheless, the expansion of state control over regions that had once been war zones allowed me to return to Colombia and conduct research in Urabá and Caquetá, in addition to

---

[30] Boletín de los inmarcesibles (2007).

Viejo Caldas, Medellín and Bogotá in recent years. In the summer of 2009, I conducted over thirty additional interviews with local labor and agrarian rights activists, government officials, union bosses, military officials, farmers, workers, displaced peasants, and others while visiting countless banana plantations, coffee fields, government offices, libraries, and military bases. I also returned to Colombia for a fourth bout of fieldwork in the summer of 2015, this time spending almost my entire time in Viejo Caldas, largely through the assistance of fellow academic traveler, Chris London, who set me up with an initial array of contacts in and around Pácora, Caldas. During this period, I interviewed another thirty+ people, including coffee farmers, activists, government officials, and extensions agents and others working with Fedecafé, largely to better understand the waves of cafetero militancy that have arisen over the past years. Finally, over the past years I have been able to supplement these bouts of fieldwork with skype and telephone interviews with key informants who have helped keep me up to date with current events occurring in the remote rural regions of this study. In total, I have conducted over 100 interviews, most of them in field sites. Rather than systematically incorporate these interviews into the narrative of each case study, I have used these interviews primarily as a guide to help clarify the dynamics of each case study as they unfolded over the broad historical periods analyzed.

Overall, this book is the product of nearly 20 years of research, including 4 rounds of fieldwork, over 100 structured and semi-structured interviews, and countless informal ones. An early version of this research was my dissertation thesis. Since then, various threads of it have been published as solo and coauthored articles in various scholarly journals, including *Politics and Society*, *Global Labour Journal*, *Journal of World-Systems Research*, *International Journal of Comparative Sociology*, *Review: A Journal of the Fernand Braudel Center*, and *Journal of Agrarian Change*. This gestation period has allowed me the opportunity to revisit the various conceptual arguments and substantive claims of the dissertation while providing greater time to familiarize myself with the historical nuances of the three regional cases through new bouts of fieldwork and deep immersion in the burgeoning secondary literatures on Colombian politics, coffee, bananas, and cocaine. Indeed, as most comparative historical sociologists would acknowledge, gaining familiarity with the complex social dynamics of the cases – including three regional regimes and three global markets – in addition to an understanding of how these dynamics were historically situated within the arc of US world hegemony requires significant reading of secondary sources and critical reflection. It is only through this book, however, that I have been able to satisfactorily knit these threads together into a coherent argument that captures the broad and deep dynamics of labor regime variation across macro-periods and micro-regions that are encapsulated here.

Chapter Outline

This book begins with a discussion of labor regimes theories that associate contemporary processes of neoliberal globalization with the rise of new forms of market despotism and forwards a new, more nuanced conceptualization of labor regime and development dynamics that arise at the margins of world capitalism. The remainder of the book is divided into three empirical parts, each of which focuses on a regional case study. The first case study focuses on the coffee regime of Viejo Caldas; the second on the banana regime of Urabá; and the third on the frontier regime of the Lower and Middle Caguán region of Caquetá. The geographic locations of these three regions are depicted in Map 1. Each case study is further segmented into two temporally distinct chapters in order to illuminate the continuities and changes in the nature of labor regimes over time. The first chapter of each regional case study examines the transformation of each labor regimes from its origins in the nineteenth century into the highpoint of US world hegemony in the postwar developmental decades of the twentieth century. The second chapter focuses on how these labor regime dynamics changed as US world hegemony unraveled and each regime was forced to adapt to world markets that have become unhindered by geopolitical regulations.

The first regional case study examines the trajectory of the coffee regime of Viejo Caldas. Chapter 2 examines the rise of Viejo Caldas as a site of coffee production for export during a period in which the global coffee market operated according to laissez-faire principles rooted in a British world hegemonic order. I highlight how two distinct structures of coffee production emerged – frontier smallholds and large coffee estates, both of which developed strategies to protect themselves from direct exposure to the market. I analyze how the large estates experiment with proletarianized labor forces triggered a wave of labor unrest that led to their dissolution by the 1930s. It was in this historical context that the National Federation of Coffee Growers took on parastatal responsibility for developing the sector based upon the smallholder structure of production. I examine Fedecafé's developmentalist interventions in the sector and argue that these interventions facilitated the emergence of a hegemonic social compact (Pacto cafetero) that transformed the region's smallholding producers into fully marketized cafetero farmers.

Chapter 3 recasts Fedecafé's hegemonic social compact in world historical perspective, asking how and why it was successful despite the increasing dependence of cafetero farmers on coffee production for the market to meet their class reproduction needs. I argue that Fedecafé was able to exploit new opportunities in the international coffee market brought on by the rise of US world hegemony. Specifically, Colombia engaged in geopolitical collective action efforts that led to

Map 1 Local labor regimes in Colombia: Viejo Caldas, Urabá, Caquetá

Sources: Esri, USGS, NOAA, Garmin, NPS

the establishment of international coffee agreements. These agreements politically regulated the market in ways that allowed Fedecafé to "move up" the coffee chain and avoid the social contradictions of peripheral proletarianization. I argue that the shift to crises of control came when the US pulled its support for the politically regulated world coffee market, essentially returning the market back to a highly volatile laissez-faire institutional structure and therefore re-peripheralizing Colombia's market location. This re-peripheralization undermined Fedecafé's social compact and thus the economic and social stability of cafetero farmers.

The second regional case study examines the trajectory of the banana regime of Urabá. Chapter 4 argues that the rise of paramilitary despotism in contemporary Urabá has been shaped by the historical geopolitics of the world banana market. It begins with an analysis of the rise and fall of the international banana market in the early half of the twentieth century. I point out that the banana market arose through the activities of a handful of powerful vertically integrated corporations that secured control of production through despotic means, but that this despotism gave way to a global wave of labor unrest and economic nationalism that forced the companies to vertically disintegrate their activities by mid-century. Next, I discuss how the banana market was restructured under the auspices of the United States, which encouraged domestic banana production as a developmentalist growth strategy but ultimately re-peripheralized the producer end of the market. Banana production in Urabá, I argue, arose during this period of developmental optimism. However, the region's movement into a highly peripheralized niche forced Urabá's banana elites to rely upon the authoritarian practices of the National Front regime to control labor and keep production costs low. Chapter 5 describes how the despotism of Urabá's banana regime endured in the 1970s, but fell into crisis in the 1980s when the central state implemented a series of democratization reforms that opened new political opportunities to Urabá's local working class. By the end of the decade, the workers succeeded in displacing elites from local political offices and using this leverage to grant concessions to banana unions. However, this crisis of labor control triggered a violent reaction from elites who relied upon paramilitarism to regain control of the region and therefore adapt to the competitive demands of the banana export market.

The final case study examines the rise and collapse of FARC counter-hegemony in the Caguán region of Caquetá. Chapter 6 analyzes the Caguán's historic transformation from a frontier region comprised of displaced migrants in the 1960s into a despotic cattle regime under the control of Colombia's Cattle Ranchers Association (Fedegán) by the 1970s and finally into a coca regime under the counter-hegemonic control of the FARC by the 1980s. I argue that FARC counter-hegemony was rooted in part in its ability to absorb populations of rural surplus labor that came to the region as a result of the dispossessing tendencies of the developmentalist politics of the state. It was also rooted in the FARC's involvement in the illegal coca market, which granted them core-like profits that they used to consolidate a protective social compact vis-à-vis local cocalero producers. In this sense, the FARC's interventions in the Caguán's coca regime provide important points of convergence and divergence to the actions of the other developmental organizations analyzed, including Fedecafé and Augura as well as Fedegán, all of whom have struggled to adapt to the competitive demands of the world market.

In Chapter 7, I analyze how FARC counter-hegemony in the Caguán collapsed in the 2000s and 2010s. I show that the adoption of neoliberal economic policies in the 1990s bolstered FARC counter-hegemony because it created new waves of displaced migrants who sought shelter in coca-producing regions like the Caguán. However, I also show how Colombian neoliberalism provided the impetus for a significant shift in the region's cattle industry from its historic production of meats and hides into the production of dry and powdered milks for export. This shift, in addition to the growth in the FARC's presence, intensified struggles over control of the region. What eventually dismantled the FARC's control of the region was a shift in geopolitics, as the FARC's involvement in the illegal coca economy gained the attention of the United States, which intensified its aid to the Colombian military through its War on Drugs and War on Terror initiatives. This militarization of the region undermined the FARC's ability to continue to protect local cocaleros, eventually leading to the collapse of the FARC's labor regime altogether. It was in this context that the peace accords were signed. And it is in this context that we can see more clearly how the state's central underlying problem is neither the FARC nor the coca economy, but rather how to respond to a crisis of surplus populations.

I conclude with a discussion of the key arguments of this book and some closing remarks on the capacity of the twenty-first- century world market to accommodate stable forms of social class reproduction and development for populations living at its margins.

I

Toward a Sociology of Labor and Development at the Margins of the Market

The focus of this book centers on explaining the stark variation in labor regime dynamics that has arisen across the rural commodity-producing regions of Viejo Caldas, Urabá, and the Caguán region of Caquetá. However, the presence of brutal violence and terror deployed to contain labor, the endemic crises and social unrest and the appearance of alternative social formations and illegal markets operating outside the effective control of the state pose significant problems for a labor regimes perspective that has been developed to explain labor dynamics in core regions of world capitalism. Indeed, this chapter argues that the existing conceptual framework typically utilized by labor regimes scholars falls far short when examining the dynamics on the ground in rural Colombia. To better grasp these dynamics, I reconstruct a labor regimes perspective that is attuned to the experiences of commodity production and development that arise at the margins of the market.

Rethinking Labor Regimes at the Margins of the Market

Analyzing capitalist trajectories over time and space necessitates clarification of what I mean by "local labor regime dynamics." Like Michael Burawoy's (1979, 1983, 1985) concept of a "factory regime," as well as more recent conceptions of "labor control regimes,"[1] the patterns of commodity production and capitalist development in each of the three rural subregions I analyze are not strictly economic phenomena. They are neither simply "labor processes" in which human labor transforms raw materials into finished products nor mere "employment relations" that describe workplace authority structures, production arrangements, and compensation systems. Instead, they are modalities of social class reproduction and labor control that bring together human labor, capital, and the state

---

[1] Jonas (1996); Anner (2015); Baglioni (2018); Pattenden (2016).

through the transformation of the natural environment into a finished commodity for the market. They are "local" because they articulate a spatially anchored segment of the world's population into global circuits of commodity production and exchange. They are "labor" regimes because this articulation occurs through a labor process that simultaneously produces a commodity and reproduces a social class whose livelihood depends on this production. They are "regimes" because the subjection of livelihoods to systems of commodity production tied to the whips and whims of the market is an inherently precarious, contradictory, and socially disruptive process that requires political-institutional strategies of labor control and class domination to ensure the continued extraction of surplus labor and the expanded reproduction of capital. Like any regime of social domination, the mechanisms of social control used to create workers and commodities are by no means guaranteed. Rather, they are projects that are institutionalized, contested, and sometimes even subverted.

Like any regime of social domination, the mechanisms of social control used to create workers and commodities vary significantly, with some regimes operating through the production of worker consent and others requiring more coercive mechanisms of labor control. Perhaps the earliest formulation of capitalist labor regimes can be traced back to the writings of Karl Marx (1976)[1867], whose descriptions of the "satanic mills" of English industrial factory life became emblematic of the despotism that results from full proletarianization and capitalist labor markets. This belief in "despotism" as the definitive experience of workers under capitalism, however, changed in the early twentieth century when labor unions and workerist parties began to wrest significant concessions from capital and gain social protections and rights from their respective states. The partial inclusion of workers' interests into capitalist states, and especially the rise of Fascist regimes that were backed by segments of the working class, gave rise to new theories of labor control that sought to explain what the Italian Communist Antonio Gramsci described as "hegemony." For Gramsci, hegemony existed as a form of class domination achieved predominantly through the acquiescence, if not active participation, of subaltern groups and classes in capitalist labor processes and capitalist systems of social control.

During and immediately following World War II, neo-Gramscian ideas were used by Western Marxists to highlight the role of propaganda and capitalist cultural practices in generating the "false consciousness" and worker political acquiescence to totalitarian regimes and practices.[2] In the postwar

---

[2]   Burawoy (2003); Jeffries (2016).

decades, neo-Gramscian theories slipped into the shadows of academic circles, as Franklin Roosevelt's "labor-friendly" New Deal social compact between capital, labor, and the state spread among the advanced capitalist states of Europe and North America and as Truman's "Fair Deal" gained traction among the emerging developmentalist states of the Third World. However, by the closing decades of the century, these theories resurfaced again in academic circles to explain what many saw as a general decline in the strength of organized labor and the emergence of increasingly despotic labor regime dynamics as firms and workers struggled to adapt to an increasingly globalized world market.

Since the turn of the century, the overwhelming emphasis of labor regimes scholarship addresses the temporal question of how and why erstwhile hegemonic labor regimes established by activist Fordist–Keynesian states in the postwar decades have deteriorated toward increasingly despotic regimes in the current era of globalization. Specifically, many labor scholars argue that today's hypermobility of productive capital has created a single, global, and highly competitive labor market that pits the world's workers against one another in a worldwide "race to the bottom" in wages and working conditions. Whereas workers were afforded some degree of protection from full exposure to the competitive tendencies of the global market during the postwar decades, today's workers must compete against one another for access to jobs with businesses that have become increasingly mobile and less beholden to local worker demands. The result of this race to the bottom of the global labor market has been a generalized *convergence of labor regimes* in the present era toward increasingly precarious forms of working-class livelihoods and more despotic working conditions.[3]

---

[3] Perhaps the most influential scholar of the new forms of market despotism that have resulted from the globalization of the world economy is Michael Burawoy. First laid out in his contemporary classic, *Manufacturing Consent: Changes in the Labor Process under Monopoly Capitalism* (1979), and later developed through subsequent writing (1983, 1985, 2003, 2015), Burawoy argues that contemporary advancements in technology, transportation, and communications infrastructure have made capitalist production increasingly mobile, affording capital the ability to move (or threaten to move) to cheaper and less regulated sites of production, thus tipping the balance of class power away from organized labor (unions, labor parties) to favor global capital. The result has been a shift away from various types of "hegemonic" social compacts that arose when activist states partially offset the costs of workers' class reproduction through provisions of social insurance, welfare, and formal labor rights and regulations toward regimes characterized by "hegemonic despotism," wherein workers submit to

To be clear, scholars disagree on the distinct mechanisms by which globalization has generated new forms of market despotism. One set of theories, what may be described as *structural globalization theory*, emphasizes how the global mobility of capital has undermined the structural power of workers, whether directly by expanding the size of the global labor market[4] or indirectly by weakening state regulatory capacities,[5] facilitating a growth in flexible production systems and global supply chains,[6] or by fostering the movement of capital out of manufacturing into the financial service industries.[7] A second set of temporal theories, what may be described as *neoliberalism theory*, posits that the decomposition of labor results from the resurgence of ideological doctrines of the self-regulating market, that is, the rise of "neoliberalism" as the dominant ideology and set of practices of national states and international development agencies.[8] Despite these differences in their proximate causes, both structural globalization and neoliberalism theorists agree that twenty-first-century capitalism is forcing workers to adjust to increasingly despotic conditions of work and economic life. The question for our purposes, however, is whether the emergence of new structures of economic globalization and the widespread adoption of neoliberal practices are useful in explaining the spatial and temporal patterning of labor regime dynamics in rural Colombia.

---

increasingly despotic forms of managerial control due to their dependence upon their jobs to meet their reproduction needs and for fear that any efforts to challenge managerial control of their labor could potentially lead to a plant closing and job loss. Whereas the despotism of early industrial capitalism arose when job-dependent workers feared their individual loss of a job, today's workers acquiesce to the dictates of capital for fear that they along with all of their coworkers will lose their jobs to more compliant workers living at the other end of the global labor market.

4   Cowie (1999); Milkman (1997); Collins (2003); Rothstein (2016).
5   Tilly (1995); Markoff (1996).
6   Gereffi (2018); Lichtenstein (2006); Petrovic and Hamilton (2006); Bonacich and Appelbaum (2000); Ross (2004); Hatton (2011); Woodcock (2017).
7   Silver (2003); Krippner (2011); Calhoun and Derlugian (2011).
8   Following Karl Polanyi's writings in *The Great Transformation* (2001)[1944], today's scholars of neoliberalism argue that efforts to force society (including land, capital, and labor) to the dictates of the global self-regulating market, subjects the very foundation of society to the dictates of the market. By reversing the natural social order in which markets serve the interests of society, neoliberal policies provoke processes of societal disintegration and destruction by rolling back workers' access to state regulatory agencies and protections (Milkman and Ott 2014; Webster et al. 2008) and by facilitating the structural processes of globalization that undermine existing sources of worker power (della Porta 2015; Silva 2009; Zolberg 1995).

Rethinking Global Market Despotism and Effective Labor Control

Undoubtedly, contemporary labor regime scholarship has opened up promising avenues of research on the diverse ways that capital has forced labor to adapt to the whip of global markets. However, viewing the structural and politico-ideological dynamics of world capitalism from the perspective of rural Colombia, a region outside the typical purview of labor scholars, allows us to rethink some of the conceptual blind spots of labor regime analysis and clarify the specific patterning of labor regime dynamics that have arisen in Colombia's coffee, banana, and cocaine regimes. Two conceptual blind spots are of particular relevance to analyses of labor regimes dynamics at the margins of the market: a bias of global market dominance and a bias of labor control.

Too often, labor scholars share the economistic assumption of the power of markets to shape and order society according to market imperatives. This *bias of global market despotism* is rooted in a set of assumptions that reify the so-called silent compulsions of the market without paying enough attention to the ways that commodity, labor, and financial market dynamics are socially and politically constructed and reconstructed by specific sets of social institutions and actors.[9] Unfortunately, labor regime scholarship, and scholars of global capitalist markets more generally, often begins with what might be called a "post-primitive accumulation moment" – when systems of commodity production are already set in motion, workers already dispossessed of the means of production, class reproduction already proletarianized, and class struggles (if indeed these exist) narrowly rooted in worker struggles at the point of production.[10] Not only does such a perspective give inordinate, if not magical, weight to the coercive powers of the market to shape social life by perennially removing and reshaping any obstacles to further economic growth. By eluding an analysis of the social foundations of markets and labor processes, it becomes susceptible to abstract and normative assumptions that are rooted in the experiences of predominantly white male industrial workers living in Europe and North America.[11]

In many regions of world capitalism, processes of dispossession do not ceaselessly result in full proletarianization, and the silent compulsions of the market often fall short as effective mechanisms of labor control. And to make global

---

[9] Perelman (2000).

[10] Smith and Wallerstein (1992); Federici (2004); Weeks (2011); Dunaway (2014); Ferguson (2015); Harris and Hough (2021).

[11] Roediger (1991); Rose (1997); Weeks (2011); Ferguson (2015).

commodity production viable, capital must rely on extra-economic coercion that often takes the form of *state and parastate violence*.[12] World-systems scholars have long pointed out how peripheral regions of world capitalism have been pockmarked by pervasive practices of coerced labor.[13] However, there is mounting empirical evidence suggesting that the systematic deployment of labor violence, state repression, policing, paramilitarism, and new forms of capitalist authoritarianism is becoming increasingly pervasive across the entirety of the contemporary global economy.[14] Reports by the International Labour Organization (ILO 2009, 2017), for example, have described "forced labor arrangements" as the veritable "underbelly of globalization," affecting some 24.9 million people in "virtually all countries and all kinds of economies."[15] Other studies have upped this number to 27 million, equivalent to the number of slaves seized from Africa during the Atlantic slave trade.[16] As this book makes clear, the systematic deployment of state coercion and paramilitary violence has been an essential weapon in the capitalist tool kit in rural Colombia. Whether to dispossess rural inhabitants from

---

[12] To be clear, dependency and world-systems scholars have long pointed out the extra-economic coercion associated with colonial labor systems and other peripheral forms of capitalist production (Frank 1966, 1967; Furtado 1964, 1970; Galeano 1973; Wallerstein 1974). Moreover, a more recent wave of scholarship draws upon Marx's writings on "primitive accumulation" to make a sense of the violent and dispossessing tendencies of neoliberal capitalism (Arrighi 2005a, 2005b; DeAngelis 2001, 2004; Federici 2004; Harvey 2003; Levien 2017, 2018; Perelman 2000).

[13] Wallerstein (1974); Tomich (2016, 2017).

[14] Indeed, a burgeoning body of scholarship analyzes the emergence of new forms of authoritarianism associated with the adoption of neoliberal policies, including the criminalization and policing of the poor (Bourgois 1995; Gowan 2010; Wacquant 2009), the mass incarceration of surplus populations and racialized underclasses (Alexander 2010; Golash-Boza 2015), and the rise in new securitization and surveillance techniques developed to protect the lives and property of the privileged (Clarno 2017).

[15] The ILO (2017) defines forced labor as

all work or service which is exacted from any person under the menace of any penalty and for which the said person has not offered himself voluntarily. It implies the use of deception or coercion, either by the state and public agencies, or by private individuals and enterprises, to force people to enter work or service against their will, to work in conditions they did not accept and to prevent them from leaving the job by using any form of punishment or threat of penalty.

For a critical analysis of the ILO's forced labor campaign, see Lerche (2007).

[16] Bales et al. (2009: vii).

the land or to repress worker militancy and political unrest, acts of extra-market violence have been regular and reliable tools of capital and states and therefore essential components of the global market at its margins.

A second blind spot of labor regime scholars is their tendency to assume that capitalist markets and systems of commodity production will continue to generate effective systems of labor control and social domination. This *bias of labor control* is evident in the market despotism perspective of Burawoy and others, who emphasize how contemporary processes of neoliberal globalization serve the interests of global capital at the expense of labor. Not only does this orientation presume a priori the durable workings of capitalist markets and therefore lead to over-deterministic explanations.[17] There is mounting empirical evidence that the workings of the twenty-first-century market are not simply generating new forms of market despotism and working-class acquiescence to capitalist labor processes. Rather, they are also precipitating deep social crises, social mobilization, and unanticipated anti-systemic social formations that challenge the supremacy of the global market and the power of capital. Indeed, the past two decades have seen waves of global protest activity that are driven by not only organized labor but also informal and precarious workers, the unemployed, and other subaltern groups that have been systematically excluded from access to stable proletarian jobs.[18] Indeed, both early protest waves such as the Pink Tide in Latin America, the Occupy Movement protests across Europe and North America, and the Arab Spring, and more recent upsurges by Black Lives Matter have chipped away at the hegemony of neoliberal practices across the globe. It is now imperative that labor scholarship account for both the precarity of labor as well as the precarity of twenty-first-century capitalism.

In Colombia, this bias of effective labor control is most evident in research that emphasizes the relationship between the adoption of neoliberal policies in the 1990s and the growth of paramilitarism.[19] Some of the richest and most compelling recent studies of neoliberalism in Colombia highlight in painful detail how paramilitarism has terrorized opposition groups, including labor unions, human rights groups, and leftist political parties, forcing them to comply with new conditions of work, opening up new spaces for foreign investment, and paving the ground for renewed economic productivity. These studies of paramilitary domination as the face of twenty-first-century capitalism in Colombia capture the terror experienced by workers and working-class communities as they face

---

[17] Stern (1988).

[18] Karataşlı et al. (2015).

[19] Chomsky (2008); Hristov (2009, 2014); Gill (2016).

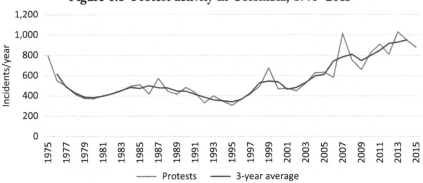

Figure 1.1 Protest activity in Colombia, 1975–2015

Source: CINEP Social Movements Database

exceptionally violent forms of despotism. However, their emphasis on class domination through paramilitarism overlooks how the present era of neoliberal globalization has simultaneously been marked by new forms of political contestation, labor unrest, and social mobilization. Figure 1.1 provides evidence indicating how social protest activity in Colombia has progressively increased rather than diminished as the country adopted neoliberal reforms since the mid-1990s. During the 1980s and early 1990s, protest activities hung far below those of the mid-1970s, when the country erupted in mass social protests aimed at toppling the authoritarian practices that remained in place under the National Front regime. However, national protests began rising steadily in the mid-1990s, as the government progressively adopted neoliberal polices. By 2013, the number of protest incidents in Colombia topped 1,000 twice, surpassing the previous peak of protest activity in the mid-1970s. In short, neoliberal capitalism in Colombia has not only resulted in new forms of class domination; it has also generated new upsurges in social unrest and new crises of labor control that have shifted the pressures of global market competition onto capital as well as onto labor.

But the crisis tendencies of capitalist development do not solely generate social crises and militancy. Twenty-first-century scholars of labor need to be sensitive to the tendencies of capital to expel surplus workers from the circuits of capitalist production and exchange, and, in some cases, to facilitate the emergence of alternative (illegal, informal) class, state, and market formations that exist outside the effective authority of the state. The expulsion of surplus workers through processes of capitalist dispossession and displacement has indeed been a major "push factor" driving global flows of migratory labor.[20] But capitalism's inability to

---

[20] Araghi (1995); Hart (2002); Harvey (2003); Davis (2006); Ness (2015); Sassen (2014).

absorb the totality of the world's workers does not simply push workers from one productive region to another. It also pushes surplus labor into conditions of advanced marginality that become breeding grounds for the establishment of alternative economic livelihoods and unruly social formations that operate in the shadows of state control.[21] Analyses of the labor dynamics of mafias and gangs, warlord economies, illegal and informal markets, for example, are typically overlooked by most labor scholars.[22]

In fact, illegal and informal activities remain significant generators of capitalist wealth and employment, especially in world regions that remain largely untouched by formal economic activities. For example, the United Nations Office on Drugs and Crime (2011:35) published a report estimating that the illicit financial flows that result from drug trafficking and other transnational organized crimes amount to some US$650 billion per year, about 1.5% of global GDP. The transnational market for illegal drugs alone accounts for some 50% of these proceeds (US$350 billion).[23] In terms of informal employment, the International Labor Organization's *Women and Men in the Informal Economy: A Statistical Picture* (2018:13–14) estimates that more than 60% of the world's employed population, more than 2 billion people over the age of fourteen, earn their living in the informal sector, in undeclared jobs that are not subject to national labor legislation, income taxation, social protection, or entitlement to employment benefits. Informality exists in all countries regardless of their level of socioeconomic development, although it is more prevalent in "developing countries," where the percentage of the employed population working informally averages at 69.6% of the total workforce. These average rates are highest in Africa (85.8%), Asia and the Pacific (71.4%), and the Caribbean and Central and South America (68.6%). Informal employment in Colombia in 2016 was 60.6%, just under the world average of 61.2%.

There are also good reasons to believe that the alternative economic livelihoods of global surplus labor will continue to grow into the future. As James Ferguson (2015:89–90) points out,

> As any observer of the contemporary world cannot fail to have noticed, more and more of the things in the world are produced by smaller numbers of

---

[21] Davis (2006); Ferguson (2015); Benanav (2019a, 2019b); Wacquant (2009).

[22] Some notable exceptions include Arrighi and Piselli (1987); Bair and Werner (2011); Bourgois (1995); Derlugian (2005); Karataşlı et al. (2015); Reno (1999).

[23] The markets analyzed include illegal narcotics, counterfeiting, human trafficking, oil, timber, fish, art/cultural property, gold, human organs, small arms and light weapons, and diamonds and colored gems (UNODC 2011).

people who specialize in it. Plastic toys for children are overwhelmingly made in China. Wheat is grown in Canada on a scale and at a price that few can compete with ... This is not simply a matter of the sort of functional global division of labor that is evoked by the phrase "comparative advantage." For the fact is that whole regions and populations find that they have no "advantage" of any kind and are (in some significant measure) simply left out of the global production regime. Even where valued products are exported, it is often in ways that do not generate much employment ... In such situations we have massive populations that are, from the point of view of the production system, "redundant."

Despite their redundancy to capital and capitalist states, these burgeoning surplus populations are indeed carving out new economic livelihoods that raise important questions about the continued viability of capitalist systems of production. Clearly, these alternative social formations should be analyzed by labor regime scholars. This book contributes to contemporary discussions along these lines by viewing alternative state, market, and class formations as "normal" dynamics of capitalist development and part of the everyday experiences of the world's workers, particularly as processes of global peripheralization push people to the margins of the market.

Toward a Theory of Labor Regimes at the Margins of the Market

To capture the broad range of labor regime dynamics that arise at the margins of the global market, I reconceptualize labor regime types along two dimensions: (1) mechanisms of labor control and (2) control of the labor process. The former distinguishes whether or not capitalists have come to rely heavily upon what Marx (1976:899) described as "direct extra-economic force" (state and parastate forms of labor repression and violence) to control labor and the labor process of a given commodity or, instead, if the labor process occurs through what Marx described as the everyday "silent compulsions of economic relations." The latter describes the extent to which these mechanisms of labor control – violent or not – are indeed effective in maintaining capitalist control of workers and the labor process. These distinctions can be seen in ideal-typical forms in Figure 1.2.

The ideal type displayed in box (1) consists of a situation in which the reproduction of the local regime does not rely upon "extra-economic" violence as a principal mechanism of labor control. Instead, systems of commodity production run largely through the everyday "silent compulsion" of the market. Drawing upon Gramscian nomenclature, I describe this type of labor regime as "hegemonic," or a situation of "hegemony," to emphasize the acquiescence of commodity-producing farmers and workers to the demands of the labor process for the commodities

Figure 1.2 Labor regime ideal types

		Key Mechanism of Labor Control	
		"Silent compulsion of economic relations"	"Extra-economic force"
Capitalist Control of Labor Process	Effective	1. "Hegemony"	2. "Despotism"
	Ineffective	3. "Counter-Hegemony"	4. "Crisis of Control"

produced. The labor regime in box (2) is the ideal-typical opposite. Here we see a situation in which state and/or parastate actors employ violent forms of labor repression, which are often effective in establishing capitalist control over the labor process. I call this ideal type of labor regime "coercive domination," or simply, "despotism."

Boxes (3) and (4) differ from boxes (1) and (2) in that they indicate a situation in which capitalists have lost their capacity to control the conditions of commodity production that constitute the labor process. Box (3) refers to a situation in which the local population establishes an economic livelihood, or class reproduction strategy, that operates outside of the effective regulatory control of the state. Under these conditions, levels of violent labor repression would be low, given the fact that the state does not exercise significant influence over the local population. I call this ideal type "counter-hegemony" to highlight the ability of the local population to establish an alternative political economy. Finally, box (4) consists of a situation in which the local population contests its articulation into the labor regime and vies for control over the labor process or the fruits of commodity production, despite efforts by capital and the state to deploy violence to retain control over their labor. I call this ideal type, a "crisis of control."

Adopting this broadened ideal-typical conceptual framework clarifies the empirical patterning of Colombia's coffee, banana, and cattle-turned-coca labor regimes across time and space (depicted in Figure 1.3). During the era of US hegemony, capitalists maintained control of producers across the three labor regimes. Yet, the primary mechanisms of labor control varied, with hegemony predominating in Viejo Caldas and despotism predominating in Urabá and the Caguán region of Caquetá. Each of these regimes gave way to crises of labor control as US hegemony began to unravel in the 1980s and 1990s. Caldas and Urabá transformed into regimes marked by waves of labor unrest while the Caguán developed into a counter-hegemonic regime under the protection of the FARC guerrillas.

Figure 1.3 Local labor regime trajectories over time and space

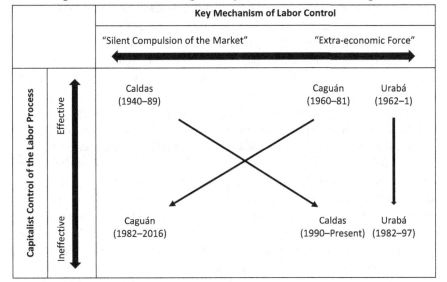

Rethinking Peripheral Proletarianization as Development
in the Twenty-First Century
==

Broadening the labor regimes framework beyond its neo-Gramscian consent–coercion dichotomy not only cautions against overdeterministic and unidimensional explanations of the causes of hegemony, despotism, crisis, and counter-hegemony. It also refocuses attention on the proximate causes of labor regime stability and crisis that have arisen in rural Colombia across broad historical periods of time. Put simply, it requires an approach that puts extra-market coercion and endemic crises of effective labor control, and the hegemonic institutions created to contain these dynamics, at the center of the analysis.

To this end, I utilize a world historical sociological approach that is rooted in three specific insights of Giovanni Arrighi in his analyses of capitalist development over the longue durée.[24] The first comes out of Arrighi's earliest work

---

[24] Arrighi's earliest work dates back to the 1960s when he analyzed labor market formation, development and underdevelopment in Southern Rhodesia. In the 1970s, Arrighi moved back to his native Italy, where he led a team of researchers who studied the varied the varied processes of market, class and state formation that arose in rural Calabria, a peripheral region of southern Italy. By the 1980s, Arrighi moved once again, this time to Binghamton University where he became a leading figure of

analyzing labor and development dynamics in Rhodesia in the 1960s, but was also later revisited at the end of his career in *Adam Smith in Beijing* (2009) and a coauthored article, "Accumulation by Dispossession and its Limits" (Arrighi et al. 2010). This is the idea that fully proletarianized labor regimes are both a heavy burden to developmental states and an obstacle to capitalist profitability. In contrast to Marxists of the left and modernization theorists on the right, both of whom viewed proletarianization as synonymous with capitalist development, Arrighi argues that populations that have been dispossessed from the means of subsistence and transformed into wage-dependent workers are prone to class conflict, invariably struggling for higher wages and redistributive social compacts that are an expensive drag on capitalist profits and a fetter on their market competitiveness. More useful to the productivity imperatives of capital are semi-proletarianized workers who subsidize their reproduction costs by retaining control of land and other assets, and are therefore amenable to processes of super-exploitation that give capital a competitive edge in the global market. Access to the means of subsistence, in turn, grants workers greater control over the conditions of their entrance into labor markets and therefore greater structural power vis-à-vis capital.

This focus on the critical role of proletarianization processes that have shaped rural Colombia's development trajectories is especially important in light of a second set of insights Arrighi later developed on the spatial dynamics of global commodity chains. In the 1980s, Arrighi agreed with Immanuel Wallerstein's assertion that the capitalist world-system was comprised of global commodity chains that linked the labor processes of core regions to those of peripheral regions. However, Arrighi and his coauthor, Jessica Drangel (1986), argued that core and peripheral positions within a commodity chain were not determined by differences in production activities or even by processes of unequal exchange. Rather, drawing from Schumpeterian insights into the nature of market competition and innovation, Arrighi argued that global disparities between core and peripheral locations under world capitalism are defined by the degree to which a nodal location in a given chain is marked by monopoly or competitiveness. Core locations are defined by capital's ability to avoid market competition and accumulate "core-like profits" that can be reinvested in innovative and promising new products while externalizing competitive pressures onto peripheral chain actors.

---

world-systems analysis, a process that culminated in the 1990s and 2000s in his trilogy on world hegemonic transitions: *The Long Twentieth Century* (1994), *Chaos and Governance in the Modern World-System* with Beverly Silver (1999), and *Adam Smith in Beijing* (2009).

Peripheral locations, in turn, are defined by their market competitiveness and therefore their continual struggle to obtain and maintain the smaller "peripheral profits" made available to them in the market.

When situating labor regimes within the core–periphery position of this Arrighian understanding of commodity chains, we see that contradictions of full-proletarianization are intensified when commodity production exists in the periphery of the chain rather than at its core. In the latter, capitalists can use their monopoly profits to reinvest in both profitability and legitimacy concerns. Core-like wealth is reinvested in the expanded accumulation of capital through more efficient production techniques and the development of new and innovative production lines. And it is also redistributed back down to workers through expensive social compacts that purchase their consent through high wages, safe working conditions, and internal labor markets, as well as through social insurance, welfare, and other social protections provided by respective states that partially decommodify their social reproduction. In contrast, peripheral locations cannot afford to redistribute their scant profits back into protective social compacts that subsidize workers' social reproduction and cultivate worker consent. Instead, labor processes and class relations become highly unstable, subject to class conflict and social unrest that can undermine capitalist production altogether.[25]

This insight was later incorporated into the intellectual corpus of world-systems analysis. In his later writings, for example, Wallerstein (1995, 2004) himself drew upon these insights in his explanation of the recurrent tendencies of the world market to make and remake exclusive boundaries around which segments of the world's population are included in protective social compacts and which are systematically excluded. He refers this boundary-drawing process as the "systems-level problem." That is, when looking at the composition of social compacts from a world-systemic perspective, we see that expensive social compacts that redistribute some of the total wealth created can only be provided to a relatively small segment of the world's working population without fundamentally threatening the profitability of the system as a whole. As Wallerstein (1995:25) described with reference to the social compacts established during the postwar Fordist-developmentalist decades, "One could cut in several-hundred-million western workers and still make the system profitable. But if one cut in several billion Third World workers, there would be nothing left for further capital accumulation."

---

[25] Silver and Slater (1999); Silver (2003).

Beverly Silver (2003) sharpened these conceptual insights in her analysis of world-systemic patterns of labor unrest and class de/formation. Poignantly, she writes historical capitalism is characterized by a "fundamental contradiction," wherein,

> on the one hand, the expansion of capitalist production tends to strengthen labor and, therefore, brings capital (and states) recurrently face to face with strong labor movements. The concessions made to bring labor movements under control, in turn, tend to drive the system toward crisis of profitability. On the other hand, efforts by capital (and states) to restore profits invariably involve breaking established social compacts and intensifying the commodification of labor, thereby producing crises of legitimacy and backlash resistance.
>
> (Silver 2003:20)

Drawing on this analytic thread, I describe the socially destabilizing convergence of processes of proletarianization and peripheralization as *peripheral proletarianization*, a situation in which the structural concerns of capitalist profitability contradict sharply with their legitimacy concerns for control over the labor process. I argue that this structural contradiction is more easily redressed for capitalists in core nodal locations, who (when confronted by demands from workers from below) can afford to reinvest in expensive social compacts that can cultivate the consent of fully proletarianized workers without threatening their market position and continued profitability. Peripheral capitalists, in contrast, must find ways to repress these demands without losing control of the labor process or losing their legitimacy vis-à-vis other market actors, including support from their respective states as well as consumers of their products, importing countries, and other market actors. In short, capitalists in the core have a greater probability of cultivating hegemonic labor regimes while peripheral capitalists are more likely to cultivate regimes that are marked by crises of labor control and repression.

If the first two Arrighian insights help contextualize Colombia's labor regimes in capitalist space, the third contextualizes them in capitalist time. Giovanni Arrighi's (1994, 2009; Arrighi and Silver 1999) later writings on world hegemonic transitions, in turn, helps situate local labor regimes temporally within the arc of rising and falling world hegemonies. Following Arrighi, we see that the world market is much more precarious and dynamic an institution than typically understood. Indeed, for the silent compulsions of the world market to function, market practices must be sustained by geopolitical institutions that govern market norms and protect enterprises and capitalist profits from threats from below. Periods of world hegemony help stabilize the workings of the world market by generating hegemonic geopolitical alliances connecting core and peripheral actors who share an interest in the expansion of specific markets but that ultimately sustain the primacy of the world hegemon at the commanding heights of the world economy. Periods of world hegemony, however, unravel when these geopolitical alliances and the hegemonic institutions that they generate fail to deliver on their promises, be they from peripheral actors seeking to upgrade to core niches in world markets or from peripheral actors who have been denied access to such opportunities for market growth and development.

Picking up on Arrighi's writings on world hegemonic transitions, Beverly Silver and Eric Slater (1999) make the explicit link between periods of world hegemony and the establishment of hegemonic social compacts. In their sweeping world historical analysis of the social origins of world hegemonies from the Dutch to the British to the American, they find a broad pattern of recurrence in that periods of world hegemonic stability are associated with the establishment of hegemonic social compacts that incorporate subaltern groups and classes as junior partners, while periods of hegemonic unraveling are associated with the breakdown of these compacts. Silver (2003) later developed this argument even further, arguing that the viability of these hegemonic pacts differs across each world hegemonic period, with more robust and inclusive social compacts created in core regions and more fragile and less inclusive pacts created in peripheral regions. This book picks up on this line of inquiry, focusing on the extent to which world hegemonic transitions impact the local labor regime dynamics of distinct global commodities.

Overall, the world historical perspective sheds light on the crisis tendencies of labor regimes that arise at the margins of world capitalism and the need to develop a broader conceptual toolkit to explain the social conditions under which labor control strategies break down, give way to extra-institutional violence, or the establishment of alternative economic livelihoods outside of the effective control of states and capital. In doing so, this book draws attention to one critical social condition driving labor regime crises: the toxic convergence of processes of proletarianization with conditions of market peripheralization, or peripheral proletarianization.

Far from assuming processes of proletarianization and peripheralization as *a priori* dynamics of labor regimes, this book draws attention to the specific sets of local, national, and global forces and actors driving processes of peripheral proletarianization as well as the struggles by workers, farmers, and even capitalist organizations and state agencies to avert the experiences of peripheral proletarianization. As we shall see, a key driver of proletarianization has been the Colombian state, which has engaged in efforts to transform the country's rural regions into sites of global commodity production through practices that have dispossessed rural inhabitants from the land and created pools of surplus labor to be exploited by local capital.

This state developmentalist strategy of promoting capitalist systems of production that rely upon proletarianized labor is a social gamble. In itself, these state development-ment practices merely articulate local labor regimes into highly peripheralized niches of the global market, thus exacerbating the social contradictions of peripheral proletarianization and contributing to the forms of endemic social crises that have pockmarked rural Colombia for decades. Only when these state developmentalist practices on the ground have been supplemented by a simultaneous set of devel-opmentalist state actions to geopolitically reconstruct the core–periphery dynamics of the global market and upgrade to more profitable market niches have they been successful in averting situations of peripheral proletarianization. However, as this book demonstrates, the ability for Colombian labor regime actors to effectively engage in developmentalist market politics and upgrade to core-like niches in global commodity markets has dwindled over the past decades due to world-systemic processes associated with the decline of US world hegemony. As processes of market peripheralization have intensified and spread across the global economy, the opportunities for economic and social upgrading have diminished, leaving the world's workers in an increasingly precarious predicament.

Analyzing Colombia's labor regimes world historically thus illuminates how the rise of US world hegemony in the mid-twentieth century expanded and stabilized the institutional workings of global markets. This market expansionary process, in turn, fostered both the *movement into* the market from emerging sites of global commodity production as well as the *movement up* the value chains of those markets to avert the negative consequences of peripheralization. However, by the turn of the twenty-first century, the United States has largely rolled back its market safeguards in ways that have re-peripheralized Colombia's niches in the global market. The contemporary crises of labor control that have arisen at the margins of the market in rural Colombia have been spawned by the state's continued efforts to retain market-dependent, proletarianized systems of global commodity production in a context of deepening peripheralization. As this book indicates, a first step out of this toxic developmental conundrum would be the formulation of new models of economic growth and development that seek not to de-peripheralize Colombia's market niches, but to de-proletarianize its systems of production and diminish worker reliance on income generated in the market to meet their subsistence livelihood needs. In other words, a first step would be to gamble not on development through the market, but development in the fortifi-cation of rural livelihoods outside the global circuits of capital.

Case Study #1

THE RISE AND FALL OF HEGEMONY IN THE COFFEE REGIME OF VIEJO CALDAS

It's like they say, I've been a cafetero since childhood and remained one during the good times and also difficult ones. That's how it goes, some good, others bad. And, us people here, we don't live merely by producing coffee. We have to continue fighting with it, whatever comes our way. We are always looking forward to see what may happen, what comes. Until now, thank God, we have had to defend what we have gained. We aren't going to say we have never reached a crisis point that is so horrible that we can't imagine a way out. No, we've been surviving and that's how we do it, alive and kicking.

(Don Jairo Rodriguez, coffee farmer, Salamina, Caldas [July 2, 2015])

The first thing we have to do is alert the national government that this is a grave crisis of the entire sector. We are producing at a loss. The ruin of all coffee growers is coming and we have to take measures to help the 800,000 cafetero families in this country. The cost of producing a coffee load is $900,000 pesos [US$285.30] and the sale price is $720,000 pesos per load [US$228.24]. This is the result of the politics of the national government. They have to be made aware of this because past commitments were made. We believe that the Federation has to deliver on this [commitment] to coffee growers. Now we see that the finance minister does not want to propose an alternative solution to this serious crisis, so we coffee growers have to organize.

(Orlando Beltrán Cuéllar, Dignidad Cafetera [March 23, 2018])[1]

In early September of 2018, the farm-gate prices of coffee had slid once again below the costs of production and the country's coffee-producing farmers (*cafeteros*) were worried that they would not survive the economic losses without another boom like the one they enjoyed in the mid-2014s, or even the smaller

---

[1] La Crónica del Quindío (2018).

one at the close of 2016. Figuring out a way to stretch their budgets, access new lines of credit, and retain faith in future bumps in coffee prices has become a significant part of the new reality for these producers. The other part of this new reality is the willingness to participate in street protest, strikes, and mass demonstrations, often in the face of police repression, in order to force the Colombian government to accept responsibility for the crisis and secure promises of protection from future whips of the market. In October 2018, the cafeteros took to the streets once again in a series of actions organized by the cafetero movement, Dignity for Colombia's Coffee Growers (*Dignidad Cafetera*), and managed to have some of their debts forgiven.

For generations, such precarity and endemic crisis did not exist. Throughout the middle decades of the twentieth century, the cafetero farmers of Viejo Caldas experienced an unprecedented degree of economic stability and upward social mobility, transforming them into one of Latin America's middle-class peasantries and a symbol of the progress attainable by capitalist development. Coffee production for export to the global market became a mantelpiece of the national developmental model, a driver of economic growth and modernization. And when most of Colombia's countryside plunged into low-intensity guerrilla warfare, state violence, and paramilitarism, the coffee region remained a bastion of traditional political party votes and largely immune to either guerrilla activity on the left or paramilitarism on the right. At the helm of this model stood the National Federation of Coffee Growers of Colombia (Fedecafé), a parastatal organization granted a mandate to regulate the domestic market, rationalize production, and vertically integrate the sector based upon a smallholding farmer structure of production. Fedecafé's measures vis-à-vis the country's cafeteros became known as the *Pacto Cafetero*, a hegemonic social compact in which coffee farmers agreed to invest in the expanded production of coffee for export in exchange for regulatory measures and institutions that were designed to reduce the risks and enhance the rewards of coffee production.

For the greater part of the twentieth century, this Pacto Cafetero was successful as an engine of economic growth and development, as a hegemonic labor regime that incorporated cafeteros as active junior partners in the expanded production of coffee, and as a moral economy that delivered on its promises of economic stability and social mobility. Fedecafé's Pacto Cafetero initiatives produced high-valued coffee for the market, stable livelihoods for its producers, and political legitimacy for the state. As a consequence, coffee production became a symbol of national pride and coffee producers came to imbue their work with greater significance. They were no longer subsistence farmers (*campesinos*) who happened to produce coffee alongside other crops in order to make a living. Instead, as noted in the quote from Don Jairo above, they became *cafeteros*. Coffee-production became a vocation and a social identity rather than simply an economic livelihood. Though it has its "difficult times," ultimately it became a way of life that one *is* rather than something that one *does*.

Since 1989, however, the ability to be a cafetero has diminished and the region has become embroiled in conflict and social unrest. As we shall see, since then the world coffee market has become increasingly competitive. Coffee prices have declined significantly and become highly volatile, fluctuating wildly by the hour, day, month, and year. This competition and volatility has strained Fedecafé's ability to maintain its part of the bargain to producers under the Pacto Cafetero, resulting in recurrent periods in which coffee prices have fallen below the costs of production and chronic crises of labor control. Yet, Colombia's cafeteros continue to figure strongly in the country's economic and political imagination as a barometer of the national economy and of the Colombian government ability to protect the livelihoods of its people.

It is this moral economy of coffee that has granted the country's cafeteros a certain degree of structural power, or political leverage, vis-à-vis the Colombian state despite the liberalization of the world coffee market. Since the 1990s, Colombia's cafetero movement has become increasingly effective in orchestrating mass street protests and strikes capable of bringing the regional, and at times national, economy to a halt when coffee booms turn to bust. As the Dignidad Cafetera's leader, Orlando Beltrán Cuéllar, noted in the quote above, any drop of coffee prices below the costs of production is indicative of the political failure of the Colombian state to deliver on its historic promises to protect the livelihoods of the country's coffee producers. Thus far, this message has been effective in galvanizing mass support for the cafetero movement's demands for immediate debt forgiveness, state assistance, and new rounds of subsidized loans to finance the upkeep of their farms, plant new and improved trees if needed, and weather the hardships until the next harvest. And they have been successful in repeatedly forcing the state to acknowledge its responsibility to uphold their commitments to cafeteros under the Pacto Cafetero.

The irony of this predicament of Colombia's cafeteros is that each new round of market bust triggers cafetero protests that are successful in recreating the *status quo ante* on ever-deeper grounds. To compensate for the increasing volatility and competitiveness of the world coffee market, Fedecafé has invested in new production technologies and specialty coffee bean varieties that gain higher prices in the market, but require increasing production costs and therefore greater risks assumed by the country's cafeteros. If the market booms during harvest, the rewards justify new rounds of loans and new production cycles. If it busts, entire coffee regions plunge into economic crisis. In this era, coffee production has become a precarious gamble that is highly dependent on the whims of a volatile market, an unreliable state, and the continued successes of the Dignidad Movement. Yet, as Don Jairo notes, it remains a vocation which makes it difficult for cafeteros to imagine a political future that is less rather than more dependent upon coffee production for the world market. While increasingly militant in terms of its tactics, the demands of the Dignidad Movement remained firmly rooted in a form of backlash resistance, or a politics of nostalgia, that seeks protection from the worst excesses of the unregulated world coffee market. But in their successes, they have also recreated the cafetero's market dependence.

In this case study, I explain how and why Colombia's coffee regime shifted from hegemony to endemic crises of labor control by recasting it in world historical perspective. I argue that today's crises in Colombia's coffee region are not simply the inevitable fate of commodity-producing farmers in the contemporary global economy. Nor are they simply emblematic of the structures of underdevelopment that have existed since Colombia's insertion into the world market centuries ago. Rather, the crises are the result of the convergence of two politically contested historical processes: the proletarianization of cafetero livelihoods and the peripheralization of Colombia's niche in the world coffee market.

Chapter 2 analyzes how Colombia's coffee-producing farmers protected themselves from the vicissitudes of the world coffee market during the previous era of market liberalism, the late nineteenth and early twentieth centuries. During this period, coffee was produced using two distinct structures of production – large coffee estates using proletarianized labor and small family farms that cultivated coffee alongside subsistence crops. The former erupted in a wave of labor militancy when world coffee prices dropped during the Great Depression of the 1930s, which led to a series of reform measures that divided the estates into small and medium-sized family farms. The latter did only weather the economic storm of the 1930s with few consequences, their durability in the face of peripheral market tendencies shaped the politics of the Colombian state. It was in this context of subsistence farmer strength and coffee worker militancy that Fedecafé, and the Pacto Cafetero in particular, arose as developmentalist solution that would both protect coffee-producing farmers from busts in the market while bolstering their productivity. I end this chapter with a discussion of the social institutions underlying the Pacto Cafetero and how these institutions transformed coffee-producing farmers into fully proletarianized cafeteros.

Chapter 3 explains how and why Fedecafé's Pacto Cafetero averted the structural contradictions of peripheral proletarianization, and instead resulted in the formation of a durable hegemonic labor regime. By situating Colombia's coffee in world historical perspective, I show that Fedecafé's successes in Viejo Caldas resulted from its capacity to take advantage of the market opportunities opened up by US world hegemony. Specifically, Colombia's position in the world coffee

Map 2 Viejo Caldas, Colombia

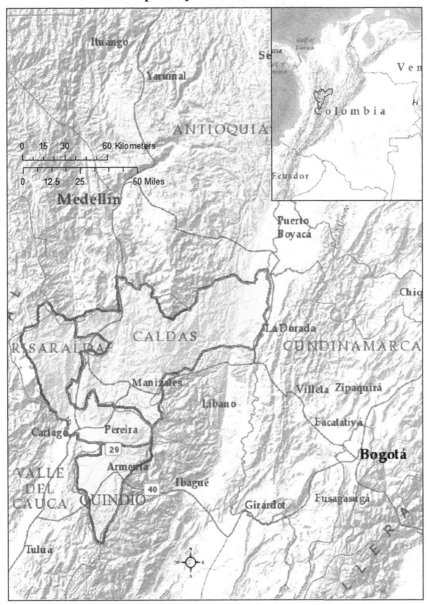

Sources: Esri, USGS, NOAA, Garmin, NPS

market was upgraded from a peripheral to a core-like niche under the Inter-American Coffee Agreement (IACA, 1941–45) and the International Coffee Agreements (ICA, 1962–89). The IACA and ICA regulated the world market by fixing prices and export quotas in an effort to promote US influence over and curtail the threat of anti-imperialism and Communism in the coffee-producing regions of the world. The central importance of US hegemony to Fedecafé's domestic regime, I argue, was demonstrated when the ICA quota system was abandoned in 1989. The deregulation of the international coffee market re-peripheralized Colombia's market niche, straining Fedecafé's capacity to maintain its commitments under the Pacto Cafetero, and giving way to today's crises of labor control. I end with an analysis of how Fedecafé and cafeteros have responded to these crises. I point out how the cafetero movement's demands for delivery of the promises of protection under the Pacto Cafetero, and their gains in restoring the *status quo ante*, have deepened the crisis of peripheral proletarianization as each new wave of mobilization deepens their dependence upon an increasingly capitalized market.

2

The Rise of Fedecafé Hegemony in Viejo Caldas

This chapter traces the social and historical origins of Fedecafé's hegemonic labor regime. I argue that Fedecafé hegemony was shaped by the experiences of an earlier generation of Colombian producers who struggled to adapt to an unregulated, volatile, and highly competitive international coffee market. I begin macroscopically by analyzing how the institutional dynamics of the world coffee market grew and expanded during the nineteenth century under British world hegemony. Second, I describe the obstacles and opportunities this burgeoning world market offered to Colombian elites and analyze the processes that facilitated Colombia's eventual insertion into this market. Third, I demonstrate how Colombia's early experiments with coffee protection for export took two forms – smallholding campesino farmers and large coffee estates, each of which developed their own types of social protections from the boom and bust pricing cycle of the market. I then argue that over time the large estates undermined their extant protections by proletarianizing their labor forces. This led to a wave of class conflict and labor unrest on the estates, which was pacified when the Colombian government passed legislation that redistributed estate lands to smallholders. Fourth, I trace the social and political origins of the National Federation of Coffee Growers, a powerful group of commercial and financial coffee elites that became the state's parastatal vehicle charged with reorganizing and expanding the coffee sector based upon a smallholder structure of production. I argue that Fedecafé's developmental initiatives, or Pacto Cafetero, provided solutions to the problems of the unregulated coffee market of the past, but gave rise to a new set of structural contradictions related to their goal of protecting smallholding producers from market risks while deepening the weight of the market in their lives. I end with a discussion of how Fedecafé's material and ideological investments in the country's cafeteros succeeded in transforming them economically from campesino farmers into fully proletarianized cafeteros and politically into bastions of support for Colombia's political establishment.

The World Coffee Market under British World Hegemony

The origins of coffee production in Colombia can be traced to the expansion of world trade that occurred during a period of British world hegemony in the nineteenth century. From the 1840s until the first Great Depression that began in the 1870s, the world economy went through a major expansion in commercial activity. At the helm of this expansion was British military and economic power. British participation in the geopolitical alliances under the Concert of Europe brought an end to the Napoleonic Wars and prevented major outbreaks of continental warfare for the remainder of the century. This, in addition to the development and expansion of railroads and telecommunication technologies, reduced the costs of ground transport, provided a peaceful climate for investment, and promoted transnational commerce in and around the continent. Beyond Europe, British naval power commanded the seas, diminishing the risks of piracy while the advent of steam-powered and industrial shipping further reduced the costs of international commerce and facilitated the integration of new world regions into what became the first truly global capitalist economy.[1]

The economic motor of this world capitalist expansion was British industrialization and manufacturing, which spread to other countries, spawning a global search for cheap raw materials, agricultural products, and industrial inputs. A global division of labor arose in which the most advanced industrial countries imported raw materials and primary products and exported them back as finished goods sold on the burgeoning world market. Industrial capitalists invested in time-saving machinery and rationalized production technologies while exploiting the pools of proletarianized labor created by processes of rural dispossession, urbanization, and mass emigration. Capital was also recirculated as financial flows, with London becoming a global financial center providing the liquid capital that greased the wheels of the world economy. Major railroads were constructed to articulate internal hinterlands to port cities. Telegraph lines traversed national geographies to communicate world prices to local producers. And the gold and silver rushes along the US and Canadian west coasts, in Australia and New Zealand, southern Africa and parts of Latin America provided capitalist states with the precious specie that backed the creation of new international currencies now pegged to silver, bimetallic, and increasingly the gold standard.[2]

---

[1] Hobsbawm (1975).

[2] Hobsbawm (1975); Allen (2001:3).

Facilitating the global flow of commodities and capital across the burgeoning market were British liberal doctrines of free trade and comparative advantage. Under British hegemony, economic liberalism became both the governing logic of world market exchanges and the touchstone political issue throughout the capitalist world.[3] Great Britain paved the way by repealing its own protectionist measures in the 1840s and opening its domestic economy to the pricing logic of the world market and the sanctity of private ownership of the means of production. In Europe, where processes of industrialization and proletarianization had gone the farthest, doctrines of economic and political liberalism appeared to provide an ideological middle ground to the burgeoning working-class radicalism that erupted during the 1848 Revolutions and the revanchist conservatism promulgated by aristocrats and the Church. Elsewhere, liberals represented the left of the political spectrum. Latin American liberals, for example, often drew upon the doctrines of free trade and private property to confiscate and privatize lands held by the Catholic Church and latifundista elites believed to be un- or under-productive. British financial support to Latin America also facilitated this process. During the years of decolonization, British capital played a key role in assisting the breakaway republics in Latin America. By the latter half of the century, British capital was extended as massive loans to newly established states now governed by Liberal leaders who used this influx of capital to build national infrastructure to facilitate their entrance into the world market as producers of primary products for export. Indeed, this burgeoning world market provided Latin American elites with opportunities to transform domestic social structures and economies that had taken form during the prior era and to ride the wave of technological innovation and modernization that was interpreted as progress. Yet, the market's laissez-faire institutionality also posed significant risks, as efforts to lure capitalist investments often recreated colonial patterns of trade and underdevelopment.

It was in this context of British world hegemony that the modern world coffee market took form. Like other tropical export commodities such as sugar and tea, the world coffee market followed a colonial pattern of trade wherein production was limited to the natural ecological conditions of the tropics (sun, rain, volcanic soils, mountainous altitude) and consumption predominating in temperate zones. Unlike sugar and tea, where the colonial systems of production

---

[3] This was the heyday of economic liberalism, championed by political economists as the economic complement to the political liberalism of the American and French Revolutions that sparked European revolution and independence movements across Latin America in the early decades of the nineteenth century.

were retained, the bulk of world coffee during this period was produced by independent nation-states and sold in a relatively unregulated world market.[4] This was because the center of production shifted from its historical centers in the Middle East, East Africa, and East Asia to Latin America, with Brazilian production growing seventy-five-fold from essentially nothing at the beginning of the century to over half of the market in 1850 and nearly 90% of the market by the close of the century.[5] Coffee production during this time was essentially a scramble to meet the growing demand for coffee, which transformed from a relatively small luxury market into a staple of the diet of North American and Northern European working-classes. While tea became the preferred staple of British workers, it was coffee that took hold in North America. US employers, for example, successfully lobbied to eliminate import duties and tariffs, as caffeine became instrumental to the regimented and disciplinary labor regimes of American industrial workers and coffee drinking became a symbol of the passage from leisure-time to work-time, the diametrical opposite symbolic function of alcohol at this time.[6]

Over the nineteenth century, the US market abounded with cheap and abundant low-grade coffee that struggled to keep up with growing consumer demand. In fact, coffee production and consumption continued to grow despite the decline of British commercial supremacy during the first Great Depression (1873–96). While the British role in the world economy shifted from commercial entrepôt to a financial entrepôt, American consumption and Latin American production expanded largely in sync. Over the course of the nineteenth century, US coffee imports grew by 2,400%. US per capita consumption reached 13 lbs/year, over 40% of the entire coffee market.[7] British consumption played a small direct role in this market, but British capital played a key role in its provisioning as loans to coffee-producing governments to finance the construction of public transportation infrastructure (primarily railways) and commercial agriculturalists to finance and expand the day-to-day costs of production (labor, machinery, irrigation, etc.).[8]

---

[4] British tea and sugar were produced in its colonies in South Asia, Dutch tea and sugar were produced in its colonies in East Asia, and French and Spanish tea and sugar were produced in what remained of its colonies in the Caribbean.

[5] Topik (2003:31).

[6] Gusfield (1996).

[7] Topik (2003:37).

[8] Stephen Topik (2003:39) describes this critical, albeit indirect, role of Britain in the world coffee market:

> There was a triangular trade. Brazilians sold their coffee in the United States and used the returns to purchase British finished goods. Americans purchased coffee

The deregulated logic of the coffee market exposed producers to risks, both natural and economic. Economically, knowledge of world prices became standardized as the London Stock Exchange, and later the New York Stock exchange, began speculative trading on coffee. As knowledge of prices became directly available to producers through telegraph lines, their vulnerability to the prices set by usurious merchants and middlemen diminished, but as is common for commodities traded in an unregulated market, new risks arose that stemmed from the volatility of prices in the market. Coffee turned into a particularly volatile market due to its natural production cycle and its exposure to various ecological dangers. The tree crop cycle for coffee arose during this time to be an especially pernicious obstacle to farmer viability in the market. Depending on the variety of coffee, it takes an average of three to four years for a coffee tree to begin bearing fruit (seeded cherries), with harvest periods occurring yearly or bi-yearly. The amount of coffee cherries produced also varies significantly from year to year, ranging from 5 to 15 lbs of unroasted green coffee (depulped cherries) per tree, while fruit production typically diminishes steadily after twenty years. Because of the length of time between seedlings and harvests, the volume of coffee in the market typically booms and busts. When harvesting happens at times of high coffee prices for the sale of unroasted green coffee, producers typically plant new seedlings with the hope that the harvest of the new trees will coincide with another period of high prices. Yet, when harvesting occurs when prices are low, producers typically decide not to plant new seedlings for fear of another bust or because they simply lack the capital to invest in new seeds and an expanded production.

The pricing volatility produced by this coffee tree cycle is confounded by ecological factors that impact yields and therefore prices. Coffee trees are persnickety, requiring specific amounts of natural sunlight, rain, and soil nutrients (especially true for Arabica varieties). Their tropical geography makes them vulnerable to destructive hurricanes and el Niño weather patterns. They are susceptible to coffee leaf rust fungus (*la roya*) that spreads quickly from tree to tree, as well as coffee borer beetles that rapidly reproduce in coffee cherries (*la broca*). Their production along mountain slopes can also expose harvests to frosts, all of which have wiped out entire crops, significantly reducing the amount of

---

with foreign exchange earned by selling temperate raw materials in Britain, as well as to the Continent. And although the British did not drink much of the coffee that they serviced, they profited from reexports to major consumers and the insurance and carrying trades, which they dominated until the 1930s.

coffee in the market and raising prices and profits for those lucky producers whose crops were unperturbed.[9]

The exceptional volatility of prices in the coffee market offered significant profits to its yearly winners and significant losses to its losers, and clearly many producers gambled on being the former. However, the overall expansion of the market during this period also tilted producers toward continued coffee production. This was especially true if and when they received support from states that reduced export taxes, made land, labor, and capital readily available, and invested in transportation and telegraph infrastructure. With production for the market believed to be the vehicle of modernization and progress, coffee appeared to provide tropical producer states with a natural comparative advantage.[10]

Colombia's Insertion and Peripheralization within the World Coffee Market

Colombia's ability to exploit these new opportunities created by British capital and American coffee consumption remained limited, however, for most of the nineteenth century. The primary obstacles to Colombia's insertion into the world market during this period were its rugged geography and its chronic political conflict. To be sure, Colombia's geography was a mixed blessing. Situated along the equatorial Andes Mountains, Colombia contains ample sunlight and rain, fertile valleys, lush temperate highlands, nutrient-rich volcanic soils, as well as tropical plains that are conducive to the development of a broad range of exportable fruits and vegetables. Its mountain slopes in particular provided a uniquely favorable ecology for the cultivation of high-valued Arabica coffee beans, later marketed as "Colombian milds." Yet, efforts to transform these fertile lands into productive and profitable agricultural enterprises with comparative advantages in the world market were hindered by this natural geography as well. Since the colonial era, the bulk of Colombia's population had settled into regional clusters in temperate highland zones that were divided by three intractable ranges of the Andes Mountains (Eastern, Central, and Western Cordilleras). East–west transportation across the steep inclines of these cordilleras was slow and treacherous, limited mostly to travel by mule until the early twentieth century. Moreover, as Colombia stands squarely on the equator, its mountains descend downward into tropical ecological zones marked by dense jungle forests, swamplands, and

---

[9] Talbot (2004:35–37).
[10] Roseberry (1995).

marshes. South–north transportation from settled central highland regions to outlets in the Caribbean occurred primarily by river on keelboats that traversed the rough waters and malaria-prone tropics of the Magdalena River. Even when human boatmen were replaced by steamships in the late 1840s and 1850s, the journey from Bogotá to Cartagena typically took much longer than from Cartagena to Continental Europe.[11] Not surprisingly, commercial planters were often beholden to usurious merchants who monopolized transportation routes and exploited their knowledge of world prices and market trends, which ultimately weakened the relative market power and profitability of those who took on the risks of agricultural production. For most of the nineteenth century, the vast majority of productive agricultural land remained concentrated in the hands of the Catholic Church and wealthy *latifundista* families who continued to sustain hacienda systems that used debt-peonage, indigenous *minga* labor, and share-cropping arrangements. Colombia's economy was largely "inward-looking," pre-serving the colonial arrangements inherited from the Spanish that operated outside of the global circuits of capital at the time.

Colombia's unrelenting geography was confounded by deeply entrenched political fragmentation that frequently resulted in sectarian conflict and partisan warfare that ultimately prevented the consolidation of political power by liberal elites seeking a seat at the "banquet of civilization" centered on the North Atlantic. Since Colombia's declaration of independence from Spanish rule in 1810, the country had become embroiled in recurrent independence struggles, chronic civil warfare, and sectarian violence between regional caudillos, aspiring national leaders, and political party factions. The number of major wars during this period are hard to count, as political conflicts blurred with other forms of social and political violence such as banditry, riots, and local *caudillismo*, though most agree that some fourteen national-scale wars erupted from Colombian independence until the turn of the century.[12] Warfare was driven primarily by the absence of a strong centralized state rather than by ideological differences between the cau-dillos who competed for local territorial control. Regional elites remained loyal to geographically isolated urban centers (Bogotá, Medellín, Cali, Cartagena) rather than to the central state. In fact, until 1886 the country was governed by a federalist constitution that granted regional governments taxing authority, distinct currencies, and the like. Chronic partisan conflict and regional warfare for control

---

[11] Safford (1965).

[12] David Bushnell (1992:13–14) counted at least fourteen national-scale rebellions in Colombia between 1828 and 1902, which does not include other forms of political violence, including riots, regional rebellions, etc.

of local land and allegiances made foreign investors and bankers skittish about any effort to develop commercial enterprises, instead preferring to make loans to finance military procurements. British capital, which rushed to Latin American entrepreneurs and states to finance national railways and shipping infrastructure, remained scant in Colombia during this period, therefore contributing to Colombia's isolation from rather than integration into the globalizing capitalist world market.[13]

Colombia's first forays into coffee production arose under these adverse political and economic conditions. The risks of coffee production were well-known, yet, as Marco Palacios (1980:13) points out, it appealed to "enlightened hacendados" who were drawn to the promise of profits and therefore planted coffee alongside traditional crops (sugarcane, maize, yuca, livestock, and cattle) using the varied debt-peonage labor systems they inherited from the past. Production on these haciendas, which began along the eastern cordilleras in the 1820s and spread westward in the 1840s and 1850s, was limited in scope and scale. Chronic warfare dried up labor supplies, destroyed plantations, closed up transportation routes, and diminished returns on investment. Capital remained scarce and production techniques and transport systems primitive, and hacendado planters were compelled to take on high-interest loans with foreign commercial import houses located in London, Paris, and New York, who offered limited amounts of credit as advances on the sale of crops to agents abroad. Despite these obstacles, coffee production for export grew steadily from an average of 1,186 60 kg bags exported in 1853–55 to 49,900 by 1868–70.[14]

The election of moderate Conservative Rafael Nuñez (1880–86) marked a decisive first step toward the removal of the domestic political obstacles to Colombia's capitalist drive. Under Nuñez, Colombia adopted the gold standard (1880) to stabilize its currency and adopted a new constitution (1886) that centralized power and paved the way for liberal economic reforms. Particularly important to the coffee sector was land legislation that privatized Church and public land (*baldíos*) and stimulated the colonization and formal settlement of vast territories. The promise of land gave rise to the great "Antioqueño Colonization," the mass migration and settlement of highlander families from the areas around Medellín down the slopes of the Western Cordilleras in a region that formally became Viejo Caldas in 1888.[15] Between 1870 and 1905, the region's population

---

[13] Safford (1965).

[14] Palacios (1980:19, 35–48).

[15] Viejo Caldas was later subdivided into three political departments: Caldas (1905), Risaralda (1966), and Quindío (1966).

jumped from 68,698 to 235,369, while the size of adjudicated lands settled jumped from 21,112 to 114,235 ha. An additional 74,875 ha were purchased but not yet inhabited.[16]

Wealthy urban families used the opening of baldío lands to purchase and formally acquire large tracts of land that were used to graze cattle and experiment with plantation agriculture, including coffee production.[17] The opening up of the agricultural frontier also provided refuge for campesino families that were uprooted by war and poverty elsewhere in the country. These frontier migrants typically carved out new swaths of jungle lands to make way for the establishment of subsistence family farms. Because they often lacked formal titles to the land or could not afford the titling and surveying fees, they typically squatted on these plots of land, cultivating coffee and other cash crops to accumulate savings to eventually obtain formal titles and/or pay legal fees. However, the lack of clarity surrounding property ownership in general created an environment that was conducive to the repeated and often forceful eviction of settler families by large-scale landowners whose political connections granted them *de facto* asylum from this type of extra-legal land acquisition.[18] Whether these land struggles resulted in large or small holdings, both contributed to the steady transformation of Viejo Caldas' mountain slopes into sites of coffee production. And though the country's production still remained centered on the large estates of the eastern and central cordilleras during this time, coffee cultivation along the agrarian frontiers expanded national production levels from roughly 50,000 60 kg bags in 1853–55 to 326,000 bags by 1892–94.[19]

Coffee's expansion in Colombia seemed poised to continue its steady growth into the twentieth century but was disrupted by the outbreak of the infamous "Thousand Day War" (1899–1902), a partisan political party conflict that arose as a civil war and broke down into guerrilla warfare led by bands of radical Liberals. By the close of the war, over 100,000 Colombians were killed, much of the country's agricultural farms lay in ruins, and the national economy had largely ground to a halt. And while it was the Conservatives who formally won, political leaders on both sides of the spectrum had grown weary of violence, eager to find a path to peace, and fearful that further conflict would encourage a US invasion of the country's Panama Isthmus region.[20] A peace treaty was signed in October

---

[16] Vallecilla Gordillo (2001:57, 60).

[17] Palacios (1980:17–18).

[18] LeGrand (1986).

[19] Palacios (1980:19).

[20] Bergquist (2001:201).

1902, leading to a period of Conservative Party rule that would continue uninterruptedly for the next three decades.

Perhaps more surprising was the fact that it was under these years of the "Conservative Republic" that both Liberals and Conservatives came to share the view that Colombia shed its feudalistic robes and transform into a modern capitalist society by adhering to the principles of economic liberalism. Between 1902 and 1930, the Colombian government courted foreign investors with promises of security, lax labor and regulatory laws, and access to vast new expansions of privatized land. During this period, Colombia developed foreign-owned export enclaves that would shape the subsequent political and economic trajectory of the country, including the banana plantations owned by the United Fruit Company and the oil fields owned by Standard Oil of New Jersey. The Colombian government also became a major recipient of the abundance of liquid capital emanating from New York and London, reaching some $260 million during the 1920s alone. This influx of capital, in addition to a threefold increase in government revenues obtained from customs duties levied on exports, financed a series of massive public projects that revolutionized Colombia's meager railway and river transport systems, energy and telecommunications infrastructures, and public health facilities. These projects helped subsidize foreign investment while stimulating domestic industrialization and foreign trade. Consequently, the annual value of Colombia's total exports and imports jumped eightfold, from roughly $26 million between 1905 and 1909 to an average of roughly $200 million between 1925 and 1929.[21]

As Michael Jiménez (1995b:262) points out, it was during this period that Colombia's coffee exporters began to envisage themselves as the country's "modernizing vanguard." Loans and investments flooded into the coffee sector, stimulating expanded production on estates and financing the cultivation of new coffee trees along the agricultural frontier. Between 1896/1890 and 1931/1935, coffee production in Colombia jumped from roughly 26.8 to 222.5 thousand metric tons, an increase of 157%.[22] Nationally, coffee exports rose to 70% of the total value of Colombian exports.[23] By then, the Colombian economy had shifted from the large estates of the central and eastern highlands to the slopes of the western cordillera highlands of Viejo Caldas, where small and medium-sized farms predominated. By 1925, this region had become the central "coffee-axis" of Colombia and the country's most vibrant center of economic growth.[24]

---

[21] Bergquist (1986:295–97).

[22] Samper and Fernando (2003:422).

[23] Bergquist (1986:295–96).

[24] Vallecilla Gordillo (2001:146–49).

Early Experiments with Social Protection and Proletarianization

With the troubles of domestic political instability and warfare swept into the dustbins of nineteenth-century history, Colombia's capitalist transformation resumed. Yet, the country's full insertion into the world coffee economy presented producers with a new set of problems that emanated from the dynamics of the coffee market itself. The first problem was increasing competitiveness among coffee producer-exporter countries, which ultimately benefitted large industrial roasting firms that monopolized the consumer end of the market by creating coffee blends sourced from various exporters. As a consequence, coffee producer countries were pressured to increase the quality of their beans without radically increasing the cost of these beans in the market. Increasing export volumes and quality thus became the way that coffee producer countries adopted to this early period of peripheralization.[25]

During this period, Colombia solidified its peripheral niche within the market. As Table 2.1 indicates, Colombian coffee production increased by a whopping 167,000 metric tons during this period, more than any other major coffee-producing country except for Brazil. However, Colombia was not the only coffee producer to significantly increase its production levels. El Salvador, Guatemala, Kenya, Ethiopia, Tanganyika, and Nicaragua each increased their production levels by over 10,000 metric tons per year, while other countries like Ecuador, Costa Rica, Madagascar, Indonesia, and Yemen also made significant advances. The overall size of the world market almost doubled, growing from 857 to over 1,500 tons.

In terms of its relative weight in the world market, Colombia's jump in production increased its overall market share from 2.7% to 12.4% during this period. This made it the second largest coffee-producing country in the world after Brazil, which retained its monopolistic control of nearly 60% of the market. These vast increases, in addition to the entrance of new producer-exporters and advances in existing ones, appeared to chip away at the market shares of Brazil, Guatemala, Costa Rica, Indonesia, Haiti, and India, all of whom increased their exports while losing their shares of the market. Faced with this competition, Jamaica and Venezuela actually reduced their exports while others like Ceylon and Portuguese Timor exited the market altogether.

If the first problem Colombian producers experienced as they entered the world coffee market was the competitiveness that arose among coffee producer-exporter countries, the second problem was the structural volatility of prices. It is widely

---

[25] Topik (2003:23–49).

Table 2.1 *Coffee export growth and world market shares, 1896–1935 (1,000 metric tons, five-year avg.)*

	1900		1930		Exports growth
	Exports	Market Share (%)	Exports	Market Share (%)	
Brazil	586.3	68.3	917.3	59.6	331.0
Colombia	*23.2*	*2.7*	*190.4*	*12.4*	*167.2*
El Salvador	22.2	2.6	58.6	3.8	26.4
Guatemala	38.2	4.4	56.7	3.7	18.6
Kenya	0.0	0.0	15.8	1.0	15.8
Ethiopia	0.0	0.0	14.1	0.9	14.1
Tanganyika	0.0	0.0	11.7	0.8	11.7
Nicaragua	4.6	0.5	15.3	1.0	10.7
Ecuador	0.0	0.0	9.4	0.6	9.4
Costa Rica	15.4	1.8	23.5	1.5	8.1
Madagascar	0.0	0.0	6.7	0.4	6.7
Indonesia	54.9	6.4	61.5	4.0	6.6
Yemen	0.0	0.0	4.1	0.3	4.1
Angola	8.5	1.0	11.8	0.8	3.3
Uganda	0.0	0.0	2.5	0.2	2.5
Haiti	32.5	3.8	34.3	2.2	1.8
Honduras	0.0	0.0	1.8	0.1	1.8
India	14.3	1.7	15.8	1.0	1.5
Belgian Congo	0.0	0.0	1.5	0.1	1.5
Peru	0.0	0.0	0.7	0.0	0.7
Guadeloupe	0.8	0.1	0.0	0.0	−0.8
Venezuela	48.2	5.6	47.1	3.1	−1.1
Jamaica	5.6	0.7	3.1	0.2	−2.5
Ceylon	1.0	0.1	–	–	–
Portuguese Timor	1.9	0.2	–	–	–
Mexico	–	–	30.7	2.0	–
Dominican Republic	–	–	4.8	0.3	–
World Total	857.4	100	1,539.2	100%	681.7

No data available (–).
Source: Author calculations based on Samper and Fernando (2003).

noted that coffee typically goes through "natural" cycles of overproduction due to both the timing of harvests and unpredictable ecological vulnerabilities to frosts, pests, and fungi that can destroy entire crops and therefore significantly reduce supplies. These boom-and-bust cycles exacerbate pricing volatility when

Figure 2.1 Pricing volatility of Colombian coffee exports to the
United States, 1899–1935

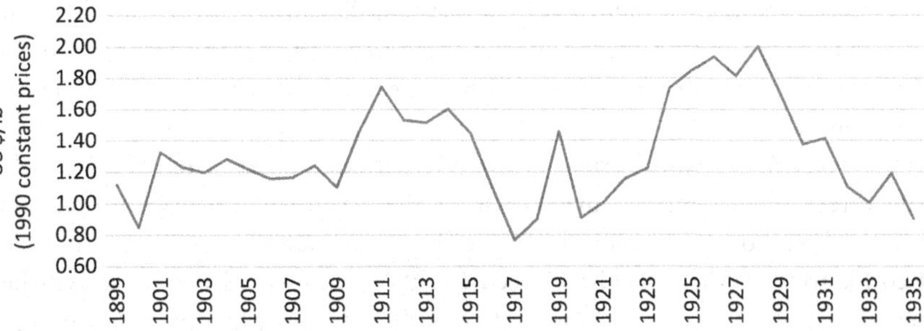

Source: Calculations based on Samper and Fernando (2003)

international purchases are governed by the laissez-faire logic of economic liberalism that predominated during this time.[26]

Figure 2.1 depicts the pricing volatility of Colombian exports to the United States point of entry in New York between 1899 and 1935.[27] It shows how average yearly prices on imports to New York varied widely from lows of less than $0.90/lb in 1900, 1917, 1935 to highs of more than $1.40/lb in 1910–15, 1919, and 1924–29. Most crippling for producers were steep and immediate busts that occurred in short periods of time, like that which occurred in 1899–1900, 1914–16, 1919–20, 1928–30, 1931–32, and 1934–35.

The impact of these pricing busts on Colombian coffee producers, however, differed depending upon whether coffee was produced by subsistence farmer families, semi-proletarianized coffee estates, or fully proletarianized capitalist plantations. In Viejo Caldas, the predominant structure of coffee production was small and medium-sized family farms that were essentially created as squatter settlements along the expanding agricultural frontier. By 1932, some 3,411 medium-sized farms (between 4.1 and 16.5 ha) and 36,475 small farms (between 4.1 and 16.5 ha) dotted the region's landscape.[28] Coffee was planted and cultivated alongside other subsistence agricultural goods and cash crops, often to accumulate the money needed to purchase formal titles, hire a lawyer, or to pay land surveying fees. After formal titles were acquired and fees paid, this influx of

[26] Giovannucci et al. (2002); Talbot (2004); Fridell (2014).
[27] Coffee imports to the United States grew from 363.68 thousand metric tons in 1899 to 791.30 by 1935, more than double the size of the second leading importing country, Germany (Samper and Fernando 2003:444–49).
[28] Vallecilla Gordillo (2001:146, 165).

cash would typically be used to purchase seeds, tools, livestock, or otherwise diversify their use of the land. Family labor was the predominant means of subsistence, though medium-sized farmer families would also hire migrant laborers during harvest periods. These workers were often recent frontier settlers who were eager to earn some cash in order to eventually purchase smallholdings of their own.

The volatility of coffee prices in the international market had comparatively little direct impact on the livelihoods of these subsistence farmers precisely because their household reproduction did not typically depend upon the sale of coffee to meet their livelihood needs. Rather, they would enter and exit the market depending upon the going rate of coffee. If and when prices were high during harvest, the incentive was created to use this cash to purchase seeds or convert some land to coffee cultivation. However, if prices dropped, they could just as easily exit the market by converting their coffee fields to grazing land or other crops, or simply let the coffee berries rot on the trees. This autonomy from the coffee market gave them an "exit option" that essentially protected them from the social risks produced by the volatility of prices in the coffee market.[29]

But it was not only this exit option that prevented Viejo Caldas' campesino settlers from becoming fully marketized cafetero farmers. The incentives to enter the market were not as compelling as the international boom in prices would suggest. Because they cultivated along the steep mountainous slopes of a geographically diffuse and sprawling agricultural frontier, they were often quite isolated from one another as well as from the commercial firms that purchased domestic beans and exported them to the world market. This made them vulnerable to merchants who specialized in purchasing local beans and transporting them across the region's rugged terrain (often by mule) to export houses in city centers and coastal towns. As a consequence of the high transport costs and the monopolization of these routes by usurious merchants, Colombia's campesino coffee producers did not often know whether international prices were high or low and did not have many options on who to sell their harvest to. In practice, this meant that they could not reap the economic rewards of the booms in international prices, peripheral as this niche was, and they did not take on the risks of coffee cultivation as their predominant form of economic livelihood. They were resolutely *campesinos* who produced coffee alongside other crops, not *cafeteros* in the sense of what this came to mean in the coming decades.[30]

---

[29] Palacios (1980); Bergquist (1986).
[30] London (1995); Hough (2007).

In contrast to coffee smallholdings, the large-scale coffee estates that predom-inated in eastern and central cordilleras and had spread to the western cordilleras of Viejo Caldas, where some 288 large coffee estates (between 16.5 and 1000+ ha) were established by 1932.[31] In contrast to coffee smallholdings, these large estates were indeed highly vulnerable to the pricing volatility of the coffee market. But even then, their ability to weather pricing busts differed depending upon the extent to which production on the estate was fully marketized or not. Prior to the Thousand Day War, the production that did arise on large coffee estates typically used an amalgam of various semi-proletarianized or non-proletarianized wage systems that some at the time described as "feudal."[32] Some estates used permanent workers (*arrendatarios*) who, like tenant farmers, were granted a plot of land (*parcela*) on or nearby the estate in exchange for work obligations on the coffee estate. Others contracted frontier settlers (*colonos*) to open new lands along the frontier regions in exchange for the sale of the coffee trees planted (plus improvements on the land).[33] Finally, some used sharecropping arrangements that granted workers access to estate lands in exchange for a portion of their harvests or rent payments.[34]

The use of fully proletarianized farm hands or even seasonal harvesters (*jorna-leros*) was less common during this period because the open frontier made it relatively easy for landless workers to avoid unfavorable labor arrangements. The fact that these estates were typically established alongside peasant squatter com-munities and frontier settlements meant that workers moved back and forth into labor arrangements on relatively favorable terms. The existence of this type of exit option made it difficult for estate owners to discipline labor or create more exploitative labor arrangements to make up for any losses during economic busts.[35] Unable to externalize the revenue losses onto their workforces, estate owners during this time protected themselves from the volatility of the coffee market by diversifying production or simply maintaining a good proportion of

---

[31] Vallecilla Gordillo (2001:146, 165).

[32] Marco Palacios (1980:13) notes that they "were thought of as feudal by all who considered themselves even moderately liberal."

[33] Frontier colonos would agree to clear forest land and then plant and cultivate coffee trees for a specific number of years (three to four) until the trees became productive and then sell these trees and improvements and renounced land . . . pushing further out into frontier forests (Bergquist 1986:315–16).

[34] Bergquist (1986:315–21).

[35] Jiménez (1995b:265–66).

surplus capital in liquid form in foreign banks, where the capital could accumulate on its own.[36]

However, the general optimism produced by the economic boom of the 1910s, combined with the availability of vast new sources of liquid capital, convinced Colombia's large coffee estates to adopt increasingly commodified labor systems, including the use of fully proletarianized workers. As Michael Jiménez (1995b) noted, the influx of foreign capital provided estate owners with the capacity to concede relatively high wages to seasonal and full-time farmhands. They also began offering loans to their labor force, which, in turn, began to cultivate coffee on the small plots of land that they came to inhabit and sell them directly to local buyers. This combination of "relative economic security" in addition to new "opportunities to engage in commercial activity" without the usual market arbitration from estate owners granted coffee workers a relatively high degree of economic autonomy. Such a system benefitted both workers as well as owners so long as prices remained high and labor remained abundant. However, when prices crashed in 1920–21 it offered no solution to buffer against the problem of fluctuating market prices. And as it happened, both estate owners and their works became saddled with losses and debts that required repayment. Estate owners responded to this crisis by trying to push the profit losses back onto their workers by demanding longer hours and less pay. Estate workers, however, responded by organizing a series of strikes demanding cheaper food and housing, shorter hours for freely contracted workers, a reduction and/or termination of the number of tasks required for payments of land rents by arrendatarios, for a complete end to the ejection of squatters from estate parcels, and for legal recognition of worker unions by the state. By 1925, Colombia's coffee estates had become sites of Communist and radical Liberal organizing drives aimed at organizing a united front of arrendatarios and jornaleros who demanded basic labor rights.[37]

At first, estate owners responded to this first wave of labor militancy by relying on the state arbitration mechanisms established from conflicts located in other sectors, such as the labor legislation of 1919 and 1920 and the Office of Labor in 1923.[38] These labor arbitration mechanisms were generally effective in quelling the appeal of some of the most radical tendencies on the estates. What was not

---

[36] This liquid capital was used to buy bonds issued on the internal debt, invest in short-term loans to import-export firms, held in foreign banks, or stockpiled as gold through bills of exchange in London Banks (Palacios 1980:8).

[37] Bergquist (1986:337).

[38] Such early labor legislation attempted to defuse and regulate labor unrest by prohibiting strike activity in certain key sectors (public service and transport), by deporting foreigners involved in the labor organizing campaigns, and by creating various

diffused by state labor offices was diffused by the massive boom in coffee prices between 1923 and 1927, which bred new optimism in both estate owners and coffee workers. Yet, as labor historian Charles Bergquist (1986:332–34) pointed out, these ameliorative mechanisms proved to be insufficient when coffee prices tanked during the years of the Great Depression and when the systemic crisis of the market "threatened the economic viability of the large coffee estates and jeopardized the very existence of the coffee hacendados as a class." Estate owners responded with an all-out offensive against their workers. In an effort to curtail the autonomy gained by the workers on their estates, they prohibited workers from cultivating coffee on their own *parcelas*, banned the sale of their agricultural commodities in local markets, and ejected the labor leaders, political organizers, and others considered to be agitators using private security forces. This in turn strengthened the resolve of the coffee workers, who not only resisted this ejection from the lands they cultivated, but also began challenging the legality of estate owner land titles and the terms of the contracts on their parcelas.

Frustrated by the failure of the labor arbitration offices to resolve the conflicts on their estates, owners turned to their political links within the Conservative Party, albeit the most reactionary ones, to garner support for repressive measures against the workers. The result was a spiraling of violence on the estates by the closing years of the decade. Liberal and Communist activists used this to publicly delegitimate and discredit the Conservative regime. The Liberal party candidates, in turn, promised concessions to the budding labor movement in exchange for votes in the 1930 presidential campaign. Riding this wave of labor unrest, the Liberal Party won the election and began to advocate a series of agrarian and labor laws that sought to end the violence and restore the profitability of the coffee sector.[39]

Foremost among these Liberal reforms were the land redistribution programs codified in Agrarian Reform Law 200 of 1936. Rather than encourage the more traditional agrarian policies of expanding the agricultural frontier regions (which avoided a political confrontation with traditional landed elites), the Liberal government instead began to actively buy out the coffee estates themselves at market value. These huge chunks of property would then be surveyed, divided, and finally sold to the squatters and coffee-growing smallholders who had been cultivating them. The estate owners, who as early as 1929 had been recommended by the Chief of the General Labor Office to sell off their holdings and instead invest in

mechanisms to conciliate and arbitrate labor conflicts at the point of production (Bergquist 1986:332–33).

[39] Bergquist (1986:338–39).

coffee bean processing and merchandising, realized rather quickly that such a strategy was not only wise in the short run but in the long run as well. This type of agrarian reform through land redistribution was appealing to liberal reformers who had become distrustful of large-scale planters' capacity to generate economic growth and social stability.[40]

The Rise of Fedecafé's Developmental Social Compact

The crash of the Great Depression in the 1930s did not only highlight the vulnerability of large-scale coffee estates to the structural volatility of the international coffee market. The 1930s marked the end of British world hegemony.[41] The world market had collapsed, the doctrine of economic liberalism failed to provide a viable strategy out of the world economic slump, and governments throughout the advanced capitalist world began to experiment with national hegemonic projects. As Silver and Slater (1999:197) note, while distinct in their political and economic policy measures, the US New Deal, Soviet Five-Year Plan, fascism, and Nazism were each "different ways of jumping off the disintegrating world market into the life raft of the national economy." Outside of the dominant centers of capitalism, economists like Raul Prebisch began to develop critiques of the theory of comparative advantage in favor of a new paradigm of "structural economics" in which the world market was composed of centers and peripheries linked by unequal and declining terms of trade. To rectify this market inequality, structural economists began to advocate a more proactive state and encourage "import substitution industrialization" policies to achieve domestic economic growth and modernization.[42]

Colombia's Liberal Party leaders, Enrique Olaya Herrera (1930–34) and Alfonso López Pumarejo (1934–38), shared this belief that the state must take an active role in cautiously engaging in world trade by protecting domestic industrialization and worker-citizens through social and labor reforms. And they were well aware that the Great Depression had afforded Colombia with an opportunity to actually bolster its coffee sector. As had happened on Colombia's large coffee estates, many of the world's coffee-producing plantations experienced similarly destructive waves of social unrest and bankruptcy during this time.[43] And

---

[40] Christie (1986); Jiménez (1995b:264).

[41] Arrighi (1994).

[42] Baer (1972).

[43] Stolcke (1995); Samper Kutschbach (1995).

perhaps fortunately for Colombian coffee producers, Brazil's large-scale plantations appeared to be hit the worst, as Brazilian coffee exports dropped from over 1 million metric tons in 1930 to just over 700 one year later.[44] The disruption caused by the Great Depression thus provided an opportunity to actually increase Colombia's share of the international market by expanding coffee production on those productive units that were shielded from the volatility of the market: its small and medium-sized farms. The question facing these Liberal reformers was how to restructure the sector along these lines.

The land redistribution occasioned by the Land Law 200 of 1936 essentially nailed the coffin of the country's large estate owners, whose economic bankruptcy had exposed their market liabilities and whose turn to violence to quell labor unrest exposed their moral bankruptcy. During the years of the Conservative Republic, these planter capitalists had been the state's most reliable partner in the growth of the coffee sector. They had long developed strong political ties to Bogotá through their participation in the Agricultural Society of Colombia (SAC, est. 1871), the country's oldest and most formidable economic interest group. However, under the Liberal regime of the 1930s, these ties were more a political burden than an asset. Thus, it was a class of commercial and financial capitalists rather than planters that proved most effective in impacting the state's politics toward the coffee sector.[45]

At first only a small group of real estate developers and financiers that rode the tide of frontier expansion by profiting from the speculative land market, this class of "Western" commercial capitalist families based in Medellín had transformed into lucrative coffee traders and marketers. In this capacity, they provided frontier settlers with credit to establish coffee farms, monitored bean quality, and undertook merchandising campaigns that touted the quality of Colombian mild beans abroad. By the mid-1920s, they were receiving "the lion's share of [state] resources for infrastructural improvements," much of which was invested in transportation routes that connected frontier producers to port cities located on the Pacific and Atlantic coasts. Because these routes were the most cost-effective way of exporting coffee, they also ended up becoming used by small and large producers in both the frontier regions of the western cordilleras as well as the older highland regions of the central and eastern parts of the country.[46]

In 1927, these commercial elites had formed the National Federation of Coffee Growers of Colombia (Fedecafé), a lobbying organization that advocated for the

---

[44] Samper and Fernando (2003:434).

[45] Christie (1978:268); Jiménez (1995b:265).

[46] Jiménez (1995b:265–66).

growth and expansion of the sector. Under the Liberal regime, Fedecafé became a semi-private parastatal organization and was given a public mandate to regulate and organize Colombia's coffee export economy based upon a smallholder structure of production. Fedecafé's first president, Mariano Ospina Peréz, was a firm believer that smallholding producers provided Colombia with a competitive edge in the world market, particularly in comparison to Brazil's reliance on large coffee plantations. In 1934, he wrote,

> Colombia, because of the enormous parcelization of its coffee properties and the multiplicity of crops grown within each coffee farm, is in very favorable position to endure a price war. Even supposing that a great part of the coffee harvest were lost or that the price of coffee were to fall considerably, the people of the coffee zone could count on a considerable part of the productions they need for their subsistence.
>
> (Quoted in Stolcke (1995:81))

Colombia's export growth during the 1930s seemed to substantiate this belief. And consequently, Fedecafé was granted the authority to tax exports and use this revenue to finance the vertical-integration, modernization, and expansion of the sector as a key pillar of the government's broader industrial development plan. Over the next four decades, Fedecafé deepened and expanded its state-like authority over the coffee region, further integrating the sector into the international coffee market while protecting local producers from problems arising from marketization.

Fedecafé's directors inherited a domestic sector that continued to face deep structural obstacles to its further growth. One set of obstacles was the geographic diffuseness of productive lands and the disorganization of the domestic commercial market. By the 1930s, smallholder farms dotted a rugged and seemingly impassable landscape that stretched across the three mountain cordilleras from the department of Santander in the northeast all the way through Viejo Caldas down to the departments of Tolima and Huila in the southwest of the country. In order to get harvested green coffee to the coffee-husking plants where they would be processed, sorted, and bagged for export, coffee smallholders had come to rely upon usurious merchants to transport them at relatively high prices. The negative impact of these predatory mercantile networks on producers and exporters was twofold. First, middle merchants siphoned off profits that could have been retained by either smallholders or by exporters. In addition, they also provided little incentive for producers to assure a degree of quality control for Colombian beans. Under these conditions, coffee farmers tended to orient their energies toward satisfying the short-term interests of the transport merchants by producing as much coffee as possible rather than producing quality beans. This was reflected in world consumer markets by the 1920s, where Colombian coffee was not only declining in price but was also perceived to be declining in quality as well.[47]

The second major obstacle was the tendency for coffee prices to fluctuate wildly in the market. Domestically, volatile prices presented Fedecafé with two problems. First, falling prices meant that coffee exporters needed to increase the levels of coffee produced and exported in order to make up for losses in per unit income. Greater volumes of coffee flooding the market cheapens its value, leading to a vicious circle wherein efforts to make up for losses are supplemented by even greater attempts to expand productivity. This crisis of overproduction required some type of regulatory mechanism in order to assure that coffee supply would be controlled in a way that followed demand. Second, as discussed earlier, was the fact that pricing volatility, in general, and busts, in particular, pressured small-holders to diversify their farms to diminish their reliance on coffee production to meet their household reproduction needs. For Fedecafé, this meant that they would have a hard time convincing coffee producers that the investments in expanded coffee production and quality beans would be worth the risks of greater market dependence.

Fedecafé responded to these problems with a number of developmentalist initiatives that served to consolidate the sector under Fedecafé control and provide an institutional framework for its rapid expansion. In order to vertically integrate domestic production, Fedecafé invested in the construction of a wide network of local cooperatives, purchasing points (*puntos de compra*), husking plants (*trilla-doras*) and storage facilities, all owned and operated by Fedecafé and located conveniently throughout the coffee-producing heartlands. These networks of local purchasing points protected growers from predatory merchants by providing them with the opportunity to sell their beans at transparent prices directly to Fedecafé buyers. Fedecafé's guarantee of purchase (*garantia de compra*) policy meant that they would purchase any beans that met their quality standards. Their price floor system (*precio piso*), in turn, prevented domestic coffee sale prices from dropping below the costs of production. The combination of the guaranteed purchase and price floor served a number of functions. First, by controlling and stabilizing prices in the domestic market, it reduced the risks and enhanced the financial gains for coffee producers. Farmers were thus incentivized to dedicate more of their labor and land to coffee rather than subsistence products. Second, it also drew producers into Fedecafé's commercial orbit, which helped them purchase greater volumes of coffee produced in the domestic market and make it easier to engage in further

---

[47] London (1995:6).

efforts at domestic vertical integration.[48] Finally, it helped them secure steady inflows of quality coffee beans. This influx of coffee supplies would allow Fedecafé to separate the choicest beans for export while stockpiling the rest in an effort to buffer against future upturns and downturns in the world market.

Early on, Fedecafé financed these initiatives by taking advantage of Colombia's relative jump in world market share.[49] However, these revenues began to dry up by the mid-1930s. In 1940, Fedecafé created a more permanent institutional solution, the National Coffee Fund (*Fondo Nacional Cafetero*, FNC). The FNC began collecting coffee export taxes and overseeing Fedecafé spending and investments. It became the lynchpin of Fedecafé's domestic purchasing initiatives, essentially stabilizing prices in the domestic market and guaranteeing a market outlet for coffee produced to allow for long-term developmental planning in the sector.

Fedecafé also invested heavily in quality control and improvement measures to standardize and add value to coffee exports. Two complementary institutions played a key role in these initiatives: the establishment of the National Coffee Research Center (Cenicafé, est. 1938) and rural extensions services. Cenicafé was created as a research institute equipped with a full-time staff of professional agronomists, scientific researchers, economists, and ecology experts aimed at increasing farming efficiency and coffee plant productivity, developing pest and disease controls, developing new plant varieties and other measures to ensure the long-term development and expansion of the sector. Fedecafé's extensions services, in turn, were created to act as a knowledge conduit between coffee farmers and Cenicafé scientists. After receiving formal training as agronomists, Fedecafé's extensions agents were assigned to specific coffee-producing locales where they gained intimate knowledge of the soil, weather patterns, pests, and other ecological features of these regions.[50] Importantly, they were also tasked with regular farm visits to individual farms in order to monitor crops, look for signs of coffee rust or coffee borer worms, inspect industrial inputs and equipment, discuss any problems or unexpected outcomes the farmer experienced since their last visit, and offer advice on how to proceed with cost-effective improvements. The continued presence of extensions agents in coffee-producing fields thus provided Fedecafé with up-to-date knowledge on local problems experienced by farmers in their

---

[48] Fedecafé's cooperatives became the predominant site of domestic coffee purchases. Their coffee quality standards and floor prices set the benchmark for all coffee bought and sold domestically. The amount of coffee purchased by Fedecafé for export grew from 1% in 1938 to 60% by 1978 (Vallecilla Gordillo 2001:206).

[49] Talbot (2004:54); Samper Kutschbach (1995:161).

[50] Today, Fedecafé's extensions agents also use satellite images to analyze the ecological terrain of each farm, collect soil samples, and monitor weather patterns and blight.

efforts to produce coffee while simultaneously promoting Cenicafé's latest research findings and developmental initiatives.

The improvements that Fedecafé, Cenicafé, and extension agents suggested to farmers typically required financial investments in their farms. In the 1930s, Colombia's coffee farmers typically took out a loan from the Agricultural Savings Bank (*Caja Agraria*, est. 1930) to finance the costs of any improvements. However, eventually Fedecafé created its own public coffee bank (*Banco Cafetero*, est. 1953) that provided credit lines with low-interest subsidized loans to coffee farmers. This access to credit with easy repayments schedules allowed farmers the ability to purchase new coffee tree seeds, water and irrigation systems, tools, fertilizers, and other items that could be used to improve the productivity of their farms.

While these initiatives helped improve the quality and flow of beans into its storage and export houses, Fedecafé began an aggressive international marketing campaign meant to increase the value and demand for quality Colombian coffee. All coffee exported from Colombian was stamped with a "100% Colombian Coffee" label so that roasters and distributors could market the price up to consumers and avoid the use of Colombian beans as simple inputs to the coffee blends sold by transnational corporations like Folgers, Sara Lee, and others. They also began to use the marketing icon, "Juan Valdez," to sell the idea that Colombia's coffee beans were produced by smallholding farmers using family labor rather large capitalistic plantations. Spending more on Colombian coffee was worth it, as it would support and protect artisanal and "traditional" livelihoods. Like Fair Trade and specialty coffees today, Fedecafé's early marketing strategies emphasized how consumer willingness to pay more for coffee would not only provide a quality cup, but also directly improve the livelihoods of rural producers.[51]

As a developmentalist set of initiatives intended to increase productivity and growth, Fedecafé's investments in Colombian coffee production were undoubtedly successful. The number of 125 kg sacks of coffee produced increased from 1,610,337 in 1932 to 4,608,569 by 1970, reaching 9,064,042 sacks by 1980. These increases in production both expanded output on existing farms and brought coffee cultivation to new regions of the country, including the departments of Tolima, Nariño, Huila, and Valle del Cauca in the southwest. However, Viejo Caldas remained the central coffee-producing axis of the country during this period, increasing its yields from 472,449 sacks in 1932 to 2,591,665 by 1980.[52]

---

[51] Talbot (2004); Jaffee (2007).
[52] Vallecilla Gordillo (2001:149).

In terms of exports, Colombia increased from 3.1 million bags exported in 1932 to 6.5 million bags by 1972.[53]

In short, Fedecafé was able to take advantage of the breakdown of the liberal world economy, offering a series of remedies and business strategies for the management, consolidation, and expansion of the coffee sector. And as history shows, their efforts were highly successful. By mid-century, Fedecafé had acquired the second largest share of the world coffee market. Its coffee was widely recognized as "the richest coffee in the world" and the figure of Juan Valdez had become an international symbol of quality beans produced by committed smallholding farmers.

The Pacto Cafetero as a Hegemonic Labor Regime

Fedecafé's initiatives were not simply successful as a set of developmentalist policies aimed at promoting economic growth through the expanded production of coffee. What was exceptional about this growth was that it occurred with the active participation of smallholding producers, who until then guarded their autonomy from the market by retaining an "exit option" when prices dropped. Under Fedecafé hegemony, these semi-marketized campesino farmers transformed into market-dependent, "full-proletarianized" cafeteros that dedicated their land and labor to increasing the quality, productivity, and growth of the sector. This transformation formed the bedrock of Fedecafé's developmentalist project, which was indeed successful in boosting Colombia's competitiveness in the international coffee market.

Fedecafé's developmental project thus needed to walk a fine line between protecting these cafeteros from the peripheralizing tendencies of the world coffee market and simultaneously deepening the influence and reach of this market in the lives of cafeteros and their communities. This task was complicated even further by the deep distrust that coffee-producing campesinos and former estate workers had of both the market and the Colombian government, which for decades sided with large landholders and coffee estate owners rather than frontier settlers and workers. To consolidate a hegemonic labor regime, Fedecafé needed to establish their legitimate authority vis-à-vis cafeteros, providing them with moral and ideological leadership by incorporating them as junior partners in a hegemonic project that benefitted both.

Fedecafé's ability to generate a hegemonic labor regime in Viejo Caldas rested upon investments in the lives of cafeteros that were both material and ideological,

---

[53] Palacios (1980:232).

economic, and sociopolitical. As discussed above, Fedecafé's material investments sought to protect cafeteros from the volatility of international coffee prices and stabilize their household incomes. This was accomplished by the FNC's price floor and guaranteed purchases, which ensured that domestic sales of unroasted coffee greens would be sold at stable prices that were over the costs of production, by provisions of technical support from extensions agents working in coordination with Cenicafé, and by provisions of credit and loans from the Banco Cafetero. The combination of these measures reduced the risks of coffee production and ensured that cafetero investments of their land and labor would generate income for their households.

Fedecafé also invested heavily in a series of broader social development projects and institutions to improve the welfare and economic stability of coffee producers and the regional economy. Some of these initiatives were direct investments. For example, Fedecafé invested heavily in social infrastructure in the region, including the construction of schools, hospitals, aqueducts, electrical grids, and the like, all meant to improve cafetero access to public education, medical attention, consumer products bought and sold on the market, and the "diverse amenities of modern life."[54] They also helped finance backward and forward linkages and economic diversification in the region. For example, the Banco Cafetero provided loans to Viejo Caldas' residents to purchase homes or finance local businesses. The NFC also became a major shareholder in various other financial institutions in the region. Over the next three decades, the FNC's Coffee Business Group (*Grupo Empresarial Cafetero*) would own the major stock in some fifty+ local businesses with holdings of over US$2.4 billion. The FNC's Financial Corporation of Caldas (*Corporación Financiera de Caldas*, est. 1961) financed the construction of some 150 local businesses (industrial, agricultural, commercial) with a patrimony of over US$70 million.[55] Its Corporation for Coffee Diversification (*Corporación para la Diversificación Cafetera*, Cordicafé, est. 1963) provided loans to local farmers who wanted to use their land for the cultivation of agricultural produce other than coffee, including sugarcane, lulo, papaya and other fruits, yuca, and others.[56]

These investments transformed the coffee-producing regions of the country into sites of rapid economic growth and development. The combined population of Viejo Caldas' key cities of Manizales (Caldas), Pereira (Risaralda), and Armenia (Quindío) grew from 246,978 in 1938 to 1,309,805 by 1985, more than double its rural population of 613,953. The percentage of people employed in agriculture

---

[54] London (1999).

[55] Robledo (1998:21).

[56] Giovannucci et al. (2002:62, 79).

likewise declined, from 68% in 1938 to 42.6% by 1973.[57] Fedecafé's investments played a key role in this social transformation. One study found that FNC investments financed the construction of 5,288 aqueducts, 16,923 school houses (*aulas escolares*), 5,387 teaching residences (*viviendas para maestros*), 12,719 sanitation dumps (*baterías sanitarias*), 1,423 bridges amenable to vehicle traffic, 1,139 pedestrian bridges, and 12,883 km of highways in Colombia's coffee regions. They also financed the electrification of 204,739 homes and the maintenance of some 50,672 km of local roads.[58] By the 1980s, with the exception of the major metropolitan centers, Colombia's coffee regions in general, and Viejo Caldas in particular, had become the most developed in the country in terms of public expenditures and social institutions.[59]

Fedecafé also made significant efforts to live up to its organization goals of being a "non-profit coffee cooperative" with a mission to protect "the well-being of Colombia's coffee growers" and "an effective, democratic and representative organization." Although Fedecafé functioned to maximize productivity and accumulate capital, it distanced itself from private capitalist business enterprises whose fiduciary responsibility was to investors and not to coffee-producing farmers. It also distanced itself from the state, whose actions were meant to protect the livelihoods of the nation at large. Instead, Fedecafé's parastatal status meant that its responsibility was to protect the lives of cafetero producers. It touted smallholders as "ideal citizens" whose dedication to coffee production formed the bedrock of the nation. In producing coffee, the country's cafeteros were producing the nation and a dignified way of life.[60] The Pacto Cafetero was therefore much more than a developmental alliance linking the interests of cafeteros, Fedecafé, and the Colombian government. It was a moral economy in which Fedecafé promised to protect coffee farmer livelihoods in exchange for cafetero compliance with Fedecafé's directives regarding coffee production.

Not surprisingly, Fedecafé invested heavily in the construction of a specifically "cafetero identity" that imbued coffee production with deep moral and social significance. As Christopher London (1999:2–5) points out, the "twin ideological pillars" of this cafetero identity were a productivist orientation to coffee cultivation and a paternalist orientation to Fedecafé. *Productivism*, he argues, is "the conceit that through continuously increasing productivity and gross output economic problems (as well as) social problems ... will disappear." Local forms of

---

[57] Vallecilla Gordillo (2001:244, 256).

[58] Robledo (1998:21–22).

[59] Junguito and Pizano (1997); Ramírez et al. (2002).

[60] London (1995).

knowledge and expertise are relinquished in favor of knowledge produced by specialists and experts who produce *technical* rather than sociopolitical solutions to problems surfacing in everyday life. *Paternalism*, on the other hand, is "an implicit agreement between capital and labor in which capital allows, and even provides for, some satisfaction of basic needs as a means of creating loyalty and increasing labor's capacity to produce and consume." Ultimately, this type of arrangement aims to establish within labor a sense of dependency on the institutions of capital for its very survival.

To cultivate a paternalistic orientation in the country's cafeteros, Fedecafé became a card-carrying membership organization. As members, cafetero farmers were issued coffee identification cards (*cédulas cafetera inteligentes*) through which they access the discounts, subsidies, and other privileges granted by Fedecafé's financial institutions, cooperatives, local stores, and storage houses (*almacenes*). Like driver's licenses in the United States, cédulas cafeteras granted cafetero farmers the means of accessing social citizenship rights in the coffee-producing regions in which Fedecafé institutions took on state-like importance.[61] Fedecafé also established municipal, departmental, and national organizational committees (*comités cafeteros*) to facilitate information flows and communication between Fedecafé's national directors and local cafeteros. Positions within this organizational hierarchy became filled through regular elections that gave some voice to cafetero interests. Like a grassroots cooperative, Colombia's municipal committees were charged with electing representatives to serve in the departmental committees, who in turn elected representatives to the national committee.[62] At the top of the organization came the National Coffee Congress (*Congreso Nacional Cafetero*), presided over by a General Director who was elected by national committee members. These democratic institutional practices have provided some opportunities for cafetero farmers to influence national coffee policy while granting them a stake in the organization's continued growth and expansion. However, as critics point out, Fedecafé's highest positions have been monopolized by a few "good families" (*buenas familias*), who have been careful to steer Fedecafé's practices away from any policies that might threaten the continued extraction of surplus labor from cafeteros or otherwise threaten the paternalism of the organization.[63]

---

[61] While the number of card-carrying members has shifted somewhat over time, there are currently some 377,000 households and over 560,000 individual members who are formal members of Fedecafé (Fedecafé n.d.-b, accessed December 28, 2020 at https://federaciondecafeteros.org/wp/?lang=en).

[62] Fedecafé now has 366 municipal committees that serve 15 departmental committees (Interview with extensions agent in Manizales, Caldas, July 2, 2015).

[63] Palacios (1980:218–19); Christie (1986:279); London (1995:7).

Fedecafé also fostered its paternalism through its extensions services. As mentioned, Fedecafé's extension agents were trained on the latest research coming out of Cenicafé and expected to promote new production technologies advocated by Fedecafé (technology transfers). However, this technical role of extensions agents was complemented by a sociological role designed to imbue coffee production with greater social significance and thus legitimate Fedecafé's project of modernizing the sector. As Christopher London (1995, 1997) notes, since their earliest issues in the 1930s Fedecafé's technical manuals have been replete with articles by or about extensions agents that discuss coffee production as a vocational calling and extension work as a form of secular proselytization meant to create both orderly fields and model citizens in the country's cafeteros. Extensions agents were trained to conduct themselves as if they were the walking embodiment of the work ethic and moral character that Fedecafé wanted to instill in the country's coffee producers. As such, they draped their technical discourse in nationalistic and quasi-religious overtones, describing their relations with farmers as "partnerships" in a shared mission of making Colombian coffee the best in the world. During farm visits, they were expected to ingratiate themselves into cafetero family and community life by familiarizing themselves with local customs and events and maintaining friendly relations with farmers and their families. Indeed, far from mere monitoring and data collection, field visits often took the form of family gatherings wherein extensions agents and farmers decided collectively how to make the most efficient use of the land, what the exact costs and future revenues accrued from household investments would be, and how prior plans had panned out since their last meeting. Given their expertise and specialized knowledge, Colombia's cafeteros were encouraged to wait for a consultation with Fedecafé agents before making any major economic household decisions regarding their land and labor.

In addition to this paternalism, Fedecafé's extensions agents also were trained to instill productivist orientations to coffee farming wherein economic hardships experienced by cafetero families would be interpreted as technical problems to be solved with technical improvements to the productivity of their farms. To be clear, imbuing Colombia's cafeteros with a productivist orientation was no small feat. As discussed earlier, Colombian campesino coffee producers protected themselves from busts in the market by retaining diversified farms and an exit option that minimized the presence of the market in their lives. Moreover, many of this early generation of cafetero farmers had experienced the economic shock of the Great Depression or had become radicalized through the wave of protests in the 1930s. However, into the postwar decades, the risks of specializing in the production of coffee for the market were significantly reduced by Fedecafé's guaranteed purchase practices, loan services, and purchasing practices. These interventions in the market, when combined with the technical expertise and assistance from extensions agents, provided a powerful formula encouraging Colombia's cafeteros to deepen their faith in the ongoing profitability of the sector and to convert ever-greater portions of their land to coffee.

This process of cultivating the cafeteros' dependence upon the coffee market to meet their class reproduction needs does not seem to conform neatly to the primitive accumulation process described by Karl Marx in *Volume 1 of Capital* (1976)[1867], in which rural land displacement in England led to the emergence of fully proletarianized industrial wage laborers. Yet, it is analytically similar as a form of dispossession and proletarianization. Under the Fedecafé's developmentalist interventions, Colombia's cafeteros formally retained control of their land and labor, but they lost control of the coffee labor process. As Farshad Araghi (2000:150) describes of processes of depeasantization that occur without land dispossession, "what they produce, how they produce, and for whom they produce" are no longer determined by cafeteros. Instead "production is carried out by the peasantry ... but not for the peasantry." In Colombia, Fedecafé, through the influence of its extension agents, acquired extensive control of the coffee labor process. Cafetero farmers, in turn, became instruments of production, producing coffee without retaining the full value of their labor.

Indeed, from the 1940s into the 1970s and 1980s, Colombia's coffee-producing lands gradually transformed from subsistence plots dotted with coffee trees into full-scale Fordist factories in the fields in which nearly every aspect of the farm became quantified, measured, and valued as an economic instrument designed to maximize productivity. Socially, this conversion of coffee lands paralleled the transformation of producer identities from campesino farmers who cultivated coffee alongside subsistence crops into fully marketized cafetero farmers. From the 1930s into the 1950s, Fedecafé influence over the coffee labor process grew slowly but steadily. They helped coffee producers purchase seeds and farm equipment at subsidized prices and using provisions of credit. Moreover, extensions agents helped them figure out the most productive ways of using their land. However, by the 1960s Fedecafé began to promote more capital-intensive technological innovations and "Green Revolution" technologies to increase productivity without relying on the renovation of new lands.

Colombia's "period of technification" began with Cenicafé's development of a new "dwarf variety" of coffee plant variety, known as *Caturra*.[64] The Caturra

---

[64] The shift from "shade-grown" to "sun-grown" coffee cultivation in the 1970s began as a general strategy to increase production. However, as Cenicafé scientists soon learned, the overall productivity of either strategy relied on the specific geography of the farm,

variety was much smaller than the traditional "shade tree" variety that had been cultivated since the nineteenth century. Its smaller size allowed for more densely planted coffee groves, and its ability to withstand direct exposure to sunlight allowed for better weed management and a more balanced use of fertilization. However, adopting sun-varieties like Caturra came with risks. Historically, shade trees were cultivated under large fruit-producing trees like bananas, coconuts, oranges, and limes, all of which would be consumed by families or sold in the local agricultural market. The adoption of the sun tree varieties thus expanded the production of coffee at the expense of shifting toward a single cash mono-crop.[65] Moreover, transitioning from shade to non-shade varieties required a certain amount of capital. This was needed both to purchase the new seeds as well as to pay the costs of chemicals to protect sun-grown trees from pests. The adoption of fertilizers thus supplanted the natural pesticide controls, such as birds, spiders, and other animals and insects that had habituated the fruit trees that shaded traditional trees.[66]

Large and medium-sized farmers had enough land to experiment with these new techniques early on without assuming any fundamental risks to their livelihoods. Smaller producers, who formed the majority of productive units in the country, were less willing to take the chance. By the mid-1970s, however, the new coffee varieties appeared to be paying off handsomely and small producers began to join the action.[67] By the close of the decade, roughly 69% of Colombia's producers had uprooted their traditional coffee trees and replaced them with new Caturra varieties. And when these new trees were struck by an outbreak of coffee rust disease (*la roya*) in the early 1980s, the country's cafeteros renovated

---

including its rainfall, sunlight, soil nutrients, and the like. So over time, Fedecafé began recommending shade-grown varieties in some regions and sun-grown in others, depending upon which strategy maximized production (Interview with Fedecafé communications and marketing officer via Skype, March 27, 2015). Either way, this decision was premised upon the productivist orientation of Fedecafé rather than the interests of farmers who might otherwise find sun-grown coffee structurally less-conducive to the family's reproduction needs as it requires more land, fertilizers, and inputs.

[65] Fedecafé began these initiatives as early as 1965 to help diversify the local economy so that it could buffer against mono-cropping and encourage economic diversification. This was part and parcel of a broad, developmental set of measures called, "Program for the Development and Diversification of the Coffee Zones" enacted in 1965 (1980:238, 247).

[66] Guhl (2008:115–21).

[67] Guhl (2008:146).

their fields once again, adopting a new variety of tree with a genetic resistance to coffee rust, *Variedad Colombia.*[68]

Fedecafé's technification strategies, in addition to the investments requiring farmers to meet their quality bean standards, increased the overall costs of production and extended the workload of cultivating and harvesting coffee beyond the family labor sources that most farmers had previously depended upon. Thus, medium-sized and larger farms (5–15 ha and above) began to hire seasonal harvesters and in some cases full-time farmhands to help meet these new production demands. In Viejo Caldas, the number of wage workers on coffee farms grew from 46,740 in 1931 to some 122,215 by 1973.[69] Nationally, estimates of these numbers grew from between 300,000 and 500,000 in 1970 to up to 700,000 by the mid-1980s.[70] Indeed, as a developmentalist effort meant to transform Colombia's coffee fields into highly rationalized and capitalized agricultural factories, Fedecafé's technification efforts were undoubtedly successful.

The Politics of Fedecafé Hegemony during the Postwar Decades

During the postwar decades of the twentieth century, Fedecafé's Pacto Cafetero was clearly successful as a hegemonic labor regime. Fedecafé's interventions transformed an erstwhile class of economically conservative and politically radical class of coffee-producing campesinos into market-dependent cafeteros who viewed themselves as junior partners in the larger project of producing coffee in order to develop the country. Fedecafé's technical interventions increased the overall productivity of the country's coffee fields, doubling the country's exports from 3 to 6 million 60 kg sacks between 1930 and 1960.[71] And, Fedecafé's continued investments in local social and economic infrastructure had transformed Viejo Caldas into one of the country's most prosperous regions of the country.[72] Less obvious, however, was how Fedecafé's domestic interventions in the coffee market facilitated a form of class domination that buttressed the country's conservative political establishment.

---

[68] Ortiz (1999:41); Cenicafé (1999).

[69] Vallecilla Gordillo (2001:197).

[70] Junguito and Pizano (1993:160–61).

[71] Fedecafé (n.d.-a, accessed February 20, 2019 at https://federaciondecafeteros.org/wp/coffee-statistics/?lang=en); Palacios (1980:232).

[72] Junguito and Pizano (1997).

The conservatism of Colombia's cafeteros first surfaced during the period of sectarian violence that erupted between 1946 and 1957. Historians have documented how *La Violencia* manifested in different ways across Colombia's diverse social and political geography.[73] In some regions, *La Violencia* took the form of class conflicts or revolutionary insurgency wars that pitted landed elites, oligarchs, and commercial capitalists against workers, dispossessed peasants, and other economically marginalized groups. In other regions, it took the form of social banditry, feuds, or paramilitarism. In Colombia's coffee regions in general, and Viejo Caldas in particular, the political violence and chaos unleashed by *La Violencia* was deeper than in most places. For example, between 1946 and 1957, Viejo Caldas had the highest number of reported deaths, some 44,255. Tolima and Antioquia, two other regions that produced significant amounts of coffee reported 30,912 and 26,115 respectively.[74] Yet, it did not take on the types of revolutionary tendencies and class conflicts that developed in other regions of the country. Instead, the violence in Viejo Caldas took on its most sectarian form, with rural groups fighting as Liberals against Conservatives and vice versa. Moreover, the chaos of the violence permitted cafeteros the ability to settle old scores with troublesome neighbors by displacing them from their farms, acquiring contested land, or simply claiming new lands along the frontier.[75] From this perspective, it is clear that *La Violencia* essentially ended the historic disputes over private and public lands that had arisen with the opening of the agrarian frontier decades earlier. By the early 1950s, the agrarian frontier had closed. Yet, Viejo Caldas continued to produce coffee as it had been doing, with its structures of production and commerce intact. Coffee production in the region actually

---

[73] Sánchez and Meertens (2001); Bergquist (1986); Roldán (2002); Green (2003); Palacios (2006).

[74] Bergquist (1986:365).

[75] Charles Bergquist (1986) argued that the sectarian nature of the violence in Colombia's coffee regions was the result of the conservative political orientation of the cafeteros themselves, who identified strongly with one or other political party and followed the directives of party leaders to wage war against the other party. In his research on the Quindío in the 1950s, Carlos Miguel Ortiz Sarmiento (1992) came to a similar conclusion, finding that class conflicts were averted because "society had not tended to structure itself in a predominantly class-based fashion." Furthermore, he points out how "intermediaries," such as foremen, estate managers, and small businessmen in the coffee region, were able to use their political ties to war-minded party leaders to manipulate the violence to their own benefit, ultimately attaining large tracts of property and accumulating capital at the expense of both smallholders and larger landowners.

increased during this period, from 104,149 tons produced in 1946 to 122,597 tons in 1953.[76]

During the years of the National Front (1958–74), Viejo Caldas remained a bastion of electoral support and legitimacy for the regime, despite the regime's growing authoritarianism in the 1960s and 1970s. As will be discussed in greater detail in the case studies on Colombia's banana and cattle-coca regimes, 1960s Colombia was a period of rapid economic growth and development. Like other developmentalist regimes, National Front leaders passed legislation meant to stimulate domestic industrialization and economic diversification. As such, the state invested heavily in the development of new agro-export zones that displaced rural inhabitants, many of whom flocked to the cities looking for decent work, housing, access to social services, education, and health.[77] By the 1970s, the National Front's agro-industrial policies were producing social unrest in many parts of the countryside, where displaced peasants, frontier settlers, and proletarianized agricultural workers also began organizing for radical reforms. At the helm of the agrarian movement was the National Peasant Users Association (ANUC), which organized a united front of displaced farmers, rural wage workers, and frontier migrants that was engaged in labor strikes and land invasions across the country.[78]

Colombia's cities, now marked by burgeoning shantytowns and informal economic activities, also became hotbeds of unrest from radicalized students, wage workers, and marginalized masses whose demands for social reform and protections were falling on flat ears under the National Front regime.[79] President Alfonso López Michelsen (1974–78) responded by expanding the size of the country's security forces to crack down on protestors. Julio César Turbay Ayala (1978–82) later intensified this trend by instituting a "security statute" that criminalized protests, defined opposition activists as subversives, and therefore permitted the use of force against protestors to instill order and protect national security. This repression unleashed by the Colombian state, in turn, contributed to a further radicalization of social activists, many of whom joined rural and urban

---

[76] From this perspective, some have gone so far as to argue that the eruption of political violence helped release demographic pressures on the land due to the rural exodus of farmers, who were implicated in the sectarian conflict and abandoned their farms for fear of retaliation (Oquist 1978:16, 19, 84; Vallecilla Gordillo 2001:296).

[77] By the early 1960s, the national population became predominantly urban rather than rural, jumping from 39% rural in 1951 to 52% in 1964 and 60% by 1970 (Mohan 1994:8–9).

[78] Zamosc (1986).

[79] Livingstone (2004:50–52); Palacios (2006:226–39).

guerrilla insurgency groups who argued that the authoritarianism of Colombia's oligarchy left them with little choice but to take up arms to defend themselves.[80]

As this social unrest and political repression deepened, Fedecafé's leaders vocalized their "non-partisan mandate" that allowed them to "remain on the sidelines" of these political battles.[81] In this historical conjuncture, their goal of "protecting coffee farmers" was interpreted as protection *from* the political and social instability experienced in other parts of the country. And in this sense, they were quite successful. As the country fell into a deepening crisis into the 1970s, Viejo Caldas proved impervious to both rural radicalization and guerrilla insurgency activities. To be sure, the ANUC and other groups did attempt to organize those working in the coffee sector as seasonal harvesters or full-time workers on the region's remaining large estates. However, these efforts generally failed to create a set of demands or political platform that could mobilize both coffee workers and cafetero farmers.[82] As Leon Zamosc (1986:140) points out, even during the height of ANUC radicalism in the mid-1970s, efforts to unify the interests of the migrant workers hired as coffee harvesters and cafetero smallholders were always thwarted by the smallholders, who "always protested against the wage increases that were the basic demands of the workers."[83] Indeed, the social

---

[80] The 1970s was a particularly chaotic period in Colombia. Social unrest swelled in the cities. New urban guerrilla groups like the student-led April 10th Movement (M-19) had formed and national civic strikes calling for political and social reform that challenged the legitimacy of the National Front and the political legacy of monopoly politics that it left in its aftermath after it was formally dismantled in 1974 (Safford and Palacios 2001:324, 332). In the countryside, the Revolutionary Armed Forces of Colombia (FARC), the National Liberation Army (ELN), and the National Popular Army (EPL) developed territorial strongholds in key agro-export zones as well as along the southern agricultural frontier regions of the country (Reyes Posada 2009:15–54).

[81] Ortiz (1999:37).

[82] Ortiz (1999) points out that some union activity from coffee workers (migrants and tenants) did arise in the coffee region in the 1960s, including land invasions and wage strikes that were often "draped in the banner of the Communist Party or the ANAPO Party" (who were becoming increasingly powerful actors elsewhere in the country in the 1970s). And, there emerged a "Union of Coffee Laborers" that had headquarters in Armenia, Quindío. Yet, such activities remained peripheral, failing to provide laborers with a platform that could help build a strong union movement.

[83] Pierre Gilhodes (1972) echoes this, stating that "an antirevolutionary climate [emerged] once the former tenants acquired land [and] became incorporated into the traditional regional life as peasants and lost their identification with the landless laborers."

protections and economic stability experienced by smallholding coffee farmers under Fedecafé's hegemonic social compact shielded them from the social dislocation, exploitation, and repression experienced by those excluded from the privileges and protections of this pact.

In summary, Fedecafé's Pacto Cafetero was effective in a number of ways. As a hegemonic labor regime, it facilitated the transformation of coffee producers into full-scale cafeteros dedicated to the expanded production of coffee for the market. Producing coffee was no longer simply something one does to earn a living, but instead became something that one is, a class identity with larger social significance and status. Under Fedecafé hegemony, Colombia's cafeteros also developed a politically conservative orientation that was critical to the longevity of the National Front regime and the political party establishment in general. In exchange for this loyalty, they became the benefactors of the privileges of both the developmentalist project of Fedecafé as well as the national developmental policies of the National Front regime. Viewed from this perspective, we see that hegemony in Viejo Caldas was a privilege that came to rest in large part on the backs of the country's marginalized and oppressed.

3

Fedecafé's Labor Regime in the Arc of US World Hegemony

In Chapter 2, we saw how Fedecafé's developmental interventions in Colombia's domestic coffee market protected cafetero producers from the destabilizing dynamics of the international coffee market. But in doing so, these interventions also deepened cafetero dependence on that market, and therefore on Fedecafé's institutions, to meet their livelihood needs. This chapter explains how and why Fedecafé was successful in consolidating a hegemonic labor regime given that this regime relied on fully marketized producers. To answer this question, I situate Fedecafé's project in world historical perspective to show how Fedecafé's domestic initiatives arose in conjunction with the rise and consolidation of US world hegemony in the decades following World War II. During this time, the United States responded to a wave of anti-imperialism, labor unrest, and economic nationalism by reorganizing the world market to promote capitalist development and expansion globally. Specifically, during this period coffee producing and exporting countries engaged in geopolitical collective action strategies to protect themselves from the worst excesses of peripheralization and create opportunities for domestic wealth accumulation. These efforts were supported by the US government, resulting in a series of international coffee agreements that stabilized and regulated the world market. In Colombia, the politically regulated international coffee market provided Fedecafé with the opportunity to "move up" the coffee chain, access core-like profits, and avoid the structural problems of market peripheralization. This process of economic upgrading, I argue, was the critical factor buttressing Fedecafé's hegemony in Viejo Caldas. The key role of US world hegemony in bolstering Fedecafé domestically became evident when the United States pulled its support from the international coffee agreement in 1989. As we will see in the closing sections of this chapter, once the geopolitical alliances buttressing the regulated international market unraveled, Fedecafé's domestic hegemony soon followed, giving way to chronic crises of labor control and waves of social unrest that continue to impact the lives of today's cafetero farmers.

The Rise of US Hegemony and the De-Peripheralization of Colombian Coffee

While Fedecafé's hegemonic project helped vertically integrate the sector at the national level, such policies did not and could not have remedied the structural problems associated with Colombia's peripheral niche in the world coffee market. Fluctuating prices, declining terms of trade vis-à-vis the coffee roasters and importers, and generally low returns on investments continued to plague the sector in the 1930s. In other words, while Colombia's coffee export sector grew and expanded under Fedecafé, it is not immediately clear how and why the sector grew so strongly, or more importantly, how Fedecafé was able to accrue enough wealth to reinvest in both further accumulation processes, as well as in its expensive social compact vis-à-vis cafetero producers.

As Figure 3.1 depicts, coffee prices remained quite low in the 1930s and 1940s. As mentioned in Chapter 2, Colombia used this period of low prices to expand its market niche by increasing production on coffee smallholdings. However, these increases in exports did not provide Fedecafé with a way to protect growers from volatile and low prices in the market. To be sure, the end of World War II brought increased demand for coffee, which helped elevate prices in the closing years of the 1940s and into the years of the Korean War. Yet, prices fell once again by the late 1950s due to overproduction in the postwar expansionary era. Not only did such ups and downs wreak havoc on the FNC's capacity to stockpile and subsidize production as a buffer within Colombia, but

Figure 3.1 Colombian coffee exports and prices, 1930–60

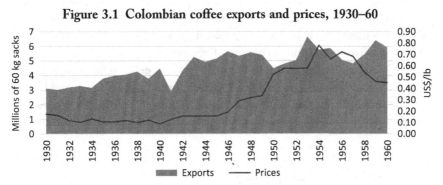

Sources: National Federation of Coffee Growers, Coffee Statistics Database (Fedecafé n.d.-a, accessed February 20, 2019); Palacios (1980: 232)

such volatility had by the late 1950s created a major crisis of profitability for coffee producing countries as a whole.[1]

Hoping a way to both boost exports and reap the rewards of these investments, Fedecafé began lobbying the Colombian government in the 1930s to engage in negotiations with the United States, the largest consumer of Colombian coffee exports, for a trade deal to provide a lucrative and stable outlet for its exports. While these talks never panned out, the outbreak of World War II did provide an alternative strategy. When Brazil's Vargas regime began to flirt with the idea of forming an alliance with Hitler's Germany, the Roosevelt Administration engaged in efforts to strengthen "Pan-American solidarity among allies" in Latin America. The result was the establishment of an "Inter-American Coffee Agreement" that set import quotas on coffee coming into the US market during the war years of 1940–45 and guaranteed higher prices for coffee exports. When the War ended, however, so did the agreement, and the United States began an active campaign to deregulate the market under the stipulations of the General Agreement on Tariffs and Trade in 1947 and the "Havana Charter" of the International Trade Organization in 1948.[2]

By this time, however, the world systemic climate had changed. A strong wave of nationalist, anticolonial, and anti-imperialist currents gained strength in many parts of Africa and the Asian subcontinent. Latin America was undergoing its own wave of militant nationalism, reflected most vividly by the institutionalization of import-substitution industrialization policies and populist-style politics that rode the tide of anti-imperialism.[3] It was within this world historical context that the major coffee producer countries, led by Colombia and Brazil, began their own efforts to find ways of using their dominance of world coffee production to their economic advantage.

The major obstacle facing major coffee producer-exporter countries like Colombia and Brazil was that the most capital-intensive and profitable nodes of the coffee commodity chain – roasting, blending, packaging, and distribution – were monopolized by consumer countries, foremost among which was the United States. Thus, exporters' capacity to "upgrade" into core-like nodes in the chain through forward linkage strategies would entail a major offensive that could have led to economic suicide, due to the recent consolidation of these niches by national roasting and processing companies.[4] Rather than attempt such a strategy,

---

[1] Stewart (1992:230); Talbot (2004:48).
[2] Bates (1997:90–92); Talbot (2004:49).
[3] Cardoso and Faletto (1979).
[4] Talbot (2004:54).

Table 3.1 *World coffee exports and market shares, 1930–60 (millions of 60 kg sacks)*

	Brazil Exports (%)	Colombia Exports (%)	Rest of Latin America Exports (%)	Asia, Africa, Oceania Exports (%)	Total Exports (%)
1930	15.3 (59.3)	3.2 (12.4)	4.8 (18.6)	2.5 (9.7)	25.8 (100)
1935	15.3 (56.3)	3.8 (14.0)	4.6 (16.9)	3.5 (12.9)	27.2 (100)
1940	12.1 (51.7)	4.4 (18.8)	4.0 (17.1)	2.9 (12.4)	23.4 (100)
1945	14.2 (51.3)	5.7 (19.5)	4.6 (16.6)	3.7 (13.4)	27.7 (100)
1950	14.8 (50.9)	4.5 (15.5)	4.9 (16.8)	4.9 (16.8)	29.1 (100)
1955	13.7 (40.8)	5.9 (13.2)	6.5 (19.3)	7.5 (22.3)	33.6 (100)
1960	16.8 (39.6)	5.9 (13.9)	7.9 (18.6)	11.8 (27.8)	42.4 (100)

Source: Junguito and Pizano (1993:64–67)

Fedecafé, in coordination with Brazil's *Instituto Brasileiro do Café* (IBC), began to engage in a different strategy, one that was based upon Brazil's coffee valorization practices of the first decades of the twentieth century. In 1906, and later in 1917, 1921, and 1926 Brazil purposefully withheld large volumes of their exports from the market. Because they produced some 70% of the world's coffee during this time, withholding their exports significantly reduced world supplies in relation to world demand, and thus brought windfall profits as prices escalated.[5]

By the 1950s, however, Brazil's world market share had shrunk as Colombia and other countries increased their exports. Table 3.1 illustrates this historical shift in the world coffee export market. In 1930, Brazil's share of the export market was still high. Their exports of 15.3 million sacks of 60 kg bags amounted to 59.6% of the market. However, by 1960 they had increased their exports to 16.8 million sacks, but their market share had dropped to 39.6%. Colombia's market share increased from 12.4% to 13.9%. However, the largest increase in market shares came from the rest of Latin America and from producers in Asia, Africa, and Oceania. Geopolitically, this meant that Brazil and Colombia needed to forge a broad alliance among producing countries in order to force the United States to accept more favorable terms of trade in the international coffee market.

The geopolitical collective action strategies of the world's coffee-exporting countries began in 1959–60 when some 94% of the world's producers (including some colonial representatives such as France and Portugal) first attempted to

---

[5] Fridell (2014:51–53).

establish fixed export quotas and collectively withhold exports to raise prices in the international market. As John Talbot (2004:58–59) points out, this first attempt at an ICA proved ineffective for two reasons. First, the export quotas they set were too high. This increased overall exports well above international demand, thus lowering rather than increasing the value of exports in the market. The second was the fact that the agreement lacked an effective vehicle to enforce adherence to the quotas and regulate the overall market system. Both problems revealed the structural weaknesses of exporters in the absence of participation by major importing countries.

However, the geopolitical tide shifted in favor of coffee exporters in the aftermath of the 1959 Cuban Revolution. Fearful of the spread of communism into "its own backyard" and the heating of the Cold War, the Kennedy Administration implemented its "Alliance for Progress" initiatives to stimulate development and economic stability across Latin America through major provisions of economic and technical aid. Viewing an opportunity to restructure the international coffee market as part of these broader hegemonic aspirations, the ICA countries immediately offered to extend their agreement to the United States. These negotiations proved successful, and a new agreement was signed in 1962 with full support and participation by the US government.[6]

Indeed, the relationship between the geopolitical concerns of the US government and their ardent support for the ICA of 1962 is well documented.[7] As Stephen Krasner (1973:496, 502) notes, the head of the US delegation to the governing council of the International Coffee Organization was a representative of the US State Department (the Deputy Assistant Secretary of State for Economic Affairs) rather than from other branches of the government that are directly involved in trade and commercial matters. And at the time, the State Department believed that "economic growth and stability were perceived as conducive to the creation of regime types favored by the United States," and that "the American government saw economic pay-offs as a device for securing Latin American diplomatic support, particularly for action against Cuba."

This prioritization of long-term geopolitics over the short-term interests of corporate roasting and trading companies in the United States was certainly noted by US coffee corporations. As Krasner (1973:502, 505–6) explains, the ICA agreement did indeed "hurt the economic interests of one sector of the American coffee industry – the coffee traders." And, it "did not help the other sector, coffee roasters, and may have hurt them." Yet, the National Coffee

---

[6] Bates (1997:120–21).

[7] Krasner (1973); Bates (1997); Stewart (1992); Talbot (2004).

Association (NCA), the lobbying group of US coffee roasters and traders, agreed to the ICA's stipulations "out of a sense of public duty." Public duty or not, the ICA was not necessarily understood to be a significant threat to corporate bottom lines. For one, by stabilizing the market, importers and roasters were granted reliable supplies of quality coffee.[8] Moreover, in exchange for their support, some leading firms were granted special deals with Brazil and Colombia to buy coffee at discount prices, thus giving them a competitive advantage within the US domestic market.[9]

Given the context of the Cold War and the possibility of social revolutionary forces coming to power in the hemisphere, the US government was willing to participate in the international coffee agreements despite the fact that they sacrificed profitability concerns for its broader geopolitical interests in hemispheric hegemony.

Managing US Hegemony through the International Coffee Agreements

Analyses of the International Coffee Agreements show that the mechanisms it used to regulate exports and prices were indeed successful in stabilizing the market and lifting prices in ways that facilitated domestic development initiatives for major exporter countries like Colombia.[10] Under the agreements, exports of unroasted (green) coffee beans to North America and Europe were fixed to a yearly quota of just under 47 million 60 kg bags. Up to 18 million bags were allocated to Brazil and over 6 million to Colombia, while the rest was subdivided among the remaining coffee-producing countries according to their export volumes of the previous years. Approval of these quota allocations and rules were overseen by an International Coffee Council composed of an equal number of exporter and importer members. These members were elected through a voting system that divvied up 1,000 votes among producers and 1,000 votes among consumer countries, depending upon the size of their exports and imports. In practice, because all decisions required a two-thirds majority approval, the United States gained de facto veto power for all decisions on imports while Brazil and Colombia obtained this power for all decisions on exports. All decisions were

---

8 Talbot (2004:59–60).
9 Bates (1997:121–27).
10 Bates (1997); Giovannucci et al. (2002); Gresser and Tickell (2002); Talbot (2004); Daviron and Ponte (2005); Goodman (2008); Fridell (2014).

binding and overseen by the International Coffee Organization (ICO), the membership group and governing body that organized the meetings, monitored market trends, and certified the origins of coffee in the market.[11]

In terms of pricing, the ICA's primary means of protecting exporters from the structural volatility of pricing that would typically occur under conditions of market deregulation was through the export quota system itself. The quotas were created to ensure that no bumper crop or coffee frost or blight could destabilize the volume of coffee in the market at any given time. To be sure, prices were not directly fixed by political negotiations and no explicit price floor system was put in place. Instead, a system of target price ranges was established so that quotas for specific exporting countries would be increased if world market prices rose above the target price range and decreased if they dropped below that range. Moreover, the ICA agreements formalized the segmentation of the world market by distinct coffee types under its "selectivity principle." Under this system, the market was broken down into distinct bean types: *Robustas, unwashed Arabicas, Colombian milds,* and *other milds.* This radically diminished, though did not completely eliminate, the market competition among coffee producing-exporting countries so that producers of lower-quality Robusta beans (ex. Africa and Indonesia) did not compete with producers of unwashed Arabicas (ex. Brazil), Colombian milds (ex. Colombia, Costa Rica, Kenya), and other milds (Mexico, Guatemala, Nicaragua).

To instill the ICA agreements with a dynamic capacity to adapt to market changes, the International Coffee Organization established temporal limits on each agreement and dates to establish new ones. Indeed, during the 1960s and 1970s this power to renegotiate the terms of the ICA worked to the advantage of exporter countries, who used US Cold War fears and nominal support for "national development" to challenge the core–periphery inequalities in the market. The 1968 renegotiation of the ICA, for example, occurred during a year of worldwide social unrest that posed a significant challenge to the legitimacy of US foreign and domestic policy. ICO producer countries used this as an opportunity to introduce a "diversification fund" clause that was financed by contributions from producer countries that were collected and redistributed back as loans to be used toward development and diversification projects.[12]

---

[11] Talbot (2004:58–66); Fridell (2014:58–63).

[12] It was during this period (1968–73) that we see how the developmental aspirations of producers began to seriously threaten the capital accumulation of coffee companies located in consumer countries. In the 1960s, US companies began to shift their efforts toward the manufacturing and sale of instant coffee to consumers. Yet, Brazilian instant coffee began to enter into the US market with a distinct advantage because of their capacity to vertically integrate both production as well as manufacturing

Efforts to renegotiate this new ICA had broken down by 1973, due to the world economic crisis that emerged following the breakdown of the Bretton Woods system of fixed exchange rates. The US's efforts to expand the supply of dollars into the world economy radically devalued the dollar, which dominated the commercial transactions associated with the international coffee economy. This led to a marked decrease in the export earnings of coffee producers. Brazil and Colombia responded by demanding a new ICA that would adjust the target prices ranges to the shift in currency markets so as to compensate for the losses in real terms. Fearful of contributing to inflation, and pointing out that prices were already escalating because of the Brazilian frosts of 1969 and 1972, the Nixon administration refused to increase the costs of coffee for consumers. Thus, no agreement emerged on a new quota system for 1973 though the administrative structure of the ICO was maintained.[13]

Fortunately for Colombia, coffee prices in the mid-1970s remained relatively high despite the derailment of the ICA due to a major frost in Brazil in 1975, civil wars in Ethiopia and Angola, and political turmoil in Uganda, all of which curtailed the supply of world coffee. Ignoring the failed renegotiation of the ICA, and empowered by a boom in prices, producers began to initiate attempts at collective action outside of the ICO as a way of gaining further leverage once negotiations resumed. During this period, Colombian representative were critical in the establishment of the "Geneva Group" (fourteen producers who pledged to uphold the 1972 quota levels), "Café Mundial" in 1973 (a multinational buffer stock company run by producers), and the "Bogotá Group" in 1978 (which later became "Pancafé," a fund established to speculate on coffee futures). While the scheduled renegotiation of the ICA again in 1976 was also unsuccessful in establishing a quota system, producers and consumers both agreed on an "automatic quota" if prices dropped to 78 cents/lb of coffee.[14]

---

processes. Brazil thus augmented their share of the US market from roughly 1% in 1965 to 14% by 1967. This growing encroachment into the most profitable niches of the coffee commodity chain was viewed as a direct threat to US companies, who lobbied against "unfair trading practices." In fact, the ICA of 1968 included a clause that prohibited "any ICA member from discriminatory treatment in favor of processed as opposed to green coffee." Brazil went along with such a clause so long as the quota system was intact in 1968 and so long as other clauses were included, such as the diversification fund. But by 1973, these issues had become intense sites of conflict (Talbot 2004:62).

[13] Krasner (1973:512–13).

[14] Talbot (2004:71–72, 77).

Figure 3.2 Average monthly price, Colombian milds, 1962–89

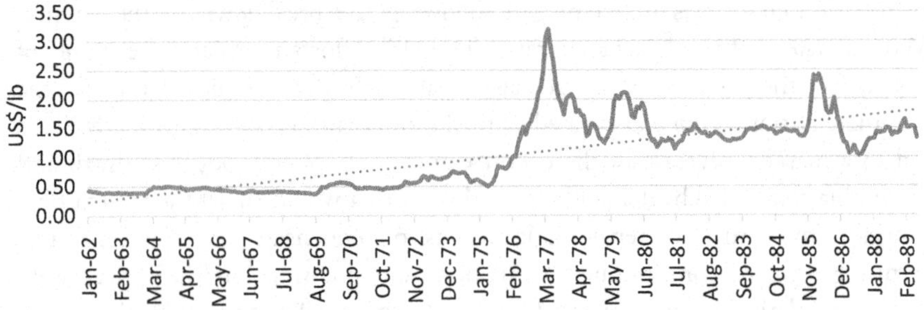

Source: National Federation of Coffee Growers, Coffee Statistics Database (accessed February 27, 2019)

By 1979, world coffee prices were rapidly dropping back to levels predating the mid-late 1970s boom, which converged with changes in the geopolitical climate that once again favored the collective action of the producers and the establishment of the new quota agreement in 1980s. A second wave of guerrilla mobilization emerged in Latin America, as the failure of the development project to deliver on its promises sparked unrest from urban-industrial workers, rural populations displaced by the introduction of capitalist agriculture, a burgeoning urban lumpenproletariat, and middle-class student radicals.[15] This situation of political unrest, including the Sandinista Revolution in Nicaragua, the escalating civil wars in El Salvador, Guatemala, and Angola, and the rising power of the guerrillas in Colombia were top priorities of US representatives to the ICO. And once again, the political well-being of producer countries and the threat of rebellion, anti-imperialism, and economic nationalism became linked to the stability of the coffee world economy. Coffee manufacturers and suppliers were once more willing to accept higher prices in exchange for steady inputs of green coffee, though their support for the ICA was rapidly waning.

Figure 3.2 depicts the international ICO price of exports of Colombian milds in the market during the ICA quota system period. Prior to the ICA, coffee prices of Colombian exports fluctuated between 10 and 20 cents/lb, with the exception of the postwar boom. Under the 1962–68 and 1968–73 agreements, prices hovered around 50 cents/lb of unroasted coffee greens exported. They rose despite the abrogation of the quota system in 1973, and then increased dramatically beginning in April 1975. Under the new quota systems that went into effect in 1976 and again 1983, prices never dropped below US$1.00/lb. Overall, the

---

[15] Wickham-Crowley (1992).

trendline shows an average growth in prices from under 50 cents/lb in the early 1960s to over US$1.50 by the 1980s. Indeed, these years of stable growth under the ICAs marked the high point of coffee capitalism.

The Collapse of the ICA Market and Re-Peripheralization of Colombian Coffee

While US participation in the 1980 ICA agreement indicates their continued willingness to sacrifice profitability concerns over broader geopolitical concerns, such a decision was becoming increasingly difficult to make. In the 1960s, the collective action of producer countries was limited to their capacity to withhold exports and drive prices up. Yet, by the 1980s they were able to move into the most profitable niches of the market, including the futures markets and the manufacturing of instant coffees, thus intensifying competition for roasters and distributors. The Reagan administration viewed these calls to withdraw from the ICA as a platform to showcase its support for unrestricted trade by appointing new "market-friendly" delegates to the ICO that sought to undermine the strategic geopolitical alliances buttressing the ICA.[16] They did so in two key ways: (1) encouraging the globalization of coffee production and consumption to undermine the export monopoly held by Brazil, Colombia, and other large ICA countries, and (2) promoting the financialization of coffee capital to undermine the structural power of exporters. By the close of the decade, these efforts were successful, and the United States pulled its support from the ICA system, with significant consequences for Colombia and other major coffee-exporting countries.

Because the ICA agreements allocated world market shares based upon demonstrations of domestic coffee productivity, the ICA quota system created an incentive structure that increased world coffee exports and spread coffee production to new countries.[17] Between 1962 and 1983, the number of coffee-exporting countries in the ICO jumped from thirty-seven to forty-eight.[18] This globalization of coffee production only intensified in the aftermath of the debt crisis of the 1980s, when indebted governments recognized that coffee revenues remained relatively high in comparison to other agricultural export commodities (due to its protection under the ICA). The appeal of coffee exports led to a major

---

[16] Talbot (2004:96–97).

[17] It is worth noting that the world coffee market has been global since its pre-capitalist origins (Clarence-Smith and Topik 2003).

[18] Talbot (2004:98).

expansion in the productive capacities of smaller exporting countries such as the Dominican Republic, Honduras, Nicaragua, and Vietnam and also encouraged the development of new coffee export zones in new producer countries such as Thailand and the Philippines.[19]

While at its surface, this leap in the number of ICO countries may appear to reflect a strengthening of support for the ICA quota system; in fact, many of these new and smaller coffee-producing countries were less attached to the ICA system, having had less experience with successful collective action efforts as a mechanism to further their own political and economic interests and feeling that their capacity to expand their share of the world market was unnecessarily limited. Additionally, many of these countries lacked the institutional framework and the class power that made collective action possible in such countries as Colombia and Brazil. Thus, as the globalization of production expanded throughout the decade, many new producers simply refused to join.[20]

Figure 3.3 illustrates how the total volume of world coffee exports as well as the regional share of that volume changed under the ICA agreements. Prior to the initiation of the first ICA agreement in 1961/1962, the total volume of world coffee exports remained under 40 million sacks of unroasted coffee greens. Under the ICA agreements, world exports grew steadily from less than 40 million sacks to a high of 80.1 million sacks in 1989. Moreover, when looking at the relative volume of exports by region, the world's largest coffee exporters – Brazil and Colombia – only increased their volume slightly in comparison to the rest of the world. Said simply, world exports doubled under the international coffee agreements, but most of this growth came from export growth in the rest of Latin America, Asia, Africa, and Oceania, where support for the ICA quota system was less pronounced.

While the globalization of production was undermining the organizational basis of the quota system, so did the globalization of consumption. Under the ICA agreements, world coffee consumption both increased in the United States and Western Europe and spread to new countries, including the Soviet Union and the satellite countries of Eastern Europe. In 1962, the ICA was comprised of twenty-five consumer countries who consumed 94% of the world's coffee. By 1983, the number of consumers in the ICA increased only to twenty-seven, while their consumption of the world's coffee dropped to 80%. This global expansion in coffee consumption provided space for incipient trade relations between the newly producing and newly consuming countries that avoided the geopolitical

---

[19] Talbot (2004:76–77, 92); Akiyama et al. (2001:86).
[20] Stewart (1992:240–41); Bates (1997:138–39).

Figure 3.3 World coffee exports by region, 1929–92

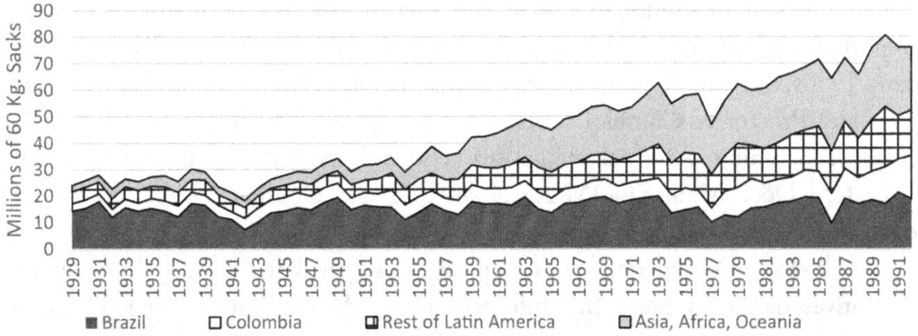

Source: Junguito and Pizano (1993: 64–67)

basis of the ICA quota system as it was formed in the 1960s therefore saw the ICA as an unnecessary obstacle to the expansion of international commerce. In fact, the intensification and globalization of production and consumption was a key factor in the consolidation of a two-tiered coffee market by the 1980s: coffee traded within the regulatory framework of the ICA and a "parallel market" of coffee traded outside of the ICA (i.e., "tourist coffee"). Smaller producers who were not ICA members, smaller producers who were frustrated by their negligible share of coffee quotas within the ICA, and larger producers who had stockpiled massive amounts of coffee greens and chose not to watch them rot or be destroyed, all began selling tourist coffee at discounted rates in legal and illegal markets across the globe. It was estimated that the United States, which had no customs regulations in place to refuse the entry of coffee that had come second-hand from the tourist market, had allowed the entry of nearly 2 million "illegal bags." The immediate effect of this was to drop the overall price of coffee, which benefited US coffee manufacturers and suppliers to the detriment of the large producers.[21]

A second set of transformations that undermined the organizational basis of the ICA quota system by 1989 came with the financialization of coffee capital. As John Talbot (2004:103–4) notes, the financialization of capital in the coffee trade took two main forms: the consolidation of capital into massive transnational conglomerates and the explosion of speculative trading in coffee financial markets. Regarding the former, the largest roaster and manufacturing companies took advantage of new opportunities to access credit in the 1980s to buy out their competitors and expand their operations through mergers and acquisitions. By the close of the decade, the largest coffee roasters and manufacturers became

---

[21] Stewart (1992:261–65); Akiyama et al. (2001:88); Talbot (2004:78–79).

incorporated into huge multi-product, transnational conglomerates (TNCs) that handled massive volumes of coffee. To meet these massive demands, coffee importers underwent their own series of mergers and acquisitions. Thus, by the early 1990s, only four major corporate conglomerates (Nestlé, Philip Morris, Sara Lee, and Proctor & Gamble) controlled over 60% of total coffee sales across all major consuming countries while five coffee importers (Neumann Gruppe, Volcafé, ED&F Man, ECOM Agroindustrial, and Goldman Sachs) controlled over 40% of total world imports.[22]

The 1980s also experienced an explosion of speculative trading in financial derivatives based on the coffee futures market. Whereas the trading of coffee futures dates back to the origins of the New York Coffee Exchange in 1882 (which merged with sugar and cocoa to form the New York Coffee, Sugar and Cocoa Exchange, CSCE by the 1970s), such financial transactions were used primarily by importers and roasters to hedge against sudden price changes.[23] By the mid-1980s, however, the CSCE introduced the possibility of trading in options on coffee futures contracts, which opened the market to a class of financial speculators with little knowledge or interest in the workings of the coffee market *per se*, but who saw in it a way to make a rapid and profitable return on their investments.[24] The increasing weight of financial speculation within the global

---

[22] Nestlé acquired Hills Bros., Chase and Sanborn, Sark's Gourmet Coffees, Zoegas, only to later sell them to Sara Lee to start a new line of gourmets under the name Nescafé. Philip Morris acquired General Foods/Maxwell House, Jacob Suchard, Gevalia, and Ajinomoto. Sara Lee acquired Superior Coffee, Douwe Egberts, Chock Full o' Nuts, Tenco, along with those bought from Philip Morris. Proctor & Gamble owned Folgers, which acquired Maryland Club Foods/Butter-Nut and Millstone Coffee (Daviron and Ponte 2005:90–95; Talbot 2004:103–4).

[23] The coffee futures contract traded on the CSCE of the New York Stock Exchange is called the "C" contract. A futures contract for Robusta coffee began to be traded on the London Commodity Exchange in the 1970s, evolving into what is now called the London International Financial Futures Exchange (LIFFE).

[24] Talbot (2004:112) described three major changes in the coffee finance markets. The first came in 1986, when the CSCE introduced the possibility of trading in options on coffee futures contracts, which were significantly cheaper than the futures contracts themselves. This opened space for speculation to smaller roasters and traders and gave the TNCs "another instrument to juggle into their integrated trading strategies." The second change came with the rise of commodity funds, "huge conglomerations of financial capital seeking the highest and most rapid profits available, by trading in financial, oil, metals, and agricultural futures markets," which were another mechanism of stimulating the participation of smaller speculators. The result of such changes in the financial coffee market was a decisive shift away from involvement by hedgers who

coffee market thus transformed the sector in two major ways. First, by separating investor knowledge of productive markets (changes in supply and demand) and financial markets, corporate profits became decoupled from actual volumes of coffee trade in the market. Second, and relatedly, the growth of financial trading propelled an overall escalation in the volatility of coffee prices, as coffee prices began following the rapid fluctuations of the financial markets. Financialization has required instantaneous and detailed knowledge about shifts in coffee prices, supplies and markets. This has been advantageous to transnational food conglomerates who have been able to better harness such flows of information.[25]

Overall, the globalization and financialization of the international coffee market converged in ways that undermined the structural power of large coffee exporters such as Colombia and Brazil and paved the way for the eventual dismantling of the ICA quota system. By the close of the 1980s, the ability to mount collective action based upon an alliance of exporters was weakened by the growth of small producing countries who felt that the ICA quotas limited their shares of the world market. Exporters ability to force prices up by withholding supplies also diminished as multi-product food conglomerates were able to easily blend higher-end coffees like Colombian milds with lower quality Arabicas and Robustas without undermining their product values. Moreover, the financialization of profits decoupled prices from volumes of coffee in the market. And even if exporters could align and withhold their exports, the expansion of coffee consumption into mass markets outside of the United States has made it more difficult to develop an institutional enforcement mechanism that would be interested in stabilizing the market. Not surprisingly then, the meetings to negotiate a fourth ICA for September 1989 were an utter failure. Major divisions among coffee producer-exporter countries emerged. Large exporters led by Brazil,

---

were involved in the coffee market itself toward a class of speculators who were interested in it in order to make rapid profits. Third, this escalation of trading on the futures market was also accompanied by a shift in the type of speculation from one based upon "fundamental analysis" to one based upon "technical analysis." The former analyzes the projections of future supplies and demands for coffee, a skill that requires detailed understanding of the coffee commodities market. The latter is solely based upon analyses on past market activity, including charts of the moving averages of prices, trends in total volume, and so forth, which require very little understanding of nature of the coffee market per se. Consequently, the rise of coffee speculation based upon technical analysis has meant that large sums of money began moving in and out of the futures markets in a manner that is only tangentially related the actual movement of commodities on the ground.

[25] Giovannucci et al. (2002:16); Talbot (2004:110–13).

Colombia, Mexico, and Costa Rica aligned with many African exporters, including Ethiopia, Uganda, Ivory Coast, Tanzania, and Kenya, who feared that their relatively small niches would diminish even further with advances in production by exporters in Asia and Oceania. This latter group, including Indonesia, Vietnam, and Papua New Guinea allied with Central American producers like El Salvador, Honduras, Nicaragua, and Guatemala whose governments were receiving US military and development aid to fight their civil wars. The United States tilted the scales to this latter group of Central American, Asian, and Oceanic countries in favor of the deregulation of the coffee market.[26] Gaining the support of the United States appeared to be central to a final verdict on the ICA. By this time, the United States had become fully implicated in its neoliberal agenda and had much to gain from its abrogation. In fact, by 1989 the US delegation to the ICO had shifted from the State Department to the Trade Policy Committee, under the office of the United States Trade Representative, whose primary mission was to cut back trade barriers that disadvantaged US exports. By the end of July 1989, ICO negotiations had broken down. And while the ICO as an organization was kept alive, its quota system was eliminated.[27]

Efforts to reinstate the ICA quotas broke down once again in 1993, as the United States was only prepared to institutionalize a "free market-oriented" ICA, free of political regulation stemming from the producers. Twenty-four exporting countries, led by the delegations from Colombia and Brazil, responded by forming the Association of Coffee Producer Countries (ACPC) in October 1993, whose members agreed to withhold 20% of their exports in a desperate attempt to drive prices up once again. And even though the ACPC countries held 85% of the world supplies, its attempts were undermined by delegations from Mexico (which was preparing to meet the requirements of the North Atlantic Free Trade Agreement, NAFTA), and Thailand and Vietnam (who were benefiting from a surge in exports to Asia). By 1994, efforts to reinstate a geopolitically regulated quota system came to a close, and its supporters began to figure out domestic strategies to weather the coming storm.[28] The era of the geopolitically managed coffee market under the ICA had ended.

Many observers agree that the dismantlement of the ICA system and the market liberalization that followed was the primary cause of an "international coffee crisis" that began in the 1990s and continues today.[29] Since 1990,

---

[26] Bates (1997:172–75).

[27] Talbot (2004:89).

[28] Talbot (2004:120, 124–26).

[29] Bates (1997); Giovannucci et al. (2002); Gresser and Tickell (2002); Talbot (2004); Daviron and Ponte (2005); Bacon et al. (2008); Fridell (2014).

Table 3.2 *World coffee exports and market shares, 1990–2017 (millions of 60 kg sacks)*

	Brazil Exports (%)	Colombia Exports (%)	Vietnam Exports (%)	Rest of World Exports (%)	Total Exports (%)
1990	16.9 (21.0)	13.9 (17.3)	1.1 (1.4)	48.6 (60.3)	80.7 (100)
1995	14.5 (21.3)	9.8 (14.5)	3.5 (5.2)	40.0 (59.0)	67.9 (100)
2000	18.0 (20.1)	9.2 (10.2)	11.6 (13.0)	50.7 (56.7)	89.6 (100)
2005	26.2 (29.9)	10.9 (12.4)	13.4 (15.3)	37.1 (42.3)	87.6 (100)
2010	33.2 (34.2)	7.8 (8.1)	14.2 (14.7)	41.9 (43.1)	97.1 (100)
2015	37.0 (32.2)	12.7 (11.1)	20.7 (18.0)	44.2 (38.5)	114.5 (100)
2017	30.6 (26.1)	13.0 (11.1)	23.2 (19.8)	50.7 (43.1)	117.5 (100)

Source: International Coffee Organization (n.d., accessed February 27, 2019 at www.ico .org/new_historical.asp?section=Statistics)

pricing volatility has increased, overall export prices have dropped, and corporate profits have become increasingly decoupled from volumes produced. The hardest hit by these changes to the international coffee market have been producers of high-quality Arabica beans, like Colombia as well as various Central American and East African countries, who have found it difficult to compete against exporters of low-end Robusta beans that can be easily blended without diminishing the overall quality of their coffee. Table 3.2 compares the world market shares of Brazil and Colombia to Vietnam and the rest of the coffee-exporting countries of the world. Overall, the size of the export market has increased from 80.7 million sacks in 1990 to 117.5 million by 2017. Brazil's exports dropped from 16.9 million sacks in 1990 to 14.5 by 1995. Thereafter, Brazil's IBC set upon a strategy to maintain its world market shares by dramatically increasing its overall exports. Over the next decade, they increased overall exports to 30.6 million sacks in 2017, actually increasing their market share from 21.0% to 26.1% over this period. The biggest winner of the post-ICA coffee market has been Vietnam, whose exports grew from 1.1 million sacks in 1990 to 23.2 million by 2017. Their shares of the market grew from 1.4% to 18.0%, overpassing Colombia as the second largest exporter of coffee. Colombia, in contrast, has struggled to maintain its exports, which dropped in the 1990s and once again in 2010, only recently coming close to its 1990 levels in 2017.

Indeed, Arabica coffee producers have experienced a growing influence of financial speculators in the market, which has increased the overall volatility of pricing. Figure 3.4 depicts the volume and percentage of Arabica coffee traded in

Figure 3.4 World coffee traded in coffee futures market, 1994–2017

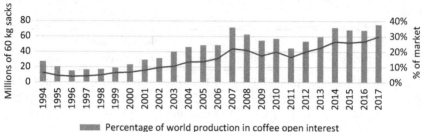

Percentage of world production in coffee open interest

—— Volume of coffee traded in open interest (millions of 60 kg sacks)

Source: Intercontinent Exchange (n.d., accessed on February 28, 2019 at www.theice.com/FuturesUSReportCenter.shtml)

the coffee "C" futures market of the New York Stock Exchange.[30] Like the volume of coffee futures, the percentage of coffee futures has increased over time since the mid-1990s. By 2007, some 35% of all coffee traded in the international market was subject to financial speculation. By 2017, the percentage grew to nearly 40% of all coffee in the market.

The Impact of Re-Peripheralization on Fedecafé's Pacto Cafetero

Indeed, the deregulation of the international coffee market following the collapse of the ICA quota system posed an immediate threat to the continued viability of Fedecafé's developmental coffee institutions and therefore its Pacto Cafetero vis-à-vis the country's cafetero farmers. Fedecafé responded to this unfavorable

---

[30] The volume of coffee traded in the futures market is calculated as the amount of coffee in the world market that is under an "open interest" contract. Simply put, coffee futures occur through contracts that are "open" to further speculative buying and selling that continue until the contract date ends and money is exchanged for actual volumes of coffee. The volume of coffee futures is a measure of how much coffee exists in "open interest" at any given time period. Figure 3.4 shows that volume of coffee futures grew steadily from 1995/1996 to 2007/2008. The world financial crisis of 2008/2009 interrupted this growth temporarily until trading in coffee futures began to grow once again beginning in 2011. The percentage of coffee futures, in turn, calculates the volume of coffee traded in "open interest" relative to the total amount of tradable coffee in the international market at a given time.

market environment by cutting its export taxes in 1990 and 1991 and using the FNC's accumulated reserves to subsidize growers for their losses. While temporarily providing a solution to meeting producer demands for prices that would cover the costs of coffee production, it proved inadequate when over 500,000 ha of coffee fields were destroyed by an outbreak of coffee rust in 1994 and a coffee berry borer worm (*la broca*) in 1995. Fedecafé then developed a renovation plan to uproot traditional Colombian varieties (*Typica* and *Bourbon*) that were hit hardest by the blight with Cenicafé's rust-resistant *Caturra/Colombia* variety. Whereas only 38.2% of coffee produced in Caldas in 1980 was Caturra, by 1997 this number shot up to 82% and 89% by 2005.[31]

To finance the costs of this recovery, the FNC lowered its price floors to growers and cut back on their services.[32] Yet, the bust in prices in 1998 and 1999 depleted their reserves. Over the decade, they lost some 80% of their total revenues and incurred a debt of over US$433.5 million. To stop the hemorrhaging, the FNC then made dramatic cuts to its advertising budget and sold off shares of its financial holdings and liquid assets, including their interests in the Banco Cafetero, which transformed from a public bank designed to support cafetero farmers into a private for-profit bank, *Bancafé*. Between 1995 and 2001, FNC assets shrunk from US$1.5 billion to $400 million. [33]

Despite these financial maneuvers, international coffee prices continued to sink, making it impossible for the FNC to continue to subsidize growers. In January of 2001, it abandoned its floor price mechanism altogether. Without its price floors, Fedecafé's competitive edge as the largest purchaser and domestic price setter of the market for unroasted green coffee diminished. In 1990, Fedecafé purchased nearly 50% of coffee exported to the world market. The remaining 50% was spread out among numerous domestic and foreign exporting firms. By 2000, Fedecafé's purchases dropped to 36%.[34] The four major foreign conglomerates (including Kraft, Cargill, Neumann, Volcafé) were perhaps the biggest winners. Between 1989 and 1996, their share of direct coffee purchases rose from roughly 8% to over 52%.[35] Fedecafé's capacity to set prices had collapsed and its efforts to control and manage yields and quality were being crushed under the weight of the deregulated market.

Yet, it was the cafetero farmers rather than Fedecafé itself who bore the brunt of the post-ICA market. The price drop of the 1990s led to a 50% drop in average

---

[31] Vallecilla Gordillo et al. (2005:33, 58).

[32] Robledo (1998:21–23).

[33] Giovannucci et al. (2002:55).

[34] Ramírez et al. (2002:55).

[35] Robledo (1998:102–3).

cafetero incomes. By 2001, when coffee prices dropped to their lowest, cafetero income was only 40% of what it had been in 1990; and, some 61% of cafetero households had fallen below Colombia's poverty line.[36] At the same time that cafetero debts were deepening, the costs of producing the new Caturra/Colombia variety of coffee were escalating.[37] While more resistant to leaf rust and more productive per tree, this variety required greater fertilization (phosphates, potash, urea), averaging up to 10–15% of total production costs.[38] Previously, these purchases of imported fertilizers were subsidized by the FNC as a measure intended to stabilize yields and increase coffee quality. By the early 2000s, however, the cost of fertilizers nearly tripled in price, from US$34.14 per metric ton in 1993 to US$50.81 in 2003 and US$89.51 by 2007.[39] Consequently, cafetero purchases of fertilizer dropped from 405,153 metric tons in 1990 to only 141,624 by 2007.[40]

The cost of labor, in turn, has historically been the most expensive for those cafeteros with farms large enough to hire full-time farmhands and seasonal harvesters (*recolectores*). In the 1980s, labor costs hovered between 60% and 70% of total farm expenses.[41] The adoption of Caturra/Colombia increased coffee yields per tree and therefore the need to hire seasonal harvesters, whose costs rose to up to 80% of total expenses by the early 2000s. As most cafetero owners of small and medium-sized farms could not afford these costs, the overall number of seasonal workers actually dropped from 750,000 in 1990 to 515,00 by 2000.[42]

Facing bankruptcy and unable to rely upon new provisions of subsidized loans from the Banco Cafetero, many cafeteros began selling off portions of their farmland. This subdividing process contributed to a process of land concentration in the region. The average farm size in Caldas, for example, dropped from 10.3 ha

---

[36] Giovannucci et al. (2002:23).

[37] Production costs are both fixed and variable. Fixed costs are the costs of maintaining and upgrading a farm, which must be incurred despite production yields and outputs. These include the preparation of soils, the cost of seedlings and seeds, insurance and overhead costs (tools and coffee processing equipment), public utilities, and land taxes. Variable costs include labor (harvesters, farm hands, truck drivers), fertilizers and pesticides (Author interview with coffee farmer in Salamina, Caldas on July 2, 2015).

[38] Vallecilla Gordillo et al. (2005:34); Ramírez et al. (2002:63).

[39] World Bank (n.d., accessed July 28, 2020 at https://datacatalog.worldbank.org/data set/world-development-indicators).

[40] DNP (n.d., accessed March 2, 2019 at www.dnp.gov.co/programas/agricultura/esta disticas-del-sector-agropecuario/Paginas/informacion-cafetera.aspx).

[41] Ortiz (1999:82).

[42] Giovannucci et al. (2002:23, 26–27).

in 1970 to 3.8 ha in 1997 and 3.3 ha in 2005.[43] Nationally, the percentage of medium-sized farms (10–15 ha) decreased between 1970 and 1997 from 15.5% to 6.1%. The percentages of small farms (under 5 ha) and very large farms (over 100 ha) increased from 3.4% to 9.4% and 62.1% to 94.7%, respectively.[44]

While some cafeteros sold off portions of their land, others gave up coffee farming altogether, preferring to sell the entirety of their farms to search for work elsewhere. Between 1988 and 1993, some twenty-three of Caldas' twenty-five rural municipalities saw a net outflow of inhabitants while its urban centers swelled.[45] In fact, the influx of rural migrants into the major cities of Viejo Caldas contributed to an estimated 8% increase per year in urban informal activity and an average unemployment rate of 22% unemployment in Pereira (Risaralda), Manizales (Caldas), and Armenia (Quindío) between 1994 and 2000.[46] Other migrants avoided the cities, preferring to migrate to the coca-producing frontier regions of the country.[47]

Finally, some cafeteros decided not to sell off their land, but instead uproot their coffee trees and plant coca on their existing land holdings. The returns on investment for coca during this period were both higher than coffee as well as less risky as an economic investment.[48] Yet, as we shall see in greater detail in the last case study, cultivating coca for the illegal cocaine export market brought social and political risks. Specifically, the emergence of coca production in Viejo Caldas in the 1990s exposed the region to the political and social violence that had plagued other regions of the country for decades but which was a distant reality for the country's cafeteros who were shielded from this violence by the Pacto Cafetero.[49]

Figure 3.5 illustrates this point, showing the incidents of combat activity and state/paramilitary repression of civilian noncombatants that occurred in Viejo Caldas between 1975 and 2017. During the years of the ICA quota system, both the number of incidents of combat between guerrillas and state forces as well as the incidents of repression hovered between low and nonexistent. These incidents grew slightly in 1989 and into the 1990s. Both escalated dramatically at the turn of the century, reaching highs between 2001 and 2005. By 2007, combat activity

[43] Vallecilla Gordillo et al. (2005:58).

[44] Guhl (2008:210).

[45] Vallecilla Gordillo et al. (2005:42).

[46] Ramírez et al. (2002:41).

[47] Richani (2002:68–69).

[48] London (1999:138–39).

[49] Rettberg (2010); Ibáñez Londoño et al. (2013).

Figure 3.5 Combat activity and state/paramilitary repression, Viejo Caldas, 1975–2017

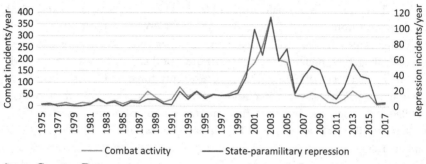

------ Combat activity ------ State-paramilitary repression

Source: Coercion Dataset

declined once again, due in large part to the military defeats of the guerrillas. Incidents of state and paramilitary repression of noncombatants, however, underwent two more waves in 2007–9 and 2013–15.

From Hegemony to Crises of Control: Waves of Cafetero Protests

By the turn of the twenty-first century, Colombia's cafetero farmers began to experience the full force of peripheral proletarianization. Under the Pacto Cafetero, they had become dependent upon the production and sale of coffee for their income and therefore the perpetuation of Fedecafé's control and management of the labor process. Yet, the international coffee market had made the Pacto Cafetero untenable. Prior to the Pacto Cafetero, when the domestic market was deregulated, Colombia's coffee farmers protected themselves from the volatility of the market by diversifying their fields, minimizing the marketization of their household reproduction, and retaining the "exit option" when prices sagged. Yet, when the market was becoming deregulated once again in the 1990s, the transformation of semi-proletarianized coffee farmers into fully proletarianized, card-carrying cafeteros made it difficult for most to envisage a future other than as a cafetero. Not only had their economic existence became marketized but so had their class identities and their political imaginations.

Christopher London's (1999) qualitative analysis of cafeteros in the 1990s demonstrated vividly how their deeply held class identification as cafeteros made it difficult for them to make sense of the causes of the crisis or how to figure out the most appropriate way to respond to it.[50] On the one hand, they experienced a clear sense of abandonment by Fedecafé, whose rollbacks of its regulatory initiatives was interpreted as a "reneging on the paternalistic compact" that they believed was at the core of Colombia's coffee industry. They also expressed frustration that these rollbacks were not simply causing economic hardship in their lives, but their abandonment by Fedecafé was "eroding the core communal values" that they themselves had preached.[51]

Yet, like many class formations that have been threatened to be "unmade" by the dismantling of protective social compacts, Colombia's cafeteros began to engage in actions to retain their rights and privileges under the political *status quo ante*.[52] As the coffee crisis deepened, Colombia's cafetero farmers shifted from passive to active responses, deploying Fedecafé's own discourse of cafetero rights, privileges, and protections as a powerful insurgent identity that has mobilized them onto the streets to force. Over the past three decades, waves of backlash resistance against the liberalization of the market, what Silver (2003) describes as "Polanyi-type" labor unrest, have spread across Colombia's coffee-producing regions. Rather than protest their dependence upon coffee production for the market or seek ways to minimize their dependence upon Fedecafé in favor of a less commodified livelihood, the country's cafeteros have directed frustrations at Fedecafé and ultimately at the Colombian government, for failing to deliver on the promises of protection under the Pacto Cafetero. In other words, they have organized to preserve their lives as market-dependent cafeteros. To do so, they

---

[50] Between 1996 and 1998, London (1997, 1999) surveyed 446 cafeteros in the departments of Caldas and Nariño and held a series of roundtable discussion with 93 of those surveyed with the intent of understanding how they interpreted the causes and potential solutions to the crisis of the sector. Seventy-six percent of growers believed that there was indeed a crisis in the coffee industry, with the three major causes sited as (1) "the broca, other pests or pathogens" (37.04%); (2) "the cost squeeze, or issues related the high cost of production and the low price for green coffee (31.04%); and (3) "bad weather conditions" (10.23%). The remaining 24% either believed that the problem of low prices did not constitute a crisis or did not know if it was. When asked to choose from various categories of solutions to the crisis, over 62% called for new actions from either Fedecafé or the Colombian government, while only 6.5% thought political-citizen action by farmers was needed and the rest had "no idea/no solution." When classifying solutions into "passive" or "active" types to determine whether the brunt of the solution should come from cafeteros or from Fedecafé, 64% of respondents responded for passive solutions. The focus group discussions echoed these sentiments from the survey data.

[51] London (1999:115, 126–27, 138–39).

[52] Silver (2003); Lee (2007); Bair and Hough (2012).

Figure 3.6 Coffee prices and cafetero protests in Viejo Caldas, 1975–2018

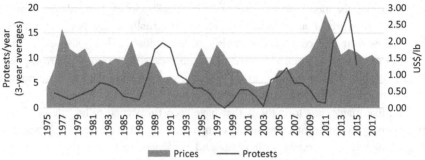

Prices ▬▬▬ Protests ——

Sources: CINEP Social Movement Database, www.cinep.org.co/Home2/servicios/sistema-de-informacion-general-sig/base-de-datos-de-luchas-sociales.html; Fedecafé (n.d.), National Federation of Coffee Growers, Coffee Statistics Database (accessed February 28, 2019)

have engaged in street actions, demonstrations, and strikes that have posed significant, albeit temporary, threats to Fedecafé's control of supplies and the labor process.

Figure 3.6 illustrates the yearly number of cafetero protests in Viejo Caldas between 1975 and 2018 placed alongside longitudinal data on the average yearly prices of Colombian milds in the international market. From the late 1970s until the late 1980s, prices remained high and protest activity remained low. This is not necessarily surprising, as coffee prices were elevated under the ICA quota agreement and Fedecafé's regulatory initiatives provided economic stability to producers. However, when looking at the peak years of protest activity in which the number of incidents rose above five per year, we see at least four waves: 1989–96, 1999–2002, 2004–8, and 2011–16, each of which followed a prior drop in prices.

The first wave built upon a social movement infrastructure that had been building up since the late 1970s. During the pricing boom period of the mid-late 1970s, some of the largest coffee farmers, including Fabio Trujillo Agudelo, Octavio Mejia Marulanda, and Fernando Londoño Londoño, established an independent organization, Association of Coffee Producers (Aprocafé, est. 1977), to protest what they viewed as Fedecafé's "discriminatory treatment" of larger farmers and to stimulate public debate over how to best spend FNC revenue. Aprocafé's leaders were activated again following an outbreak of *la roya* coffee fungus in the early 1980s. Fearing that Fedecafé was abandoning its responsibility to finance the costs of renovating fields destroyed by blight, they organized a series of protests in front of Fedecafé's departmental committee offices and the "First Meeting of Campesino Leaders from Antigua Caldas against the

Roya" in December of 1984. By 1985, they were successful in recruiting over 900 cafetero delegates from across the coffee-producing regions of the country to join a new organization, the United Colombian Coffee Growers (*Union Cafetera Colombiana*, UCC). The UCC was designed to be an autonomous protest organization that could pressure Fedecafé to respond appropriately to any further shake-ups of the coffee sector.[53]

In early 1989, when news spread that negotiations over the ICA quota system were breaking down, fierce debates arose in Fedecafé's municipal and departmental committee meetings on what to do. A group called Coffee Growers in Alert (*Cafeteras en Alerta*) began organizing street protests in coordination with the remnants of Aprocafé and UCC activists. Following the abrogation of the ICA, as prices began to collapse, these three groups fused to become the National Unity of Coffee Growers (*Unidad Cafetera Nacional*, UCN) with headquarters in Manizales and under the leadership of Aprocafé's Fabio Trujillo Agudelo and activist Jorge Enrique Robledo. During this first major wave of cafetero protests, the UCC organized region-wide street protests and marches demanding forgiveness of debts and promises of continued provisions of financial and technical support. The organizational capacity of the UCN was not clear, as its activity remained sporadic and limited mostly to regional centers. However, by May of 1995, coffee prices began to rise again and the UCN was able to use this to pressure the Fedecafé's *Comite Nacional* to approve the forgiveness of 25% of cafetero debts (roughly $10 million pesos) and provide $40 billion pesos in subsidized loans to help cafeteros finance the renovation of their fields that had been blighted by the broca berry borer worm. Inspired by this success, the UCN organized its first "Paro Civico Cafetero Nacional" (national coffee shutdown) in June of 1995. A 24-hour protest was held, with participation of over 100,000 people from 151 municipalities and 10 departments, including solidarity protests from transport workers, local businesses, teachers, students, and even some local political representative (*diputados* and *concejales*) and elements of the Catholic Church. Colombian lawmakers responded to the shutdown by passing Law 223 of 1995, which granted total debt forgiveness on loans under 3 million pesos. Dissatisfied with this repayment cap, the UCN called for another round of protests to take place in the coming months. In 1996, the FNC finally caved, granting full debt forgiveness for all of the 86,783 cafetero families impacted by the pricing crash.[54]

---

[53] Robledo (1998:32–35).

[54] Robledo (1998:40–42); Author interview with former UCN activist in Bogotá on July 30, 2004.

Coffee prices remained relatively high and protest activity in the region declined in 1996 and 1997. By 1998, however, prices began to decline precipitously once again. This bust was exacerbated by a massive earthquake in January of 1999 that devastated large parts of the department of Quindío. The UCN responded with a second wave of protests in 1999 and 2000 that demanded debt forgiveness and loan provisions to those farmers who lost their harvests in the earthquake. During this period, the UCN began staging a number of coordinated actions alongside other agrarian producers, all of whom were struggling to make ends meet in a national agrarian sector that was subject to market deregulation. These movement alliances developed into a broad federation of large and small agricultural producers, called the National Association for Agricultural Salvation (*Salvación Agropecuaria*, SA).[55] Salvación Agropecuaria began organizing national, regional, and local protests against governmental efforts to negotiate a "Free Trade Area of the Americas" agreement (FTAA) with the United States.[56] By July 2001, anger at the FTAA negotiations converged with plummeting coffee prices that reached levels not seen since 1992–93. The UCN took to the streets alongside other agrarian groups in massive protests and demonstrations, including a two-day civic shutdown (*paro cívico*) wherein over forty national highways were blocked and closed, bringing protesters into direct clashes with police equipped with tanks and antiriot gear. They came out *en masse* once again for a *paro cívico* in October of 2002. In an effort to help save the coffee sector from collapse, in 2002 the Colombian Government agreed to finance an aid package providing producers with a direct subsidy pegging local to world prices, and access to "refinancing credit" to help renew coffee trees and cover technical assistance needs. The FNC resumed these responsibilities in 2003. However, they announced that their price floor mechanism would remain pegged to world market prices rather than adjusted to meet production costs. Moreover, they promised future access to credit, though this would no longer come from the publicly mandated Banco

---

[55] The agricultural sectors most active in Salvación Agropecuaria tend to be those who would have the most to lose from a full opening of the domestic agricultural market to international competition. This includes the canaleros (cinnamon), paperos (potatoes), cafeteros (coffee), and cerealeros (cereals) (Author interview with former UCN and Salvación activist in Manizales, Caldas on August 17, 2004).

[56] Salvación Agropecuaria's mandate can be summarized in seven key points: (1) the guarantee of agricultural self-sufficiency for the nation; (2) stable and sufficient remuneration of prices for agricultural products; (3) effective control of production costs; (4) cheap, available lines of credit; (5) debt forgiveness and the dismissal of judicial charges; (6) state protection, regulation, and intervention in the agricultural sector; and (7) unification of production under the state (Salvación Agropecuaria 2015).

Cafetero, which had become dissolved by then. Finally, the FNC agreed to finance a major overhaul of the sector that would include the costs of renovating some 300,000 ha of coffee land.[57]

Between 2004 and 2006, prices began to rise slowly once again, though they were still only slightly above $1.00/lb and well below the average costs of production for most farmers. The slow pace of recovery, coupled with their prior successes in forcing the central government to take on the protective measures of the Pacto Cafetero in the face of a weakened Fedecafé, convinced the UCN to participate in national protests in April 2004 that were organized by Salvación Agropecuaria, labor unions, and indigenous organizations against Colombia's adoption of free trade policies.[58] The steep rise in coffee prices that began in 2007, however, returned the country's cafeteros to the fields. By then, the original 300,000 ha of renovated coffee had doubled to 600,000 ha.[59] By the close of the decade, coffee prices were rising to levels well beyond their heights during the ICA years, protests de-escalated, and the newly renovated coffee trees were producing high-quality coffee that promised to fetch a good price in the market.

The latest wave of cafetero protests came after the highs of the years 2010 and 2011 began sliding downward again in 2012. By early 2013, the country's cafeteros had plunged back into debt. The new coffee trees required expensive fertilizers and pesticides that they paid for with loans, many from private banks. The hope was that these new high-yielding trees would generate greater volumes of beans that could buffer against any drop in prices. However, the harvest period in 2012 converged with a steep glut in prices and escalating labor costs, which dropped farmer revenues once again below production costs. By then, however, the political context had shifted. Colombia's cafeteros had become integrated into a national agrarian movement federation called the Movement for the Defense and Dignity of Agricultural Producers (*Dignidad Agropecuaria*). This was a broad coalition of agricultural producers, agrarian wage workers, and campesino farmers demanding a reversal of the government's support for neoliberal agrarian policies, an end to free trade agreements, and investments in the agricultural sector to promote national food sovereignty. The *Unidad Cafetera* organization, now called *Dignidad Cafetera*, was at the forefront of the *Dignidad* movements because they already had over a decade of experience and success mobilizing farmers and

---

[57] CONPES (2004:6).

[58] Author interviews with ANUC-UR activist in Bogotá on July 28, 2004 and with Salvación activists in Bogotá on July 30, 2004 and August 4, 2004.

[59] Caracol Radio (2007).

supporters onto the streets and pressuring the government to meet their movement demands.[60]

Thus, when prices fell in 2012, Dignidad Cafetera engaged in a series of actions that brought cafeteros alongside other agrarian producers, workers, and supporters that effectively shut down the coffee-growing regions of the country through road blocks and civic strikes. By February, these actions spread to the rest of the country, becoming a national agrarian strike that was joined by the Colombian labor union federation (*Central Unitaria de Trabajadores*, CUT), university and high-school students, teachers and administrators, healthcare workers, truckers, and political activists. Dignidad Cafetera was protesting again for debt forgiveness and provisions, but this time was demanding a radical democratization of the FNC and the establishment of a new payment subsidy system that would keep farm-gate prices for unroasted beans above production costs.[61] These demands became part of a larger set of demands from Dignidad Agropecuara for a fundamental overhaul of the country's agrarian institutions. They also converged with another mass mobilization by indigenous communities and landless farmers in the Catatumbo region of the country, who engaged in land invasions, demanded land reforms and an end to rural displacement driven by government-support for extractive mining developments, oil excavation, and hydro-electric power plants. The protests brought hundreds of thousands of people onto the streets, many of whom were met by Colombian security forces who clashed with protestors, leaving at least four dead, dozens of security forces injured, and hundreds arrested.[62] By March, the Santos Administration (2010–18) caved to protestor demands. Regarding the coffee sector, Santos agreed to forgive debts, institute a government commission with Dignidad leaders to better understand and ultimately address the structural problems of pricing, and to preserve key provisions of the Pacto Cafetero in order to protect farmers from future price shocks.[63] In exchange for these promises of protection, Colombia's

---

[60] Author interview with Dignidad activist via Skype on February 18, 2014.

[61] Sheridan (2013); Author interview with Dignidad activist via Skype on December 24, 2015.

[62] Sheridan (2013); Melo (2013).

[63] Hough (2015); these protests resulted in (1) the creation of a new subsidy program (*Proteccion al Ingreso de los Caficultures*, or PIC) for coffee growers to make up for any shortfalls between the selling prices of coffee beans and the costs of production, (2) forgiveness of all debts on interest and capital payments to the *Banco Agrario*, the public bank that holds approximately 90% of loans to the country's coffee growers, and (3) government agreement to participate in a series of negotiations with leaders of the *Dignidad Cafetera* movement to discuss problems of chronic coffee farmer debt, price

cafeteros agreed to take on a new round of loans and renovate their fields in accordance with new development planning directives of Fedecafé.[64]

This wave of protests in 2013 marked the biggest outburst of social unrest and political militancy in modern Colombian history. It was a turning point for Colombia's agricultural producers in general, as it put the question of agrarian production at the center of the political agenda. For the country's cafeteros, it also marked a high point in the sense that the central government was acknowledging that the Pacto Cafetero had been insufficient as it was to protect the livelihood of producers and their communities.

The Contemporary Crisis of Peripheral Proletarianization in World Historical Perspective

This chapter recast the contemporary struggles of Colombia's cafetero farmers in world historical perspective. Doing so clarified how Fedecafé's success in establishing a hegemonic labor regime during the middle decades of the twentieth century rested upon the International Coffee Agreements, which protected Colombia from the worst excesses of pricing volatility and competition that had characterized its market niche until then. Moreover, we saw that the ICA quota system itself was created to extend US world hegemonic influence over the tropical coffee-producing regions of the world. Its collapse in 1989 swept away the protective blanket that had become essential to the national development measures of Colombian and other coffee-producing governments. International market liberalization since the 1990s thus intensified competition among exporters, which re-peripheralized Colombia's market niche and ultimately undermined Fedecafé hegemony in Viejo Caldas. Since the 1990s, coffee prices for Colombian coffee exports have fluctuated wildly in the international market, often dropping well below production costs. And as production costs increased, so has the vulnerability of cafetero farmers.

A return to a geopolitically regulated international coffee quota and pricing system seems unlikely. South–South relations among exporters remain competitive, fragmented between those who benefitted from the previous system and

---

controls for agro-inputs, agricultural trade policy, and national development policy (Sheridan 2013). The FNC also agreed to increase the size of annual field renovations from 84,000 to 90,000 ha. The costs per hectare of these renovations are estimated to be between $8 and $12 million Colombian peso (US$2,860–$4,285) (USDA 2016).

[64] Author interview with Dignidad activist in Chinchina, Caldas on June 30, 2015.

newcomers whose productive capacity and profits were stunted by small export quotas. The rise of Vietnam and other exporters that can produce coffee at significantly lower costs has diminished the leverage of large powerhouses like Brazil and Colombia. This, in addition to the politics of the US government, which is no longer willing or able to sacrifice profits for broader legitimacy concerns, has intensified competition in the production-exportation niches of the market while benefitting transnational corporate importers and roasters. Power in the industry as a whole has become concentrated, with three companies – ECOM Agroindustrial, Neumann, and Volcafe – purchasing about 50% of all coffee exports, while ten roasters, including Nestlé and Jacobs Douwe Egberts, process nearly 40% of world consumption.[65] These multinational food corporations now purchase coffee for less than a third of the price they paid under the ICA system in the 1980s. Meanwhile, the costs to consumers have gone up in major consumer markets like in the United States from an average real cost of US$1.40/lb to US$3.61 today.[66] In other words, core–periphery inequalities in the international coffee market have increased since the abrogation of the ICA.

In the absence of a geopolitically regulated market, some have advocated new efforts to redistribute some of the wealth through Fair Trade and other coffee-certification processes meant to diminish transaction costs, retain price floors, and provided farmers with higher rents from coffee.[67] The rising presence of Starbucks and other cafes, specialty coffee houses, and coffee culture in general, has given the impression that the coffee trade has become a leader of ethical trade and poverty reduction.[68] Since the crash of the ICA quota system, the number of Starbucks cafes increased from under 20 to 27,399 by 2017.[69]

However, critics have pointed out the serious structural limits of Fair Trade as a sustainable strategy for the world's 25 million coffee farmers and 125 million people whose lives depend on coffee production for the market.[70] Namely, despite their marketing presence, Fair Trade, specialty, and other ethically certified coffees constitute about 20% of global coffee production.[71] Moreover, supplies of ethically produced coffee far outweigh demand for it. In their 2015 report, for example, Fair Trade International itself noted that the amount of their coffee produced

[65] Fairtrade International (2015).

[66] Morales-de la Cruz (2017).

[67] Gresser and Tickell (2002).

[68] Giovannucci and Koekoek (2003); Luttinger and Dicum (2006); Fellner (2008).

[69] Starbucks (n.d., accessed March 14, 2019 at www.starbucks.com/about-us/company-information/starbucks-company-timeline).

[70] Jaffee (2007); Bacon et al. (2008); Fridell (2014).

[71] Echavarría et al. (2014:11).

increased by 16% between 2012 and 2014, up to 549,000 million tons. Yet, the amount they sold had only gone up by 6% over that period, up to 150,000 million tons.[72] Finally, despite the spread of specialty coffees and café locations, overall coffee imports to leading consumers have actually undergone a long-term decline since the 1940s. In the United States for example, coffee drinking peaked during World War II and has been declining ever since as consumers have replaced it with carbonated sugary beverages and soft drinks.[73]

In Colombia, all of the coffee purchased by the FNC at its cooperatives – roughly 30% of all coffee produced nationally – has always required certification of its quality standards and production conditions. However, Fedecafé has invested heavily in the development of fair trade and other certified sustainability programs over the past two decades. These initiatives, developed with Nestlé's Nespresso AAA, UTZ-Rainforest Alliance, 4C, CAFÉ Practice (Starbucks), Fair Trade, and organics, grew from some 1,745 certified farms in 2004 to 235,574 farms by 2017. This is about 40% of the country's coffee farms. Colombia now exports the most ethically certified and ecologically sustainable coffee in the world. However, specialty and sustainable coffees amount to only 1 million 60 kg sacks, roughly 14% of all of the coffee produced in the country.[74] Critics point out that the limited demand for these coffees makes it impossible to generalize this strategy to Colombia's coffee sector as a whole. Rather, given the flood of low-quality coffee in the international market from places like Vietnam, Fedecafé should develop a price floor system that extends to lower-quality coffees produced that do not meet either FNC or third-party certification standards. Likewise, cafeteros that have invested in the heavy costs of producing high-valued sustainable coffee have no guarantee that their beans will be purchased as sustainably certified coffees, especially as more cafeteros take on sustainable production systems and competition for access to the market increases.[75]

Currently, the international coffee market is bifurcating into a high-end specialty market centered largely in Europe and a low-end market of blends and packaged coffees elsewhere, leaving Colombia's high-quality but standardized exports threatened from both ends. To meet growing demand for high-end specialty coffees, Fedecafé has moved away from its historic commitment to build and market a national brand of high-quality Colombian mild Arabicas toward specialty niche markets of varying standards. As mentioned, they have partnered

---

[72] Fairtrade International (2015:77).

[73] USDA (2016).

[74] Haye (2018).

[75] Author interview with coffee farmer in La Merced, Caldas on June 30, 2015 and with two campesino activists in Riosucio, Caldas on July 5, 2015.

up with various ethical, social, and ecological certification organizations to produce coffees that meet their specific ethical standards. These efforts have required both financial investments in renovation and technical assistance from extensions agents that have been both costly and risky in that they entail sunken costs to cafeteros that might not pay off at the time of harvest.[76]

Fedecafé has also invested heavily in "single origin" coffee that markets its coffee like regional wines to add value. These efforts require empirically verified scientific evidence that the beans produced indeed vary in terms of their chemical composition, taste, and other properties and that the ecological conditions of each region vary in terms of soil nutrients, sun and precipitation, local flora and fauna, and the like. These initiatives have not only required investment of time and money from teams of Cenicafé scientists, but they have essentially redirected the focus, role, and importance of extensions agents for local populations of cafeteros, who must trust the micro-knowledge about the conditions of production that they do not have. Coffee that is not purchased as specialty-certified or single-origin types is exported with the Fedecafé quality standard and sold as it has done historically. Or, increasingly, it is sold in the low-end market where it is blended with cheaper quality coffees and does not therefore result in value-added revenues.[77]

Finally, Fedecafé has made significant movement into the consumer end of the market. Following the Starbucks café trend, they have established Juan Valdez cafes in key markets in the United States, Europe, Canada, Japan, as well as through major urban centers in Latin America and Colombia. To enter the growing Keurig "Green Mountain" coffee pod market, they have begun selling single-serving freeze-dried pods. Additionally, they have developed partnerships with Starbucks and other distributors to sell their single-origin and Juan Valdez specialty coffee brands. Finally, to stimulate domestic coffee consumption of their specialty coffees, Fedecafé developed a partnership with Starbucks to open coffee houses in Colombia that would only serve FNC coffees.[78]

---

[76] Author interviews with two coffee farmers in Salamina, Caldas on July 2, 2015 and with the commercial coordinator for Fedecafé's coffee cooperative in Chinchina, Caldas on July 3, 2015.

[77] Author interviews with Fedecafé' Chief Communications and Marketing Officer via Skype on March 27, 2015 and with the Caldas Departmental Extensions Officer in Chinchina, Caldas on July 3, 2015.

[78] González (2014); USDA-GAIN (2018); Author interviews with Fedecafé' Chief Communications and Marketing Officer via Skype on March 27, 2015 and with Fedecafé's Treasurer General in Bogotá on June 25, 2015.

Despite these new developments, Colombia's coffee crisis has only deepened, as Fedecafé's efforts to adapt to the international market above has been met by an increasingly powerful cafetero movement from below. Labor movement scholars have developed useful ways of analyzing the forms of worker power vis-à-vis capital and states. Structural power accrues to workers when their actions can disrupt the broader functioning of the workplace or the economy. Associational power accrues when workers form collective organizations such as trade unions and political parties that can mobilize workers onto the streets or to the ballot boxes.[79] Symbolic power, a form of associational power, derives from the ability of workers to draw upon culturally held claims about rights, political and ideological idioms, and identities rooted in moral economies, to mobilize workers onto the streets.[80]

In general, the structural power of Colombia's cafeteros has clearly declined over time as the relative value of coffee exports in the economy has diminished and its role in development policy has been overshadowed by industrial diversification during the postwar decades, illegal narcotics, and a more recent turn to oil, mining, and other extractivist industries.[81] Cafetero strikes and shutdowns, while disruptive to the regional economy, have lost their ability to significantly impact the productivity of the rest of the national economy. Yet, despite this weakening of their structural power, the cafeteros' symbolic power remains strong and their associational power has increased. Coffee continues to be associated with Colombia's national identity. Moreover, Fedecafé's lobbying power and national political presence shows no signs of diminishing. Both the country's cafeteros as well as Fedecafé itself have been able to use this symbolic association of coffee with nationalism to their advantage. Because the economic crisis of the sector is viewed as a crisis of the national economy, the fate of the country's cafeteros and the stability of the country's coffee regions, in turn, have become economic barometers of the national economy and political barometers of the legitimacy of presidential administrations.

The cafeteros' most effective power, however, seems to be associational. The recurrent waves of cafetero unrest have allowed them the opportunity to build a

---

[79] Wright (2000); Silver (2003).

[80] Lee (2007); Webster et al. (2008).

[81] For example, coffee reached a high of 77% of the value of Colombian exports in 1945 (Beyer 1949). In 2018, this value shrunk to 6.6% (Banco de la República n.d., accessed December 28, 2020 at www.banrep.gov.co/es/-estadisticas). In terms of its contribution to GDP, coffee reached nearly 10% by 1950 (Junguito and Pizano 1991:43–44). By 2014, its contribution to total GDP is now only 1% (Echavarría et al. 2014:3).

powerful social movement infrastructure that extends well beyond the coffee region. Whereas *Unidad Cafetera* was able to mobilize cafeteros, their families, and community members onto the streets in response to the post-ICA pricing plunge in the early 1990s, a decade later they were able to successfully organize national protests including demonstrations in the national capital, Bogotá. Moreover, their leaders had become entrenched figures in the political landscape. Movement activist Oscar Gutierrez Orozco, for example, became a powerful and popular representative on the city council of Manizales. The UCC's leader, Jorge Robledo Castillo, was elected as national senator from the leftist Polo Democrático political party. In these positions, both developed social movement networks with trade unions, human rights groups, indigenous and Afro-Colombian activists, and other social movement organizations. They also developed political and social networks at the regional and national levels with government officials, academics, and interest groups to pressure for change from inside and outside of government. UCC activist and trained economist, Aurelio Suárez Montoya, developed detailed research on the sector that has been critical to the movement's claims and policy recommendations. By the early 2000s, these networks had become pivotal to the formation of the broad anti-neoliberal coalition of groups protesting Colombia's free trade negotiations with Europe and the United States and to the establishment of the agrarian movement federation, Salvación Agropecuaria. Thus, by the time that coffee prices dropped again in 2012, Colombia's cafeteros were able to mobilize these alliances, this time through the Dignidad Agropecuaria federation, to mount the largest national protests in modern Colombian history.

The strength of Dignidad Cafetera and the Dignidad Agropecuaria movement has only intensified the contradictions facing Fedecafé. In fact, the 2013 protests were so disruptive and powerful that the Santos Administration responded by establishing a commission to analyze the structural problems of the coffee sector, evaluate the effectiveness of Fedecafé's regulatory interventions, and develop a plan to radically overhaul it. The commission, headed by former Fedecafé director Juan Jose Echavarría, recommended radical reforms that would privatize some of Fedecafé's most important institutions (including the FNC) and do away with some of its market interventions (guaranteed purchase policy) in order to increase Colombia's international market share and overall productivity. Fedecafé, coffee farmers, and Dignidad activists criticized the Commission for its neoliberal orientation and its unquestioning faith in the corrective capacity of the market. Fedecafé's marketing director, Luis Fernando Samper, took issue with the commission's hostility to regulatory institutions with a point that could have been taken right from Fedecafé's playbook in the 1930s:

It is important to highlight that the Commission sees value in FNC's commercial activities, but believes the FNC should operate exclusively with private incentives and no use of public resources. We [Fedecafé] believe in the market, but, unlike the Commission, we do not blindly believe in the free market as a solution to everything and everybody's problems. There are recent examples of clear market failures in the United States and Europe. Unlike the Commission, most of the world has come to realize that free markets on their own do not perform miracles.

(Quoted in Sheridan 2015)

As it turned out, pushback against the Commission's report appears to have strengthened Fedecafé's resolve to deepen, rather than diminish, its regulatory interventions in the market. In August of 2018, Fedecafé's Chief Executive officer, Roberto Vélez Vallejo, argued that the root causes of the coffee crisis in Colombia had to do with the liberalized nature of pricing in the international market and called for the establishment of an "international ideal floor price" system for all coffee sold in domestic markets.[82] More recently, Fedecafé has been exploring ways to pull Colombian coffee out of the New York Stock Exchange's "C" market altogether to both reduce the volatility of prices and increase their value. This was part of a larger set of policies, including establishing higher floor prices to Colombian farmers and efforts to grow domestic consumption, in order to grow the sector into the twenty-first century.[83]

In short, both Fedecafé and the Dignidad Movement seem wedded to the idea that coffee production for the twenty-first-century market can be both a strategy of development and a stable modality of class reproduction of the country's cafetero farmers. At this point, there is no evidence showing that the cafetero movement is seeking ways to diminish cafetero reliance on coffee or minimize their dependence upon the market to meet their economic livelihood needs. For example, every single cafetero farmers I have visited during my fieldwork knows the exact quantity used and costs of the seeds, fertilizers, and other inputs they use. They all rely on soil tests collected by extensions agents and passed on to Cenicafé's scientists to assess the nutrients, moisture, and acidity of every square meter of their land. They all have maps of their farms that detail the plant life and spatial location of their coffee trees in relation to other flora. It is not uncommon

---

[82] Morales-de la Cruz (2017) argues that this international floor price was significantly lower than it should be, relative to the profits made by transnational importing and roasting firms.

[83] Brown (2019).

now for cafetero farmers to open up their laptops and show you excel spreadsheets with these details, or to open up planning programs that determine their daily, monthly, or seasonal responsibilities for the day. When asked what his work has been like recently, one farmer I interviewed, for example, simply showed me his laptop, smiled and said, "it's all in there."[84]

Extensions agents, in turn, remain a persuasive and influential presence on cafetero farms and in their communities. They continue to view their involvement in cafetero decisions as "partnerships" and "friendships." As one extensions agent told me, "when you arrive at someone's farm, you are not only expected to say hello to the husband, wife, and each kid. You should also know the names of their dogs and cats. If you know all of their names, and they know you, you are part of the family."[85] Moreover, extensions agents remain supportive of cafetero demands that are expressed in Fedecafé's municipal and departmental committees, even if and when cafeteros express their support for the Dignidad movement.

Yet, there are other signs that the cafetero class identity is threatened. For example, the average age of cafetero farmers is now fifty-six years old.[86] This appears to be the first generation of cafetero parents who are encouraging their children to leave the farm when they finish secondary school because they fear that coffee may remain a risky and precarious occupation in the future. Older cafeteros, while often proud of their accomplishment, also have expressed the feeling of being stuck producing coffee due to a lack of alternatives. For example, as one older farmer explained,

> What happens is that since there is a family tradition of 50, 70, 80 years [producing coffee], they have no other skills ... It is the only thing they know how to do, so they keep waiting for the bonanzas that do arrive at some point, waiting for subsidies, government aid, and now the achievements of Dignidad Cafetera ... My dad who is 83 years old still has a farm that he works. When you see him, he is either excited about his harvest or patiently waiting for the next.[87]

Interestingly, however, there has been a segment of the coffee-producing population that has avoided the boom-and-bust cycles of the sector. Colombia's

---

[84] Author interview with coffee farmer in Salamina, Caldas on July 2, 2015.

[85] Author interview with municipal extensions agent in Salamina, Caldas on July 2, 2015.

[86] Haye (2018).

[87] Author interview with coffee farmer in La Merced, Caldas on June 30, 2015.

Association of Indigenous and Peasant Producers (Asproinca) is a group of some 350 indigenous farming communities that was founded in 1995. The regional chapter in Viejo Caldas was formed out of frustrations with Fedecafé's extensions services and quality standards, which required them to specialize in coffee productivity rather than diversify their land holdings. As one Asproinca farmer pointed out,

> [Fedecafé extensions agents] came to my farm, telling me "you have to knock down everything there and plant coffee or else they would stop providing support." This made us angry because we knew the [risks] of coffee, so we cultivated banana, yucca, arracacha [vegetable roots], fruit trees and all those things. But, then the [local] committee made us knock down these plants to put only coffee. That was when I decided not to participate in [Fedecafé's] initiatives. This coffee crisis that these poor cafeteros are experiencing, that has nothing to do with us. We have cane, coffee, banana, yuca to collect, and we are more or less well.[88]

In other words, like the coffee-producing farmers of the 1930s, Asproinca's farmers have essentially avoided the contemporary busts of the coffee market by cultivating coffee alongside subsistence agricultural goods to diminish their reliance on the market. And, their successes have not gone unnoticed. For example, their organization's dedication to ecologically and socially sustainable farming won recognition from the United National Development program as a model for rural development in 2008.[89] Dignidad Cafetera's leader, Oscar Gutierrez Reyes, while advocating a deepening of regulatory protections for cafetero farmers, has also noted that Aspoinca's approach provides a more sustainable future and is therefore essential to any longer-term efforts to establish national food sovereignty.[90] Indeed, the development of low-quality coffees (in addition to high-quality ones) as well as overall governmental investments in agricultural diversification and domestic production have become central demands of the Dignidad Cafetera movement.

In summary, rather than simply "survive the coffee crisis, alive and kicking," as Don Jairo Rodriquez explained at the beginning of this case study, the rise of

---

[88] Author interview with Asproinca activist and coffee farmer in Riosucio, Caldas on July 5, 2015.

[89] UNDP (2008).

[90] Author interview with Oscar Gutierrez in Manizales, Caldas on July 16, 2015.

Asproinca and the growing militancy of the Dignidad movement are suggesting an alternative solution to the coffee crisis that diminishes the role of the market in the lives of the country's coffee-producing farmers. Whether the country's cafeteros deepen their proletarianization and diminish it remains an open question at this point, one that appears to hinge on the agrarian politics of the country at large.

Case Study #2

DESPOTISM AND CRISIS IN THE BANANA REGIME OF URABÁ

I was appointed by the Estado Mayor [AUC Central Command] to retake "el Calima" five years ago. But the Bloque Bananera was initiated by me as a measure of self-defense. I started here and will have finished my task when I turn in my arms.

(Hernán Hernández, Commander of the AUC Paramilitary's "Banana Bloc" upon their demobilization on November 24, 2004)[1]

A Return to Despotism in Colombia's Banana-Enclave Region of Urabá

The experiences of Colombia's cafetero farmers with the global market, the state, and commodity production stands in stark contrast to another set of rural producers living some 350 miles to their north: the agricultural workers of Colombia's banana export region of Urabá. Unlike the hegemony of Fedecafé's coffee regime, Urabá's banana plantations became focal points of paramilitary groups that engaged in some of the most despotic forms of labor repression in the country. On March 14, 2007, Chiquita Brands International, the contemporary successor company of the United Fruit Company, was fined US$25 million as part of a settlement with the US Justice Department for payments their Colombian subsidiary (*C.I. Bananas de Exportación*, or Banadex) made to the United Self-Defense Forces of Colombia (*Autodefensas Unidas de Colombia*, AUC), an umbrella paramilitary organization with ties to banana plantation owners, drug traffickers , cattle ranchers, and Colombian military forces.

According to Banadex statements, these payments of approximately $1.7 million between 1997 and 2004 were made in exchange for "employee protection," which company executives described as "the cost of doing business" in Colombia's

---

[1]   El Tiempo (2004).

banana-producing enclave of Urabá – a region of the country that has been embroiled in decades of political violence between leftist guerrillas and national security forces. As evidence of their discomfort in making these payments, Banadex executives pointed out that they made similar payments between 1989 and 1997 to leftist guerrilla groups, including the Revolutionary Armed Forces of Colombia (FARC), National Liberation Army (ELN), and Popular Liberation Army (EPL), all of which operated in the area prior to the appearance of the AUC. The AUC's leader, Carlos Castaño Gil, however, disagreed with Banadex's rationale that the payments were simply the cost of doing business in Colombia. Instead, he testified that he met with Chiquita executives in late 1996 and early 1997 to clarify to them that "the Colombian army was ineffectual in removing the guerrilla groups" and that the payments were explicitly intended to "drive the leftist guerrillas out of the Santa Marta and Urabá banana-growing regions."[2] He added that the AUC's control of the region would "protect the company, its executives, employees, and infrastructure from future attacks by leftist guerrillas ... and create a business and work environment that would enable Chiquita's Colombian banana-growing operations to thrive."[3]

As it turned out, the AUC did engage in various bouts of low-intensity combat to force the guerrillas from the region while on Chiquita's payroll. However, the bulk of AUC activity was rooted in a violent strategy Castaño referred to as "draining the water to catch the fish." That is, the AUC engaged in a brutal campaign of terror comprised of targeted killings, death threats, torture, forced displacement, and massacres of unarmed civilians who the AUC claimed were guerrilla sympathizers. By 2004, it became clear that the AUC had not only "caught the fish," meaning that they successfully purged the region of the FARC, EPL, and ELN. They also "drained the water" by forcing some 60,000 people from their homes, killing, maiming, and torturing approximately 4,000 people, over 400 of whom died in some 62 mass slaughters.[4]

The worst hit by the wave of paramilitary violence was the region's banana worker union, SINTRAINAGRO, a union with a historically leftist leadership and militant stance vis-à-vis banana plantation owners. Prior to the AUC's campaign of terror, SINTRAINAGRO engaged in a series of strikes in the late 1980s and early 1990s that forced the region's banana plantation owner association (*Asociación de Bananeros de Colombia*, Augura) to (1) recognize their right to represent some 95% of Urabá's approximately 17,000 banana workers and (2)

---

[2] Barker et al. (2009:47).
[3] Nielson (2012).
[4] Verdad Abierta (2008); see also Cohen (2014).

finance a sector-wide "social compact" that would redistribute some of the profits back to workers in the form of social programs and local development initiatives. By the end of the AUC's campaign of terror, however, an estimated 844 union members and leaders had been assassinated.[5] And, observers began to note a fundamental transformation in SINTRAINAGRO's political orientation and organizational campaigns. Instead of readily engaging in mass strikes to leverage concessions from banana plantation owners as they had done in the past, they adopted a new stance of "harmony and good will" toward local bosses and refused to strike when Augura failed to uphold its promises under the "social compact." Moreover, SINTRAINAGRO's leadership distanced itself from the national union movement at large, becoming outspoken supporters of the presidential administration of Álvaro Uribe Vélez (2002–10), a staunchly antil-abor and anti-leftist politician with alleged family connections to the AUC. SINTRAINAGRO's General Secretary, Hernan Correa, summarized the union's political transformation and the consolidation of paramilitary domin-ation over the region in an interview, stating simply, "we came to see that the boss was not an enemy, he was a partner."[6]

In 2005–06, President Uribe signed a "peace accord" with the AUC that resulted in the group's formal demobilization and reintegration back into Colombian society with near total impunity.[7] Since then, a number of splinter paramilitary groups (*Bandas Criminales*) have arisen in former AUC territorial strongholds. One group, called the *Urabeños*, continues to carry out acts of labor repression in the banana region. In fact, SINTRAINAGRO has been Colombia's most "most targeted union" with the "highest murder rate" of any group of workers in the country.[8] This is particularly striking in light of the International Trade Union Confederation's Global Rights Index report (2016:31) that found Colombia to be "the country with the highest number of [trade unionist] murders of any country. Over 2,500 unionists have been murdered in the past 20 years, more than in the rest of the world combined."

Explanations of the rise of paramilitary terror in Colombia, and in Urabá in particular, abound in the scholarly literature. Some view paramilitarism as a response by local elites to the rise of guerrilla insurgency and protracted armed conflict in the region. Violent repression is consequently considered an organic

---

[5] This number includes the total number of SINTRAINAGRO unionists reported assassinated between 1986 and 2009 (Correa Montoya et al. 2009:24).

[6] Quoted in Chomsky (2008:211).

[7] Kline (2009:68–73).

[8] Correa Montoya et al. (2009:24–25); Delgado (2020).

response to the need to establish order in the midst of social and political chaos.[9] Others view paramilitarism as a result of the institutional weaknesses of the state, which is unable to enforce labor contracts, quell militancy, or obtain territorial control of marginalized regions of the country.[10] Still others view it is a determined outcome of the power of transnational capital, the logic of neoliberalism, or the entrenched conservatism of local elites.[11] This case study shows that a full explanation of paramilitarism in commodity-producing export centers like Urabá must recast local labor regime dynamics in comparative and world historical perspective. Doing so shifts the central questions and core theoretical assumptions from why regions like Urabá became entrapped in despotic state and paramilitary violence to why the historical processes that produced hegemony in other agro-export regions of Colombia, such as the coffee regime of Viejo Caldas, did not produce similar outcomes in Urabá. What is distinct about the nature of banana production and the banana market that lends themselves to despotism? And specifically, why didn't the geopolitics of US world hegemony in the postwar developmental decades ameliorate the peripheralizing tendencies of the banana market as it had done for the cafeteros of Viejo Caldas?

This case study analyzes Urabá's despotic labor regime from a comparative and world historical perspective. Chapter 4 examines the geopolitics of the world banana market from its early inception during the period of British laissez-faire capitalism in the nineteenth century into the period of US-backed developmentalism in the middle decades of the twentieth century. I analyze the rise of a prior period of banana production in Colombia, when the US-based United Fruit Company (UFC) established a banana-enclave zone in the Santa Marta region of the country in addition to other enclaves in the Caribbean, Central America, and South America. I point out enclave production produced deep contradictions of peripheral proletarianization that erupted in a hemispheric wave of labor unrest and economic nationalism that forced the UFC and other banana monopolies to vertically disintegrate their firms. I argue that this process of vertical disintegration was fostered by the US government and global multilateral agencies that promoted the establishment of independent domestic banana producers and exporters as a mechanism of national development. I then show how this period of developmental optimism stimulated the formation of a geopolitical alliance of banana-exporting countries that tried to restructure the banana market in order to capture

---

[9] Rangel Suárez (2000); Pécaut (1999, 2001).
[10] Chernick (1999); Safford and Palacios (2001); González et al. (2003); Leal Buitrago (2004); Restrepo (2004).
[11] Richani (2002); Brittain (2010); Hristov (2014); Chomsky et al. (2007).

Map 3 Urabá, Colombia

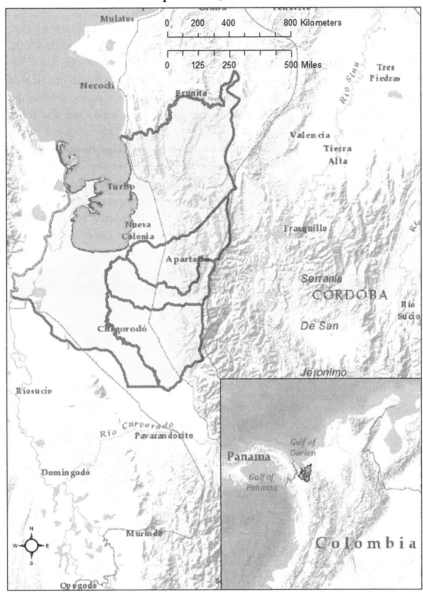

Sources: Esri, USGS, NOAA, Garmin, NPS

greater rents. The failure of these efforts, however, only further peripheralized the production and exportation niches of the banana market.

Chapter 5 examines how banana production for export emerged in the Urabá region of the country during the period of developmental optimism in the 1960s. With active state support, Urabá's banana sector was able to grow into the 1970s and early 1980s. But this growth rested heavily upon the authoritarian practices of the National Front regime, which repressed banana worker efforts to unionize the plantations and stymied their efforts to mobilize at the ballot box for social reforms. Urabá's despotism, however, shifted to a crisis of labor control in the 1980s when Colombia's political system underwent a period of democratization. Democratization, I argue, facilitated a growth in banana worker militancy that triggered a violent backlash by local elites that took the form of paramilitarism. I conclude this chapter with a discussion of how paramilitarism returned control of the banana region back to local banana elites, and how this control was essential to the continued viability of Colombia's banana export sector under conditions of peripheral proletarianization.

4

The World Historical Origins
of Despotism in Urabá

Colombian political leaders have probably been no more capable and no more repressive than those of other countries. Rather ... the reasons for the historical weakness of the left are to be found in the lived experiences of the majority of Colombians ... The revolutionary insurgents of the 1960s in Colombia, like their middle-class intellectual supporters, tended to equate Colombian history with that of other countries such as Cuba, whose economies revolved around industries owned by foreign capitalists and worked by proletarianized labor. If the Colombian economy had come to depend on banana or oil exports [rather than coffee], the twentieth-century history of the nation in general, and the fate of leftist third parties in particular, might have been different.

Charles Bergquist (2001:204)

In his reflections on Colombia's "contemporary crisis" of spiraling violence, guerrilla insurgency, and paramilitary terror in Colombia at the close of the twentieth century, labor historian Charles Bergquist argued that proletarianized workers in foreign-owned corporate sectors tended to give rise to powerful working-class movements across Latin America that subverted the power of traditional elites and forced a radical democratization of their country's developmental trajectory. Colombia's social crisis was therefore not a product of an exceptionally repressive regime. Rather, it stemmed from the deeply rooted hegemony of its political establishment that resulted from the lived experience of Colombia's cafeteros.

This chapter follows Bergquist's line of inquiry about the impact of the structure of banana production on the emergence of despotism in Colombia's banana regime of Urabá. Like Bergquist suggests, it analyzes the distinct developmental ecologies of coffee and banana production and their implications for processes of class formation and class politics. However, as we saw from the last case study, the structure of agro-export production alone does not determine an industry's labor regime dynamics. As we saw for Viejo Caldas, the core–periphery structure of the coffee market had important causal implications on the extent to which Fedecafé was able to sustain its hegemonic social compact vis-à-vis the country's cafeteros. To explain Urabá's labor regime dynamics, we must therefore go beyond Bergquist's approach to analyze how banana production in Colombia has been impacted by larger world historical processes. Specifically, we must analyze the impact of US world hegemony on the structure of core–periphery relations in the world banana market and ask why this process intensified the contradictions of peripheralization in Urabá rather than ameliorate them as it had for the country's cafetero farmers in the coffee market.

I begin this chapter by comparing the ecologies and developmental prospects of bananas and coffee. Both are tropical export commodities that link peripheral regions of the global south to advanced centers of capitalist consumption. Yet, their ecological and physiological differences have important ramifications on their development into profitable global commodities. In the next section, I examine how these differences shaped the rise of the global banana trade in the late nineteenth century and into the early decades of the twentieth century. Here, I highlight how the trade transformed from a risky niche market into a major global market dominated by vertically integrated transnational banana companies backed by US hemispheric power and domestic authoritarianism. Next, I describe the social contradictions of these vertically integrated systems of production and the strategies employed to control labor and sustain stable supplies of bananas for the market. I then describe how this labor despotism gave way to a global wave of labor unrest and crisis that forced the banana corporations to vertically disintegrate their holdings and externalize production onto local producers. I then analyze how this restructuring of the banana market opened the way for the emergence of a new site of banana production across Latin America and the Caribbean in the 1960s. Inspired by the success of the International Coffee Agreements, nascent banana planters participated in the establishment of a geopolitical alliance among banana-exporting countries. However, their efforts to restructure the market to capture more wealth in the 1970s fell short, leaving producer-exporters to fend for themselves in the market. Rather than *move up* the banana market to avoid the contradiction of peripheralization, many banana producers at the time *moved into* the banana market's most competitive niche without providing an opportunity to shield themselves from the full impact of market peripheralization. It is precisely this competitive market niche that Colombia inserted itself into in the 1960s and 1970s. Understanding the geopolitical construction of this market, I argue, clarifies how and why the Colombian state actively repressed labor militancy in the region during the years of the National Front regime.

The Divergent Ecologies of Coffee and Banana Production

Bananas are one of the earliest plants domesticated by humans, dating back more than 7,000 years. Their production and cultivation first arose in South Asia, spreading thereafter eastward to Southeast Asia and the Pacific Islands and westward to tropical Africa, eventually reaching the Americas. As they expanded, bananas became one of the most important agricultural staples of those rural populations that settled the tropics, as they are relatively easy to cultivate and provide needed shade for smaller subsistence crops like yuca, beans, legumes, and other fruits and vegetables. Today, bananas are the world's largest fruit crop and the fourth largest agricultural commodity, after wheat, rice, and corn.[1] The largest producers of bananas in the world are Brazil, Indonesia, Mexico, and India. Yet, in these countries the market for bananas is primarily local and national in its geographic scope. The bananas cultivated are sweeter, smaller and thinner-skinned variations of the globally traded Cavendish bananas. And, they are predominantly produced on small farms using family labor systems and noncapitalized farming techniques.

The global banana trade, on the other hand, is dominated by massive transnational fruit conglomerates who grow thick-skinned and starchier Cavendish bananas, often as a mono-crop on large plantations that use proletarianized labor systems, regular inputs of agrochemicals and fertilizers, and highly capitalized and rationalized cultivation systems. The market for these global bananas has remained under the monopolistic control of a small number of companies whose names and organizational structures have changed over time, but who are the parent companies of today's Chiquita Brands, Del Monte, and Dole corporations. Like coffee, the geography of the banana trade follows colonial and neocolonial patterns in which bananas are produced and exported from the tropical export zones scattered throughout the Caribbean, Latin America, Africa, and Southeast Asia and consumed predominantly by North Americans and Europeans.[2] Consequently, struggles over control of the international banana market have had important ramifications on whether the banana market reproduces core–periphery inequalities or provides opportunities for national development and economic growth.

Like coffee, the origins of the world banana market date back to the heyday of British world hegemony and market liberalism in the nineteenth century. Yet, the biological and physiological features of bananas and coffee differ starkly in ways

---

[1] Koeppel (2008:xiii).
[2] Raynolds (2003).

that have shaped their subsequent development since then. One major difference is in the environmental conditions that each crop requires. As we saw from the last case study, coffee thrives in tropical highland regions that are agreeable to human settlement and diverse agricultural production systems. Coffee's development and expansion therefore rode the wave of frontier expansion, as subsistence farmer families could cultivate coffee alongside stable products without massive inputs of capital. Bananas, in contrast, thrive in harsh, hot and humid tropical lowlands, with average temperatures of 80° Fahrenheit, yearly rainfall of between 78 and 90 inches, and consistent air and ground moisture. They grow best in equatorial swamplands, marshes, and other forested tropical lowland regions that are prone to malaria, dengue, and other mosquito-based diseases and venomous pests. Because these ecological regions are difficult to inhabit by human populations, the development of banana export sectors has typically arisen in sparsely populated regions that were often considered unproductive wastelands by local governments prior to their transformation into plantations. Clearing seemingly impenetrable and disease-ridden lowlands to establish large plantations with outlets to the sea was incredibly labor-intensive. Workers were therefore imported from neighboring regions and even other countries in order to clear the forests, cultivate banana plants, cut and harvest them, pack and ship them, as well as to lay down the infrastructure required to transport them to ports. And rather than establish dispersed farming settlements that could minimize workers' dependence upon the sale of their labor to banana plantation owners, the harsh tropical conditions made it difficult to establish viable subsistence farms in regions adjacent to the banana groves. Indeed, contract farms have arisen alongside large-scale banana plantations. However, banana workers themselves have typically been fully proletarianized workers whose housing, amenities, and social class reproduction have been intimately tied to, if not entirely dependent upon, the banana plantations that they worked.[3]

The ecology of bananas has also made banana producer more wedded to land-intensive value-added strategies than coffee. As we saw from the last case study, coffee has been subject to quality standards and innovations that have segmented the market into distinct types – Robustas, Arabicas, Mild Arabicas, blends, organics, etc. – with different sales values. Because of this, coffee farmers have been able to develop new ways of generating additional value without requiring significant changes to their land holdings. Bananas, in contrast, have been less amenable to similar types of value-added innovations. Consequently, banana

---

[3] For case studies of class formation in the banana zones of this period, see LeGrand (1998); Striffler (2002); Moberg (2008).

companies have kept consumer prices low while developing growth strategies designed to increase the overall volume of sales by producing ever-greater supplies. Historically, this pushed banana companies into the marketing end of the banana trade by advertising what had otherwise been an exotic tropical fruit as a vitamin-rich food for babies, a healthy snack for schoolchildren, and an essential part of North American and European breakfasts.[4] Overall, this growth strategy compelled banana companies to develop strategies involving the procurement, felling, and renovation of new ever-larger tracts of land that could be used for future expansion.

Expanding banana plantations into tropical frontier regions has exposed companies to significant environmental risks. The mono-cropping of bananas, for example, depletes soil nutrients after about a decade of cultivation. Just as destructive are tropical pests like the root-eating *taltuza* rodent and banana funguses that have blighted entire plantations at a time. Perhaps most problematic has been black leaf disease (Black Sigatoka) and yellow and green leaf syndromes (Panama Disease), both soilborne funguses that devastated many plantations throughout the Caribbean and Central and South America until the *Gros Michel* variety was replaced by the more disease-resistant *Cavendish* variety in the 1950s.[5] Other risks have been weather-related, as the tropical geography of bananas made them vulnerable to tropical storms, hurricanes, and floods that have wiped out entire plantations in a matter of days.[6] Acquiring uncultivated land and shifting primary production sites both within enclaves as well as jumping production from one enclave to the next acted as protection against these environmental risks and assured that any environmental destruction arising in one site of production would not impact the overall supply of bananas to the world market. As one former lifelong United Fruit Company engineer explained to anthropologist Philippe Bourgois (1989:7),

> The Panama Disease used to kill everything. The only solution was to get a hold of new lands. It was not possible to maintain bananas once the disease struck. So when one farm died another was planted ... That's how we ended up in Ecuador.

While clearing tropical brush to establish ever-growing banana plantations has been labor-intensive processes, the construction of the canals, roadways and

---

[4]   Soluri (2003); Bucheli (2003, 2005); Chapman (2007); Koeppel (2008).

[5]   For analyses of banana blight and land uses, see Kepner and Soothill (1967:31–32); Striffler (2002:31–32); Wells (2003:320–24); Ploetz (2005).

[6]   For example, the thirty-year period between 1903 and 1933, Jamaica alone suffered from ten major hurricanes that destroyed over 486 million tons of the country's banana exports (Roche 1998:261).

railways linking the bananas to the ports, not to mention the ports and shipping, has been extremely capital-intensive.[7] Investing in the construction of this logistical infrastructure created enormous "barriers to entry" that facilitated the monopolization of the trade by large, highly capitalized companies with bases in the United States and Europe. In part, these investments in expensive infrastructure were simply a response to the logistical problem of shipping heavy volumes of bananas from plantations located inland to the ports. However, it was also a response to the physical properties of bananas themselves. Unlike coffee, whose durability as unroasted green beans allows it to be stored for long periods of time and shipped over large distances to where they are roasted and ultimately consumed, even the most modern varieties of exportable bananas are highly perishable. This means that they need to be shipped quickly to consumers before they decay. Banana companies therefore invested in capital-intensive technologies including railroad lines, trucks, and refrigerated steam ships that could transport heavy volumes of bananas quickly so that they would ripen upon arrival in consumer markets.[8] Thus, banana company success had rested upon the ability to keep production costs down, transport ever-larger volumes of exports in a timely fashion, and stimulate demand through marketing directly to consumers.

Once a banana plantation is linked to international shipping routes, processes of production and capital accumulation become significantly easier to develop into economies of scale than coffee. As we saw in the last chapter, in the absence of market regulation, the coffee tree crop cycle has had a direct and immediate impact on prices and production. The long period of time between seedlings and harvests leads to cycles of overproduction and underproduction, resulting in intense pricing volatility in the market that poses stark risks for producers. Coffee is also a fruit tree that grows from seeds that are planted and cultivated. This means that coffee farmers need access to credit in order to regularly purchase new seeds, seedlings, and seed varieties when renovating their farms. Bananas, in contrast, are perennial crops whose plants produce fruits in a relatively short period of time (nine to twelve months after planting) that can be harvested year round. Exportable bananas are also asexual in terms of their reproduction, seedless, and therefore exact genetic replicas of their parents. As the world's largest herb, they multiply when mature branches are cut and replanted. And they also

---

7   In fact, bananas were initially cultivated as a staple food along railway lines as a cheap food for workers. It was only later that this relationship between tropical railways and bananas was reversed, with banana production driving railroad construction (Chapman 2007:25–58).

8   For analysis of the adoption of new banana technologies, see Soluri (2003); Striffler (2002, 2003); Chapman (2007).

reproduce new bunches of fruit (hands) composed of single bananas (fingers) when new branches grow in the place of older ones.[9] Because bananas can be produced both steadily throughout the year and cheaply once planted, they do not suffer from the type of harvesting cycle and pricing volatility associated with coffee.[10] In fact, relative to most other agricultural commodities, banana prices are generally stable over time, as they respond more to dynamics of demand and consumption than production.[11] Because prices are relatively stable, the companies that have risen to the top of the global banana market became those that had access to large swaths of land, could master the process of producing large quantities of bananas cheaply, transport them rapidly to consumers abroad, and develop economies of scale.

The Rise of Vertical-Integration during the Era of British World Hegemony, 1860–1930

It took decades for the global banana trade to develop into a transnational capitalist enterprise with profitable economies of scale. The deregulated nature of the world market combined with the ecological and geographic specificities of bananas made it difficult to overcome the overall risks associated with transporting perishable tropical bananas to consumers living hundreds and even thousands of miles away.[12] Until the 1860s, the market essentially piggybacked on other commercial activities. Merchants operating out of Cuba and other Caribbean Islands would load bunches of bananas onto their schooner vessels, transporting them alongside other tradable goods where they would be sold as individually wrapped red dessert bananas in New York, Boston, and other major coastal port cities. By the 1860s, schooners began regularly carrying small amounts of red bananas cultivated by locals from Colón (Panama), Cuba, the British West Indies (Jamaica) to ports in Boston, New York, and New Orleans. Though still a luxury that few North Americans had tasted, by the 1880s over 100 companies had

---

[9] Koeppel (2008:xii–xiii, 11–14).

[10] See FAO (1986, 2003, 2018) for a detailed analysis of pricing dynamics of the world banana market.

[11] For example, except for the periods at the beginning of World Wars I and II and the early years of the Great Depression in the 1930s between 1909 and 1963, retail prices for bananas sold in the United States rarely rose above US20¢ or fell below $15¢ per pound (USDA 1965).

[12] Roche (1998:37); Chapman (2007:43–58).

forged distinct niches in the banana market as fruit distributors, steamship operators, tropical railroad companies, or early banana exporters.[13]

It was not until the turn of the nineteenth century, following a wave of mergers and acquisitions, that banana companies transformed from niche importers, transporters and distributors into vertically integrated transnational corporations that controlled and systematically organized entire banana commodity chains from production and transport to distribution and marketing. The largest market was in the United States, where the United Fruit Company (est. 1899), Standard Fruit (est. 1924), and the Cuyamel Fruit Company (est. 1911) controlled the flow of bananas imported from Costa Rica, Nicaragua, Honduras, and Colombia to the ports of the United States and Canada.[14] Across the Atlantic, Fyffe and Company (est. 1888) and Elder Dempster and Company (est. 1898) controlled banana imports from the British West Indies. Over the next three decades, bananas transformed from a luxury dessert into a staple of American and European working-class diets, and the United Fruit Company, Standard Fruit, Cuyamel, and Fyffes became some of the most powerful and highly profitable capitalist enterprises in the hemisphere. As one US government report on the rise of the United Fruit Company noted,

> The organization of the United Fruit Company marked the end of the era of pioneering, of risks and hardships, easy profits as well as total failures, and the beginning of a new era that converted the highly perishable tropical banana into an important item of world trade.[15]

---

[13] Adams (1911:847–48).

[14] Lorenzo Baker and Andrew Preston's Boston Fruit Company (est. 1885) specialized in shipping and domestic distribution. Minor Keith's Tropical Trading and Transport Company (est. 1873) shipped bananas from railroad construction sites in Costa Rica, Nicaragua, Honduras, and Colombia to New Orleans and New York. In 1899, these companies merged, becoming the United Fruit Company, the parent company of today's Chiquita Brands International. That same year, a distribution company run by Joseph, Luca, and Felix Vaccaro in New Orleans began to import large quantities of bananas from Honduras. By 1924, the Vaccaro Brothers Company became the publicly traded giant, Standard Fruit Company, the historic predecessor of Dole Fruit Company and Del Monte Foods, Incorporated. The Cuyamel Fruit Company, owned by Samuel Zemurray, also imported bananas from the Cortés region of Honduras and marketed its bananas jointly with Standard Fruit to compete more effectively with the UFC (Roche 1998:37–38, 41, 50–51). Fyffe and Company (est. 1888) and Elder Dempster and Company (est. 1898) began importing bananas from the British West Indies to the United Kingdom. By 1902, both companies were amalgamated with some 45% of its stock owned by United Fruit (Davies 1990:34–35).

[15] May and Plaza Lasso (1958:7).

Extending corporate control into the production, transport, and distribution ends of the market was a strategy meant to secure the transnational flow of bananas while minimizing the risks that emanated from the dynamics of the laissez-faire market during this period. To stabilize production, the banana companies acquired massive amounts of tropical swamplands throughout Latin America and the Caribbean from local governments that were eager either to sell off or concede unproductive domestic territory to pay down government debts, obtain new revenues through land sales and leases, obtain rents from export taxes, and stimulate the construction of expensive and otherwise unaffordable transportation and communication infrastructure.[16] Indeed, the first few decades of the twentieth century were a veritable "green gold rush" in which the major banana companies grabbed land even when the majority of it would never become future sites of banana cultivation.[17] More often than not, this competitive corporate land grabbing both drove and was driven by the geographic expansion of railroads, which served as launching points to expand into new regions that would have otherwise been viewed as too disconnected to be put to productive use. By the early 1930s, the banana companies had become some of the largest landowners in their host countries and in the hemisphere at large. The United Fruit Company, for example, had acquired over 3.5 million acres, only 3.2% of which (114,920 acres) was actively producing bananas.[18] Some 11.6% (414,093 acres) was reno-vated but not actively producing bananas, and the rest was idle land with no clear future plan for renovation or cultivation.[19] Standard Fruit, while smaller, also acquired over 500,000 acres that included both productive and potentially pro-ductive lands.[20] Collectively, the banana corporations owned land that stretched from the Caribbean Islands and the coasts of Central America into the North Atlantic coast of South America in Colombia and Pacific coast of Ecuador.

Vertical integration also brought United Fruit, Standard Fruit, Cuyamel, and Fyffes into the transportation node of the banana commodity chain. As

---

[16] For analysis of the land acquisition practices of the banana companies, see Langley and Schoonover (1995:14–15); Moberg (2003:147–56); Soluri (2003:41–52).

[17] Perhaps the most noteworthy example of this occurred when United Fruit and Cuyamel engaged in a competitive land grab frenzy between 1927 and 1930, wherein the former gobbled up some 1,400,000 acres in the Upper Ulua region of Honduras in response to Cuyamel's plans to acquire 13,459 acres along the west coast of Guatemala (Kepner and Soothill 1967:86–87).

[18] In 1900, for example, the largest corporate landowner, United Fruit Company, owned roughly 200,000 acres of land (Bucheli 2005:82).

[19] Kepner and Soothill (1967:86–87).

[20] Karnes (1978:105).

mentioned, ownership of railroads was essential to their ability to transport ripening bananas out to sea and building material, production inputs, and workers into their inland plantations. By 1934, the UFC alone owned and operated over 1,500 miles of large-scale railroads and over 800 miles of light-rail tracks (tramways) that ran over 7,200 railway cars.[21] They also dredged, constructed, and privately owned extensive networks of ports scattered across the Caribbean and Central American littoral. They also dominated sea routes, becoming some of the largest owners of steamships operating in Caribbean and Atlantic waters.[22] By 1930, for example, the United Fruit Company operated over 115 ships, amounting to roughly 25% of the company's total assets.[23] Collectively, the banana companies did not only ride the waves of new seafaring technologies. They also developed and pioneered new technologies like refrigerated shipping boats (reefers) and transnational commercial radio-operations that significantly reduced the risks of large-distance transportation, brought banana export production to new far-reaching geographies, and increased the overall volume of bananas in the market.[24]

Finally, the banana companies moved into the consumer and distribution ends of the market, becoming major fruit marketing companies over this period. Because bananas could be produced cheaply and abundantly once a plantation was established, the major obstacle to continued growth in the market was demand. As mentioned, bananas remained a relatively exotic food eaten in upscale hotels and restaurants at the turn of the century.[25] The banana companies thus engaged in massive advertising and promotional campaigns in recipe books, nutritional information packets, as well as in popular art and music to familiarize North Americans and Europeans with the nutritional and economic perks of

---

[21] Kepner and Soothill (1967:19).

[22] As far back as the 1850s and 1860s, steamships began replacing schooners as the preferred shipping vessel for transnational banana merchants. In terms of their carrying capacity, they increased the overall volume of bananas transported from some 2,000 bunches carried by schooners to between 12,000 and 20,000 bunches by the 1880s. They were also much quicker than schooners, which reduced the risks that cultivated bananas would perish before reaching their final destinations and expanded the geographical distance and scope of banana production from the Caribbean and Central American into South America (Abbott 2009:5).

[23] In 1901, for example, the UFC alone owned 100 ships (Bucheli 2005:54; Roche 1998:40).

[24] For an in-depth historical analysis of the use of banana company shipping, see May and Plaza Lasso (1958); Davies (1990).

[25] Bucheli (2005:27–28).

Table 4.1 *World banana exports and country market shares, 1900–29 (thousands of bunches)*

Exporting Country	1900 Exports	1900 % of Market	1929 Exports	1929 % of Market	Growth (1900–29) Exports	Growth (1900–29) % of Market
Honduras	4,772,417	24.0	28,221,463	29.0	23,449,046	+5.0
Jamaica	7,173,890	36.1	22,020,877	22.6	14,846,987	−13.5
Colombia	273,882	1.4	10,300,021	22.6	10,026,139	+21.2
Guatemala	0	0.0	6,545,695	10.6	6,545,695	+10.6
Brazil	0	0.0	6,192,667	6.7	6,192,667	+6.7
Costa Rica	3,332,125	16.8	5,784,724	6.4	2,452,599	−10.4
Mexico	0	0.0	5,602,499	5.9	5,602,499	+5.9
Panama (Colón)[a]	2,215,709	10.7	4,722,426	5.8	2,506,717	−4.9
Nicaragua	1,324,727	6.7	4,160,700	4.9	2,835,973	−1.8
Cuba	845,942	4.3	3,682,900	4.3	2,836,958	0.0
Total	19,848,692	100	97,233,972	100	77,295,280	

[a] Production in the Colón region of Panama was part of Colombia until Panama's independence in 1903.
Source: Kepner and Soothill (1967:37)

eating bananas.[26] As John Soluri (2003:58) points out, bananas were promoted as "an affordable, nutritious, self-packaged 'fast food'" during an era when working people in the United States were becoming more health-minded and more harried." Between 1900 and 1910, banana consumption in the United States tripled from about 15 million to 40 million bunches. By 1913, they outsold apples and oranges.[27] And by 1929, Americans were eating a per capita average of 20.7 lb of bananas per year, over 26% of the total fresh fruit they consumed.[28]

Overall, this process of vertical integration in the global banana industry contributed to both the geographic expansion of the market and to a major increase in its overall volume. Table 4.1 shows the overall geographic and economic growth in the world banana market between 1900 and 1929. The total volume of exported bananas nearly quintupled from 19,848,692 bunches in 1900 to 97,233,972 by 1929.[29] New banana-exporting countries arose, including

---

[26] Soluri (2003); Bucheli (2005); Chapman (2007); Koeppel (2008).

[27] Koeppel (2008:67).

[28] Bucheli (2005:33).

[29] A "bunch" of bananas (also known as a "stem") is a hanging cluster of bananas made of various "hands." They typically weigh between 66 and 110 lb.

Brazil, Mexico, and Guatemala, with Guatemala controlling over 10% of the total export market by 1929. Notably, some of the most productive banana exporters in 1900, like Jamaica, Costa Rica, Panama, and Nicaragua, increased their overall exports but dropped in terms of their market share due to rise of new producers and larger growth in others. Colombia's and Guatemala's shares grew the most during this period, by 21.2% and 10.6%, respectively, while Jamaica and Costa Rica saw their shares decline by over 10%.

In sharp contrast to the dynamics of the world coffee market, this early period of growth in the size and geographic reach of the banana market did not give rise to new economic producers who could challenge the market monopolies of the major banana companies. Rather, the barriers to entry into the banana trade resulted in ever-greater monopolization. Table 4.2 depicts the monopolization of the banana market by the major transnational companies in 1932. Overall, the United Fruit Company sat atop the banana market, supplying nearly 60% of the total market. Standard Fruit slightly supplied just over 17% and other fruit companies supplied the remaining 23% of the market. In terms of exporting countries, Honduras and Jamaica were the largest. Together, they supplied over 50% of the total market, amounting to 57.0% of United Fruit's exports and 55.6% of Standard Fruit's exports at this time.

Overall, the vertical integration of the banana market provided the banana companies with vast monopolies that allowed them to grow the market while keeping production costs and retail prices affordable to working-class consumers in the North Atlantic and Europe.

Banana Despotism and the Global Crisis of Vertical Integration, 1930–1960

While economically profitable, the vertically integrated nature of the banana market proved socially unstable. Vertical integration required continued access to large tracts of land that were often occupied and settled by locals, low production costs that ran up against an increasingly militant class of proletarianized enclave workers, and the continued support of local governments that would side with the banana companies over locals in these land and labor disputes. Banana company responses to these social and political contradictions were vital to their continued growth and expansion, yet the institutional remedies they used ultimately exposes the global banana market's coercive and despotic underbelly.

The earliest social unrest on the banana plantations arose as the consequence of the banana companies acquisition of land. The creation and expansion of banana enclaves often required the dispossession of indigenous groups, maroon colonies,

Table 4.2 *World banana exports and company market shares, 1932 (thousands of bunches)*

Exporting Country	United Fruit		Standard Fruit		Other Companies		Totals	
	Exports	% of Company Exports	Exports	% of Company Exports	Exports	% of Company Exports	Exports	% of World Market
Brazil	0	0.0	0	0.0	6,873	33.1	6,873	7.6
Colombia	6,900	12.8	0	0.0	463	2.2	7,363	8.2
Costa Rica	4,100	7.6	0	0.0	213	1.0	4,313	4.8
Cuba	0	0.0	2,211	14.2	2,440	11.7	4,651	5.2
Guatemala	5,248	9.7	0	0.0	0	0.0	5,248	5.8
Honduras	20,200	37.5	5,077	32.6	2,619	12.6	27,896	30.9
Jamaica	10,500	19.5	3,583	23.0	6,278	30.2	20,361	22.6
Mexico	500	0.9	2,522	16.2	1,184	5.7	4,206	4.7
Nicaragua	1,100	2.0	1,621	10.4	657	3.2	3,378	3.7
Panama	3,000	5.6	546	3.5	54	0.3	3,600	4.0
Canary Islands	1,700	3.2	0	0.0	0	0.0	1,700	1.9
Other Regions	600	1.1	0	0.0	0	0.0	600	0.7
Total Exports	53,848	100	15,560	100	20,780	100	90,188	
Company Share of World Market	59.7%		17.3%		23.0%		100%	

Source: Kepner and Soothill (1967:37)

fishing and peasant villages, or other local inhabitants who either lacked formal titles to the land or whose formal titles were simply ignored by companies and local governments. These land grabs, thus, triggered ongoing land struggles against dispossession between locals and the banana companies that took the form of land invasions, squatter movements, and in some cases armed rebellion. While the banana companies often relied on public and private security forces to evict squatters and squelch resistance, some land conflicts became pitted legal battles that spilled onto the national political scene, turning national public opinion against domestic governments and the banana companies.[30]

As these tracts of land transformed into sites of banana production, the nature of the unrest shifted to struggles by proletarianized workers who struggled to improve the harsh nature of working and living conditions in the enclaves. To contain outbreaks of labor unrest and worker radicalization that threatened company profits and domestic government legitimacy, the banana companies used both carrots and sticks. On the one hand, the wages offered to enclave workers were typically higher than those available to them in their local labor markets. And because the banana enclaves were geographically isolated from their national host societies, the banana companies ran their enclaves as private "mini-states within states." They constructed their own hospitals and health clinics, housing units for workers, managers and their families, schools, churches, and entertainment zones. Moreover, they viewed themselves as "civilizers of the tropics" and instituted norms within their enclaves that were meant to encourage a form of "benevolent paternalism" between workers and bosses.[31] For example, to promote its middle-class "breadwinner ideal," United Fruit had a policy of hiring a plantation labor force that was exclusively male, providing salaries meant to sustain a family, banning female employment, and only selling company-constructed homes to married men.[32]

Yet, despite these efforts to create Fordist-style arrangements in their enclaves, the working and living conditions were notoriously harsh and company paternalism was often oppressive rather than benevolent. Charles Kepner and his colleagues' (1936; Kepner and Soothill 1967[1935]) early analyses of the social conditions of United Fruit Company's enclaves have provided scholars with a unique window into the despotism of this world. Worker housing, for example,

---

[30] For analyses of land struggles between locals and banana companies, see Bourgois (1989); Striffler (2002); Moberg (2008); LeGrand (1998); Langley and Schoonover (1995); Forster (2003).

[31] For analyses of the early labor struggles of Latin American banana workers, see Kepner (1936), Kepner and Soothill (1967), Striffler (2002), Bucheli (2005, 2008).

[32] Striffler (2002:46–51).

Table 4.3 *United Fruit Company death rates, 1927–31 (per 1,000 employees)*

Enclave	1927	1928	1929	1930	1931
Panama (Chiriquí Region)	–	–	7	14	14
Panama (Other regions)	19	16	14	11	20
Colombia	9	7	7	7	6
Costa Rica	13	14	14	13	15
Cuba	12	7	7	6	7
Guatemala	13	11	14	10	8
Honduras (Tela region)	10	12	7	8	6
Honduras (Trujillo region)	12	14	15	18	22

Source: Kepner (1936:116–17)

often deteriorated rapidly under the harsh tropical weather conditions and access to clean water and sanitation utilities were negligent. And despite the construction of health clinics, so many workers and others living in the banana enclaves were dying of mosquito and water-borne illnesses like malaria, dengue fever, cholera and typhoid, snake bites, and pestilential diseases that the United Fruit Company kept statistics on its "employee death rates" per enclave. Table 4.3 provides glaring insight into the precarious nature of life in the banana enclaves. It depicts the United Fruit's formally reported death rates by regional enclave between 1927 and 1931.

Such harshness of living was not solely environmental in nature. The wages provided, though high enough to lure workers to the enclaves, were often low in relation to the cost of local goods and services provided by the company stores. And to make matters worse, much of employment within the enclave was intermittent because the banana fruit was not cut down every day, longshoremen were only needed when ships were in port, lumberjacks only when forests required clearing, etc. Thus, the wages per job were often insufficient to cover yearly costs of living in the enclave and workers became subject to the hiring whims of the company's enclave managers, who used competition among workers to reduce wages.[33]

To ensure labor discipline under these adverse conditions, the banana companies engaged in three key labor control strategies during this period. First, the company's relied heavily on the virtual absence of national labor rights and social protections afforded to workers under host governments. In fact, domestic government typically ceded these responsibilities and regulatory oversights to the

---

[33] Kepner and Soothill (1967:126–35).

companies themselves. Thus, workers were often fired at will with no arbitration mechanism, labor unions were banned, and public demonstrations and collective gatherings of workers required company authorization.[34] And even when national labor laws did exist on the books, as in Panama's overtime and eight-hour day laws and Guatemala's six-day workweek laws, the banana companies were essentially "given carte blanche to disregard any labor legislation" that butted against its own desire to maximize productivity and keep costs low.[35] Second, company policies promoted ethnic divisions and racial antagonism to dissipate worker efforts to build class-based solidarity in the enclave. It is widely recognized that United Fruit, for example, adopted racially segmented labor markets, dividing plantation jobs and housing by race and ethnicity and offering different pay grades for ethno-racially distinct segments of the enclave workforce. They also relied heavily on host governments that used the racial backgrounds of enclave workers, who were often immigrants or indigenous peoples, to stigmatize worker organizing efforts, justify the denial of labor rights, and militarize the banana zones.[36] Third, their ownership of large tracts of land and monopolization of local transport provided the banana companies with ready-made capitalist tools to discipline and control enclave labor, thwart governments seeking land rents and export taxes, and ensure low production costs. Like the "spatial fix" strategy used by today's global corporations, the banana companies were early pioneers of the use of the ideology and practice of the runaway factory to leverage power over workforces that were more anchored in local geographies.[37] They also used their control of the land as a weapon of labor control by engaging in contract farming with local farmers who planted bananas in uncultivated peripheral regions surrounding their banana enclaves. Contracting out to local farmers in this way served a double function. On the one hand, when confronted with labor unrest on their plantations, the harvests supplied by local contract farmers diminished the structural power of enclave workers by buffering against the negative impact of strikes and work stoppages.[38] On the other hand, it provided the companies with cheap supplies of bananas without assuming the risks and responsibilities of production. In this

---

[34] See Langley and Schoonover (1995) for the role of Central America's authoritarian comprador states in the expansion of the banana market during this time.

[35] Kepner and Soothill (1967:141–42).

[36] There is a rich body of literature on the use of racial divisions to control enclave labor (Botero Herrera 1990; Bourgois 1989; Euraque 2003; Grossman 1998; Moberg 1996; Steiner 2000).

[37] See Harvey (1989) and Silver (2003) for elaborations on the spatial fix as a strategy of labor control.

[38] Kepner and Soothill (1967:190–92); Striffler (2002:32–33); Raynolds (2003:33–34).

sense, the banana companies were not only early pioneers of the spatial fix strategy of globalization. They were also early pioneers of the global subcontracting system that became an increasingly common strategy of sourcing and labor control in the closing decades of the twentieth century.[39]

Indeed, these early strategies of labor control were mostly effective in maintaining labor discipline during the early decades of the twentieth century. However, they became less so in the aftermath of World War I when worker militancy heated up. By the 1920s, nascent socialist and communist parties, national labor organizations, and internationalist labor and racial consciousness publications like Marcus Garvey's *Negro World* were gaining broad popularity and influence across Latin America and the Caribbean, often finding widespread support among banana employees.[40] Banana workers strikes erupted across Costa Rica and Panama in 1918 and 1919. The American Federation Labor's Pan-American labor congress (est. 1918) and the Central American Federation of Labor (est. 1921) established national labor organizing committees in Guatemala, El Salvador, Costa Rica, Colombia, Mexico, Honduras, Nicaragua, which began organizing plantation workers, railroad workers, and other segments of the workforce across their respective enclave zones.[41]

Facing worker radicalization, the banana companies became increasingly reliant upon a fourth strategy of labor control: the use or threat of violence to enforce labor discipline. Like Russians dolls, this repression was reinforced by a coercive apparatus that was fortified by different protective layers. Within the enclaves, the Fruit Companies used private security forces that specialized in antilabor surveillance actions to weed out agitators, protect strike breakers and terrorize workers and peasant squatters. However, when large-scale strikes erupted across the enclaves, the banana companies became reliant on national security forces, often militaries and police forces supplied by their host governments to repress labor activity. For example, martial law was declared, soldiers dispatched, strikers arrested, shot down, or imprisoned in response to extensive strike activity that arose in Colombia, Guatemala, and Honduras between 1928 and 1932. Similar labor repression occurred in Costa Rica and Panama during this period.[42] The immediate reasons why host governments called in their militaries to put down labor unrest during this period were clearly contingent upon domestic political calculations. However, in general, governments across Latin America and the

---

[39] See Gereffi and Korzeniewicz (1994), Ross (2004), Dicken (2015), Gereffi (2018), Suwandi (2019) for good overviews of the rise of global subcontracting.

[40] Bourgois (1989, 2003); Bucheli (2005).

[41] Kepner and Soothill (1967:180–206).

[42] Kepner and Soothill (1967:164–65, 197–98).

Caribbean tended to see their primary role as providers of social order and security in order to encourage foreign investment.[43] Lax land and labor laws and unflinching support for the dominion of the banana companies was a powerful incentive that brought the companies to their shores in the first place. Forcibly repressing labor agitation and political radicalization in the enclaves was therefore a logical extension of the terms of this agreement.[44] Indeed, their willingness to use violence against their own populations gained them notoriety as "banana republics" that served the interests of foreign corporations through corrupt, antidemocratic, authoritarian practices.

However, if and when local government's capacity to protect the ongoing interests of the banana corporations broke down, the last layer of protective covering for the banana companies was US imperial might. Indeed, the banana companies had strong and favorable relations with the US State Department and various presidential administrations. Thus, when local governmental strongmen collapsed, the US military was sent out to protect banana company interests without fearing a serious confrontation with locals or without significant repercussions on further US influence in the region.[45] The US government's willingness to send its troops and naval vessels southward into the tropics was similar to the decisions made by domestic governments to militarize their enclaves. Formal decisions to use military forces were contingent upon domestic political calculations. This said, US interests in accessing, if not, controlling the flows of capital, labor, and commodities in the Caribbean and Latin America have a long history.

Indeed, US hemispheric imperialism dates back to the independence wars of the 1820s when the United States adopted its "Monroe Doctrine" opposing European colonial interventions in the Western Hemisphere while extending its own influence via financial aid to revolutionary governments. By mid-century, the US government was more interested in its own westward colonial expansion rather than any endeavors that would implicate them inchaotic wars and internal strife of its southern neighbors. But as British world hegemony heated up in the closing

---

[43] Langley and Schoonover (1995); Wells (2003:318).

[44] For example, before the outbreak of World War II, US imports constituted some 49% of Costa Rica's exports, 53% of from the Dominican Republic, 27% from Guatemala, 87% from Honduras, and 55% from Panama (Bucheli 2008:439).

[45] During the first three decades of the twentieth century, the United States had become implicated in at least twenty-two significant military interventions in the banana zones of the Caribbean and Central America. These include: Honduras (1903, 1907, 1912, 1919, 1924), Colombia (1903), Dominican Republic (1903, 1914, 1916), Haiti (1914, 1915), Nicaragua (1907, 1909, 1915), Cuba (1906, 1912, 1917), Panama (1912, 1918, 1925), Guatemala (1920), and El Salvador (1932) (Bucheli 2008:439).

decades of the century, the practices of "free trade imperialism" led European processes of war making and state making into a scramble for colonial control of Africa, the Middle East, and South Asia, the United States actively sought to impede this expansion into what it considered to be "its own backyard." Its war with Spain in 1898 facilitated this process, expelling their influence from the region and opening unimpeded access to the vital shipping routes of the Caribbean basin. To be clear, it was not politically popular for US leaders to encourage the formal expansion of national territory southward through the types of colonial engagements of its counterparts across the North Atlantic. Instead, it opted for neocolonial relations that externalized protection costs onto local governments while granting access to local resources, labor, and wealth. The growth of banana corporations like United Fruit thus provided a useful roadmap to move in this direction, as the banana industry was acquiring new and more distant swaths of land, tapping new sources of wealth, establishing foreign relations with domestic governments, and extending the power and influence of the United States in ways that resonated with imperialist notions regarding America's manifest destiny. As such, the neocolonial presence of the US military in the Caribbean Basin provided both the banana companies with the confidence to continue their expansion throughout the region and local governments that supported this expansion with the confidence of US backing if confronted with calls for social change or a transfer of political power within their own countries.

While these strategies of labor control did facilitate the expansion of the international banana market during the early decades of the twentieth century, by the late 1920s these strategies were failing to contain what was becoming a global wave of labor militancy and economic nationalism. As Kepner and Soothill (1967[1935]) point out, major outbreaks of labor unrest arose across all of the United Fruit Company's enclaves, including Guatemala (1927, 1928), Colombia (1928, 1930, 1931, 1933), Honduras (1931–32, 1933), Panama (1932, 1933), and Costa Rica (1934).[46] These outbreaks were often organized by burgeoning socialist and communist organizers who found the harsh conditions of plantation work, the insularity of enclave life, and the imperialist practices of the foreign company presence to be fruitful breeding grounds for worker radicalizations. Not only did banana workers during this period challenge the monopoly power of the fruit companies within their enclaves. They also become politicized voters who played a critical role in the rise of numerous reform-minded liberal governments that swept across Latin America and the Caribbean in the 1930s. These governments were

---

[46] Other enclave zones, like Mexico in 1929, avoided the outbreak of strikes by offering various labor concessions to union leaders.

not only supplanting Conservatives that had previously provided unflinching support to foreign investors like the banana companies. They instituted social reforms that challenged the ideological doctrines of laissez faire liberalism in favor of state-directed economic regulations meant to protect national workforces, stimulate domestic industrialization, and overcome structural problems such as the declining terms of trade and export specialization in the market.[47]

Nowhere was this crisis of labor control more evident than in the United Fruit Company's banana enclave zone in Santa Marta, Colombia. By the 1920s, the region became a hotbed of labor militancy and socialist agitation. This culminated in the infamous "Great Strike of November 1928," wherein a 30,000-person strike led by UFC workers under the (*Unión Sindical de Trabajadores de Magdalena*, USTM) was forcibly repressed by the Colombian military under the orders of the Conservative government. While "order" was restored on the plantations, news spread that hundreds of banana workers and their allies had been massacred during the chaos, sparking popular outrage at the Conservative government that forced the secretary of war to resign. In the ensuing months, the politicization of the massacre by populist radicals like Jorge Eliécer Gaitán, helped elect a reformist Liberal, Enrique Olaya Herrera, to the presidency (1930–34), thus formally ending three decades of Conservative rule and ushering in nearly two decades of Liberal Party rule.[48]

Overall, the spread of outbreaks labor unrest and economic nationalism like those that occurred in Santa Marta challenged the dominancy of the banana companies in the region during this period by exposing the despotism underlying their vertically integrated system of production. Over the next few decades, it became increasingly clear to these companies that they needed to radically change their business practices in order to continue to secure access to Latin America's bananas.

Vertical Disintegration, US Hegemony, and the Rise of Banana Developmentalism

The United Fruit Company led the response to this hemispheric threat by vertically disintegrating its corporate structure and shifting its investments more heavily into the importation, distribution, and marketing of bananas, thus externalizing the risks of production onto locals. As Marcelo Bucheli's (2003, 2005)

---

[47] Bucheli (2005).
[48] LeGrand (2003).

detailed analyses of the United Fruit Company's investor documents and internal memos show, the decision to vertically disintegrate the company was driven by fears that its investors would sell off their shares in response to unrest on its plantations. Moody's credit-rating agency, for example, put out a 1954 publication called "United Fruit's Prospects under Political Pressures" that deemed UFC stocks to be especially risky investments. In response to the CIA-backed overthrow of Jacobo Arbenz in Guatemala in 1954, Moody's wrote that "further political disturbances in the Caribbean area can never be ruled out" and that "unfortunately the company's operations are subject to natural and foreign political hazards beyond its control." Other risks cited included the passage of "unfavorable tax policy" in Costa Rica, the threat of land expropriation in Cuba following the revolution of 1958, labor strikes in the Santa Marta region of Colombia, in Guatemala, and in Costa Rica, and so on. Overall, investors were worried that the UFC's involvement in further enclave production posed a series of risks that required some immediate form of industrial restructuring.

Moreover, the 1960 appointment of Thomas Sutherland as company president proved to be a critical turning point in this company restructuring. Sutherland believed that by encouraging nationals to enter the banana industry "United Fruit could contribute to the development of stable conditions in the tropics (i.e., aid in the creation of a growing middle class), gain partners who would be valuable allies in the development of joint interests, and reduce the frequent attacks by 'trouble makers' against United Fruit as a large land owner and employer." He also pushed for the UFC's further expansion into Ecuador, a country that had already made great strides toward developing its own domestic plantation and exportation system. And, he also led efforts to diversify the UFC's operations and change the company name to United Brands (UB). Though Moody's response was initially cautious of the changes, by the time of its 1967 report it came to view the UFC's future "with optimism," advising investors to "hold the stock because of its potential growth." In 1970, the UB's new president, Eli Black, reported,

> While these operations are in stable countries with enlightened governments, the fact is that all Latin American countries are being swept by strong winds of nationalist aspiration. (The Company) knows that it must adjust to change in Latin America. It is adjusting ... Since 1952 the Company has divested itself of 65% of its holdings in the four countries (i.e. Costa Rica, Guatemala, Panama, Honduras). Many thousand acres have been given to the governments for distribution; the remainder has been sold to individuals and firms ... In several countries land has been given to unions to build low-cost housing financed by the company.
>
> (Quoted in Bucheli (2003:95–96))

Table 4.4 *United Brands acreage owned and leased, 1958–66 (acres)*

Country	1958	1966	Land Sold	% Sold
Colombia	6,954	0	6,954	100
Costa Rica	26,946	21,046	2,900	10.8
Dominican Republic	2,584	0	2,584	100
Ecuador	7,516	0	7,516	100
Guatemala	25,489	7,350	18,139	71.2
Honduras	29,043	25,618	3,425	11.8
Jamaica	1,464	539	925	63.2
Panama	29,409	26,322	3,087	10.5
Other	937	214	723	77.2
Total	130,342	81,089	49,253	37.8

Source: Arthur et al. (1986:144)

Other banana companies followed the lead of the UFC (renamed United Brands) by selling off their own lands and reprioritizing their efforts at the marketing and distribution end of the market. By the 1960s, an industry-wide process of vertical disintegration had led to a veritable reverse-land grab. Table 4.4 provides evidence of this process by tracing the land owned by United Brands (formerly the United Fruit Company) in selected countries between 1958 and 1966. Overall, the UB sold off 37.8% of its land, with greater sales in South America (Colombia and Ecuador) and the Caribbean (Dominican Republic and Jamaica) than in Central America.

Indeed, from the perspective of banana-producing countries, the vertical disintegration of the global banana industry provided an opportunity to enter the world market as independent banana producers and exporters. And over the course of the 1960s, the establishment and expansion of domestically owned banana plantations became central pillars of national development policy throughout Latin America and the Caribbean. Taking over ownership of lands that had previously been owned by "imperialists" was itself a symbolic political maneuver that legitimated liberal reformist regimes throughout the region. However, governments also began to strategize policies that would bolster economic growth by expanding the productivity of their banana export zones, thus transforming the economic vitality of domestic banana production into a barometer of national development.[49]

Importantly, this entrance into the market was advocated by the US government and the multilateral development agencies, which promoted domestic

---

[49] Wells (2003).

industrialization and export growth as a mechanism of US world hegemony in the postwar decades. As we saw from the last case study, US support for the International Coffee Agreements and coffee-based developmentalism facilitated its hegemonic control over the world's coffee producer countries. To retain control of banana producing countries, the United States engaged in a different set of world hegemonic actions. First, the US State Department played a supportive role in the United Fruit Company's initial decision to abandon their enclaves. As noted earlier, during the first decades of the twentieth century, the United States regularly sent its military forces to retain order in the banana enclaves and to pressure unwieldy governments not to implement reforms that would threaten the ongoing profitability of the banana companies. By the 1930s and 1940s this type of unwavering US military support for the companies declined, as the US government was careful not to anger its hemispheric allies in Latin America and the Caribbean. However, it was revamped again as the Cold War heated up, ultimately reaching a significant turning point following the 1954 coup d'état that ousted land reformer Jacobo Arbenz in Guatemala and the involvement of the UFC's Great White Fleet ships in the 1961 Bay of Pigs Invasion. By the 1960s, such interventions only fueled the fire of anti-imperialist radicalization across the tropical banana-producing regions of the Third World. This, in addition to deepening US military involvement in Southeast Asia, convinced State Department officials that the sale of banana company land and assets would help minimize the possibility of further military actions in the region.[50]

Second, since the close of World War II, the United States and US-backed multilateral institutions had been providing vast amounts of development aid to governments as a geopolitical antidote to the appeal of Soviet-backed communism and radical nationalism that threatened the continued expansion of world capitalism. This aid became a critical source of income to many banana-producing countries that used it to purchase extant banana land and assets from the banana companies, construct new enclave zones, and capitalize nascent domestic exporting firms. Between 1960 and 1980, the critical years of banana developmentalism, US developmental agencies including the United States Agency for International Development (USAID), the Inter-American Foundation, and the African Development Foundation, and others provided over $66 billion in economic aid to countries that by 1980 had become the leading banana exporters in the world.[51] The World Bank estimates that at least $149 billion in overall net

---

[50] Chapman (2007:143–72).

[51] This was calculated using the USAID's Foreign Aid Explorer Database (n.d., accessed April 9, 2019 at https://explorer.usaid.gov/aid-trends.html). It included economic aid

flows of development aid and assistance streamed into these same countries during that period.[52]

To be sure, only a portion of this overall aid was used to finance the establishment of domestic banana production and export industries. Moreover, the process of vertical disintegration and the emergence of independent banana producer and exporting firms was an uneven process across the banana regions of the world. Some countries, like Colombia and Ecuador made significant advances in the establishment of their own domestic banana plantations as well as exporting and marketing companies. Others, including the Central American banana-producing countries, had not yet developed into domestic players in the market. On the whole, however, the combination of vertical disintegration of the banana companies with the influx of development aid ushered in a period of developmental optimism and a major rush of new entrants into the world banana market.

Table 4.5 illustrates the growth in the world banana market during this period of developmental optimism. In the decade between 1961 and 1971, the volume of bananas exported skyrocketed upward from 3,718,000 tons to 6,200,000 tons, reaching 6,600,000 by 1981. The largest exporting regions of Central and South America at the beginning of this period led the market's growth, increasing their exports by 1,740,000 tons and 695,000 tons, respectively. Asia and Oceania, led by the Philippines, arose as major banana exporters during these years, jumping from 187,000 tons in 1961 to 1,056,000 tons two decades later. Other world regions, including US exports from Hawaii, also increased their exports from 149,000 tons to 265,000 tons.[53] The only significant declines in production came from African and Caribbean exporters, both of which had longer histories of

---

from the following funding agencies: African development foundation, Civil Corps of Engineers, US trade and development agency, US Agency for International Development, US Departments of Agriculture and Treasury, and the Inter-American Foundation. Recipient countries included the top twenty-five banana exporters in 1980, excluding the US and re-exporter Ireland: Ecuador, Costa Rica, Honduras, Philippines, Colombia, Panama, Guatemala, Côte d'Ivoire, Nicaragua, China, Taiwan, Brazil, Cameroon, Somalia, Suriname, Saint Lucia, Jamaica, Malaysia, Saint Vincent and the Grenadines, Mexico, Belize, Thailand, Grenada, Pakistan, and Dominican Republic. Aid was measured in constant 2017 US dollars.

[52] This calculation includes "Net official development assistance and official aid received (constant 2015 US$)" (World Bank n.d., accessed July 28, 2019 at https://datacatalog .worldbank.org/dataset/world-development-indicators).

[53] See Sutton (1997) for an in-depth analysis of this European banana market system.

Table 4.5 *Regional banana exports and world market shares, 1961–81 (10,000 tons)*

Country	1961		1971		1981		Growth (1961–81)	
Central America	110.9	29.8%	282.9	45.6%	285.1	42.8%	174.2	+13.0%
South America	144.1	38.8%	179.4	28.9%	213.6	32.1%	69.5	−6.7%
Caribbean	39.1	10.5%	25.1	4.0%	14.7	2.2%	−24.4	−8.3%
Africa	44.2	11.9%	39.5	6.4%	20.5	3.1%	−23.7	−8.8%
Asia and Oceania	18.7	5.0%	71.3	11.5%	105.6	15.8%	86.9	+10.8%
Other	14.9	4.0%	22.1	3.6%	26.5	4.0%	11.6	0.0%
Total	371.8	100%	620.4	100%	666.0	100%	294.2	

Source: FAOSTAT (n.d., accessed August 1, 2019 at www.fao.org/faostat/en/#home)

independent contract farming and found it difficult to compete in what was becoming an increasingly competitive market.[54]

The Rise of Banana Developmentalism in Urabá and the Return of Market Peripheralization

It was in this context of vertical disintegration and US support for the establishment of domestic banana export production that Colombia's Urabá region transformed into the country's banana-axis and a key site of national development. Indeed, since the years of banana enclave production in the Santa Marta region, the United Fruit Company had set its sights on Urabá as a potential new site for future banana production. The region was located just outside the hurricane belt and was free of Panama disease. Moreover, its climate, precipitation and soil type, flat piedmont topography, and proximity to the Caribbean Atlantic made it perfectly suited for banana cultivation and export. And when the Highway to the Sea connecting Urabá to the country's populated highlands was completed in 1954, the region's economic value increased as it was expected to be able to bring in cheap sources of labor and raw materials. The hemispheric wave of social and political unrest that erupted across its enclaves, however, spoiled these plans to transform Urabá into a new enclave. Instead, the company engaged in a series of measures that would externalize the costs of production onto locals while monopolizing the export market.

---

[54] Raynolds (2003).

As early as 1959, the UFC took its first steps in this direction by creating a local subsidiary company, the *Compania Frutera de Sevilla* (CFS), that began providing credit and technical assistance to Colombian entrepreneurs that were interested in becoming banana plantation owners. Over the next decade, the CFS granted over US$10 million of loans through Colombia's *Corporación Financiera de Desarollo Industrial* (Industrial Development Finance Corporation). These loans were used to acquire seed stock, purchase land, fertilizers and equipment, pay surveying and development costs, and finance the labor needed to clear forests, plant and harvest the bananas, and construct drainage and other plantation infrastructure. Large tracts of public *baldío* lands were purchased from the government and converted into large plantations in the four main banana-producing municipalities of Apartadó, Carepa, Chigorodó, and Turbo. Forested lands were cleared, swamps drained, irrigation systems dug, and roads and transport systems constructed by regional migrants who had been evicted to make way for the plantations themselves. This regional development in turn stimulated a land grab driven by urban Colombian elites, mostly Antioqueño businessmen based in Medellín, who took advantage of the tenfold increase in land values by purchasing even greater tracts of land and either selling it off or transforming it themselves into banana plantations or cattle grazing sites administered by local managers.[55]

Urabá's transformation into a new site of banana production was not, however, driven solely by the narrow capitalist interests of the United Fruit Company or by urban real estate investors. Rather, Urabá also became ground zero for the National Front's new developmentalist initiatives that were intended to stimulate domestic agro-export production as a key generator of foreign exchange and employment. State support that was crucial to the growth of Urabá's nascent banana plantations took several forms. Foremost among them, Decree 444 of 1967 created the legal infrastructure needed to regulate trade policy, control foreign investment, and protect national industries. Under Decree 444, the export exemptions that had been historically granted to the UFC during the period of banana production in Santa Marta were eliminated and a new export refund tax was implemented in its place.[56] In the same year, the National Front introduced a new export promotion development strategy known as "Plan Vallejo" that provided tax incentives and government subsidies for selected national exporters in an effort to diversify against the country's strong dependence upon coffee as the dominant source of foreign exchange. Under this plan, Urabá's banana planters were granted tax breaks intended to reduce their production costs to increase their

---

[55] Parsons (1967:77–80).
[56] Bucheli (2005:108).

competitiveness in what was becoming an increasingly saturated market niche.[57] By April of 1964, the region had begun exporting its first shipments of roughly 2,500 tons of bananas. Only two years later, the region was exporting between 1,320 and 3,080 tons on two full ships per week.[58]

Perhaps the most important political step in the development of Urabá's domestic banana sector was the formation of the *Asociación de Ganaderos y Productores de Banano de Urabá* (Association of Cattle Ranchers and Banana Producers of Urabá, Augura, est. 1963), a lobbying group created to advocate the interests of local banana planter, exporters, and other major land owners in the region. Like Fedecafé for the coffee sector, Augura charged itself with the responsibility of overseeing the continued growth of the sector by collecting detailed information on banana production and exports, debating policies relevant to the sector, and lobbying the interests of banana planters and exporters.

Augura's advocacy of Urabá's banana producers resulted in a rush of financial and other state support for the sector. To directly address the issue of Urabá's competitiveness in the market, Augura procured a line of credit from the Ministry of Agriculture that subsidized the conversion of banana plantations from the older *Gros Michel* variety to the disease-resistant *Cavendish* variety that had become the market standard by the early 1970s. To break the CFS monopoly over local purchases, Augura established a new domestically owned and independent marketing company, the *Unión de Bananeros de Urabá* (Union of Banana Producers, UNIBAN, est. 1968). Pumped with government subsidies and loan money, UNIBAN was able to offer exceptionally favorable export contracts to local planters. By 1969, UNIBAN established its own import-marketing company, the TURBANA Corporation (est. 1969), with headquarters in Miami, Florida. To facilitate this domestic takeover of the sector, the National Front created the *Corporación para el Desarrollo de Urabá* (Development Corporation of Urabá, Corpourabá, est. 1968) to coordinate public investments in the area as well as the *Instituto de Fomento Industrial* (Institute for Industrial Development, est. 1971), a local development bank that granted UNIBAN-TURBANA loans to finance the construction of its own maritime transportation equipment and shipyard.[59] By 1973, UNIBAN-TURBANA was exporting 58% of the shipments of Cavendish bananas from the gulf of Urabá.[60] By 1984, the CFS was squeezed out of the region altogether. For the next five years, Urabá's bananas were 100%

---

[57] FAO (1986).

[58] Parsons (1967:77).

[59] UNIBAN's shipyard was completed in 1973.

[60] FAO (1986:15); Bucheli (2005:174–75); Botero Herrera (1990:117).

national in terms of ownership of plantations and the first stage of marketing, and 80% national in terms of the final stages of marketing.[61] And even when transnational companies returned to the region, as in the case of Chiquita Brands' subsidiary *C.I. Bananos de Exportación* (BANADEX, est. 1989), such competition was viewed as "normal business" by Augura's leaders, rather than the type of developmental threat that the transnational presence appeared to be in the 1960s and 1970s.[62]

Economically, governmental support for Urabá's banana planters has proved to be successful. Between 1970 and 1984, Urabá's production skyrocketed upward from 282,000 tons of bananas cultivated on 15,860 ha of land in 1970 to 847,000 tons of bananas on 20,092 ha of land by 1984. Moreover, Urabá's rapid growth also led to government support for the expansion of production back into the Santa Marta region of the department of Magdalena by 1975. Santa Marta's enclaves thus grew in tandem with Urabá, growing from 62,100 tons exported in 1975 to 73,900 tons by 1984. By then, Colombia was exporting nearly a million tons of bananas per year on over 22,600 ha of banana plantations. Following coffee, bananas became the second most important legal agricultural export in the country, generating some US$200 million or 5% of the total value of Colombian exports.[63]

However, it became increasingly obvious to Augura that their domestic economic successes were weighed down by trends in the international banana market that were pushing Colombia once again into peripheralized niche. As it turned out, rather than reduce global inequalities, the vertically disintegrated world banana market of the 1960s and 1970s was transforming into a highly polarized global subcontracting system much like that of other global industries at the time, including the apparel, retail, electronic, and other fruits and vegetables.[64] Domestic exporters like UNIBAN were confronted with pressures to minimize their production costs in order to ensure access to the sales contracts offered by the major banana importing and distributing companies. Simultaneously, they sought ways to continually expand their productivity to outcompete rival exporters and increase their overall shares of the export market, which led to chronic problems of overproduction in the market that ultimately benefitted the major banana

---

[61] Botero Herrera (1990:101–4); FAO (1986:15).

[62] Author interview with a former Augura representative in Bogotá on November 16, 2004.

[63] FAO (1986:12–13, 136).

[64] Gereffi and Korzeniewicz (1994); (Gereffi 2018); Ross (2004); Lichtenstein (2006); Dicken (2015); Suwandi (2019).

Figure 4.1 World banana imports, annual average growth, 1950–83

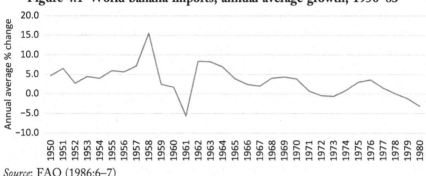

Source: FAO (1986:6–7)

transnationals. As evidenced from Table 4.5, this competition among exporters resulted in a major jump in total world banana exports from roughly 3.7 million tons in 1960 to 6.7 million tons by 1982.

To make matters worse for producers, the overall growth in banana export production was occurring precisely during a period in which the rates of growth in banana imports were slowing down. Figure 4.1 illustrates this slowdown in the growth rates of world banana imports during this period. The annual growth rate for world imports hovered around 5% between 1950 and 1956, jumping briefly upward in 1957 and 1958 but plunging thereafter into negative growth rates in the early years of the 1960s. It rose again in the early years of vertical disintegration, but steadily declined with few exceptions from the mid-1960s until 1980. Not surprisingly then, world banana market's tendency toward overproduction ended up reducing the overall value of banana exports that producer countries had come to rely on. Between 1960 and 1980, real export prices amongst producer countries fell by between 55% and 62%. Some countries, like Ecuador, were less impacted by this pricing drop due to their ability to outcompete other exporters. Most, like Colombia, however, saw their profit margins shrink as they struggled to find lower cost systems of production.[65]

By the early 1970s, the reality of the structural limitations of banana developmentalism was becoming all too apparent and many banana producer-exporting governments began to meet to discuss ways to minimize competition among themselves and generate greater revenues from their exports. Naturally, they saw the successes of both the International Coffee Agreements as well as the Organization of Petroleum Exporting Countries (OPEC) as potential models

---

[65] FAO (1986:vi–vii, 6–8).

for any geopolitical collective action they might take.[66] However, it was not clear how they might harmonize their export promotion policy objectives. These discussions heated up in 1973 and 1974. The worldwide recession that followed the oil crisis led to a drop in demand for bananas. This drop in overall demand was exacerbated by Hurricane Fifi, which devastated significant portions of banana plantations across Central America. In March of 1974, the governments of Colombia, Costa Rica, Guatemala, Honduras, and Panama formally met to discuss how to collectively respond to the crisis. They came out of these talks with what became known as the "Panama Agreement," a first step toward generating a collective strategy to restructure the banana market. Under this agreement, they committed themselves to an industry-wide increase in export taxes on banana companies, a universal modification of the tax and land concessions previously granted to banana transnationals, and to further collective action efforts to eventually control world banana supplies and drive export prices up.

In the ensuing months, however, intense debates arose over the details of how these policies might be implemented. The issues were particularly contentious in Central America, where production was still largely vertically controlled by the major banana transnationals.[67] Following the agreement, the Central American countries coordinated the passage of national legislation to break their contracts and annul the concessions previously granted to United Brands, Castle & Cooke, Del Monte, and other companies. They also agreed to implement a region-wide

---

[66] The developmental optimism underlying the UBPC's actions was, of course, part of a larger process of economic nationalism that was spreading across what was then described as the Third World. The International Coffee Agreement, Organization of Petroleum Exporting Countries, and other geopolitical market interventions were in full swing, generating profits for exporting countries that were stimulating processes of domestic industrialization and growth that had not been attainable under the laissez-faire logic of the previous era. The decision-making apparatuses of the United Nations was being challenged by the G-77, who advocated for a New Industrial Economic Order (NIEO) that would fundamentally alter the role of the world market from a mechanism reproducing core–periphery inequalities into one that would diminish those inequalities. And the US government and multilateral agencies were actively financing these efforts through provisions of economic aid to stimulate this growth, while the United States was supplying military aid and engaging in warfare against those, like Vietnam, that were experimenting with developmental alternatives that threatened to undermine the continued growth of the market (McMichael 2008:120–22).

[67] As the last holdout of vertical integration, they were only getting an average of 11% of the income generated in the banana trade, while the TNCs captured 37% and retailers located in consumer countries captured 19% (FAO 1986:12, 40).

export tax in 1974 that would shift some of the production costs onto the banana transnationals. The banana corporations responded by interrupting shipments, threatened workers and governments with layoffs and export strikes, and even with destroying crops. This situation reached a high point of tension when officials of the Panamanian Government accused United Brands of conspiracy to murder their president, Omar Torrijos, a fiery speaker known for his staunchly nationalist politics and his close friendship with Fidel Castro. Torrijios responded by further fanning the fire, declaring that he would "take the war to its last consequences." By September, however, a settlement was finally reached when the banana transnationals backed down and producer countries formally established the *Unión de Países Exportadores de Banano* (Union of Banana Producing Countries, UBPC) with strong resistance from Torrijos and no support from the US government. Over the next eight years, the UBPC would use its collective strength to break existing contracts and forge new ones between domestic producers and the banana transnationals without significant retaliatory measures.[68]

However, there were significant structural obstacles facing UBPC countries that limited their capacity to obtain national development and growth through banana production for the market. These obstacles are quite clear when comparing the political restructuring of the banana market to that of the coffee market during this time. First was the perishable nature of bananas, which made it difficult to stockpile and hold off the market to raise prices as coffee producers did with coffee. Any bananas purposefully taken out of the market would rot or be replaced rather easily by new supplies that could be produced throughout the year. In other words, unlike coffee that was withheld from the market for a period before it could be sold, withholding bananas from the market essentially destroyed value that could not be easily reconverted at a later date.[69]

Second, coordinating geopolitical interventions to raise prices required a level of trust among producers that had to be built from scratch. As we saw from the last cases study, the coffee market had a long history that dates back to the Brazilian valorization schemes in the early twentieth century and the Inter-American Coffee Agreements during World War II. The ICA agreements thus built off the successes of these interventions for both producer-exporter and importer countries. Banana exporters, in contrast, were new to such coordinated actions. And rather than build off a legacy of cooperation and trust, the legacy they inherited was rooted in competition and distrust. This distrust was exacerbated by

---

[68] Bucheli (2005:72–73).

[69] See Dicken (2015:9) and Campling and Havice (2019) for an analysis of value destruction in global production networks and value chains.

the growing disparity in production costs and competition brought on by the consolidation of the global subcontracting nature of the market, which made it difficult to agree upon a mutually beneficial pricing structure.[70]

Third, and relatedly, even if the UBPC countries could agree to collectively withhold their supplies or reduce their export volumes, they were not able to obtain the support the majority of banana exporting countries. Notably, Ecuador and the Philippines, whose relatively low production costs established the market standard for how low production costs should be, did not participate in the UBPC. Without these and other leading exporters, the UBPC's ability to control world supplies and raise prices was severely weakened. Again, comparing the banana market to the coffee market is instructive. Whereas the ICA of 1961 included 94% of the world coffee market, the UBPC only controlled 42.9% in 1974 and reached only 50.0% at its peak in 1982. Included were only eight countries during its critical formative years (1974–82): Colombia, Costa Rica, Dominican Republic, Guatemala, Honduras, Nicaragua, Panama, and Venezuela. Absent from the UBPC on the producer end were five countries in South America (with 23.5% in 1974), seven countries in the Caribbean (with 7.4%), eight countries in Africa (with 6.9%), eleven countries in Asia and Oceania (with 13.5%), in addition to others located in other regions.[71]

Fourth, the nature of US hegemony had changed between its earlier years when the IACA and ICA were established and the mid-1970s when the UBPC arose. During the 1940s, 1950s, and even early 1960s, the United States dominated the world economy and its support for development posed no immediate threat to this dominance. However, by the 1970s, US economic dominance was coming under threat from resurgent industrial powers in Europe and Japan, the world was in the midst of a worldwide recession, and the developmental policies of import substitution industrialization and agro-export production that were advocated for the Third World were producing industrialization without expected forms of social development, welfare, and well-being.[72] In other words, the formation of the ICA arose during the high period of US global hegemony, when the United States was in a better position to sacrifice economic profits for global political legitimacy. By the late 1970s, however, the question of profits was certainly beginning to trump concerns about political legitimacy and fears of social revolution in the periphery. As a result, the

---

[70] Bucheli (2008).

[71] FAO (1986:12–15).

[72] See Arrighi (1994, 2002); Arrighi et al. (2003), analyses of US world hegemonic decline and national development policy in the global south in the 1970s.

Table 4.6 *Regional banana imports and world market shares, 1961–81 (10,000 tons)*

Country	1961		1971		1981		Growth (1961–81)	
United States	156.5	30.9%	191.8	32.0%	253.4	37.3%	96.9	+6.4%
Europe/Euro. Union	161.2	41.0%	222.1	37.1%	214.7	31.9%	53.5	−9.1%
Asia	13.9	3.5%	109.6	18.3%	104.5	15.5%	90.6	+12.0%
Other Regions	61.0	15.5%	75.1	12.6%	100.0	14.9%	39.0	−0.6%
Total	392.6	100%	598.6	100%	672.6	100%	280.0	

Source: FAOSTAT (n.d., accessed August 1, 2019 at www.fao.org/faostat/en/#home)

United States was more hostile to the demands of the UBPC and ultimately refused to become a signatory to their efforts.

Fifth, even if the United States had agreed to participate in the UBPC's demands, it is not clear that the United States had the market power required to control and enforce the flows of bananas across the market as it did for coffee. As we saw from the last case study, in the lead up to the establishment of the ICA, the United States dominated the global consumer markets with 62.8% of world imports of green coffee. As such, coffee producers could force the United States to accept a quota system in order to ensure US geopolitical influence. As Table 4.6 illustrates, the US share of the world banana market indeed grew from 30.9% to 37.3% between 1961 and 1981, but it never came close to matching the share it had over the coffee market. Moreover, while Europe's overall share decreased from 41.0% to 31.9%, other world regions, including Asia, radically increased their world market shares. This globalization of the world banana import market made it difficult for the UBPC to control the market. Lacking a central enforcement mechanism, the UBPC could neither enforce adherence to politically determined export niches nor harmonize export tax levels across producer countries to reduce competition among them.

Finally, it was not only that the world banana market had become more global in terms of its production and consumption. The market actually fragmented into three largely distinct trade regime circuits: a geopolitically regulated Africa, Pacific, and Caribbean (APC) market that centered on Europe and two unregulated "dollar markets" centered on North America and East Asia. This fragmentation was due in large part to European efforts to diminish the hegemony of the United States across the banana-producing regions of the world by creating a market system that provided exporters with more favorable developmental conditions. This APC market has a long history as an informal trade network rooted in colonial, and later postcolonial, relations between Europe and its former colonies Africa, the Pacific Islands, and the Caribbean. During the colonial era, European rulers were able to force their colonies into producing banana solely for the mother country. Yet, the emergence of national independence movements in the twentieth century convinced Britain, then France, Germany, and Italy that they would soon lose access to banana producers due to the market power of the US-based United Fruit Company. In response, European states agreed to use "bananas as a central vehicle for continued colonial rule in the region" by channeling smallholder peasant production in their former colonies into Europe with the help of state-backed banana grower associations.[73] The British state gave UK-based Fyffes Limited a guarantee of 75% of the British market and exclusive contracts with banana producers in Jamaica, Belize, and Suriname. After World War II, Britain financed the development of a similar pattern of trade with the Windward Islands, who traded under the UK-based Geest Corporation. Local producers and markets in turn gained preferential access to British markets. Similar types of circuits were established linking France to Martinique and Guadeloupe, Germany to its former colonies in East Africa, and Italy in Somalia.[74]

This system became formalized in 1973–74, following Britain's admittance into the European Economic Community (EEC). Rather than rely upon informal and bilaterally negotiated trade deals, the EEC representative began to formulate formal rules that granted former colonies preferential access to Europe's market under quota and licensing agreements. This culminated in the signing of the first "Lomé Agreement" in 1974 by nine EEC member states and forty-five countries located in Africa, the Pacific, and the Caribbean. Lomé sought to "create a model for relations between developed and developing states" by setting forth a number of trade provisions including duty-free entry for many agricultural imports and special protective measures for a number of key commodities of which bananas was one.[75] The Lomé Agreement set the stage for the institutionalization of the preferential treatment given to APC bananas entering into the European market. Like the ICA agreements in the coffee sector, the APC system grants producers and state marketers preferential access to the EEC under quota and licensing agreements that regulate the quantities, prices, and labor/ecological production standards of banana exports. Because the APC market provides institutional assurances regarding the import–export volumes and price rates for banana

---

[73] Raynolds (2003:27–28).

[74] Myers (2004:38–40).

[75] Myers (2004:41).

imports, it is the highest valued segment of the world banana market. Ecological and quality standards tend to be higher. Yet, these costs are offset by higher labor standards and export values that result in more favorable domestic growth.

In sharp contrast to the APC market, the dollar market connects mostly Latin American exporters to importers in the United States and Canada. Unlike the politically regulated APC market, the dollar market is characterized by an absence of quantitative restrictions and quotas on the origins and volumes of bananas imported and an overall adherence to laissez-faire market norms to determine import–export prices and quality standards. Because most Latin American and Caribbean producers are denied access to the European market, they forced into the distribution circuits of the dollar market, which tends to pay lower costs for banana exports and lack the high regulatory standards for labor and the environment offered by the APC system. However, the EU developed some conditions that allow the importation of bananas beyond what APC producer countries can supply. This has permitted large Latin American exporters, like Colombia and Ecuador, some limited access to their market. Finally, a third market system arose with the rise of Japanese (and later Russian) banana imports in the 1970s and 1980s. Bananas in this circuit operate through bilateral trade agreements between importing and exporting countries, the latter of which includes the Philippines and China. However, because the Japanese and Russian markets impose no limitations on imports, they also source bananas from Ecuador and other countries that have high production rates. Table 4.7 illustrates this geographical patterning of imports and exports in the world banana economy in 1983.

Given the structural fragmentation of the world banana market along these lines, it is not surprising that the initiatives of the Union of Banana Producing Countries in the mid-1970s proved to be a short-lived and largely ineffectual. To be sure, UBPC efforts to organize a collective strategy to restructure the world banana market did help boost the export growth and taxation rents of Central American countries. For example, it created the possibility of renegotiating local contracts between foreign banana companies and domestic producers. It also generated more earnings from banana export taxes.[76] Finally, it granted them greater autonomy from the oligopolistic contracts of the foreign multinationals, which led to their creation of their own exporting corporation, COMUNABAN, in 1977.

However, these measures did not only fail to boost the developmental growth of countries like Colombia and Ecuador that already had long-established strong

---

[76] Central American producers increased their export earnings from $25.4 million in 1974 to $51.4 million in 1976 (Bucheli 2005:73).

Table 4.7 *Import–export matrix, 1983 (1,000 metric tons)*

Importer Exporter	North America	Europe (APC)	Europe (non-APC)	Japan	Other	Total Volume	Share of World Exports (%)
Latin America	2684.3	440.5	932.7	5.7	233.9	4279.1	69.4
Caribbean	0.7	441.5	0	0	0	442.2	7.1
Africa	0	147.1	0	0	10.0	157.1	2.5
Asia	0	0	0	565.9	156.0	721.9	11.7
Other	9.7	24	449.6	4.3	89.1	576.7	9.3
Total Volume	2694.7	1053.1	1382.3	575.9	489.0	6195.0	100
Share of World Imports (%)	43.5	17.0	22.3	9.3	7.9	100	

Source: FAO (1986)

domestic producer-exporters. By essentially completing the hemispheric process of vertical disintegration, the UBPC's actions only intensified the peripheralization of this market niche. Thus, within five years of the implementation of the UBPC measures, the state-led marketing firms that arose in the Central American markets as the result of UBPC efforts in the mid-1970s began to lower their export taxes once again by 1983. Likewise, COMUNABAN also ceased its operations as it failed to develop a solid niche in what was becoming an increasingly competitive market niche. And while the UBPC continues to exist as an organizational platform for banana-exporting countries, it has not instituted any significant changes to the structures of the world banana economy.[77]

The failure of the UBPC to restructure the dollar market, in addition to the successes of the APC market, essentially established the institutional tracks upon which the world banana market would develop over the next three decades. The only significant exception was the eruption of the so-called banana wars of the 1990s and early 2000s, when the United States and its allies challenged the legality of Europe's APC market regulations under the General Agreement on Tariffs and Trade (GATT) negotiations in 1986 and later under the trade rules of the World Trade Organization. By then, however, the geopolitics of the world banana market had swung so far from the anti-imperialism of the 1960s and the developmentalist optimism of the 1970s, that Central and South American exporting countries actually sided with US efforts to force the European Community to deregulate the European market. Particularly vociferous supporters of this new

---

[77] FAO (1986, 2003).

Figure 4.2 World banana production and imports, 1961–2016

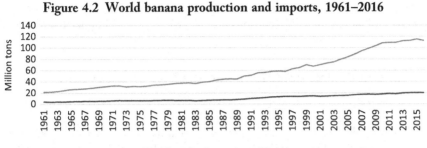

——— World production   ——— World imports

Source: FAOSTAT (n.d., accessed August 5, 2019 at www.fao.org/faostat/en/#home)

geopolitics of trade liberalization in the banana market were Colombia and Ecuador, who launched a series of lawsuits against the European Community's use of tariffs and import quotas that limited imports from the South American producers. The first banana war ended in 1993 when the European countries, now aligned as a Single European Market, agreed to a "framework agreement on bananas" (FAB) that increased import volumes and lowered tariffs for Colombia, Costa Rica, Nicaragua, and Ecuador. A second banana war arose in 2001 when the same group of banana exporters along with the United States claimed that Europe's continued adherence to the APC regulations violated World Trade Organization (WTO) rules. By 2002–3, these lawsuits also resulted in some greater flexibility in the APC market's rules regarding imports from dollar-market banana producers. Europe agreed to drop all quotas by 2006, but retain its tariff import system thereafter.[78]

During this period, banana-exporting countries that operated in the dollar markets of North America and Asia increased their production in anticipation of greater and greater access to the European market as well as rising consumption levels in the former Communist countries (Russia, Eastern and Central Europe) and in East Asia. This growth in world banana production is depicted in Figure 4.2. World production grew relatively slowly from the 1960s into the mid-1980s, from under 5 million tons in 1961 up to 6.5 million tons by 1985. Thereafter, as the banana wars heated up, the import market began to grow steadily, reaching over 20 million tons by 2016.

In short, it was precisely this increasingly competitive, unregulated market niche that Colombia entered as part of the country's efforts to transform a new region, Urabá, into its leading site of banana-based developmentalism. Rather

---

[78] FAO (2003:37–41).

than avoid the problems of peripheralization by moving up the market, Urabá became emblematic of the despotism associated with peripheral proletarianization.

Peripheral Proletarianization and the Rise of Despotism in Urabá, 1963–1982

The peripheralization of Colombia's niche in the international banana market had a direct impact on Urabá's labor regime dynamics. Unlike the hegemony established in Viejo Caldas during this period, where Fedecafé was able to finance the *Pacto Cafetero* by accessing core-like profits in the market, Augura's growth was not only heavily reliant upon access to development aid, tax breaks, and subsidies provided by the Colombian government. To maintain their competitive edge in this market niche, they needed to find ways to keep production costs low and therefore subvert actions like export taxes and other redistributive measures that could threaten their continued profitability. And this was no small feat. The region's population jumped some 15,700 residents in the 1950s to over 150,463 by 1985, with some 35,000 working full-time on just over 20,000 ha of banana plantations.[79] Given this explosive concentration of labor, Augura had to develop innovative ways to maintain control of the region and block what was becoming the growing structural power of labor. Yet, each strategy Augura deployed to maintain control of labor gave rise to new social contradictions that have only deepened the class conflicts of the region.

During Urabá's first decade of production, Augura's primary mechanism of labor control stemmed from the existence of large pools of landless and economically vulnerable migrants seeking employment in the banana sector.[80] Like the UFC's early labor control strategies before it, Augura was able to exploit the social and economic vulnerabilities of indigenous, mulatto, and Afro-Colombian communities who were displaced by government development initiatives in the region.[81] By 1979, for example, roughly half of those who migrated to Urabá to

---

[79] FAO (1986:12–13); Carroll (2011:59, 67); CAJSC (1994:36).

[80] To be sure, the wages provided to Urabá's nascent proletariat were indeed higher than those available in neighboring labor markets (Botero Herrera and Sierra Botero 1981:3). However, this pull factor to the region must be considered in light of the push factors that have resulted from a deep and troubled history of land dispossession, ethnic strife, and social-political marginalization (Ballvé 2019).

[81] The existence of such a pool of uprooted migrants has a long history in the region, due to the strategic location of the Urabá region as a gateway to the Caribbean and the Atlantic and Pacific Oceans (via the Panama Canal) as well as to its history of land and

work in the banana sector were displaced Afro-Colombians from the neighboring department of Chocó, roughly 20% were mulattos from Cordoba or Urabá natives, and a little over 20% were mestizos or whites from surrounding rural regions of Antioquia.[82]

In additional to using these pools of landless migrants to keep productions costs low, Augura also came to rely heavily upon both the exclusionary political practices and agrarian development policies of the National Front regime (1958–74). Regarding the former, the National Front formally banned the participation of "third parties" in presidential and national congressional elections and had mayoral and departmental executives appointed "top-down" by party chiefs at the national level rather than elected locally. Augura used its regional economic weight, its role in the country's national developmental plan of expanding agro-exports, and its political influence at the departmental and national levels to fill local positions in Urabá with business-friendly politicians. Since the period *La Violencia*, the region had become a Liberal Party political stronghold. Over time, Augura became a core constituency of what became known as the "Guerrista faction" of Antioquia's Liberal Party, an entrenched

---

ethnic conflict. During the nineteenth century, for example, the region's indigenous Cuna, Embera-Catio, and Zenue indigenous communities were subject to pirate raids from the sea and displacement from mestizo migrants involved in brief economic booms in rubber tapping, tagua nuts (vegetable ivory), and timber. Afro-Colombian and mulattos displaced from the neighboring departments of Chocó and Cordoba also migrated to Urabá where they struggled to establish subsistence farms and fishing communities along the region's main rivers and tributaries. The outbreak of sectarian political violence during La Violencia brought a new wave of mestizo peasant refugees to the region in the late 1940s and early 1950s, many of whom were Liberals fleeing Conservative repression in the highland regions of Antioquia and Viejo Caldas to the north. Their efforts to establish cattle grazing lands brought them into direct conflict with subsistence farmers and peasant communities who claimed this land as their own. By the late 1950s, these land conflicts were exacerbated by a new wave of colono migrants who were displaced by the construction of the *Carretera al Mar* (Highway to the Sea), a public development project that connected the region and its port in the town of Turbo to the departmental capital city of Medellín. Thus, by the early 1960s when the United Fruit Company (via its Compania Frutera de Sevilla) began to purchase and sell off land that would become large-scale banana plantations, the region was already subject to ongoing and often violent land conflicts between the region's mestizo, Afro-Colombian, and indigenous communities. See Parsons (1967); Botero Herrera (1990); Ramírez Tobón (1997); Steiner (2000).

[82] Carroll (2011:60).

political bloc with deep ties to Medellín's industrial capitalist class and Catholic church.[83] Highly conservative despite their affiliation with the Liberal Party, the Guerristas acquired their *nom de guerre* due to political influence of Senator Bernardo Guerra, a figure with racist views of the country's coastal populations and a staunchly anticommunist politics that associated demands for social reform with Cuban and Soviet aggression.[84] Like Reagan-era conservatives that drew upon racist "culture of poverty" arguments to divest public monies from urban communities in the 1980s, Guerristas used their influence to ensure that departmental spending tilted toward urban industrialists in Medellín rather than to meet the needs of Urabá's working class.[85]

Through the Guerristas, Augura was able to make sure that there was minimal governmental oversight of labor contracts and working conditions on Urabá's plantations. Only one labor court existed in the region, and it was located on the outskirts of Turbo. In addition to its physical remoteness from the banana plantations and worker neighborhoods, the court was also biased against workers because it granted employers the strange right to miss the first two appointments – a luxury that could not be afforded to workers who feared dismissal for such an absence. Moreover, Guerrista influence within Antioquia's departmental assembly ensured that the region's planters were protected by a heavy police presence that was there to protect and enforce property rights, evict squatters on from both rural

---

[83] For an analysis of local Liberal Party politics, see Ortiz Sarmiento (1999, 2007).

[84] For example, in 1982 a prominent Urabá plantation owner and board member of Unibán was elected to the national House of Representatives as a Guerrista Liberal, while others held House and Senate seats in the national parliament between 1982 and 1986. At the departmental level, the Guerristas held eight of the thirty seats in the Departmental Assembly (Carroll 2011:60).

[85] As one prominent Guerrista Liberal, Bernardo Jaramillo Sierra, noted:

> We in Antioquia are pledged to the colonization of Urabá, an enterprise that already has cost the department huge sums ... the result to date is a few openings in the selva, and even these may turn out to have calamitous consequences that will later be costly to repair.... It may well be more desirable for Antioquia to leave its resources in Urabá intact, for possible later and more effective use in support of its economy. It is rather in the valley of Medellín where agricultural colonization ought to be initiated ... it is near the centers of population that such efforts are most needed and it is there that they will be most successful.
>
> (Parsons 1967:109)

Also, see Steiner (2000) and Ballvé (2019) for analyses of the history of racism associated with Urabá's Liberal Party.

and urban spaces, and control what many politicians described as the "social chaos" of the region's working-class neighborhoods.[86]

Augura was also able to use its political influence within the Liberal Party to shape state developmental actions in ways that would ensure new flows of dispossessed and economically vulnerable migrants into the local labor market. In 1961, the Colombian government had passed legislation that established a set of agrarian development agencies meant to distribute public *baldío* lands to landless farmers (Colombian Institute for Agrarian Reform, INCORA) to stimulate agricultural productivity and local markets (Agricultural Market Board, IDEMA), and to provide financial assistance to farmers (*Banco Agrario*). These agencies had a government mandate to formalize land titles and redistribute public lands, and therefore might have ameliorated the land conflicts in the region. Yet, the region's Guerrista Liberals used their local political monopolies to co-opt these developmental agrarian institutions and further concentrate land ownership in the region.[87] By the 1970s, the greater Urabá region had consolidated into a regional political economy dominated by large-scale banana plantations in the central flatlands (Apartadó, Carepa, Chigorodó, and Turbo) and giant cattle ranching estates in the hilly grasslands of Northern Urabá (Arboletes, Necoclí, San Juan de Urabá, and San Pedro de Urabá). With the exception of a mountainous jungle region just south of the banana zone of Urabá, the region had become highly urbanized.[88]

Urabá's rapidly changing geography directly impacted conditions for workers on the plantations. During its early years in the 1960s, for example, the region's migrants consisted predominantly of single, adult males who worked as piecework and day laborers and lived in local work camps. As the lands surrounding the plantations were occupied, some 80% of these workers ended up living directly in work camps located on the plantations themselves. These workers, like many of today's migrants, left their homes looking for work that could provide them with enough earnings to send back to their families still living in their home communities. This meant that they could work for wages that were significantly lower than the family wages required to sustain a worker's family living at the site of employment.[89] Yet, as Urabá's banana planters pulled workers from further

---

[86] Parsons (1967:96–97).

[87] See Botero Herrera (1990:1), Ramírez Tobón (1997:4), CAJSC (1994:5, 13–18, 25–32) for analyses of land struggles in Urabá during this time.

[88] By 1985, over half of the region's 150,463 population lived in the region's urban centers (Carroll 2011:59, 67).

[89] See Arrighi (1970), Arrighi and Piselli (1987), Arrighi et al. (2010), and Bair et al. (2019) for a discussion of the impact of semi-proletarianization on economic growth and development.

geographies, the predominant pattern of migration and settlement became families that sought permanent forms of employment and housing. This shift in the labor pool quickly led to worker demands for higher wages to support their families, access to adequate housing and formal living conditions, and provisions of social and public services. That is, the region's migrants were transforming into a prototypical class of fully proletarianized workers with livelihoods hinged to the banana market and that began to mobilize as a class along two fronts: labor organizing for family wages and better working conditions on the banana plantations and civic organizing through political activity seeking public services in the neighborhoods. Both sets of movements, labor and civic, demanded greater reinvestments of the wealth generated by the banana plantations and therefore became subject to labor control.

Government reports on the working conditions on Urabá's plantations during these years described them as substandard and in need of greater attention. Not only was there little to no regulatory oversight of working conditions the plantations, but plantation owners demanded complete control of the labor process, often using guard dogs and foreman armed with pistols and machetes to force workers to keep up the pace of work.[90] Moreover, government reports on the conditions of the plantation work camps showed them to be deplorable living spaces. Only 6.6% had running water, 33% had latrines, and 50% electricity.[91] In response, the region's workers began to form labor unions demanding better regulatory oversight of work conditions, higher wages, improvement of the work camps, and formal collective bargaining rights. The first banana plantation worker union to arise was SINTRABANANO, a group affiliated with the labor federation of the Colombian Communist Party (PCC) that began organizing workers in 1964. By 1970, SINTRABANANO grew to some 1,500–1,600 members. In 1972, a second banana plantation union arose, SINTAGRO, which was affiliated with the country's conservative "business-union" federation, *Union de Trabajadores Colombianos* (Colombian Workers Union Federation, UTC). In 1982, a third union also arose in the region, SINTRAEXPOBAN, which was also associated with the conservative UTC-affiliated union but which organized workers in the export and marketing companies operating in the region. Finally, around the same time, SINDEJORNALEROS, union affiliated with the Independent Revolutionary Workers Movement (MOIR) began competing against SINDEJORNALEROS to organize banana export workers.[92]

---

[90] Ortiz Sarmiento (1999:98–99). See also Botero Herrera and Sierra Botero (1981).

[91] Carroll (2011:60–63, 69).

[92] Botero Herrera (1990:156–70).

The bleak conditions of life for workers in their neighborhoods became the focal point of a second arena of working-class militancy: urban politics. Given the lack of planning for adequate worker housing, the region's urban centers swelled with informal shantytowns (*barrios de invasión*).[93] By 1985, some 22.1% of banana workers on the banana plantations lived in *barrios de invasión*. And like the work camps, government reports on the quality of life in these *barrios* showed them to be deplorable. Only 30–31% of the region's homes were connected to running water, sewage systems, or electricity. Access to social services, including health and education, were likewise abysmal. As one study noted, between 1984 and 1986, the monetary value of the region's banana exports reached US$185 million per year. Yet, social spending in the region was little more than US$1 million.[94]

Thus, in the neighborhoods, banana workers and their families began to organize politically to demand investments in subsidized and public housing, the rights to public services, and formal titles to their properties. A patchwork of different neighborhood-delineated politics arose across Urabá's urban informal centers during this time, especially as different factions within the Liberal Party competed over access to their votes in exchange for clientelistic perks such as recognition of urban property rights. However, by the mid-1970s, these neighborhoods had become strongholds of leftist political parties. The earliest experiments with radical party politics came with the independent and other radical Liberal Party factions, including the Liberal Revolutionary Movement (*Movimiento Liberal Revolucionario*, MLR).[95] Over time, the Colombian Communist Party (PCC) began to create Liberal party fronts that gained traction in the neighborhoods, including the National Oppositional Unity party (*Unión Nacional de Oposición*, UNO) and the Democratic Front party (*Frente*

---

[93] Between 1962 and 1984, Botero Herrera (1990:43–46) estimates that there were roughly nineteen major urban land invasions in the four municipalities of the banana zone in which fifteen or more families occupied an urban space, set up crude housing, and demanded formal deeds for this property from local governments. Of these 19 major urban land invasions, some 8 entailed over 100 families at a time and 3 entailed over 1,000 families at once.

[94] By 1987, only 25% of the population was fully literate while 50% had attained some functional reading and writing skills. Some 43 primary schools had been constructed, but these schools only served 4,213 kids (CAJSC 1994:18, 36–37, 44–45).

[95] The MLR was the radical faction of the Liberal Party that was ultimately led by Colombian President Alfonso López Michelson (1974–78). For an overview of formal party politics in Urabá during this period, see Ortiz Sarmiento (1999:3).

Democrático, FD).[96] By the close of the decade, the PCC's party front had become the predominant political influence in the region's barrios and the region gained a reputation as "the red corner of Colombia."[97]

These working-class mobilizations on the plantations and in the political sphere in the 1970s forced Augura to find new strategies to contain the growing organizational power of labor. At first, Augura came to rely more heavily on its influence within the most reactionary faction of the Liberal Party to obstruct worker demands for better more government assistance and regulatory oversight of working and living conditions in the region. And while the National Front regime formally ended in 1974, thus legalizing the election of third-party candidates in municipal council positions, the Guerristas were able to take advantage of the continuing practice of appointing local and departmental executives (mayors and governors) to minimize the influence of the leftist parties.

Augura also engaged in a wave of labor repression meant to rid the plantations of these early union drives. Plantation owners closed ranks, engaging in discriminatory firing and hiring, bribery of labor leaders, subcontracted labor arrangements, arbitrary detentions, and threats of violence against activists. Augura also used its political influence to lobby for the construction of a military base in Carepa, which helped turn the municipality into a bastion of conservative militarism to keep watch over the entire region.[98] This powerful backlash of labor repression had an immediate and negative impact on the workers struggles on the plantations. SINTRABANANO's membership, for example, dropped from a high of 1,500–1,600 members in 1970 to a mere 350–450 by the end of 1977. In 1979, SINTRABANANO attempted to regroup, but the military was called in to occupy a banana plantation and the workers were forced to sign, what was widely regarded as, an "employer-imposed" collective bargaining pact. Another plantation owner offered the union representative a bribe of roughly US$1,000 to drop their demands and sign a similar pact – which he refused. Five days later, the union representative was found dead and a one-day strike was organized in his

---

[96] The MOIR party gained some political traction during the mid-late 1970s but declined in influence as the PCC and *Frente Democrático* gained ground. Also, the PCC's local political influence was strong due to the fact that the Maoist Colombian Communist Party (PCC-ML) that was affiliated with the EPL guerrillas and SINTAGRO was unwaveringly abstentionist (Carroll 2011:66–68; Ortiz Sarmiento 1999:3).

[97] The red corner referred to both the hegemony of the PCC in Urabá as well as to the political bloodshed that was spilled in the region in the 1970s and into the 1980s (Ballvé 2019).

[98] Carroll (2011:62).

honor. Three days after the strike, a SINTRABANANO leader was held personally responsible for the disturbance and held for twelve days in detention. By the early 1980s, an estimated 46% of Urabá's plantations had formal labor agreements, though 77% of these were unfavorable contracts imposed by employers that did grant favorable concessions to banana workers. In total, only 11% had collective bargaining agreements that were in fact negotiated between workers and management rather than dictated by management.[99]

A similar fate was experienced by the more conservative-leaning unions, SINTAGRO and SINTRAEXPOBAN. For example, when SINTAGRO struck on the neighboring African palm plantation of the Dutch company Coldesa in 1976, the palm groves were immediately militarized, union officials were threatened, and military county executives were appointed for the municipalities of Apartadó, Chigorodó, Turbo, and Mutatá. This triggered a response by a Maoist-leaning guerrilla group, the *Ejercito Popular de Liberación* (Popular Liberation Army, EPL), that had established a territorial stronghold in the rural mountainous regions just north of Urabá in the years prior. In an effort to politicize the region's repression and gain traction among the region's working class, the EPL killed Coldesa's Director of Industrial Relations. Despite this overt expression of EPL support for the Coldesa strike, the strike ultimately failed and two of SINTAGRO's top leaders were exiled from the region. After another attempt at organizing met with similar bouts of repression in 1979, the union decided to carry out its union activity clandestinely. In 1982, a union representative of SINTRAEXPOBAN was killed after presenting a list of demands to the banana plantation manager. Fifteen days later, the union's treasurer was killed and its president was wounded. Subsequently, SINTRAEXPOBAN dropped its demands, its locals were closed for a period of time, and some 250 of its members withdrew from the union.[100]

Midway through the 1970s, then, it became clear to Urabá's workers that their access to local political offices was blocked by the political stranglehold of the

---

[99] The inability for Urabá's banana unions to establish themselves as a powerful force in the face of local labor repression in the 1960s and 1970s is well documented in the literature (Beltrán 1996; Botero Herrera 1990; Carroll 2011; García 1996; Ramírez Tobón 1997).

[100] As it turned out, the only union to survive this period of intense repression was Sindejornaleros, which was affiliated with the *Movimiento Obrera Revolucionario y Independiente* (Revolutionary and Independent Workers Movement, MOIR), a splinter Maoist party faction with no attachments to any guerrilla insurgency group. Sindejornaleros, however, remained marginal in its capacity to organize in the face of such repression (Botero Herrera 1990:156–58; Carroll 2011:62–65).

Guerristas while their access to national politics was blocked by the continuing authoritarian and exclusionary legacy left by the National Front party system. Moreover, their efforts to mobilize on the plantations by forming representative unions were met with stiff repression. Given this economic and political oppression, it is not at all surprising that the region became a hotbed of leftist guerrilla activity by the closing years of the decade. Indeed, the appearnce of armed guerrilla insurgency groups in the region represented the harsh reality that local workers and their families had "no other way out."[101]

The first to come was the *Ejercito Popular de Liberación* (Popular Liberation Army, EPL), originally founded in the neighboring department of Cordoba in 1967 as the "armed wing" of the Maoist-leaning *Partido Comunista Colombiana – Marxista-Leninista* (Colombian Communist Party-Marxist-Leninist, PCC-ML). Though the EPL's presence was first known in 1970, their intervention in SINTAGRO's strike on the Coldesa plantation in 1976 solidified their association with the union by the end of the decade. A similar relationship emerged with the *Fuerzas Armadas Revolucionarios de Colombia* (Revolutionary Armed Forces of Colombia, FARC), who arose first as Liberal and Communist guerrillas during the period of *La Violencia* and later became affiliated with the Soviet line of the Colombian Communist Party (PCC) in 1966. The FARC already had a strong territorial presence in the agricultural frontier regions located along Colombia's southeastern Llanos, Orinoco river valley, and tropical piedmont regions of Caquetá, Meta, Huila, and Putumayo. By 1972, the FARC expanded northward into the Urabá region through the formation of its *Frente V* (5th Front), which became a primary vehicle of peasant protection against their displacement from cattle ranchers. Similar to the EPL with SINTAGRO, the FARC aligned itself with the local working-class population through its involvement with SINTRABANANO and used this alliance to influence its political work through the *Union Nacional Obrera* (UNO) and later the *Frente Democrático* (FD) parties.

In other words, Augura's strategy of militarizing the plantations and monopolizing local political power worked for a few years to contain the growing power of Urabá's working-class. However, it backfired by the mid-late 1970s, as Urabá's social conflicts were spilled over into the broader regional and national spheres. To be sure, the EPL and FARC guerrilla groups remained limited in their capacity to challenge the power of banana elites in the political realm and on the plantations. However, they were becoming more successful in organizing landless peasants in

---

[101] For a good overview of this line of argumentation, see Goodwin's *No Other Way Out: States and Revolutionary Movements, 1945–1991* (2001).

the rural regions directly outside of the banana-axis municipalities of Urabá and were making some inroads organizing the region's urban squatter settlements. Once established in the region, the guerrillas became a central organization tool of the region's political left. They protected rural and urban squatters from further processes of dispossession while acting as an organizational link connecting these struggles to the labor and political struggles of banana workers.

The formation of this broad leftist alliance of guerrilla groups, unions, and left political parties, however, soon gave rise to a powerful alliance on the political right that brought together Urabá's banana planters, the cattle ranching elites that dominated the surrounding rural regions of Urabá, urban landlords and politicians, as well as military officers, plantation managers, and other professionals that lived and worked in Carepa.[102] Also, it was during this time that Urabá became a major export pipeline for cocaine and other illegal drugs that were being transported from Colombia's urban drug mafias in Medellín out to the Caribbean coast. In their efforts to control rural spaces in and around Urabá, urban drug-trafficking mafias like the Medellín cartel ran into direct conflict with the FARC and EPL guerrillas that had transformed these spaces into rural strongholds. Making matters worse, the drug traffickers began to funnel money into local cattle ranching in order to launder the vast amounts of wealth they had been accumulating in the illegal drug economy. Attacks by guerrillas against local cattle ranchers and landed elites thus spiraled into low-intensity combat between the guerrilla groups and what had become a "newly minted agrarian (narco) elite."[103] Put simply, by the close of the 1970s and early 1980s, the broad left alliance linking banana worker unions, left political parties, and guerrilla groups was met by a broad right alliance between Augura's banana planters and exporters, cattle ranchers, drug-trafficking mafias, and the Colombian policing and military forces. At the heart of this struggle between political left and right was control of the banana plantations, and Augura and its allies were committed to using their access to the authoritarian institutions of the National Front regime to continue to repress banana worker mobilization to ensure their continued growth in the world banana market.

Figure 4.3 depicts this transformation in Urabá's class struggles from the first wave of social protests that culminated in 1975 until the spiraling of violence by

---

[102] The growing importance of banana planters in this alliance was reflected in the change in Augura's name from *La Asociación de Ganaderos y Agricultures de Urabá* (The Association of Cattle Ranchers and Agriculturalist of Urabá in 1963 to *La Asociación de Bananeros y Agricultures de Urabá* (The Association of Banana Producers and Agriculturalists of Urabá) by 1966 (Carroll 2011:61).

[103] Ballvé (2019).

Figure 4.3 Social protests and state repression in the Greater Urabá Region, 1975–82

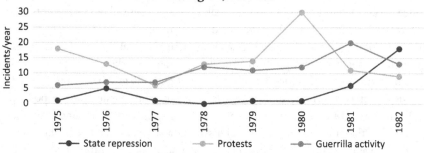

Sources: Coercion Dataset; CINEP Social Movement Database

1982. Between 1975 and 1977, guerrilla activity in the region remained low. However, social protest activity (including labor, peasant, and urban-civic protests) dropped as incidents of state repression increased slightly. Between 1977 and 1980, state repression dropped back down as guerrilla activity grew and social protests skyrocketed up to thirty protests in 1980. This wave of left activity triggered an upswing in state repression that diminished protest activity and reduced guerrilla activity back down to prior levels.

Overall then, we see that Urabá's insertion into the international market as a domestic banana producer and exporter in the 1960s brought hopes for a new surge of developmentalist growth that would mirror the successes experienced during that same period in Viejo Caldas. However, the vertical disintegration of the market, while effective as a strategy of US hegemony, threw up major obstacles to banana exporters that re-peripheralized the producer-exporter niche of the market. This reperipheralization combined with processes of proletarianization in Urabá that proved to be socially explosive. By the close of the 1970s and into the early years of the 1980s, Augura was able to contain banana worker demands by relying heavily on the repressive and exclusive practices of the Colombian state. As long as banana worker militancy was contained through repression, the politics of production would be rechanneled into guerrilla insurgency activities with little bearing on the banana labor process.

5

Despotism, Crisis, and the Social Contradictions of Peripheral Proletarianization in Urabá

Chapter 4 recast the formation of Colombia's banana market in world historical perspective. Doing so brought attention to the fact that the establishment of independent domestic banana producers and exporters throughout Latin and the Caribbean was part of a larger macro-historical process in which banana developmentalism was intended to both pacify a hemispheric wave of banana worker militancy and economic nationalism and buttress US world hegemony during the postwar decades. However, unlike the way that US hegemony manifested itself in the world coffee market during this time, in which the International Coffee Agreements facilitated Colombia's *movement up the coffee commodity chain* into a core-like niche, the restructuring of the world banana market facilitated Colombia's *movement into* a highly peripheralized market niche. In this chapter, I analyze how Colombian independent banana producers – organized in the Colombian Banana Growers Association (Augura) – struggled to adapt to this competitive market niche.

I draw upon as well as extend existing research detailing Urabá's plunge into a chaotic situation of heightened political violence, guerrilla insurgency, state repression, and labor militancy in the 1980s and 1990s. On the one hand, I substantiate insights made by scholars about the ongoing despotism of Colombia's banana sector. Aviva Chomsky (2008:181–82), for example, described Urabá's banana sector as "an extreme version of the neoliberal dream: an ample supply of very poor migrant workers, virtually no government regulation or taxes, and ready access to military force to crush any kinds of protest." During its formative years in the 1960s and 1970s, Urabá's workers were subject to heavy repressive measures that stymied their efforts to organize labor unions and gain access to local political power. And the ongoing repression became painfully evident by the 1990s and early 2000s, when Augura, the Colombian military, and transnational companies like Chiquita's subsidiary BANACOL had all become implicated in waves of paramilitary violence that terrorized Urabá's workers and their communities.

However, such analyses of Urabá's despotism overlook the social contradictions of this system of labor control. Specifically, when viewing Urabá's dynamics through the lens of labor regimes, we see that Urabá's labor regime oscillated between distinct periods of despotism and crises of labor control. In Chapter 4, we saw how Urabá's labor regime was marked by a predominance of despotic mechanisms of labor control that were generally effective in containing banana worker militancy in the 1960s and 1970s. In this chapter, however, we will see how Augura's despotism broke down in the 1980s and early 1990s when the region transformed into a major site of labor militancy and leftist political activity that was only contained once again through acts of paramilitary terror in the 1990s and early 2000s.

These shifts from despotism to crisis and back are evident in Figure 5.1. During the first period, worker protest activity (including labor and civic protests) in the four banana-producing municipalities of Urabá remained under four incidents despite low levels of state repression. Between 1982 and 1993, protest activity skyrocketed, and was followed by an equally massive wave of state-paramilitary repression. By the mid-1990s, protest activity declined once again to its 1970s-levels, followed by a similar drop in the incidents of repression. Brief and smaller waves of worker protests arose again in 2002–3 and 2009, while incidents of repression rose up again to levels experienced in the 1980s. Since then, repression remains high while protests have subsided.

In this chapter, I argue that these historical shifts in Urabá's labor regime dynamics from despotism to crisis and back again resulted from domestic social and political factors, foremost among which was the democratization of the political system and the deployment of paramilitary terror as a strategy of labor

Figure 5.1 State/paramilitary repression and worker protests in Urabá, 1975–2017

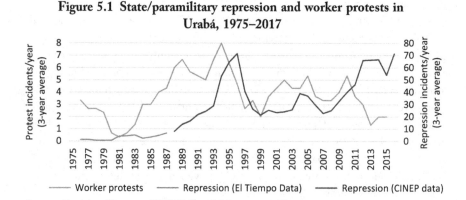

Sources: Coercion Dataset; CINEP Social Movements Database

control. The first section analyzes how Augura's despotic mechanisms of labor control unraveled in the 1980s when the political system was democratized and Urabá's banana workers were granted formal rights to organize on the plantations and in the political sphere. I then argue that the shift back to a despotic regime resulted from Augura's increasing reliance upon paramilitary terror to dismantle the collective power of labor and regain control of the region's banana plantations. I conclude with a comparison of contemporary dynamics of Augura despotism in Urabá with the chronic crises of control experienced by Fedecafé in the coffee region of Viejo Caldas.

Democratization and Augura's Crisis of Labor Control, 1982–1992

From its origins in the 1960s into the 1970s, Augura was highly effective in transforming Urabá into an axis of banana production for export while containing social unrest on its plantations. State interventions were critical to this success, as Augura received both economic assistance and protection under the National Front's developmentalist policies as well as military backing when confronted with threats to their economic and political power from Urabá's banana workers and their allies. Yet, the escalation of class conflicts and political radicalization that was arising in Urabá during the 1970s was in fact a larger national trend that was affecting the country's major urbans centers and other sites of rapid agro-industrialization in the countryside. Urban unrest, labor protests, and student radicalization culminated in massive national "civic strikes" by 1977 and 1978.[1] In the countryside, landless peasants, agricultural workers, and rural communities were mobilizing for national agrarian reform through the *Asociación Nacional de Usuarios Campesinos* (National Association of Peasant Users, ANUC).[2] And as the state responded with growing intransigence and repression, older guerrilla groups like the FARC, EPL, and ELN guerrillas expanded their influence to new regions of the country while new guerrilla groups like the urban-student-based *Movimiento 19 de Abril* (M-19, est. 1970) and indigenous *Quintín Lame* (est. 1974) were created. With the exception of Colombia's cafetero farmers who were experiencing their heyday of coffee developmentalism at this time, broad sectors of Colombian society in the mid-late 1970s were rising up against

---

[1]   For an analysis of the national civic strikes (*paros cívicos*) of the late 1970s, see Archila Neira (1995); Archila Neira et al. (2002); Archila Neira and Pardo (2001).

[2]   See Zamosc (1986) for an analysis of the ANUC movement in the 1970s.

the political monopolies of the traditional parties and the developmentalist economic policies established under the National Front system.

The presidential election of hardliner Julio Cesar Turbay Ayala (1978–82) reflected the national party establishment's last ditch effort to salvage their control of the political system. Turbay instituted a "State of Siege" that criminalized popular protests and granted the Colombian military a central role in the maintenance of what he described as problems of "public order." Granted institutional autonomy, the military began jailing vocal opponents of the regime, activists, and social movement actors, which further legitimated guerrilla insurgency as an appropriate vehicle for mass mobilization. By the end of Turbay's term, the legitimacy of the political establishment was on very thin ice and calls for sweeping social reforms dominated the national political discourse. Not surprisingly, Conservative Belisario Betancur was elected by a landslide to the presidency in 1982 on a campaign promise of instituting sweeping social and political reforms and engaging in peace negotiation talks with the country's leftist guerrilla groups. True to his promises, the Betancur Administration granted unconditional amnesty for political prisoners and armed insurgents in 1982. President Betancur then launched separate cease-fire agreements and peace negotiations in 1984 with the guerrillas, first with the FARC in May (which lasted until December of 1987) and next with the EPL in August (which lasted until November of 1985).[3]

Both groups immediately founded state-sanctioned political parties and mass organizations as a step toward greater participation in the institutional political realm. The FARC founded the *Unión Patriótica* (Patriotic Union, UP) in 1985 in order to broaden support for the Colombian Communist Party (PCC). Though the FARC had been associated with the PCC since 1966, and though it formed various other smaller parties (including the UNO and FD), neither the PCC nor its smaller party fronts placed much weight in electoral politics at the local level due to institutional impasses established under the National Front and that continued during this period. The UP thus became the first significant effort by the FARC-PCC to amass support for both the revolutionary as well as the electoral struggle. As such the PCC intended to "combine all forms of struggle" through the state via the UP party, at the point of production via unions, and through the armed insurgency actions of the FARC. In contrast to such efforts by

---

[3] Betancur also negotiated with the M-19 guerrillas, though this ended tragically with the group's occupation of the Palace of Justice in downtown Bogotá and the Colombian military's destruction of the building, killing guerrillas and justice officials alike (Chernick 1991, 1999).

the FARC, the EPL's *Frente Popular* (Popular Front, FP) was also formed in 1985, but it remained a mass-based political organization because of the EPL's decision to stay clear of electoral politics. They would later rescind this principle, fronting FP candidates for local elections in 1988.

In 1985, Betancur initiated a series of public discussions about social and political policy, or 'National Dialogue,' that included the participation of guerrilla groups. Out of this emerged the central government's decision to permit the direct election of departmental governors and county executives (akin to mayors) beginning in 1988. The period culminated with the demobilization of a number of guerrilla groups, including the EPL in July of 1990. Shortly thereafter, calls for the formation of Constitutional Assembly from a broad base of the Colombian population were met, and a new national Constitution written by a popularly elected assembly comprised of demobilized guerrilla groups, unions, activists, and other sociopolitical and cultural groups went into effect. By 1991, Colombia's political system had been fundamentally reconfigured, marking the final blow to the legacy of the National Front and ushering in high hopes for a new period of peace and greater political participation.[4]

These national-level political reforms had a direct impact on Urabá's labor regime dynamics. The central state's recognition of the political nature of the guerrillas and the implementation of cease-fire agreements offered the insurgents an opportunity to openly organize on the plantations with promises of protection by the central state. Emboldened by these promises of state protection, Urabá's labor activists came out of the shadows and began massive organizing campaigns on the plantations. To be sure, Augura and its allies were not fully compliant with the state's mandate of permitting such labor activity. A number of horrific incidents of repression occurred in and around the municipalities of Apartadó and Carepa during this period, including the assassinations, torture, and death threats of labor and political activists by the Colombian army.[5]

---

[4]   Chernick (1988:53–54); Sánchez (2001).

[5]   According to Leah Carroll (2011:76–77), the repression included the assassination of the president of the Frente Democrático in Apartadó and a banana worker by the Army during the joint SINTAGRO-SINTRABANANO strike of July 1985, the torture of a human rights lawyer, death threats against the president of SINTAGRO and against the president and other leaders of SINTRABANANO, a threat by the army against all members of the Colombian Communist Party, the killing of two activists in the teachers union in Carepa, the death threat of a peasant from soldiers, and the announcement of massive operations by the Colombian military in response to their belief that the guerrillas were infiltrating the unions. Between 1986 and 1987, such incidents included the assassination of a SINTAGRO leader, the assassination of

The repression deployed by Urabá's elites during this period was a horrific indication of their desire to suppress labor unrest and political dissent. Unfortunately, it paled in comparison to the violence they inflicted in the years to come, as evident in Figure 5.1. Moreover, as a mechanism of labor control, it remained largely ineffective during this period. In fact, labor militancy on the plantations was growing during these years. For example, SINTAGRO's membership jumped from 300 in August of 1984 to 2,700 members by December, skyrocketing to 8,000 by June of 1985 and 9,000 by the end of 1986. By 1985, SINTAGRO had organized up to 49.5% of banana plantation land in Urabá. SINTRABANANO, though smaller, leaped from 100 members in 1984 to 2,000 by 1985 and 4,000 by 1986. By 1985 it covered 8.9% of Urabá's banana plantation land.[6]

It was not only the promises of state protection from the central government that emboldened Urabá's working-class. The fact that Betancur was negotiating simultaneously with both the EPL and FARC helped unify the region's political left and facilitated coordinated actions between SINTAGRO and SINTRABANANO. For example, one particular strike in Apartadó in 1985 spread to 12 plantations (1,100 workers). Another one in Carepa involved two plantations, one of which was organized by SINTAGRO and the other by SINTRABANANO. In July of the same year, Urabá's first region-wide strike occurred, which included plantations organized by SINTAGRO, SINTRABANANO, and SINDEJORNALEROS. Despite a slew of arrests, these actions ended up forcing Urabá's military executive to recommend that the unions negotiate with Augura.[7]

Even when the negotiations between Betancur and the EPL had broken down by the end of 1985, union activity in Urabá continued to accelerate at unprecedented rates for another year. SINTAGRO, whose legal charter had been deactivated following the coordinated strike of July 19–20 of 1985, became especially militant. They organized a mass strike in November of

---

three peasants in rural Unión Patriótica strongholds, the torture and imprisonment of a UP activist, two death threats against the president of SINTRABANANO, a death threat against a UP county council executive, the military occupation of a striking banana plantation that led to the arrest of seven SINTRABANANO activists, and death threats from paramilitary squads of UP activists who had participated in the earlier strikes. The assassination of the EPL's spokesperson Oscar William Calvo on November 30, 1985, which brought a sudden halt to the EPL–Betancur negotiations was also a notable incident of repression (although this did not occur specifically in the Urabá region).

[6] Carroll (2011:72–73).
[7] Carroll (2011:71–72).

1985 demanding a reactivation of their charter and another on a plantation in Carepa that lasted thirty-five days, which won them 85% of their demands. Other major strikes included one on December 5, 1985, that included 100% of Apartadó's and 80% of Urabá's banana workforce, one on April 30, 1986, that included 120 plantations, one on December 13, 1986, with 1,500 worker participants, and one on February 20, 1987, when 8,000 workers participated in a work stoppage.[8]

This rise in labor militancy helped Urabá's banana workers win a number of key concessions. First was the state's guarantee of an eight-hour workday by 1985. Also in the same year was the establishment of two new labor courts in the banana axis itself (Apartadó and Chigorodó), reflecting the central state's efforts to intervene more directly and pacify the wave of militancy in the region. Other gains (in wages, bargaining contracts, work conditions) were won through direct mobilization on individual plantations. Most notable, however, was the increase in real wages for the region, which jumped from an estimated $3,700–3,800 pesos Colombianos/month in 1978 to $5,900/month by 1984 and $7,700 by 1986, constituting a direct hit to planters' bottom lines.[9]

Similar gains were also won on the electoral front during this initial reform period. The FARC-CCP's new electoral party, the *Union Patriótica*, made major advances in the region's county council votes in comparison to their earlier experiments with the *Frente Democrático*. In 1986, the UP won 48% of the county council votes in Apartadó (up from 23% held by the FD in 1984), 30% in Chigorodó (up from 8%), 32% in Turbo (up from 18%), 17% in Carepa (up from 0%), and 89% in Mutatá (up from 62%).[10] These electoral advances by the FARC caught the attention of the newly elected president Virgilio Barco (1986–90), who instituted a decree that would mandate local governors to appoint a Patriotic Union representative to any county executive position where the UP had won most of the county council votes as a concessionary mechanism to show his support for the peace process. In 1986, Antioquia's governor was forced to appoint a UP county executive to Apartadó. And in that very year, Apartadó's municipal government passed legislation that created the region's first municipal tax on banana packing to finance public investments. Similar production/packing tax legislation was passed in Chigorodó and Carepa. The packing plant owners (affiliates of Augura) were infuriated by the tax, and they responded by suing

---

[8] Botero Herrera (1990:57–62).

[9] Rey de Marulanda and Córdoba Garcés (1990:32).

[10] RNEC (n.d., accessed July 25, 2019 at www.registraduria.gov.co/-Historico-de-Resultados-3635-).

the local government to reverse it. And when this failed, they simply refused to pay it.[11] Jaime Henrique Gallo, a plantation owner, Guerrista Liberal (elected to the departmental House of Representative), and key figure of Unibán, responded by arguing that the tax was "a strategy against the economic system in which we live," was "undermining the system and the regime," and was "a clear-cut class struggle that has been unleashed against us in the zone."[12]

By the end of 1986, it was evident to Augura and its allies that the government's democratic reforms and peace negotiations with guerrilla groups were threatening the region's balance of class power. Guerrista Liberals were being displaced at the ballot box by the Patriotic Union and the power of Augura to quell labor reforms on the banana plantations was being undermined by the growing strength and unity of Urabá's labor movement. The stage was set for a massive counter-attack against the rising power of workers, but the national political trend was favoring further democratization of the system, which made further militarization of the region politically unviable. As it turned out, Augura responded in three key ways. First, Augura's planters began to "vote with their feet" by reestablishing banana plantations in the Santa Marta region as a way of diversifying their investments and circumventing the growing power of local labor. To be sure, small enduring pockets of banana production had existed in Santa Marta since the first wave of labor protests in the 1970s.[13] However, between 1984 and 1992 Santa Marta's production jumped from 73,900 tons to 540,280 tons exports, roughly 33% of total banana exports. This said, by 1991 SINTRAINAGRO had successfully established their first local in Santa Marta.[14]

As this strategy of moving production to Santa Marta to circumvent the power of banana unions began to fall flat, Augura turned to two more repressive mechanisms. First, at the behest of Henrique Gallo and other political elites, Augura lobbied for the further militarization of the region. By 1984, the military headquarters at Carepa had already been strengthened when the IV Brigade was fortified with the establishment of the *Batallón Voltigeros* (an additional 800

---

[11] Leah Carroll (2011) notes that similar types of tax legislation were passed in 1988 by Liberal-dominated governments in Chigorodó and Carepa, which the banana capitalists paid willingly. She thus concludes that it was not necessarily the tax itself but the fact that elites were becoming displaced politically by "the Left" that triggered such alarm and indignation.

[12] Quoted in Carroll (2011:75–76).

[13] Santa Marta's production grew from 62.1 thousand tons exported in 1975 to 28.4 thousand by 1984. However, the percentage of total exports this represented fell from roughly 18% in 1975 to only 8.7% of exports by 1984 (FAO 1986:12).

[14] FAO (1986:12, 2003:25); MINAGRO (2002).

troops). Yet, Henrique Gallo and the Guerrista Liberals argued that further military involvement was necessary to regain control of the region.[15] In this regard, he found common ideological ground with the country's national military leaders, who scoffed at the executive branch's efforts at negotiation and continued to advocate militarized rather than political responses to workers' threats from below.[16] Indeed, these calls were answered over the next two years, as Urabá transformed into the most heavily militarized region of the country in terms of troops per square kilometer. By 1989, the X Brigade was operating alongside the XI Brigade (est. 1987), *Jefatura Militar de Urabá* (Military Headquarters of Urabá) (est. 1988), and the *Batallón Francisco Paula de Velez* (est. 1989), each of which held an average 800 soldiers.

Second, Henrique Gallo and the Guerristas turned to paramilitary violence against Urabá's working class. Gallo wrote, "as long as (the president, the ministers, the governor, and the armed forces) give us slow, late solutions that make us despair, we must form our own strategies."[17] Gallo himself regularly equated the elected officials and peaceful activists of the UP with the guerrillas themselves, all of whom he called "subversives" and "anarchists." These sentiments reverberated all the way up to the leadership of Augura as well. In fact, the president of Augura, Jose Manuel Arias Carrizosa, himself was a former Justice Minister who openly pleaded for governmental sanctioning of civilian "self-defense groups."[18] These calls for "our own strategies" thus set a dangerous precedent for other elites in Urabá who also felt threatened by the wave of protest and guerrilla activity and abandoned by the executive branch of the central state.[19]

---

[15] Carroll (2011:90–91).

[16] For analyses of the social class origins of Colombia's paramilitaries, see Chernick (1988, 1999); Romero (2003); Medina Gallego (1990); Cubides (2001); Hristov (2014).

[17] Quoted from Carroll (2011:76).

[18] Ramírez Tobón (1997:126–27).

[19] In a particularly telling speech, Henrique Gallo argued that, "the apathy of the agricultural and banana sectors have allowed the Liberal and Conservative parties . . . to weaken to such an extent that they lost (Apartadó's county elections) to anarchic forces that have been gaining ground rapidly and dangerously; today they control the administration of the most important county in Urabá. If we do not become aware of the urgent and unpostponable need to participate, the county of Apartadó will not only have a Communist county executive appointed by the Governor (and removable by him), but one directly elected for a period of two years . . . not subject to any kind of supervision. These men [the elected officials of the UP] have to proceed in accordance with a philosophy, a doctrine and a discipline which is dictated to them from a place far from Urabá . . . The order and the philosophy of the Communist Party are dictated . . . in Moscow and Peking." Quoted in Carroll (2011:75–76).

Augura thus began to draw heavily on its strategic political alliance with local cattle ranchers and narco-traffickers to repress the rising power of labor. During this time, this coalition of elites began to form privately funded paramilitary militias to obtain and protect their lands from guerrillas operating in the region. These paramilitaries repeatedly cited their reason to exist as "self-defense" against the onslaught of the guerrillas. However, the "self-defensive" character of these militant reactionary groups became more and more "offensive" and more geographically unified as they consolidated into regular paramilitary armies that operated across large tracts of the Greater Urabá region.[20] This was the case for the *Autodefensas Campesinas de Córdoba y Urabá* (Peasant Self-Defense Group of Córdoba and Urabá, ACCU), the dominant paramilitary force in the region that later became the central bloc of the infamous national paramilitary organization, the *Autodefensas Unidas de Colombia* (United Self-Defenses of Colombia, AUC). The ACCU began under the leadership of Fidel Castaño, a staunch anticommunist and key figure in the military wing of Medellín's drug cartel during its heyday (1986–90). A large landowner by birth, Castaño dedicated two of his many ranches in the adjacent department of Córdoba as the center of his paramilitary operations following the FARC's abduction and assassination of his father in 1984. He began with 300 regular fighters, whom he trained and equipped using a monthly allowance provided by the Medellín Cartel. After Castaño's break with the Cartel in 1989, the ACCU began to depend more upon its alliances with individuals with links to Augura and other elite organization in the region. By 1990, the ACCU had paramilitary bases in all four of the banana-axis municipalities in addition to those held in neighboring Arboletes and Necoclí.[21]

The paramilitary alliance linking narco-landowners to Urabá's banana capitalists led to a massive increase in incidents of terror perpetrated by paramilitary forces, often operating with direct and indirect assistance from the Colombian army, against Urabá's banana workers and their families. The most atrocious incidents of paramilitary violence during this period were two massacres. The first occurred in March of 1988 on two banana plantations in the municipality of Currulao (adjacent to Apartadó), when the army along with paramilitaries with links to the ACCU killed twenty-eight people, including workers affiliated with SINTAGRO and *Frente Popular* activists. A second massacre occurred in the paramilitary stronghold region of Puerto Boyacá (Magdalena Medio), in which paramilitary assassins associated with narco-traffickers were found to be linked to

---

[20] Romero (2003).
[21] Ramírez Tobón (1997:127–34).

Figure 5.2 Incidents of state-paramilitary repression by perpetrator in Urabá, 1975–2017

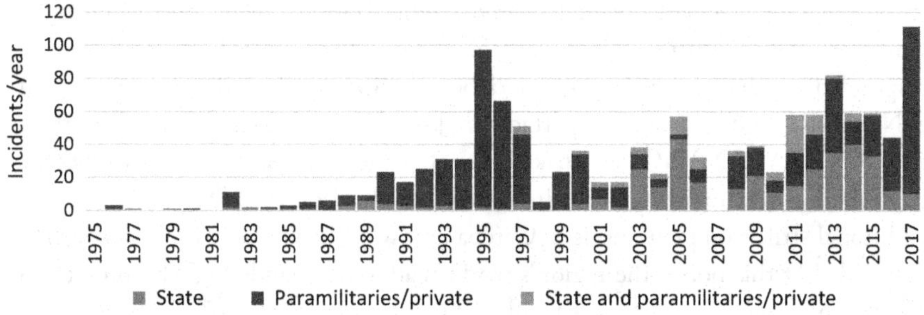

Source: Coercion Dataset

the *Batallón Voltigeros of Carepa.*[22] Other incidents included: the killing of an activist associated with the CCP-affiliated *Juventud Trabajadora Colombiana* (Colombian Worker Youth, JTC) by an assassin who fled into the local police station for protection (March 1988); the killing of nine and the disappearance of sixteen peasant squatters in Turbo (April 1988); a series of five collective killings that occurred in the banana-axis in the days immediately following military actions (August 1988–June 1989); the disappearance of forty-two peasants in a *Frente Popular* stronghold region of Turbo, seven of whom were found dead on the properties of Fidel Castaño in Córdoba (January 1990); two massacres in EPL stronghold regions of Necoclí (January and March 1990); and two massacres in Apartadó (March 1990).[23] Figure 5.2 illustrates vividly how paramilitary repression became the primary form of labor repression in Urabá during this period.

Despite this escalation in the number of incidents of labor repression in the late 1980s and early 1990s, Urabá's working class continued to press forward with their militancy and organizing activities. This was due in large part to growing political unity among the region's unions and leftist political parties. For example, the breakdown of the government's cease-fire agreement with the FARC in December of 1987 led once again to the alignment of the statuses of the two guerrilla groups vis-à-vis the central government. With the EPL and FARC on the same side in the war against the state, SINTAGRO and SINTRABANANO began to coordinate actions on Urabá's banana plantations. A list of demands was negotiated between SINTAGRO and SINTRABANANO and presented jointly

---

[22] Botero Herrera (1990:182–86).
[23] America's Watch (1990:21).

to Augura later that year, which led to wins on wages, daily and weekly working hours, housing and benefits, provisions for job security and the curtailment of subcontracting practices meant to weaken unionization drives. And when individual plantations were slow to accept the regional agreement, both unions responded with an explosion of labor militancy, including a series of SINTAGRO-led strikes in Apartadó in June that involved over 500 workers and SINTRABANANO-led strikes on 63 plantations of over 4,000 workers, culminating in a regional strike in September. In 1988, SINTAGRO led two additional strikes on plantations in Carepa that won the workers over 90% of their demands. At this point, the region's workers added demands for state protection for striking workers and respect for their human rights.[24]

---

[24] As Leah Carroll (2011:91–95) aptly points out, perhaps the most notable among the strikes of the period, one that cemented labor unity and thus strengthened rather than weakened the collective action efforts of Urabá's banana workers, was the "Military ID-card strike" of September 1988. It was only one month after the March massacre of over twenty banana workers in the municipality adjacent to Apartadó (Currulao) that the new Jefatura Militar was established in Urabá. This was not only objectionable given the military's complicity in the massacre, but additionally, the new military chief of Urabá, General Arias Cabrales, ordered that all banana workers (male/female, union/nonunion) wear special ID cards that included personal information about each individual worker. Workers were also commanded to inform the new Battalion about any movements they or their families made to and from the region in order to control nonemployees' access to the plantations. Fearing that these ID cards would make them easy targets, labor leaders demanded the withdrawal of the ID cards and the immediate resignation of General Arias. On September 15, 1988, SINTAGRO and SINTRABANANO jointly organized a strike that spread to the rest of the banana-axis region and included 26,000 workers. A week later these protests had morphed into a massive region-wide strike that brought commerce and transportation in the four banana-axis urban centers to a halt. The confrontation coincided with the mass exodus of 5,000 rural farmers who had been displaced by the guerrilla-military combat that was occurring in the surrounding regions and joined the protests. The strike ended with mediation from Apartadó's county executive, resulting in the withdrawal of General Arias' proposal but with union and Augura agreement over separate ID cards administered by individual plantations (which had already been the policy of most plantations at the time). General Arias was allowed to keep his position. Immediately following the strike, many plantation owners began to call for the cancellation of the legal charters of the region's banana plantation unions. Their calls were answered when the national government cancelled the legal charters of SINTAGRO, SINTRABANANO, and SINDEJORNALEROS following their participation in a national day of protest that had been declared illegal.

Ironically, the state's efforts to criminalize the region's unions only helped fortify the unity of the labor movement. All of Urabá's workers that were released from the three dominant banana unions ended up pouring into the ranks of SINTRAINAGRO, a small union of agro-industrial workers that held a legal charter since 1974. SINTRAINAGRO was recognized as the legal bargaining agent for Urabá's banana workers by the Ministry of Labor by May of 1989 and immediately set forth with a series of smaller strikes that protested the escalation of repression in the region. It held its first major region-wide strike in June of 1989, when they presented a unified list of demands that covered 186 plantations to Augura's offices in Bogotá. Augura's new president responded by refusing to represent the plantation owners, claiming that Augura's role was limited to a "trade organization" rather than a legal representative of plantation owners. After a month of negotiations, however, SINTRAINAGRO had won almost all of its demands regarding health, housing, education, and transport subsidies. As for the remaining demands (including salaries, bonuses, and "right to life" protections against worker repression), these negotiations came to a standstill that lasted for months. In October, two members of SINTRAINAGRO's negotiating committee were assassinated and the union responded by holding a strike in November that culminated in a region-wide protest. Peasants and workers took over the county administration buildings of Turbo, Apartadó and Necoclí, where they set up tents, remaining there for over a month. As sanitation conditions degenerated, the protest sites became afflicted with cases of cholera. Negotiations resumed thereafter, leading to an agreement by the end of November in which the workers won 70% of their demands. Moreover, it is widely claimed that this particular strike paved the way for the commencement of a new era characterized by institutionalized labor–capital bargaining activities. Rather than occur on individual plantations, future labor disputes would take place between Augura and SINTRAINAGRO, at two-year intervals, in the relative safety of Bogotá. This institutionalization of Urabá's labor–capital conflicts brought a steady decline in strike activity in the coming years, but did not negatively impact SINTRAINAGRO's union membership, which obtained a high point of roughly 90% of the total banana labor force of Urabá. This institutionalization of Urabá's labor–capital conflicts had an immediate impact on protest activity at the point of production. On the one hand, with the exception of a number of one-day work stoppages to protest the persistence of labor repression, incidents of major strike activity on the plantations began to slide downward beginning in the closing months of 1990. Furthermore, the capacity for guerrillas to regulate union activity according to their geopolitical and military needs was sharply reduced by the formalization of the biannual negotiating interval.[25]

---

[25] Rivera Zapata (2004:28).

Similar gains were made on the electoral front by Urabá's working class. The first direct elections of county executives came in March of 1988. The Patriotic Union, who had now formed a coalition with the *Frente Popular*, easily won the election in Apartadó (with 46% and 11% of the vote, respectively). Though they did not win a majority of votes in the other four municipalities of the banana-axis, the UP-FD managed to siphon off a greater portion of county council positions, including 27% in Carepa. By 1990, the coalition persisted, allowing the UP-FD to maintain their positions at the local level as well as to win one member each to the House of this access to local political power continued to buttress the movement of unions on the plantations as well as working-class districts in the neighborhoods and rural peasant sectors. Leah Carroll (2011:68–81) notes that Patriotic Union executives were much more likely than their Liberal predecessors to intervene favorably in strike activity as well as use their fiscal resources to finance public works projects and developmentalist-type investitures in the region. Such efforts included the purchase of land to legalize urban squatter settlements, subsidized housing initiatives and home improvement loans, the construction of public schools (with more teachers and school *cafeterías*) in peasant and worker areas, and the provision of basic infrastructure such as drainage systems, paved roads, electrification and water systems, and so forth.

By the early 1990s, Urabá's working class was winning the war over control of the plantations and local political offices and they were using this power to obtain key victories and concessions from Augura. Yet, these labor gains were coming at increasing costs, as each labor action triggered intense backlashes of violence and repression. And this wave of paramilitary terror and drug-infused violence was not only occurring in Urabá. During this time, Colombia was undergoing its worst period of social and political violence brought on by the addition of drug-trafficking cartels and paramilitary forces that "multiplied" what was already an intense armed conflict between leftist guerrillas and the state.[26] Three national presidential candidates had been assassinated, including the popular Liberal Luis Carlos Galán (August 1989), the Patriotic Union's Bernardo Jaramillo (March 1990), and the M-19's Carlos Pizarro León-Gómez (April 1990). The Patriotic Union party of the FARC was particularly vulnerable to campaigns of terror and reactionary violence orchestrated by paramilitary groups affiliated with drug-traffickers. In 1987, a little more than a year after their entrance onto the political stage, an estimated 111 UP militants had been assassinated. In 1988, another 276 were killed, and by 1989

---

[26] For analyses of the expansion of Colombia's armed conflict in the 1980s and 1990s, see Bergquist et al. (1992, 2001); Chernick (1999, 2003); Richani (2002).

138 were added to the death march.[27] Gonzalo Sánchez (2001:6) notes that "their entire party ... was decimated between 1989 and 1992."

National frustration with the Barco Administration's apparent inability or unwillingness to control the country's spiral of political violence led to the election of Cesár Gaviria (1990–94), the Liberal Party candidate who rode the wave of electoral support for frontrunner, Luis Carlos Galán, a political reformer and staunch enemy of the country's drug cartels who was assassinated by one of their *sicarios* (hitmen) in August of 1989. Upon his election, Gaviria brought to fruition efforts by the previous administration to demobilize several of the country's guerrilla groups, including the M-19, most of the EPL, the indigenous Quintín Lame, and an offshoot of the ELN called the *Partido Revolucionario de Trabajadores* (Revolutionary Workers Party, PRT). He also oversaw a national plebiscite that called for the formation of an elected Constituent Assembly to rewrite the country's constitution in order to make it more inclusive of the interests and demands of nontraditional parties and marginalized groups. As it turned out, demobilized guerrilla groups were granted significant influence in the constitutional assembly.[28] Guerrilla groups that refused to demobilize, including the FARC, ELN, and a dissident faction of the EPL, were excluded from this process.[29]

Once again, these national-level political processes had a direct impact on Urabá's labor regime dynamics. Importantly, the peace talks and eventual demobilization of the EPL guerrillas granted them a number of concessions from the Gaviria administration. Among these was the executive's mandate to pull the *Jefatura Militar* from the region, leaving only the two remaining battalions and the X Brigade from the state's coercive arsenal. The EPL were also granted two representative positions within the Constituent Assembly, providing them with a greater opportunity to directly affect the politics of the new national constitution. And while a total of 2,149 EPL guerrillas turned in their arms and applied for government programs for demobilized insurgents (*reinsertados*), the opportunity allowed the group to form a new political party, called the *Esperanza, Paz y Libertad* (E.P.L.), which was granted promises of greater state protection in order to avoid the type of dirty war that had decimated the FARC's Patriotic Union party some years earlier.[30]

---

[27] Dudley (2004:130).

[28] The M-19 won 26.4% of the vote and nineteen delegate positions; the Quintín Lame won 2.7% and two delegates; the EPL won two delegates; and the PRT won one delegate.

[29] Bejarano (2001:56).

[30] Livingstone (2004:188–89); Author interview with former EPL leader in Medellín, Antioquia on November 8, 2004.

In addition to this newfound status vis-à-vis the central government, the workers affiliated with the E.P.L. continued to comprise an estimated 71% of SINTRAINAGRO members, and SINTRAINAGRO's power at the point of production was arguably at an all-time high by 1990–91. This put Augura in an awkward position vis-à-vis the central government, which prioritized regional peace and therefore pressured Augura to cave on some of labor's demands. Sandwiched between pressures from SINTRAINAGRO as well as from government, Augura granted a number of major concessions to Urabá's banana workers. For the first time, Augura invited representatives from SINTRAINAGRO to its annual Banana Conference held in Cartagena in order to partake in discussions about the future of the regional economy. Also, with the mutual aid of the departmental government of Antioquia, Augura donated the equivalent of US$33,000 to finance a special "peace fund" to facilitate the reinsertion of demobilized EPL guerrillas. Finally, Augura collaborated with the E.P.L. party activists and the regional Catholic Diocese to design a social pact for the region that would seek to address the basic needs of the population through redistributive measures financed by Augura. This "Pacto Bananero" was a major win for the region's workers because for the first time Augura's directors admitted some form of responsibility for the social and economic development of Urabá.

In return for these concessions, SINTRAINAGRO agreed to promote Augura's demand of increased productivity on the plantations and both sides vocalized a "mutual commitment to compromise."[31] The acreage of banana production expanded to a record high of some 44,000 ha in the ensuing years, with 51,000 boxes exported and the 42.9 tons of bananas produced per hectare by the end of 1991, as Augura had wanted. And for the first time in Urabá's history, concessions were gained by Urabá's banana proletariat in the absence of strike activity. SINTRAINAGRO asked for a 55% pay raise and accepted 30%, asked for 50% improvements in benefits and accepted 31%, including 40% of what they requested in improved organizing conditions.[32]

As it turns out, this was the historic high point of banana worker strength in Urabá. The democratization and peace negotiation processes facilitated significant increases in labor and political activism and Augura was forced to abide by the sector's first and only redistributive social compact. However, the central government's failure to effectively demobilize and incorporate the country's largest guerrilla

---

[31] As Leah Carroll (2011:94–95) notes, AUGURA' directors were planning to increase production in order to take advantage of the opening of the Eastern European and Russian markets following the fall of the Soviet Union in 1989.

[32] Carroll (2011:95–96).

groups, the FARC and ELN as well as dissident EPL factions, created the context for a new wave of militarization. And, Augura's alliance with drug-trafficking cattle ranchers was strengthening, as both came to view paramilitarism as the only viable solution to the growing power of Urabá's political left. The stage was set for a massive elite backlash set upon uprooting the presence of the guerrillas and therefore lifting the protective blanket off of the region's working class.

"Finishing the Task …": Paramilitarism, Militarism, and the Return to Despotism, 1993–2007

The Pacto Bananero helped pacify labor unrest on Urabá's plantations for the first few years of the 1990s, but other factors continued to pose an immediate threat to the region's ruling class. In contrast to the demobilized EPL, the FARC continued to maintain a territorial hold over the rural southern half of Urabá and their national territorial presence and organizational strength was growing rapidly.[33] Moreover, escalating violence against Patriotic Union party affiliates taught the FARC's leadership that they should be cautious to demobilize without first providing measures to prevent a repressive backlash. For their refusal to disarm, the FARC were excluded from the Constituent Assembly despite their desire to participate and negotiate. Perhaps as punishment for this refusal to disarm, Gaviria ordered a military attack on the FARC's national headquarters in the southern department of Meta in December of 1990 at the same time the Constitutional Assembly was busy debating reforms in Bogotá. To complicate matters worse, the demobilized EPL itself also feared the type of repressive terror that had annihilated the Patriotic Union after disarming some five years earlier. In fact, they were brought to the bargaining table in the first place only after repeated massacres of its rural peasant base and its near total defeat on the battlefield by the ACCU in their former rural stronghold in the northern part of Urabá. This explains why the EPL leadership negotiated a separate nonaggression agreement directly with paramilitary leaders Ariel Otero and Fidel Castaño during the time of their demobilization talks with the government. Though this was a preventative measure that benefited E.P.L. party activists, in effect it ceded the remaining portion of EPL territory in Urabá to the ACCU and thus helped strengthen paramilitary control in the region.[34]

---

[33] Echandía Castilla (1999).

[34] Carroll (2011:93–94); Author interview former EPL leader in Medellín, Antioquia on November 8, 2004.

Figure 5.3 Combat activity in the greater Urabá Region, 1975–2016

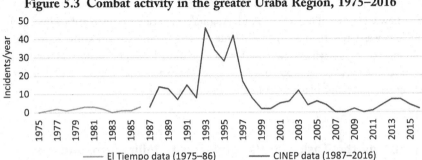

Source: Coercion Dataset

With the consolidation of the northern part of Urabá in the hands of the ACCU and the strengthening of the FARC's territorial presence to the south, it comes as no surprise then that combat activity between these two regional giants escalated during this period. Figure 5.3 depicts this period of heightened combat activity between guerrilla groups and state-paramilitary forces.

In fact, by the middle of 1991, the FARC began to coordinate their combat activity with the country's remaining insurgency forces (the ELN and the dissident faction of the EPL led by Francisco Caraballo), forming an umbrella guerrilla organization, the *Coordinadora Guerrillera Simon Bolivar* (The Simon Bolivar Coordinated Guerrilla Group, CGSB). And despite the fact that the CGSB entered into further negotiations with the Gaviria administration by the end of 1991, neither the guerrillas nor the state agreed to a cease-fire.

The escalation of conflict on the military front was matched by consistent displacement of the Guerrista Liberals in the electoral front. For one, the Patriotic Union continued to hold onto its county executive position for Apartadó throughout the period, winning the election once again in 1992 and increasing their share of county council position to 44% by 1990 and 48% by 1992. Though less popular than the UP, the E.P.L. party managed to win 16% of the county council vote in 1990 (under the *Frente Popular*) and 19% by 1992. Both parties continued to use these positions to support the labor and urban squatter movements by pressuring the state to intervene in property and labor conflicts and to invest in public infrastructure and local development projects.[35] In contrast, the Guerrista

---

[35] The UP executive for Apartadó, for example, played a leading role in the construction of a new marketplace, transportation terminal, a paved and beautified main street, and the provision of cable television. The UP also led mass demonstrations in May of 1991 to protest Liberal Party plans to establish a "free trade zone" in the region as well

Liberals continued to lose ground at the local level, dropping from 45% of the county council vote in Apartadó in 1984 to 15% by 1992. Such losses came at the national level as well. When a special congressional election was held in October of 1991, neither Jaime Henrique Gallo nor Bernardo Guerra Serna nor any other banana plantation owner was elected to National Senate or House of Representatives.[36]

These advances by Urabá's working class continued to elicit repressive counter-responses by local elites allied with the military and paramilitary forces. Most of this repression focused on UP politicians, activists, and unionists. Acts of violence committed against E.P.L. party affiliates were much more limited due to the nonaggression pact between themselves and the ACCU. Nonetheless, state and paramilitary violence persisted against them as well, including the assassination of eight E.P.L. party activists in Urabá in July of 1991. By 1992, Augura was able to convince the Gaviria Administration to order a re-militarization of the region immediately following the breakdown of governmental talks with the CGSB in May.[37] A new Operations Command was added to the military base in Carepa to fill the void left by the absence of the *Jefatura Militar*. As Augura planned to break the banana social pact through the use of outright coercion if necessary in November, the President Gaviria ordered a "Decree of Internal Commotion" that granted the military greater freedom to carry out counterinsurgency operations in war zones like Urabá without the restraints of due process of the law. It also reduced the autonomy of county executives by threatening removal from office for any elected official found to be an auxiliary to the guerrillas. This decree, only meant to last three months, was renewed three times before being written into permanent law by late 1993. And as if these measures were not enough to regain control of the region, by late 1992 the government declared an all-out "Comprehensive War" on the guerrillas and significantly increased the number of military troops in all combat zones, including Urabá.[38]

Meanwhile, the unity and strength SINTRAINAGRO had developed began to steadily deteriorate as the Gaviria administration strengthened relations with the E.P.L. political party, while simultaneously militarizing relations with the

---

as to support urban squatter protests. The E.P.L. party, for example, organized its first urban squatter invasion in mid-1991 on land that turned out to be owned by a banana plantation owner (Carroll 2011:96–97).

[36] Carroll (2011:101–2).

[37] This was part of a larger military campaign by Gaviria, the crux of which entailed heated operations against the stronghold of the FARC's central command in La Uribe, Meta (Bergquist 2001:xiv).

[38] Carroll (2011:102–3).

FARC. At first, the FARC respected the E.P.L. party's relations with the government despite the fact that the UP was being systematically slaughtered while the E.P.L. was being protected by state forces. They also respected SINTRAINAGRO's labor peace with Augura despite the FARC's desire for more far-reaching concessions to labor. In fact, when the CGSB was formed, the FARC actually used its dominant military weight to restrain the radicalism and militarism of the remaining armed wing of the EPL insurgency group in an effort to maintain "good diplomatic relations."[39] Yet, such influence loosened as time passed while paramilitary violence escalated against the dissident EPL faction. By late 1991, the EPL dissidents had come to believe that their assassinations at the hands of the ACCU were due to military secrets E.P.L. party activists passed on to the Colombian military (and thus to Castaño of the ACCU). The first incident of violence perpetrated against E.P.L. party members occurred in November of 1991. By April of 1992 an estimated 60–70 E.P.L. activists had been slain by their former comrades.[40]

Augura appeared to seize this moment by formally breaking from their commitments under the Pacto Bananero in 1992, less than two years after it came into being. By then, the region's labor-left alliance had broken down completely. The state responded to the demobilized E.P.L.'s appeals for protection by granting them armed escorts, called *Comandos Populares*, who held gun permits and reportedly received support from Colombia's national criminal intelligence agents.[41] These *Comandos* soon came to resemble small militias, which exacerbated the suspicions held by both the dissident EPL insurgents and the FARC that E.P.L. party activists had aligned themselves with the state–paramilitary nexus. By January 1993, it became clear that the FARC had become implicated in this "left-on-left violence" when they were found to have assassinated SINTRAINAGRO's president and E.P.L. activist, Alirio Guevara. The *Comandos* immediately responded by killing the General Secretary of SINTRAINAGRO, who was also a Central Committee Member of the FARC-affiliated Colombian Communist Party. By the end of the year, Gaviria was stepping up the militarization of Urabá, while numerous activists affiliated with one or another guerrilla group were being systematically shot down by armed actors of both the political right and left.[42]

---

[39] Leah Carroll (2000:227) notes that a CGSB communiqué denounced the EPL dissident's kidnapping of the former Minister of State, Argelino Duran, who later died in captivity.

[40] Romero (2003:180); Author interview with SINTRAINAGRO activist in Medellín, Antioquia on November 11, 2004.

[41] This unit is called the *Seccional de Investigación Criminal* (SIJIN).

[42] Romero (2003:181).

In fact, the number of incidents of labor repression during this time began to skyrocket upward at an alarming rate. As Figure 5.3 depicted, the total number of incidents of labor repression jumped from nine in 1989 and twenty-eight by 1993 to a whopping ninety-five incidents by 1995. Some 95% of these incidents were perpetrated by the ACCU and allied paramilitaries, which had come to comprise roughly 4,000–5,000 regularly paid and well-armed soldiers. By 1997, the ACCU's estimated 8,000 soldiers assimilated into what was now a nationally unified paramilitary organization, the United Self-Defenses of Colombia (AUC). They were now the AUC's *Bloque Bananero* operating under the local leadership of Hernán Hernández, who understood his primary task to be the elimination of the political left from the Urabá region.[43]

The Bloque Bananero's *modus operandi* of "draining the water to catch the fish" meant that they fought a two-pronged approach: undermining the guerrillas' territorial hegemony by attacking civilian host populations and fighting low-intensity battles alongside the Colombian military. Regarding the latter, the AUC was quite successful. As early as 1995, they had forcibly wiped the remaining EPL insurgents from the local map. By 1997, even the FARC were forced to succumb, retreating their fifth Front and essentially ceding the entire region to the military–paramilitary nexus. Paramilitary domination of the region was becoming the new social and political reality of Urabá and the Colombian state seemed to be unwilling to stop them. In fact, human rights reports provide evidence showing how the paramilitaries operated during this time with the implicit consent of Colombian military leaders and even coordinated actions.[44] Thus, by 1997 we begin to see coordinated actions involving both paramilitaries and Colombian military units operating together in Urabá. Between 1997 and 2006, the CINEP database detailed no less than thirty-eight incidents of state–paramilitary acts of repression. And while the paramilitaries were officially designated an "illegal armed group" and placed on the US' list of terrorist organizations in 2001, none of the 2,548 incidents of political violence documented in my dataset indicated combat activity or any other act of violence committed by the Colombian state against the paramilitaries or paramilitaries against the state occurring in the four banana-axis municipalities of Urabá between 1975 and 2017.

Without the protective blanket of the guerrillas, the closing years of the 1990s and early years of the 2000s were essentially years of massive paramilitary terror used against civilian noncombatants who had been previously affiliated with the

---

[43] The AUC grew to a peak of some 20,000 regular soldiers by 2004 (Human Rights Watch 2010).

[44] America's Watch (1990); Human Rights Watch (2010).

region's political left, including banana unionists, community activists, human rights workers, and leftist party officials. The Samper Administration (1994–98) essentially followed in the footsteps of Gaviria by maintaining the military affront against the guerrillas despite evidence that the military was operating in cahoots with the AUC. And even the Pastrana Administration (1998–2002), which forged a peace negotiation strategy with the FARC between 1999 and 2002, eventually became disgruntled and sought military solutions to the guerrillas' territorial expansion. On the one hand, both of these administrations were successful in lobbying the United States government for increasing doses of military aid to quell the armed insurgency groups, who themselves had become reliant upon involvement in the illegal narcotics economy to finance their organizational growth. On the other hand, the central state continued to turn its eyes away as paramilitary forces engaged in massacre after massacre. As both sides grew, levels of combat activity and repressive violence rose with it. And as the deaths of noncombatants escalated, and as the involvement of the guerrillas in such tactics as kidnappings and taxation of narcotics production intensified, so did the frustrations of the political Left with armed insurgency as the appropriate modality for winning concessions for the country's working class.

Between 1993 and 2002, the AUC's *Bloque Bananero* is reported to have carried out 65 massacres with 449 victims in Urabá alone. Apartadó and Turbo in specific bore the brunt of 20 massacres each, with 170 and 120 dead, respectively. By the turn of the century, it was clear that Hernán Hernández had "finished the task" of effectively purging the region of leftist and radical elements within the union movement, in the electoral arena, and on the battlefield. The Liberal party had regained its stronghold over departmental, county executive, and county council positions while the Patriotic Union and E.P.L. either fled for safety or succumbed to paramilitary terror. SINTRAINAGRO, which had only ten years earlier managed to force Augura to finance a social compact that recognized labor and redistributed some of the profits back down to workers, had once again fallen to accepting contracts that offered little to no concessions. The dissident EPL guerillas had been wiped out of the region in combat, and the FARC, who had once controlled the majority of the territory, were forced to retreat to their territorial strongholds in other regions of the country.

A major turn in the national political context came with the election of Álvaro Uribe Vélez in 2002, a hardline conservative who promised a full-scale war against the country's guerrilla groups. In fact, as Uribe launched this war against the country's guerrillas, he engaged in "peace negotiations" with the AUC that began formally in 2003. Critics point out that the entire process of a government–AUC peace negotiation was farcical, as Uribe's claim that the AUC was an "illegal armed group" that was autonomous from the state rather than a paramilitary extension of the Colombian state flew in the face of the evidence. Indeed, Uribe's familial connections with the paramilitaries and drug-traffickers of his home department of Antioquia are well-documented.[45] So it was no big surprise that his dealings with the AUC were characterized by negotiations rather than military violence. By 2005–6, the Uribe administration signed off on the AUC's formal demobilization and "reinsertion" back into Colombian civil society. Demobilized paramilitaries were granted a government stipend, protection from any possible attacks from guerrillas, and guaranteed training and educational services. Paramilitary leaders that were found to be engaged in drug-trafficking were extradited to the United States. However, critics pointed out that extradition actually helped absolve these paramilitary perpetrators from the human rights violations and terrorist activities they had committed against civilian noncombatants over the past decade.[46] In Urabá, by the time of the AUC's demobilization in 2006, the *Bloque Bananero* had not only successfully eliminated the armed left from the region, but they had brutally purged leftist elements from SINTRAINAGRO, local political parties, and community organizations. It was in this context that the "Chiquita Papers Scandal" broke, documenting Chiquita's role in financing paramilitarism in the region since the mid-1990s. Despite this mounting evidence of paramilitary terror, the Uribe government allowed demobilized *Bloque Bananero* members the right to hold onto any land holdings or property they had acquired through their expansion into the Greater Urabá region and were granted impunity for their crimes so long as they agreed to disarm.[47]

In this context of complete paramilitary domination, SINTRAINAGRO's leaders were put in an awkward situation of both representing and advocating for the rights of the region's rank-and-file banana workers while ensuring that these demands would not threaten the continued profitability of the sector or Augura's ability to control labor and the labor process on the plantations.[48] This was no small feat, as the region's workers began to engage in a series of wildcat strikes during the peak years of government–AUC negotiations in 2003–5. However, as Figure 5.3 depicts, this mini-wave of labor unrest was put down by a new wave of labor repression. By then, state military forces arose again as the predominant perpetrator of labor repression in the region. Moreover, even following the formal demobilization of some 31,671 AUC combatants nationally by 2006, it became clear that new smaller paramilitary groups were emerging to fill

[45] Hylton (2006); Hristov (2009, 2014).

[46] Oquendo (2004a, 2004b, 2004c).

[47] Author interview with labor lawyer in Apartadó, Antioquia on July 12, 2009.

[48] Chomsky (2008).

the void left by the AUC. In Urabá, a new group called the Urabeños, and sometimes referred to as *Autodefensas Gaitainistas de Colombia* (AGC) or the *Clan del Golfo*, began to engage in increasing amounts of violence against civilian noncombatants, banana workers, and community and human rights activists.[49]

Trapped once again by a wave of repression, SINTRAINAGRO's leadership has taken the union in two directions. On the one hand, SINTRAINAGRO began to denounce its former political radicalism and association with the region's political left in favor of overt expressions of right-wing politics and support for Augura. As early as 1997, for example, SINTRAINAGRO participated in a "peace march" organized by the Colombian military, despite evidence that General Rito Alejo del Río, commander of the army's Seventeenth Brigade, was openly colluding with the region's paramilitaries. When the General was forced into retirement in 1999 as a result of this collusion, SINTRAINAGRO's president Guillermo Rivera spoke at his retirement party organized by Augura. And when Colombia's National Labor Federation organized a series of national boycotts and strikes calling for an end to labor repression in Colombia in 2003, SINTRAINAGRO broke ranks and publicly opposed the strikes. SINTRAINAGRO's leaders denounced the human rights organizations that were reporting on the rise of right-wing violence and openly sided with President Uribe. Regarding Augura, SINTRAINAGRO's leaders issued public statements emphasizing the "harmony and good will" between Urabá's workers and plantation owners. When asked why the union seemed to ardently support the planters in 2004, SINTRAINAGRO's General Secretary, Hernan Correa, responded by simply stating that "we came to see the boss was not an enemy, he was a partner."[50]

It is not exactly clear why SINTRAINAGRO's leaders have become such open supporters of Augura and the political right, whether this was simply a calculation meant to survive what had become total territorial domination by the paramilitaries or if instead they believed that labor's role should be as a partner to capital. Either way, SINTRAINAGRO also engaged in a second survival strategy during this period, one that also avoided direct conflict with Augura and the paramilitaries. Beginning in the early 1990s, the union began to participate in international union confederation discussions with other Latin American banana unions. By 1993, SINTRAINAGRO joined labor groups from Honduras, Guatemala,

---

[49] The Urabeños have been led by a non-demobilized AUC member, Daniel Rendon Herrera (alias "Don Mario"), brother of the former leader of the "Elmer Cardenas" block of the AUC that had demobilized in 2006. The group is reported to have grown to some 1,120 members by 2009 (Human Rights Watch 2010).

[50] For a detailed analysis of SINTRAINAGRO's rightward shift, see Chomsky (2008:199–211).

Nicaragua, Panama, and Costa Rica to form the Latin American Coordinating Committee of Banana Worker Unions (COLSIBA). Rather than challenge planter control directly, COLSIBA has organized for market-wide labor and regulatory standards meant to minimize the negative impact of competition among producers. Thus, by 2001, COLSIBA was able to forge a voluntary standards agreement with Chiquita Brands to guarantee minimal labor standards and worker rights across the plantations that it purchased its bananas from. Since then, SINTRAINAGRO has engaged in various cross-border solidarity actions in coordination with European and North American transnational labor rights groups in order to draw attention to labor rights issues in the industry, including gendered pay inequality, environmental regulations, and the right to organize.[51]

Augura, for its part, seems to have viewed SINTRAINAGRO's presence in the sector as a permanent fixture of the social and economic landscape.[52] Indeed, it has generally supported SINTRAINAGRO's international efforts to establish market-wide standards, including Fair Trade and other voluntary certification systems. For example, Augura did not intervene in 2005 when a small number of UNIBAN-contracted farms joined together to form the *Bananeras de Urabá* Fair Trade cooperative. Since then, Fair Trade production has grown to over thirty-six Fair Trade-certified banana organizations operating in Urabá and Santa Marta, including eight Fair Trade cooperatives and twenty-eight Fair Trade labor-certified plantations that sell their bananas to the region's major exporters like UNIBAN and Fyffes. These organizations have not only established a set of working and environmental standards for their farms. They have also engaged in various social development initiatives through collectively operated "community development funds" that have financed affordable housing, provided micro-loans to families, and invested in schooling for the children of bananas workers.[53] This said, Augura it is careful to avoid any significant redistributionary efforts such as major taxes on exports that could dull its competitive edge relative to other competitors in the market. Thus, it has supported efforts to use departmental and national finances to invest in local social programs that would serve the needs of banana workers and their communities, including sports fields, parks, schools, health clinics, and the like. However, they remain adamantly opposed to local property taxes and banana export taxes.[54]

---

[51] See Frank (2005); Chomsky (2008); Frundt (2009).

[52] Author interviews with Augura representatives in Bogotá on November 16, 2004, and in Apartadó, Antioquia on July 15, 2009.

[53] Ostertag et al. (2014).

[54] Author interview with two SINTAINAGRO activists in Apartadó, Antioquia on July 15, 2009.

As a growth strategy, Augura's efforts have been relatively successful in adapting to a highly competitive niche as banana exporters. Between 1984 and 2001, Urabá's exports grew from 847,000 tons of bananas on 20,092 ha of land to over 1.14 million tons produced on 29,927 ha. Including Santa Marta's growth, Colombia's banana exports in the early 2000 averaged some 1.6 million tons of bananas per year, making Colombia the sixth largest banana exporter to the world market, supplying 5.4% of the US market and 24.3% of the European Market by 2017.[55] Even still, the competitiveness of the banana market makes such efforts a precarious balancing act. Any evidence that the region's workers may fall back into more radical demands or engage in acts of labor militancy threatens Augura's sense that it can provide these concessions without losing its edge in the market. It is perhaps this sense of precarity that has convinced many of Urabá's banana planters to simply pull out of banana production altogether in favor of the production of African Palm for export. The AUC's *Bloque Bananera* had long encouraged the cultivation of African Palm in the region as a way of laundering money they amassed through their involvement in the illegal drug trade.[56] By the early 2000s, it became clear that African Palm production in the region was killing two birds with one stone. On the one hand, it was helping to break the power of the region's unions by eliminating their jobs. On the other hand, it was facilitating a concentration of capital as narco-dollars were cleaned and new cycles of capital accumulated through the production and sale of African Palm to the world market.[57] It is not clear the extent to which African Palm will replace bananas as the region's primary export commodity. If it does, the potential for despotism and crisis may diminish, at least in the short term. However, given its inability to absorb labor, it would make it even more difficult to ensure that commodity production for the market can act as larger mechanism of social mobility, welfare, and development for the region's workers.

Comparing the Labor Regime Trajectories of Caldas and Urabá

This analysis of Urabá's labor regime highlights the structural contradictions that arise under situations of peripheral proletarianization. Faced with a competitive market, Augura has been pressured to keep banana production costs low and therefore avoid the type of redistributive social compact that proved so critical to

---

[55] FAO (2003:24–25, 2018:13–15).

[56] Human Rights Watch (2010:78–79).

[57] Author interview with human rights activist in Apartadó, Antioquia on July 15, 2009.

the stable social reproduction of Colombia's cafeteros in Viejo Caldas. As As this chapter demonstrated, these efforts rested heavily on ongoing support from the Colombian state, whether this support came in the form of developmental aid, state-directed land grabs, exclusionary and authoritarian political institutions, the militarization of the banana plantations, or the implicit approval of, if not explicit collusion with, paramilitary terror. Importantly, labor dynamics in both the coffee regime of Viejo Caldas and the banana regime of Urabá were shaped by macro-historical processes of US world hegemony in the postwar decades. However, the nature of US hegemony varied significantly across the two cases. In coffee, US hegemony manifested itself in the creation of the International Coffee Agreements that regulated the world market and provided Fedecafé with the ability to avoid the experiences of peripheralization – namely, the extreme pricing volatility of the coffee market – that proved so destabilizing in the periods both before and after the ICA agreements. In bananas, than permit the *movement up* from a peripheral to a core-like niche of the banana chain, US world hegemony facilitated Colombia's *movement into* the market as one of many independent banana producing and exporting countries that compete against one another for access to the distributionary markets controlled by a few monopolistic trans-national fruit companies. This movement into a peripheral niche of the market, and no further, has made it structurally difficult for Augura's banana planters to finance the full demands of the sector's workers without cutting too deeply into their razor-thin profit margins. Augura's balancing act has come with dire consequences for the region's workers and their communities.

This said, the rise of hegemony in Viejo Caldas and despotism in Urabá cannot be explained by macro-structural processes alone. Fedecafé's institutionalization of the Pacto Cafetero was just as much a production of US world hegemony as a response to a prior wave of class conflict that forced the organization to push competitive pressures in the market upward in order to satisfy the demands of what had become a highly radicalized and politically organized class of coffee producers in the 1930s. No such class of radical militants existed in Urabá during the sector's formation in the 1960s. To be sure, there existed such a class of militants in the Santa Marta region during the 1920s and 1930s, and their militancy was part and parcel of the hemispheric wave of unrest that undermined the vertically integrated system that predominated during the first decades of the twentieth century. However, this class had long been dissolved by the time that banana production had moved to its new site of Urabá. Thus, it was not until at least a decade into production that processes of class formation in Urabá consolidated and the region's workers began to organize to pressure Augura and its Guerrista allies to meet their demands. Thus, in sharp contrast to the shifts in the labor regime dynamics of Viejo Caldas that resulted from local and global processes, the major shifts in Urabá's labor regime dynamics arose as the consequence of national political processes. Put differently, Urabá's shift from despotism to crisis and back was neither the result of processes of banana market globalization nor from the adoption of neoliberal policies that were meant to privatize state functions and open the economy to deregulated markets. As we saw clearly in this case study, the US-centered dollar market had been global and deregulated since Urabá began producing bananas in the 1960s. Moreover, the state's economic interventions in the sector came early on as development aid to facilitate the rise of independent banana producers and exporters and later on in the form of intransigent politicians associated with the Guerrista Liberals and military bases. Thus, Colombia's adoption of neoliberal policies intending to deregulate markets, privative public assets, and roll back state protections had little bearing on Urabá's workers, whose only brief experiment with anything that resembled state protections for its population of workers – the Pacto Bananero – existed fewer than two years before Augura was able to retract it with the help of paramilitary terror.

Clearly then, Urabá's shift from despotism to Augura's crisis of labor control resulted from the democratization of the political system, including the dismantlement of the political legacy of the National Front regime and politicization of the guerrilla movements in the 1980s. These processes, at least initially, permitted the region's workers to organize on the plantations and in the political arena without facing an immediate backlash from the state and its security and military forces. Thus, it was not militarization that brought the regime back under the control of Augura in the 1990s, but paramilitarization. The rise of the ACCU and AUC, regardless of its stated *raison d'etre* as "self-defense forces" meant to counter the threat of violence from leftist guerrillas, became the only effective response by local elites to worker demands during a period of political democratization. Thus, paramilitarism in Urabá was a capitalist response to the convergence of a number of historical processes including labor's strength locally, political democratization nationally, and a waning US world hegemon that was unwilling to permit collective action from banana producers to further restructure the market in ways that might threaten the profitability of US fruit transnationals.

Finally, it is important to clarify that the two case studies analyzed thus far are not "isolated" from one another, but must instead be understood as causally interrelated. Labor dynamics in Colombia's coffee regime impacted those of Urabá's banana regime, and vice versa. And these intraregional effects occurred in three key ways. First, the state's ongoing support to Augura since the 1960s was due in large part to the general feeling that agro-export production was not simply a modality of capital accumulation, but that it held the promise of providing locals with a stable livelihood. Indeed, at the time of Urabá's early transformation into a site of banana production, coffee had already transformed regions like Viejo Caldas into highly developed and stable rural communities. Indeed, the successes of Colombia's coffee sector provided both departmental and national political-economic elites with a sense of developmental optimism that clearly shaped the politics of the banana sector. This belief, articulated most strongly by Guerrista Liberals, was that the state should actively invest in the development of the banana sector so that profits would eventually trickle down to the local economy and the pockets of the industry's workers and their communities. When such monies did trickle down to workers and their communities, as had occurred in the coffee sector, the ends would justify the means. Or put more starkly, even if paramilitarism was required to squelch worker radicalism, it would eventually result in a social outcome that was favorable to all, not just to local elites. For Augura and its allies, in other words, there was no alternative form of local development than through the continued expansion of banana production for the market.

Second, it was not only that coffee provided Colombia's political and economic elites with a ready-made case of how capitalist development can lift all boats. It was also that the success of Colombia's coffee regime created a significant bastion of electoral support for the traditional Liberal and Conservative parties. This support continued throughout the years of the National Front regime, when Urabá's workers were denied meaningful access to local political office. And it continued into the 1970s and 1980s when Liberal and Conservative administrations militarized the banana-axis and used repressive force to quell the region's burgeoning labor, squatter, and peasant movements. Put differently, since Colombia's cafeteros were incorporated as junior partners in Fedecafé's Pacto Cafetero, and since Fedecafé took on the responsibility of protecting cafetero livelihoods, their economic lives were largely unaffected by the exclusionary politics of the National Front system or by the democratization process of the 1980s. As we saw from the last case study, it was the abrogation of the International Coffee Agreement's quota and tariff system in 1989, not national political endeavors, that put an ax to their social and economic stability.

Finally, it was not only that the cafeteros' experiences shaped the developmentalist illusions of Colombian state officials or that the cafeteros themselves supported these illusions at the ballot box. The conservative leanings of the country's cafeteros also forged a political wedge in what had become a formidable and highly radicalized national social movement calling for fundamental social, political, and economic rights by the middle of the 1970s. As we shall see in greater detail in the next case study, the developmentalist politics of the Colombian state during the postwar decades had created vast swaths of disaffected urban proletarians and unemployed subproletarians as well as landless farmers and rural migrant workers, all of which became increasingly organized politically by the 1970s. Rather than side with these movements and support national efforts for political and agrarian reforms, the country's cafeteros sided with the political establishment, the result of which was increasing militarization of the countryside and criminalization of protests. By the late 1970s and early 1980s, what had initially arisen as mass protest movements and political organizations had transformed into armed insurgency rebellions that increased the stakes of the conflicts as well as their outcomes. In Urabá, the rise of paramilitarism was indeed one unintended consequence of such processes. As we shall see in the next case study, another consequence to arise out of the ashes of the conflicts of the 1970s and 1980s was leftist guerrilla insurgent hegemony.

Case Study #3

THE RISE AND FALL OF FARC COUNTER-HEGEMONY IN THE COCA REGIME OF CAQUETÁ

"If the coca market ends, this place will become a shithole (*mierdero*) again," María, cocalero (coca farmer) from San Isidro, Caquetá.[1]

"We have accepted it. We will earn less with other crops ... But what choice is there?" Edward, 23, cocalero from Los Ríos, Caquetá.[2]

Unquestionably, the 2016 Peace Accords marked a colossal turning point in Colombian history. With the demobilization of the AUC paramilitaries formally completed in 2006, hopes were high that the demobilization of the country's most formidable guerrilla army, the FARC, would overcome the next major hurdle to a final resolution to what had been nearly six decades of protracted armed conflict.[3] With the FARC's pacification and incorporation into the formal political arena with a new name for the same acronym, the *Fuerza Alternativa Revolucionaria para el Común* (the Common Alternative Revolutionary Force, est. 2017), the final steps to lasting peace in Colombia would come from robust political and institutional reforms and rural development plans that would, among other things, replace Colombia's vast narcotics industry with legal alternatives.

Yet, rather than usher in a period of optimism, the years since the passage of the peace accords have brought uncertainty and fears of an even more precarious future. On the one hand, this uncertainty stems from compelling evidence of the continuation, and recent escalation, of targeted assassinations, death threats, and other acts of political violence against Colombian leftist activists, including some of the FARC's demobilized political party candidates.[4] As we saw from the last case study, some of this violence has been perpetrated by re-formed paramilitary

---

[1] Quoted in Ciro (2018).
[2] Quoted in Casey (2017).
[3] The conflict is estimated to have cost approximately 250,000 lives and roughly 8 million internally displaced persons (IDMC n.d.).
[4] Daniels (2019).

groups like the *Urabeños*, which arose to fill the social and political vacuum left by the disbanded AUC paramilitary federation in 2006. Human rights organizations note that Colombian state security forces have also been implicated in many of these incidents.[5] Adding to the complexity of this process, a splinter faction of the FARC that refused to demobilize continues to operate in some pockets of the country and there is evidence that the National Liberation Army (ELN) and factions of the Popular Liberation Army (EPL), Colombia's last remaining Marxist guerrilla groups, have established operations in some regions previously held by the FARC.[6]

Popular support for the peace agreement, which had been flimsy from the start, appears to be waning as time goes on. President Iván Duque Márquez (2018–22), a vocal opponent of the peace process from its beginnings, has since stymied its implementation at every turn by blunting the investigation of paramilitary connections with various conservative politicians and military leaders, declawing the crop replacement and FARC re-incorporation initiatives, and demanding a return to negotiations that would allow former FARC guerrillas to be extradited and sentenced for crimes they had committed during the war.[7] As recently as August of 2019, two FARC leaders that had been central negotiators in the peace process, Iván Márquez and Jesús Santrich, called for a return to arms, arguing that the upsurge in violence proves that the Colombian government has failed to live up to its promises under the agreement.[8]

The quotations above, from Maria and Edward, highlight the fears and frustrations that coca-producing farmers (cocaleros) have had with the crop substitution and rural development initiatives that have come out of the peace accords. As they make clear, illegal coca production was one of the few viable economic livelihood strategies available to them. While they are not opposed to its substitution for another livelihood strategy, including other agricultural crops, whatever replaces coca must at least provide enough income to meet their household survival needs as coca did in the past. Otherwise, they may be forced to go back to producing it, which would then create the conditions for the return of illegal armed groups to protect and regulate transactions in the local coca market.

But uncertainty about the future of the peace process also raises deeper questions about the *raison d'etre* of the guerrillas and the coca economy in the

---

[5] From the FARC's demobilization in 2016 until the end of 2018, for example, some Colombian 702 activists and social leaders, including 135 FARC ex-combatants, were murdered (FLIP n.d.; Human Rights Watch 2010).

[6] Romero Sala (2019).

[7] Murphy and Vargas (2019).

[8] Escobar Moreno (2019).

Map 4 Upper and Lower Caguán regions of Caquetá, Colombia

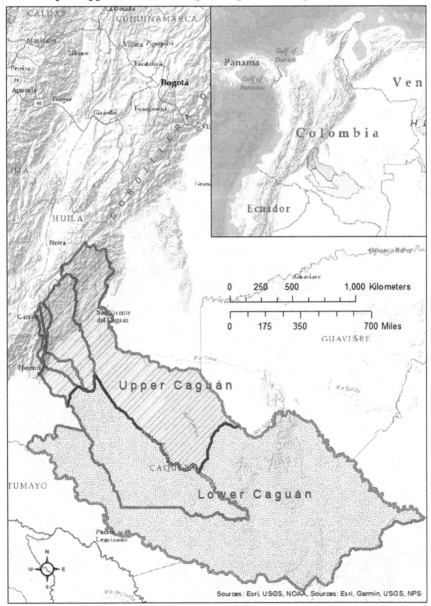

Sources: Esri, USGS, NOAA, Garmin, NPS

first place. How and why did illegal political and economic activities gain such deep traction in rural Colombia? What livelihood possibilities were actually available to those people pushed to the margins of Colombian society by the country's development processes? What role did the FARC and coca play in this larger developmental trajectory? And perhaps most importantly, what type of development is possible under a form of twenty-first-century capitalism in which new modalities of economic growth seem to create ever-larger pools of surplus labor?

This case study sheds light on these questions by analyzing the rise and demise of what I describe as FARC counter-hegemony in one of its most entrenched regional territorial strongholds and crucial sites of coca production, the Caguán region of Caquetá. In Chapter 6, I demonstrate that the rise of the FARC's counter-hegemonic coca regime was in fact a local response to an enduring failure of Colombian development – the unwillingness of the state to find ways to incorporate or stabilize the livelihoods of masses of rural surplus labor that had been displaced by capitalist growth. After national agro-industrial policies of the 1950s and 1960s first pushed uprooted rural migrants to the region, these migrants became further displaced and marginalized as industrial cattle ranching consolidated a despotic grip over the region into the 1970s. It was only when the FARC established its counter-hegemonic presence in the region and began to regulate the local coca economy that the region's migrants gained some semblance of economic stability. Chapter 7, in turn, analyzes how FARC counter-hegemony in the region was undermined through a massive militarization of the region under the aegis of the US wars on drugs and terror that opened the region once again to capitalist investment.

6

From Despotism to Counter-Hegemony in the Caguán

Thus, historically we have two principal processes of colonization in twentieth-century Colombia. On the one hand, the Antioqueño coffee colonization of the first half of the century, a great transforming and integrative force that created the basis for a middle peasantry, consolidated the links with the international market, and made possible the early industrialization of the country. And, on the other hand, we have the colonization of the contemporary era, which is permeated by guerrilla activity and drug cultivation and plays in many respects a destabilizing role. The political options for the peasantry are today very limited. They are trapped between traditional patronage networks and armed insurgency.

Gonzalo Sánchez (2001:3–4)

In his reflections on Colombia's protracted social crisis and political violence, historian Gonzalo Sánchez contrasted the "great transforming and integrative force" associated with the rise of the coffee export sector in the early twentieth century and the "destabilizing role" of the cocaine sector by the close of the century. Both arose through processes of frontier expansion, but the former gave rise to a middle peasantry and stable capitalist industrialization while the latter became permeated with guerrilla activity and violence. Indeed, explanations of guerrilla involvement in Colombia's illegal drug trade have been highly politicized, with some arguing that the FARC was a popular grassroots response to the exceptionally repressive nature of the Colombian state and class system[1] and others arguing that they are "narco-terrorists" intent upon securing their own organizational survival even if and when these actions result in civilian death and social disorder.[2]

To better understand the relationship between illegal drugs and illegal armed actors, this chapter takes Sánchez's comparisons seriously by analyzing the labor

---

[1] Chernick (1999); Richani (2002); Gutiérrez Sanín (2008); Brittain (2010); Leech (2011).

[2] Rangel Suárez (2000); Pécaut (2001).

regime dynamics of one of the FARC's most important territorial strongholds, the coca-producing Caguán region of Caquetá. As I will point out, there are indeed important points of convergence between the FARC's role in the expansion of the Caguán's coca economy over the past three decades and Fedecafé's role in the growth of the coffee economy during the postwar decades. In part, these similarities are rooted in the social and ecological determinants of coffee and coca whose respective structures of production and market dynamics are both labor-intensive commodities and, therefore, natural absorbers of rural surplus labor. However, while coffee was able to absorb labor as a critical component of Colombian national development efforts into the twentieth century, coca production arose as an unintended consequence of the failings of Colombian development.

As we shall see, in the 1980s and 1990s the FARC were not only able to incorporate the rural surplus populations that had been displaced by agro-industrialization and large-scale cattle ranching into their counter-hegemonic coca regime. They were also able to articulate the local population to the international cocaine market while avoiding the social contradictions of peripheral proletarianization. In fact, the FARC's revolutionary project shaped the nature of their interventions in the local coca market in ways that ironically mirrored Fedecafé's Pacto Cafetero vis-à-vis the country's cafeteros. The FARC provided economic security and protection to the region's migrants, who came to specialize in the cultivation and transformation of high-valued coca and coca paste that they then sold through highly regulated market channels to urban drug-trafficking organizations that would further process it into powdered cocaine for export. This control of coca production and sales granted the FARC access to vast amounts of core-like income that bolstered their revolutionary war-making, local de facto state-making activities, and their capacity to protect cocaleros from encroachment from the state and cattle ranchers. Thus, contra Sánchez, at least for the case of the Caguán, far from playing a destabilizing role, coca production and guerrilla activities worked as a "great transforming and integrative force" that created the basis for a relatively stable class of cocaleros.

Figure 6.1 provides evidence of this shift from the despotism associated with the Caguán's developmentalist cattle regime that predominated in the 1970s to a period of FARC counter-hegemony that persisted over the next two decades. During the heyday of FARC counter-hegemony, the number of incidents of state and paramilitary violence against civilian noncombatants remained virtually nonexistent. It was not until the early years of the twenty-first century, when the region became a strategic site of militarization under the War on Drugs and War on Terror that state security forces gained enough power to overwhelm the FARC's protection activities and to re-engage in acts of state repression against the local population.

Figure 6.1 State/paramilitary repression in the middle and lower Caguán, 1975–2018

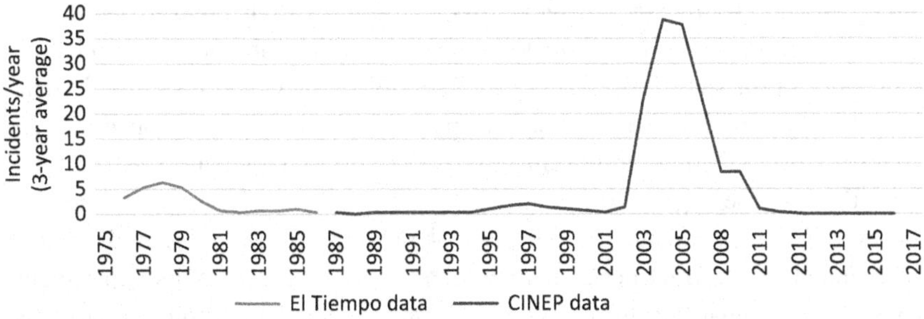

Source: Coercion Dataset

This chapter begins by recasting the problem of rural surplus labor historically, showing how the Colombian state has viewed frontier development as a safety valve meant to release social pressures accumulating in the country's main areas of development. It then analyzes the rise and demise of the Caquetá Colonization Project, the National Front regime's shabby efforts to redress the problem of rural surplus labor created by its industrial developmental initiatives. It then analyzes how the Caguán region became a site of cattle ranching under the direction of Fedegán, highlighting important points of convergence and divergence between Fedegán despotism in the Caguán and Augura's despotism in Urabá. Next, I describe how the FARC and the coca economy became the great absorbers of rural surplus labor, pushing back against the cycles of displacement and despotism of Fedegán and leading to the consolidation of a counter-hegemonic labor regime under the auspices of the FARC. From this perspective, we see that FARC counter-hegemony arose in inverse relation to the failure of Colombian agrarian development policies to address the problem of rural surplus labor. I close this chapter with an analysis of the FARC's counter-hegemonic social compact vis-à-vis cocalero farmers and workers as well as the social contradictions of the coca labor regime in the Caguán.

Agrarian Development and the Rise of Fedegán's Despotic Cattle Regime in the Caguán, 1963–1978

The Caguán region of Caquetá has been one of Colombia's quintessential external frontier zones. Located in the Greater Amazonian Basin region of the country, the Caguán is situated in a piedmont area that connects the mountainous highlands of the Western Cordillera of the Andes in Caquetá's northwestern edge down into the vast tropical grasslands, swamps and jungle forests of the Amazon river basin to the south and southeast. The region has long been sparsely populated with few incursions from colonial and postcolonial settlers and near absence of the territorial presence of the state.[3] As early as the 1930s, following Colombia's brief Leticia War with Peru in 1932–33, the northern parts of Caquetá had developed into an extensive cattle ranching zone centered on the city of Florencia; and the total population of the region was a mere 45,471 residents altogether by 1951.[4] However, Caquetá remained a subnational province (*intendencia*) until it was incorporated as a formal department in 1981 with Florencia as its department capital. The Caguán, in turn, is a rural frontier region of Caquetá that runs southeastward along the Caguán River as it flows into the Caquetá River to its south, and eventually into the Brazilian Amazon. The Upper Caguán (*Alto Caguán*) is the northern part of the larger piedmont region that includes Florencia and other more settled municipalities in the department's northwest, including parts of San Vicente del Caguán, Puerto Rico, El Doncello, El Paujíl, la Montañita. The middle and lower half of the Caguán region (*Medio y Bajo Caguán*) is the most remote region that typically refers to the municipalities of Cartagena de Chairá, Solano, and parts of San Vicente del Caguán.

During the 1950s, some 100,000 or more migrants flooded to the Caguán region to either flee persecution during the years of *La Violencia* or because they had been uprooted from economic development initiatives elsewhere. By 1956, the *Caja Agraria* attempted to regulate this migration by providing credit to settlers to help them formally acquire land.[5] However, as more and more migrated to the Caguán and other marginalized rural frontier region over the decade, National Front leaders began to fear that the presence of vast numbers of surplus rural populations would become breeding grounds for the social revolutionary guerrilla groups that were gaining traction across Latin America and the Caribbean. In an effort to curb the social revolutionary threat while promoting

---

[3]   Caquetá is home to numerous ethno-linguistically distinct indigenous communities, including Cabiyara, Embera, Inga, Witoto, Coreguaje, Macuna, Andoque, and Paez, about 3,000 people that now live on some thirty-four communal reserves (*resguardos*). The region underwent a few short-lived periods of Mestizo settlement, including two caucho booms (1887–1920 and 1930–46) and the Colombia–Peru War (1932–33). For excellent early histories of Caquetá, see Ariza et al. (1998:28–34, 89–112); Niño et al. (2000); and González Trujillo et al. (2003).

[4]   SINCHI (2000:25).

[5]   Only roughly 1,000 families participated in the Caja Agraria's initial credit-titling program (Marsh 1983).

the further industrialization of the country, President Alberto Lleras Camargo (1958–62) signed the Agrarian Social Reform Law 136 of 1962, which created the country's two key agrarian development agencies: the Colombian Institute for Agrarian Reform (INCORA) and the Institute for Agricultural Marketing (IDEMA), both of which were meant to complement the actions of the public *Caja Agraria* bank that had been providing credit to rural producers since 1956. INCORA was created to assist in the reconstruction of a stable peasantry by titling public land to landless campesinos and overseeing state-directed land colonization initiatives to populate and settle the country's unproductive frontier zones. IDEMA was established to promote agricultural productivity by granting producers technical assistance and agricultural extensions services, promoting the formation of rural cooperatives, and facilitating sales of crops through various marketing initiatives. Economically, INCORA and IDEMA were designed to promote the formation of a class of agricultural producers that would supply the rapidly urbanizing population with cheap produce.

National Front leaders agreed that the frontier region of Caquetá would provide a good opportunity to test these new state-directed agrarian development initiatives. The newly established INCORA was charged with the responsibility of overseeing and regulating the frontier colonization process in order to ensure the formation of a stable and productive class of farming families and expand the territorial control and legitimacy of the state into its southern border. And by 1962, it embarked upon its first directed frontier settlement initiative, the "Caquetá Colonization Project" (CCP).[6] The project itself entailed two phases. The first phase, called "Project Caquetá No. 1" (1963–71), continued the titling efforts initiated by the *Caja Agraria* but with the assistance of INCORA and IDEMA. The official goal of Project Caquetá No. 1 was to "assist in the settlement of new groups of 'spontaneous' colonos (with the) construction of penetration roads and the provision of land titling services, supervised credit, technical assistance, social development programs, and financial support for the Caquetá marketing cooperative, COOPERAGRO." This portion of the project was designed to stabilize the southeastern third of Caquetá, a region covering approximately 1 million hectares and with an expected settlement of roughly 90,000 inhabitants. This second phase consisted of five objectives: (1) stabilize and equalize the regional land tenure system by legalizing migrant land holdings and using the provision of credit to induce them to establish viable farm enterprises; (2) increase the productivity and worth of small farmers by importing

---

[6] For analyses of the National Front's frontier development policies, see Brücher (1974); Marsh (1983); Zamosc (1986); Jaramillo et al. (1989).

breeding cattle from other regions of Colombia; (3) raise the nutritional, health, and educational standards of the colonos; (4) connect the frontier hinterland to central towns by constructing roads and bridges; (5) encourage more efficient planning within INCORA and between INCORA and other rural development agencies.

While the Colombian government had originally intended to finance the CCP entirely, the developmentalist nature of the project appealed to the United States, which saw in it an opportunity to promote pro-capitalist transformation in Latin America. Thus, midway through the first phase of the project, INCORA's budget was supplemented with external funding from the United States Agency for International Development (USAID). By the early 1970s, the project had also caught the eye of the World Bank, which saw in it the opportunity to try out its new "integrated rural development" strategy of stimulating the economic product- ivity of the rural poor.[7] With such ideas in mind, the World Bank granted the Colombian government a loan of US$8.1 million in 1971 and another in 1975 for US$19.5 million, the latter of which helped create the Integrated Rural Development (DRI) agency within INCORA.[8]

On paper, the CCP incorporated the latest insights from the burgeoning field of developmental economics in order to cultivate a stable class of productive frontier farmers akin to the cafeteros of Viejo Caldas. INCORA would title land at subsidized rates to landless migrants. IDEMA would provide credit and extensions services to facilitate agricultural productivity and access to markets. And the *Caja Agraria* would invest in local infrastructure needed to connect the region's produce to local and national markets. In practice, however, the CCP suffered from a series of major problems. One problem stemmed from the project's inability or unwillingness to finance the full costs of agricultural produc- tion in what proved to be difficult ecological conditions. The acidic nature of the region's tropical soils made it easiest to grow grasses and herd cattle rather than cultivate staple agricultural products, which require expensive fertilizers to main- tain crop yields. Most settlers thus wished to acquire cattle as a long-term strategy

---

[7] Rather than define rural development as a simple increase in agricultural productivity, a policy that led to "top-down" assistance to only the largest and most competitive agribusinesses, reformers like World Bank President Robert S. McNamara had come to believe that an emphasis should also be placed on promoting the productivity of the rural poor. Higher productivity should therefore be combined with state interventions to stimulate job growth, transportation, storage and marketing facilities, educational and health services, land tenure reform, and community organizing (Escobar 1995; McMichael 2008).

[8] Marsh (1983:70–77).

out of poverty, but the CCP agencies did not provide the credit needed to cover the costs of purchasing cattle. Thus, settlers ended up using their credit to purchase expensive inputs that cut into their profits and ultimately made their produce uncompetitive in regional and national markets. And rather than allocate more national public funds to the CCP to help subsidize these losses, the Colombian government actually began steadily curtailing both provisions of funds and personnel to INCORA over the course of the decade. Thus, even when USAID and World Bank money began to help lift INCORA's financial burdens in the late 1960s, INCORA staffers still complained of an inability to adequately address the process due to "severe lack of funds."[9]

The CCP's lack of adequate financing was compounded by IDEMA's inability to overcome the barriers presented by the region's diffuse and complicated geography. Connecting the region's farms to regional and national agricultural markets required the construction of expensive transportation infrastructure that could traverse alluvial waterways and dense tropical forest. Such infrastructure projects would require vast amounts of capital, planning, and labor costs, which the Colombian government was unwilling to finance, especially since the project's end result – the formation of smallholding farmers – was neither a significant developmental priority nor a financially lucrative long-term investment. Quite early on then, IDEMA's inability to bring local produce to market left a void that was quickly filled by a class of usurious merchants who charged a high percentage of the sale to producers in exchange for the transport of their produce to distant markets. Many merchants became creditors as well, offering cash to CCP settlers in exchange for future yields. These settlers would use this cash to buy fertilizers that were sold to them at exceptionally unfavorable prices by the merchants themselves, resulting in the accumulation of debts that were nearly impossible to repay.[10]

Finally, the state offered no mechanism to stabilize and equalize the land tenure system. Because it established neither guarantees to prevent the future land displacement of colonos from the lands nor limits on the landholdings of a single individual, which as we saw from the example of the early land conflicts in Greater Urabá, landed elites used the titling services of INCORA to acquire vast amounts of land for their own purposes. Thus, a class of landed elites followed the arrival of frontier migrants – elites who came with both capital and contacts within the central state, both of which they used to obtain vast areas for cattle grazing. Many of these landed elites were merchants who acquired land as a method of payment

9   Marsh (1983:78–80); Jaramillo et al. (1989:25, 105–7).
10 Marsh (1983:39); Molano Bravo (1994:30).

from indebted colono migrants. Others were large-scale cattle ranchers who acquired land through INCORA because the agency had no legal limits set on the number of titles attainable. Still others simply evicted settlers from the lands they tilled by using faulty land titling claims or threats of violence. Regardless of the mechanism of dispossession, the end result was the same. The colonos were pushed further into the tropical jungles where their cycle of settlement and displacement would begin again.[11]

If the goal of the project was to establish a hegemonic labor regime akin to that of Fedecafé in Viejo Caldas, then the CCP was undoubtedly a miserable failure. By the middle of the 1970s Caquetá had become home to some of the strongest concentrations of land holdings and highest rates of poverty in the country. Álvaro Delgado (1987:100) calculated that between 1963 and 1977, INCORA granted 4 million hectares of titled lands to settlers, 3 million of which went to large cattle ranchers and *latifundistas* instead of to precarious colonos. Of these 3 million, only 200,000 (less than 2% of the total) were subject to INCORA's expropriation initiatives. Moreover, Robin Ruth Marsh (1983:22) found that these landed elites used INCORA's initiatives to gradually and steadily expand their own holdings by buying the surrounding farms of the colonos and cutting off their avenues to local markets. One cattle ranching family in particular, the Lara family, had by the early 1980s amassed over 40,000 ha of land in Caquetá alone. Indeed, their gigantic *Hacienda Larandia* was touted as the largest estate in the country and one of the largest land holdings in all of Latin America.[12] With such vast concentrations of land occurring through cycles of dislocation, it is not surprising that this wealth resulted in similarly large concentrations of poverty. The National Statistics Department (DANE 2004:4), for example, found that some 70% of the region's settlers lacked the means – land, capital, and wages – to live above subsistence levels. The national average of households living with their basic needs unmet (NBI) at the time hovered around 25.9%, while the southeastern region part of the country (including Caquetá, Meta, and Guaviare) had averages that reached up to 54.9%. And while 8.4 % of the national population lived in "misery," the percentage of the population in this southeastern region of the country who lived in misery reached up to 12.2%.

By the mid-1970s, Caquetá's frontier region was neither a hegemonic agrarian labor regime nor a mere safety valve for the class conflicts of other regions of the country. Instead, a new despotic labor regime had taken root, one that found ways

---

[11] This point is well established in the scholarly literature (Carroll 2011:124; Jaramillo et al. 1989:22; Marsh 1983:42).

[12] Ariza et al. (1998:29); Arley Bolaños (2017).

of accumulating capital through ongoing processes of primitive accumulation driven by an expanding cattle ranching industry that supplied low-cost meats and hides to the domestic market. The region's frontier migrants initiated the first steps of this cattle regime. As frontier settlers seeking access to land, they would typically clear uninhabited frontier jungle lands using family labor, with the plan of establishing a subsistence smallhold and eventually obtaining formal ownership of the land through private purchases or through INCORA's titling services. However, these frontier settlers would be followed by cattle ranchers interested in converting these new farms into extensive cattle grazing lands. The cattle ranchers would find ways, legally or otherwise, to evict these settlers from their farms, forcing them deeper into the agricultural frontier where the cycle would begin anew. At the helm of this process were some 300 or more family-owned cattle ranching companies, like the Lara family's *Compañía Ganadera Limitada*, that adopted the latest intensive-cattle ranching techniques to maximize the production of low-cost meats and hides that would be purchased in what was becoming an increasingly urban and proletarianized nation.[13]

The cattle industry's growth required access to ever-greater extensions of grazing lands, so naturally the acquisition of new land became the industry's primary focus. However, because raising cattle for slaughter does not require significant amounts of labor (the most labor-intensive part of the labor process being the slaughterhouses and meat-packing plants that were concentrated in and around the urban nucleus of Florencia), the industry had little use for the populations of rural settlers. Ultimately, colono family labor did constitute the first step of the cattle ranchers' labor process, as they transformed the region's thick jungle forest into farmlands that could become amenable to cattle grazing. Yet, once this first step was completed, the rest of the ranching process had little use for them. In short, the industry was highly land-intensive but labor-expulsive. Consequently, the expansion of the industry southward into frontiers of the Middle and Lower Caguán was motored by ongoing cycles of displacement, frontier settlement, and further displacement, as land was continually incorporated into the regime and labor spit out.

Of course, extensive cattle production in Caquetá has a long history that dates back to the 1930s, when the grasslands in and around San Vicente del Caguán were transformed into grazing zones to feed the burgeoning urban centers of Florencia and Neiva in the neighboring department of Huila. And as early as 1955, the state began to engage in efforts to modernize the industry, creating the

---

[13] Author interview with former INCORA-Caquetá employee in Florencia, Caquetá on July 6, 2009. See also CNMH (2017).

Caquetá Cattle Rancher Fund (*Fondo Gandero de Caquetá*, est. 1955) to inject local ranches with capital to increase their production.[14] Moreover, the consolidation of Caquetá's cattle industry at this time was part of a larger national trend in which landed elites and cattle ranching families were accumulating vast amounts of land through public titling services and private purchases. In 1963, the country's cattle ranchers formed the business group Fedegán (*Federación Colombiana de Ganaderos*, Colombian Cattle Ranchers Federation), which like Fedecafé and Augura assumed responsibility for lobbying the state on behalf of their industry. Over the next decade, Fedegán established a network of regional offices in key cattle ranching regions of the country and a national office in downtown Bogotá, just down the block from Colombia's Liberal Party headquarters. They used their political influence to lobby the central state for subsidies and credit to modernize the country's cattle industry. With state technical and financial assistance, Fedegán oversaw the construction of slaughterhouses equipped with the latest sanitation and septic technologies, regional networks of refrigerated storage and warehouses, improvements in grasses and nutrient soils, veterinary services, and a vast communications system to increase ranchers' understanding of market trends.[15]

Like Augura in Urabá, Fedegán's ability to accumulate wealth and territory rested heavily upon the exclusionary politics and interventions of the National Front regime. In Caquetá, the region's cattle ranchers became a powerful constituent of the clientelistic web of the local Liberal Party that monopolized the region's political institutions. Leah Carroll (2011:126) notes that as far back as the early 1960s,

> Hernándo Turbay Turbay, the patriarch of the Turbay family, had consolidated his position as the ultimate regional strongman, winning appointment as an *intendente* (governor of an *intendencia*, one step short of a department), from 1962–1965, then using his perennial Congressional post and family connections to key Liberal Party leaders to faithfully represent cattle ranchers and *latifundista* interests in Caquetá after 1968.

Allying with the Turbayistas provided assurances that the state would turn a blind eye if and when the region's cattle ranchers used questionable means to coercively expel colonos from the land. It also provided ranchers with powerful friends and allies in the judicial system, foremost among which were cattle-rancher-friendly judges who would consistently rule in their favor when legal disputes over land titles arose. These "Turbayista Liberals" also used their political power to gather

---

[14] González Trujillo et al. (2003:68–69).

[15] González Trujillo et al. (2003:63–65); Author interviews with Fedegán representatives in Bogotá on October 10, 2004 and in Florencia, Caquetá on July 6, 2009.

state assistance for the development of infrastructure that would assist in the expansion of the cattle ranching economy, including the opening of roads to cattle markets, which in turn would raise the value of property that would be soon be acquired and sold for a hefty profit.[16]

By the 1970s and early 1980s, Caquetá's cattle industry had become one of the most important and productive centers of cattle ranching in the country, with the meat and hides of some 150,000 cows supplying the regional and national market.[17] Like Urabá, Caquetá's cattle industry consolidated into an economic enclave zone that operated according to the dictates of capital. Unlike Augura's labor regime in the enclave zone of Urabá, it was not cattle ranchers that bore the brunt of despotism. Rather, it was the frontier settlers.[18] As Alfredo Molano Bravo (1994:31) poignantly noted, the colono settlers of the Caguán and other neighboring tropical frontier regions became "solitary, alienated, disorganized, wounded, timid, generally illiterate, incapable of imposing or developing a power of negotiation in the face of an opponent that had organized with all of the influences, capacities and unscrupulousness imaginable." Far from trusting the local political establishment or bureaucrats affiliated with the Caquetá Colonization Project, the region's settlers grew to become increasingly distrustful of the state, feeling that the best form of organization is one that is autonomous from the government and from local forms of class domination.[19]

Viewed comparatively, it is clear that Fedegán's cattle regime in Caquetá differed in key ways from both Fedecafé's hegemonic coffee regime in Viejo Caldas as well as from Augura's banana despotic banana regime in Urabá. As we saw from the first case study, continued growth in the coffee regime rested upon the articulation of cafetero land and labor to the market. Moreover, what made it hegemonic was Fedecafé's capacity to also incorporate the social reproduction needs of the region's cafeteros into a protective hegemonic social compact rather than externalize these costs onto the producers and their families. As we saw from the second case study, Urabá's banana regime was also labor and land intensive. However, what made the regime despotic was the fact that Augura were neither willing nor able to subsidize the social class reproduction needs of the region's banana workers. Fedegán's cattle regime, in contrast, was land-intensive but labor-expulsive, which meant that the region's ranchers were neither willing nor able to finance the full costs of production. Instead they found ways to

---

[16] Delgado (1987:44–48); Molano Bravo (1994:35, 38–39).

[17] Niño et al. (2000:133).

[18] Reyes Posada (2009).

[19] LeGrand (1994:14–18).

externalize these production costs onto the frontier migrants themselves, who were neither compensated for their labor in clearing the forest nor paid the full market-value of their land. Likewise, Fedegán assumed no responsibility for subsidizing the social reproduction costs of the region's frontier migrants who suffered a double whammy from the consolidation of this mode of capitalist development. The cattle industry incorporated their land through coercive processes of dispossession. And, because their labor was not exploitable, they were not afforded the type of structural power vis-à-vis capital that Urabá's workers mobilized on the plantations and in the ballot boxes. Instead, they became chronically uprooted pools of rural surplus labor living at the social and political margins of Colombian economy and society.

The Social Contradictions of Fedegán Despotism in the Caguán

The failings of Colombia's rural development agencies to redistribute land to those who needed it most became a major national issue for National Front leaders. In fact, as was evident in both the Caguán and Urabá, despotism and rural instability were spreading across many regions of Colombia into the 1960s and 1970s. President Carlos Lleras Restrepo (1967–71), a long-time advocate of limited land reform, responded to this problem by using his executive powers to circumvent the stranglehold of landed elites and agro-industrialists in Colombia's congress. In May of 1967, Lleras Restrepo issued "Presidential Decree 755," which established the *Asociación Nacional de Usuarios Campesinos* (National Association of Peasant Users, ANUC), an organization of sharecroppers, tenant farmers, migrant colonos, and rural agricultural workers that was encouraged to "create external pressures [on the ground] to undermine the position of the landowning class, thus changing the balance of forces within the National Front and creating a more favorable climate for the implementation of agrarian reform."[20] Emboldened by its advocacy from the President, the ANUC grew rapidly in its first few years of existence. They organized rural workers and landless communities, staged labor and civic protests, and engaged in legal battles in the courts over land titling and labor disputes. However, it was not long before the ANUC shed its bourgeois-reformist skin, becoming a powerful, autonomous mobilizing tool of the Colombian peasantry that demanded a radical redistribution of rural property and agrarian reforms that prioritized the economic rights of rural families over the interests of agro-industrialists and cattle ranching elites.

---

[20] Zamosc (1986:50).

By 1970–71, ANUC activists began to engage in direct actions such as land invasions that were met with reactionary violence from local elites, resulting in their further radicalization. By then, a number of regional factions of the ANUC had become influenced by Maoist groups like the Marxist-Leninist New Communist Party (PCML) and the Marxist-Leninist League (Liga ML), and began demanding a radical restructuring of property and an end to the state's support for agro-industrialization.

In the Caguán, Fedegan's consolidation of control of the region made it a fertile ground for the rise of agrarian social movement activity. The ANUC-Caquetá branch of the national movement was one of its most vibrant since its inception. At first, the bulk of their energies were dedicated to squatting on unused public and private lands. However, over time their actions expanded to civic strikes and occupations of local state agencies to demand access to credit, agricultural services, and the construction of rural infrastructure. ANUC's mobilizations in Caquetá climaxed in 1971 after a series of floods in the region devoured numerous settler farms along the Caguán river. The ANUC organized civic strikes demanding government relief, debt forgiveness, and new provisions of credit for the families that had been dislocated in addition to a general call for more roads, better agricultural services, and fixed prices for rice and maize. When negotiations between ANUC representatives and the provincial government failed, the ANUC organized a regional civic strike in July of 1972 in which some 10,000 colonos occupied the regional capital of Florencia for eight days. President Pastrana responded by sending in three army battalions and inviting a delegate from ANUC-Caquetá to Bogotá to negotiate. The strike ended when the government increased the price of maize and rice and promised to extend their services and road construction in the region.[21]

As it turned out, however, ANUC-Caquetá's civic strike of July 1972 was their apex of organizational strength. By then, Colombian President Miguel Pastrana (1970–74), responded to the country's agrarian unrest by calling a meeting between leaders of the Liberal and Conservative parties along with key business groups to discuss how to reverse the land reforms initiated by the Lleras Restrepo administration. The meeting culminated in what has been called the "Pact of Chicoral" (1972), an agreement that the government would limit its land redistribution efforts and unequivocally support the expansion of agribusinesses by providing favorable credits and loan policies in exchange for the paying of taxes on their properties.[22]

---

[21] Zamosc (1986:30–33, 46, 93–94).

[22] The "Pact of Chicoral" (1972) was an agreement that the government would limit its land redistribution efforts and unequivocally support the expansion of agribusinesses by

In Caquetá, Pastrana's war against the agrarian movement came in two forms that proved effective in dividing the movement and isolating its leaders. First, the Pastrana administration began stimulating the growth of government-sponsored civic organizations, *Juntas de Acción Comunal* (JAC), that organized at the neighborhood level and provided a channel to voice local concerns through governmental channels. Between 1966 and 1979, the number of JACs doubled throughout the country, but multiplied five and six times in those regions characterized by radical ANUC activity, including in Caquetá. These JACs were designed to break the autonomous class-based politics of the ANUC while pushing the region's problems into the clientelistic channels of the state and its local political bosses. Given the Liberal Party's monopoly over political posts in Caquetá, the JACs soon became a clientelistic tool of the Turbayistas, who used them to marginalize movement radicals and reward those with conservative and reformist orientations. Second, the Pastrana administration legitimated what had already been ranchers' use of local authorities or armed men to evict squatters. As Leon Zamosc (1986: 103) points out, under Pastrana, this policy of repression became "clear official policy" as INCORA functionaries who would have otherwise supported colono land occupations were instructed not to interfere, granting police and army forces free reign to regain control of the municipalities affected.

As the Colombian government cracked down on the squatters and civic activists, the national alliances that constituted the ANUC movement began to unravel. In 1972, the ANUC formally split between a reformist "Armenia line" that remained loyal to the government's promise of incremental agrarian reforms and a radical "Sincelejo line" that challenged the authoritarianism of the state and viewed their struggle for land as part of a broader Maoist revolutionary set of politics. This factional split weakened the movement as efforts to coordinate actions and strategies broke down into bitter debate and growing distrust. By the mid-1970s, Caquetá's ANUC branch leaders had become firmly aligned with the "Sincelejo Line," understanding their efforts to obtain land as part of a set of larger social revolutionary

---

providing favorable credits and loan policies in exchange for the paying of taxes on their properties. Law 135 was also modified to assure that expropriated lands would be reimbursed according to their market value rather than on their census value (as was the norm earlier). Other guarantees included the subsequent passage of Laws 4a and 5a of 1973, which created the Agricultural Financial Fund to provide services to agribusiness, and Law 6a of 1975, which made it more difficult for lands to be appropriated by muddling the standards by which land could be considered to be "legally occupied" by squatters (Richani 2002:32).

demands. As their demands and actions became more militant, they became subject to greater militarization and policing, which in turn stimulated further radicalization. ANUC-Caquetá was particularly influenced by the fragmentation of the movement, as its radical leaders became more defensive in the face of state repression and its rank-and-file militants became more isolated. Thus, when confronted with Pastrana's divide-and-conquer strategy, the ANUC movement – both nationally and locally – crumbled. Between 1971 and 1978, more than 100 of the ANUC's national leaders were killed by assassins (*pájaros*) associated with state security forces. By the closing years of the 1970s, the ANUC movement had weakened to the point of dissipation.[23]

The Rise of the FARC in the Caguán

Over time, the political void left by the ANUC movement in Caquetá became filled by guerrilla insurgency groups, foremost among which were the *Movimiento 19 de Abril* (April 19 Movement, M-19) and the FARC, which found a rugged geography that offered them safety from the attacks of the Colombian public forces and a population of precarious peasant settlers with deep-seated distrust of the actions of the state and local elites. The first to enter the region was the M-19, a group that initially arose in response to claims that General Gustavo Rojas Pinilla's left-populist party, the *Alianza Nacional Popular* (National Popular Alliance, ANAPO), actually won the 1970 presidential election. Predominantly composed of middle-class students and urban intellectuals who were inspired by Che Guevara's Foquista theory of revolution in which a small and disciplined vanguard could activate the latent revolutionary potential of the peasantry, the M-19 raided the rural municipality of Belen de Andaquíes in 1979. From there, they tried to establish a territorial stronghold that would stretch throughout the Upper Caguán region between the Caquetá and Orteguaza rivers from Belen to San Jose de Fragua, Albania, and Currillo. However, because they were poorly armed and had little military training, they were forced to retreat to hideouts in the region's municipal centers when attacked head-on by the Colombian military.[24] Over the next two years, they continued to try to make headway into the countryside but with little success. As a result, they were more successful in engaging in political types of activities,

---

[23] Zamosc (1986:202–3).
[24] Valencia (1998:138).

including organizing rural and urban voters around the ANAPO ticket and organizing neighborhood groups to press the government for civic reforms, often in alliance with the Communist's UNO party. However, these actions exposed them to military repression, which minimized their influence. By the early 1980s, the group began to withdraw from the region altogether in order to focus on high-profile actions in the country's major cities.[25]

The FARC, contrast, did not only establish roots in the frontier regions of Caquetá, the Caguán transformed into one of their sturdiest territorial strongholds and bases of national operations. Since their forced dislocation from their initial strongholds in Marquetalia, Rio Chiquito, and El Pato in the neighboring departments of Tolima and Huila, the FARC had been moving into new regions of the country where they would create insurgent camps, establish connections with local populations who they considered class allies, and engage in actions against local elites. By the middle years of the 1970s, FARC leaders began to move into Caquetá as part of a larger effort to control the eastern cordillera region of the country and physically encircle the national capital city of Bogotá. Their first local action came in 1974 when they took over the rural municipality of Puerto Rico. They then expanded their operations into the vast territories of the Middle and Lower Caguán, where they established their fourteenth and fifteenth fronts to oversee operations in the frontier municipalities of Cartagena del Chairá, San Vicente del Caguán, and Solano. They also began engaging in actions in the Upper Caguán region, including the department capital in Florencia. Like the M-19, the FARC's more urban actions were mostly political in nature. In coordination with the Colombian Communist Party (PCC), they established the UNO party as their electoral front and began to establish a presence in the local unions and the student movement. And like the M-19, these efforts proved to be quite ineffective. Electorally, they found it difficult to displace the Turbayistas from local county council positions. The heavy presence of security forces that criminalized social movement activity, in turn, made it difficult to openly organize urban workers and students.[26]

While the FARC's entrance into the urban struggles of the Upper Caguán region were met with stiff and generally effective resistance, their efforts to establish roots in the remote rural regions of the Lower and Middle Caguán proved to be much more successful. The region's remote geography provided protection from military attacks and its intricate jungle waterways provided them with the means to easily transport soldiers and supplies. And most

---

[25] Delgado (2020:10).
[26] Olaya (1998:96–98).

importantly, they found a sizable population of displaced peasants that were not only seeking protection from land hungry ranchers but were also deeply distrustful of the intentions of the state. Moreover, unlike the M-19 and most other Foquista-based insurgency groups in Colombia, the FARC was at its core a rural peasant movement. It originated as a group of armed peasant self-defense communities in the 1960s. Its leadership was almost entirely composed of campesinos rather than urban intellectuals. To be sure, the FARC has continually advocated the doctrine of "combining all forms of struggle" in which insurgency activities existed alongside political and ideological work organizing rural and urban communities, workers, and peasants. Yet, they were most effective in their efforts to protect peasant access to the land, both when existing rural communities became threatened by the entrance of capitalist transformation into the Colombian countryside and through their own "armed colonization" actions in which they facilitated the settlement of colonos in agricultural frontiers.[27] Their territorial control and authority over a region thus provided rural peasant communities with a degree of stability and protection from agro-industrialization processes.[28] The FARC's successes in the rural regions of the Caguán, therefore, divided Caquetá in half in the closing years of the 1970s. The areas in and around Florencia and the Upper Caguán remained firmly controlled by Fedegán and the Turbayistas. The more remote regions such as those along the Middle and Lower Caguán, in turn, became strongholds of the FARC.[29]

However, it was the FARC's political actions in the region's urban centers that provoked the most hostility from the Colombian government. An "all-out war" was declared on the FARC after it became clear that they were involved in coordinating Florencia's participation in the national *paro cívico* (civic strike) in 1977. Immediately following the strike, President López Michelson (1974–78) sent in thousands of counter-guerrilla forces into the rural regions of San Vicente del Caguán, Puerto Rico, and El Puajil, where the FARC had been most active. From there, the military began to take over the functions of the municipal government, beginning a series of "psychological warfare" tactics aimed at winning the hearts and minds of the frontier migrants by organizing the community to build schools, hospitals and roads. Secret Agents from the F-2 and DAS police units were also sent in to disrupt union and peasant organizing. Two months later, in December of 1977, the troops ransacked the UNO

---

[27] Richani (2002:67).

[28] Brittain (2010); Leech (2011).

[29] Valencia (1998:135–37).

headquarters in Florencia, detaining the regional secretary of the Communist Party, Feliciano Pachón. At the same time, a military operation organized by the *Comando Unificado del Sur* sent 1,500 troops into El Paujil, el Doncello, and La Montañita, where they occupied various schools and state offices, destroyed crops, and detained numerous peasants, students, and teachers thought to be affiliated with the guerrillas.[30]

The 1978 election of President Julio Cesár Turbay Ayala (1978–82), a relative of Caquetá's regional strongman Henrique Turbay Turbay, fore-shadowed what was to come to the *intendencia* over the next four years. Turbay Ayala instituted a national "state of siege" that criminalized social protests and granted the Colombian military greater powers to combat guerrilla insurgents and protesters alike. In September, Turbay Ayala designated military man, Colonel Campo Elías Bocanegra, as *intendente* of Caquetá, a position normally held by civilians. Over the following month, roughly 100 individuals were detained in San Vicente de Caguán under the pretext that they were collaborators of the FARC. Other acts of state repression include: the military assassination of the UNO leader of El Doncello in October; the killing of a suspected guerrilla in his home in Florencia in November; and the torture of three leftist activists, including the opposition council member (*concejal*) of San Vicente in December. This overt use of repression was further fortified with the establishment of the counter-insurgent Comando Operativo No. 12 in 1978 and the Batallón Juanambu in 1979. By 1981, Comando Operativo No. 12 had grown to include seven battalions and more than 6,000 troops, becoming what Álvaro Delgado (1987:110–11) described as a "permanent fixture in Caquetá's politics [and] nearly always intervening against reform initiatives, in concert with Turbayista politicians."

President Turbay Alaya also declared Caquetá to be a "war zone," in which rural settlers were indistinguishable from the guerrilla insurgents themselves. This repressive rhetoric quickly transformed into action, as the region's rural settlers that were noncombatant civilians fell prey to numerous incidents of state repression, including: the military's assassination of an entire colono family in November of 1979; the disappearance of Álvaro and Vicente Monje (two frontier migrants considered to be communist collaborators) in the same month; the detention of a group of colonos by the Batallón Juanambu in January 1980; the beating and torture of two locals of Curillo by the police in February 1980; the torture and killing of a boy in El Doncello by the military in the same month; the military assassination of two farmers accused of belonging to the FARC in El Tigre; the

---

[30] Delgado (1987:108–9).

use of military helicopters to drop cadavers over Cartagena del Chairá to intimidate guerrilla supporters in February 1980; the subsequent beating and detention of five farmers and one small businessman from the region by the military; the arrest of one student and three professors accused of belonging to the FARC in June 1980; the detention and torture of a prize-winning poet and union leader that had been affiliated with the ANUC movement by the *Brigada de Institutos Militares*; the detention of fourteen colono farmers in San Vicente for lacking identification documents; and the detention of an UNO Concejal, his wife, and others who participated in a protest against state violence in May 1979, among other incidents.[31]

This brutal wave of state repression from 1975 until 1980 (evident from Figure 6.1) was mostly effective in stomping out the lingering embers of the agrarian movement, keeping the political actions of the FARC and M-19 at bay, and retaining the Turbayista's monopolization of local political power in Florencia and other urban centers. Nonetheless, the FARC's territorial expansion into the more remote regions of the Middle and Lower Caguán proved to be much more difficult to repress during this period. The armed conflict between the state and the guerrillas in Caguán was much more of a precarious stalemate than a victory for either party. Direct incursions of Colombian military forces into the frontier were too difficult for the FARC to stop head on, meaning local settlers were exposed to the coercive arm of the state. Yet, maintaining territorial control over local frontier communities was also beyond the capacity of the military, which would be pulled into new rural territorial fights in a game of cat and mouse with FARC forces who were more familiar with the region's jungle terrain. Given this tentative stalemate between the FARC and the state, the conflict over land between Fedegán's cattle ranchers and local settlers became a low-intensity and highly precarious struggle comprised of continuous evictions and land invasions. As we shall see, it was not until the entrance of coca production into the region that the balance of local power began to shift in favor of the settlers and the FARC.

The Emergence of Coca Production in the Caguán

Colombia's involvement in the production of illegal narcotics for export dates back to the early 1970s when Colombia became a leading exporter of marijuana to the United States. Most of this production of "Colombian Gold" occurred in remote

---

[31] Delgado (1987:101, 114–16).

rural regions of the Guajira Peninsula, whose lush mountainous jungle provided producers with a cover for their clandestine cultivations and whose location on the Caribbean coast provided traffickers with an easy outlet to the north. Production also arose in other frontier regions, including in some small pockets of Caquetá, where the marijuana plant was intermeshed with the staple crops of the colono families who tended them. Here, marijuana production provided frontier settlers with some additional income that could be used to purchase fertilizers, seeds, cattle and other farm animals, or pay the titling fees that were essential to avoid further dislocation and impoverishment.

However, even at its peak years between 1972 and 1975, the income frontier farmers could generate from marijuana production remained quite low. Because marijuana can be produced in a broad range of ecological contexts, does not require massive amounts of capital, and can be easily hidden from authorities when produced in small scales, it is quite easy for producers to enter and exit the market. Consequently, marijuana production is both more competitive and less profitable than other illegal commodities.[32] As it turned out, the boom in marijuana production lasted only until the middle of the decade. By then, buyers in the United States had begun to find less costly, alternative supplies of the narcotic in Mexico, Northern California, Appalachia, and other places where production took root. By 1976, marijuana production for export from Colombia began a rapid decline. However, only a few short years later, the craze for Colombian marijuana had given way to a new craze for cocaine. Cocaine had become a fashionable party drug used by a nascent class of yuppies, entertainers, business elites, and upscale consumers who were driven by the stimulating rush of energy achieved after snorting it. As demand for global cocaine rose, the illegal market infrastructure that had been created through the marijuana trade became flooded with cocaine and Colombia rapidly became the world's leading exporter.[33]

Coca, the plant from which cocaine is processed, was cultivated historically in the Andean highlands regions of Bolivia and Peru where it was chewed by native indigenous populations as a mild stimulant to help them cope with the arduous workdays imposed upon them by Spanish colonists and *Criollo* elites. In the 1970s, producers in Bolivia and Peru began to sell coca leaves to Colombian merchants, who transported it to "laboratories" run by the major marketing cartels,

---

[32] To be sure, Colombia's most notorious narco-trafficker, Pablo Escobar, had won his first fortunes in the marijuana trade. Yet, Escobar's early fortunes in the trade were in large part due to his willingness to use exceptionally heinous acts of violence to threaten competitors and monopolize the exportation end of the market. By the late 1970s, Escobar had moved into a more profitable line of business: cocaine (Bowden 2001).

[33] Díaz and Sánchez Torres (2004).

where they were processed into coca paste and then powdered cocaine using inputs of gasoline and ether, before being exported. By 1978, however, US efforts to crack down on coca production in Bolivia and Peru pushed coca production into external frontier regions like Caquetá, where the distinct ecological and social geography proved to be a uniquely advantageous site of production.[34] In terms of its geography, Caquetá was home to a diffuse rural populations, a precarious economy, countless waterways, and a history of illegal activity that made it a prime location for such clandestine economic activities. The region's remote jungle location and vast waterways provided both coverage from government interdictions and market access to the country's urban centers. The coca plant requires large amounts of sunlight and rainfall, and the Caguán's hot, humid and eternally damp ecology proved exceptionally conducive to the plant's healthy growth. Finally, as we have discussed, the settlers of the region had been subject to ongoing bouts of settlement and dislocation. They lived highly precarious and marginalized lives and were deeply distrustful of state interventions in the region. Coca cultivation, like coffee during its early days, held the promise of providing settlers with the additional income needed to pay titling and surveying fees to legalize their property, finance the purchase of seeds and farm equipment to boost their productivity, and otherwise stabilize their subsistence smallholdings.[35]

Indeed, the structure of coca production is strikingly similar to that of coffee and both are highly amenable to the economic experiences of precarious frontier settlers. For example, neither is particularly capital-intensive, as both coffee trees and coca plants can flourish and produce vegetation with little initial inputs other than seeds, water, and natural soil nutrients. Coca plants grow quickly and can be harvested within seven to eight months. And when mature, they produce enough leaves for two to three harvests per year. Once plucked, the leaves are dried until brittle and processed into coca paste, and finally sold to merchants who transported it to urban centers where it is transformed into powdered cocaine for export. But even the processing of dried coca leaves into coca paste is not highly capital-intensive. With some initial investments, coca-producing farmer families or local collectives can process these leaves into coca paste themselves, as the process only requires inputs of water, sulfuric acid (cement lime), gasoline, mixing buckets and tarps, and perhaps a small weed-wacker, among other things. To make about a kilogram's worth of coca paste, harvests from roughly 2 acres of coca plants (about 500–1,000 kilograms of leaves) are threshed and then placed in a water pit, mixed with sulfuric acid and stomped on to further thresh the leaves,

---

[34] Walker (1989:196–97).

[35] Vargas Meza (1999:89–95).

placed in buckets and stirred with gasoline, and finally strained, pressed and heated on a stove, and packaged in kilo-sized bags.[36] And though prices for cocaine like coffee are notoriously variable from month to month and year to year, depending upon interdiction efforts and demand fluctuations, in general it takes about a ton of coca leaves to make a kilo of coca paste (2.2 lbs.), which can be sold for roughly US$900.[37] Thus, like coffee production, coca production in Colombia is uniquely amenable to family labor systems. Not only does the additional income aid in the family's social reproduction costs, the crop itself can be easily planted densely alongside subsistence crops, thus providing an additional cash revenue to an otherwise relatively self-sufficient plot of land. And because both coca and coffee are labor-intensive and conducive to the dense cultivation strategies of subsistence peasant households, their production facilitates frontier colonization and settlement processes without radically disturbing the existing lines of land tenure and property rights. And in sharp contrast to cattle ranching, the structure of coca production has the physical capacity to absorb rather than expel rural surplus labor.

But it is not simply the social ecology and labor-absorbing structure of coca production that facilitated its rapid expansion into the Caguán region during this time. The structure of the coca market has also contributed to its growth. Unlike marijuana or cattle ranching, coca is a tropical agricultural export commodity that cannot be produced in large amounts in the world's major consumer countries. This provides tropical exporters with a comparative market advantage through their structural leverage vis-à-vis importers that can facilitate domestic wealth accumulation.[38] However, cocaine is significantly different from other tropical agro-export commodities because it is an illegal narcotic that operates outside of formal legal and juridical rules and regulatory institutions of international and national governing bodies. Since market rules and norms are not enforced by third-party legal entities, cocaine's market dynamics, including its labor–capital relations, domestic and international market transactions, and property rights, become enforced by market actors themselves, who must acquire the appropriate means of coercion in order to participate effectively in the market.[39]

---

[36] Author interview with farmer outside of Florencia, Caquetá on July 6, 2009.

[37] Woody (2017).

[38] See Talbot (2004, 2009) for an elaboration of the comparative advantages of tropical agro-exports for developmental regimes in sub-Saharan Africa, Latin America and the Caribbean, and South and Southeast Asia.

[39] For analyses of the use of state coercion and private violence-wielding organizations to sustain market activities, see Lane (1979); Tilly (1985, 1990, 2002); Arrighi (1994, 2005a, 2005b); Perelman (2000); Volkov (2002); Harvey (2003).

Cocaine's illegal status, however, brings both advantages and disadvantages to its market participants. Participation in the cocaine market invites repressive incursion from national states and international governing bodies that engage in interdiction, forced eradication, and incarceration efforts tied to its adherence to international drug laws. Such "supply-side" drug war policies that attempt to diminish supplies by cutting off international flows of narcotics have undoubtedly produced a certain volatility in the cocaine market, as producers and traffickers are forced to find ever-changing and innovative strategies to evade policing and surveillance. Additionally, as mentioned, because formal juridical institutions cannot legally arbitrate conflicts that arise in the market, among competing trafficking organization, between buyers and sellers, or labor conflicts that are internal to any one organization, these conflicts often do result in drug-related violence. The cocaine market is at its core a risky endeavor. However, like other international illegal commodity markets, cocaine is highly lucrative precisely because it is illegal. For example, between 1978 and 1981 when coca production entered the Caguán region, the average price of one kilo of coca paste could go as high as US$16,000–$20,000.[40] This was, and continues to be, an amount of income that is unmatchable for most legal commodities produced in Colombia.

Cocaine's illegal status does not only impact the overall amount of wealth that can be accrued in the market. It also impacts its distribution. By its very nature, the cocaine market does not adhere to international laws regarding intellectual property rights. It is not subject to tariffs, import-export taxes, or trade rules that typically influence patterns of international trade. And, producers and traffickers cannot formally or openly receive government subsidies, investments, protections, or other forms of state assistance that often protect and sustain domestic industries otherwise threatened by market competition. Moreover, as world-systems scholars point out, such state interventions have not only played an essential role in the domestic industrialization activities of core and peripheral states alike. Such political and geopolitical interventions in global commodity markets have also played a critical role in the historical reproduction of core–periphery inequalities in general.[41] In the cocaine economy, any producer or purchaser that is willing to engage in the risks of the market can enter or exit the market at their own will. And those that do enter the market must find ways to operate at its margins, outside of the formal purview of the international juridical gaze. Because of its relatively low financial barriers to entry, in addition to its concentration in only a

---

[40] Carroll (2011:128).

[41] Arrighi and Drangel (1986); Arrighi and Piselli (1987); Wallerstein (2004).

handful of countries, the illegal cocaine market has the potential to provide peripheral market actors with access to core-like profits that cannot typically accrue to those very same market actors if they were to engage in the formal economy. Thus, at the height of the cocaine boom in the 1980s, Colombian drug-traffickers were amassing unimaginable amounts of wealth. Pablo Escobar's Medellín cartel, for example, was at one point supplying some 80% of the US cocaine market. Escobar himself was turning over an estimated US$21.9 billion per year, making him the wealthiest person in Colombia and one of the wealthiest people in the world at that time.[42]

While capable of producing vast wealth, the cocaine economy has its structural disadvantages. As mentioned, it is prone to violence as a primary mechanism of settling disputes and therefore the emergence of large-scale violence-wielding organizations, including gangs, mafias, narco-bourgeoisies, and other "violent entrepreneurs" that specialize in using terror to obtain market advantages.[43] It also creates an uneasy relationship between these narco-bourgeoisies and formal political institutions and state actors. On the one hand, when governments comply with international drug laws, they must therefore engage in direct and often viciously bloody "dirty wars" with domestic traffickers that are often better armed and equipped than their own police and armed forces. On the other hand, when state leaders ignore international drug-trafficking practices they themselves become the objects of international criminal procedures that can result in the loss of access to international aid, trading relations, or even indictments by international drug courts. Moreover, states that become sites of illegal narcotics trafficking also become subject to endemic corruption, as drug-traffickers evade international drug enforcement agencies with the direct or indirect support of national or local government officials. In any case, the political ramifications of illegal drug production tend to result in a delegitimization of national police, juridical institutions, and of the actions of the state in general.[44]

But more to the point, just because the structure of coca production has the capacity to absorb surplus labor and stabilize livelihoods in frontier regions like the Caguán and just because the structure of the market makes it amenable to accessing core-like profits does not mean that a coca-based labor regime will invariably become hegemonic. As we saw in the first case study, hegemony in Viejo Caldas arose only when the interests of the region's cafetero farmers were meaningfully incorporated as junior partners into the hegemonic developmentalist

---

[42] Macias (2015).

[43] Volkov (2002); Tilly (2002); Gallant (1999).

[44] Arlacchi (1986); Gambetta (1993); Thoumi (2002, 2003); Carpenter (2003).

project of the National Federation of Coffee Growers. By accessing core-like wealth through the International Coffee Agreements, Fedecafé was able to finance a protective social compact that ensured that production costs would remain lower than sales, extensions services and credit were readily available, and outlets to the market unhindered by usurious merchants. As coca production entered Caquetá in the late 1970s, the relationship between cocalero farmers and the urban drug-trafficking organizations that monopolized cocaine exports was far from hegemonic. For one, drug-traffickers did not invest in the acquisition of land in the region. Instead, they operated as urban mafias that purchased coca and coca paste from producers through their own networks of hired transport merchants who would receive commissions based upon how much coca they were able to pull in. Neither urban mafia bosses nor their local purchasing agents had a vested interest in ensuring that cocalero producers received ample reimbursement for their harvests. Rather, because these merchants were the only buyers in town, and because they often were the very persons selling producers seeds and other needed inputs, the region's cocalero farmers remained highly vulnerable to the prices that were dictated to them. And even if and when cocaleros were disgruntled by these prices, they could be forced to sell at the barrel of a gun.[45] In other words, the risks of production were externalized onto coca producers, who were not only subject to market coercion from local buyers affiliated with drug-trafficking organizations. They were also subject to incursions from the state, which could destroy a crop that came to its attention. And finally, they were also subject to any efforts by cattle ranchers to evict them from their lands. Evidence of coca production provided cattle ranchers with a useful tool that could bring in antidrug police forces to arrest cocalero farmers as a step toward acquiring their land.[46]

Thus, during the years of coca's entrance into the frontier regions of Caquetá in 1978 and 1979, coca production arose alongside staple agricultural crops where it was produced by some of the region's more enterprising and risk-taking settler families. And while the cultivation of coca provided the possibility of acquiring additional income that could be used to stabilize their economic livelihoods, it also exposed them to new insecurities and threats. Not only did they remain vulnerable to ongoing processes of land dispossession driven by cattle ranching elites. They also became subject to violence perpetrated by drug traffickers and antinarcotics policing measures of the state. These vulnerabilities, however, were to change in the coming years as the revolutionary project of the FARC converged with the market dynamism of the cocaine economy.

---

[45] Krauthausen and Sarmiento (1991); Molano Bravo (2004); Linton (2014).

[46] Carroll (2011:130–32).

De-Peripheralization and the Rise of FARC Counter-Hegemony in the Caguán

Scholars who have researched the actions of the FARC in the Caguán point out that they were in fact originally opposed to the frontier peasantry's involvement in the production of illegal narcotics for a number of reasons. Ideologically, they were opposed to the vacuous consumer capitalism and hyper individualism that the cocaine economy had come to symbolize. But more practically, as we saw from their actions in the Greater Urabá region in the last case study, the FARC's efforts to establish rural territorial strongholds by protecting precarious peasant communities from land displacement put them in direct conflict with drug-traffickers if and when these traffickers acquired land as one of their money-laundering schemes. Indeed, in some regions of the country, the FARC were engaged in intense low-intensity warfare against drug mafias.[47] Yet, during this period of time, drug-traffickers were not engaged in land acquisition and money laundering in Caquetá. As a result, the FARC did not engage in the type of direct confrontations with drug-traffickers over land in Caquetá that they did in regions where landed narco-bourgeoisies took root. This, in addition to demands by cocalero producers for protection against raids from government narcotics agents and from cattle ranchers, eventually convinced the FARC's high command to change its mind about the matter. By the early 1980s, the FARC was not only protecting cocaleros from dispossession and state repression. They began to take on parastatal oversight of the local coca economy in ways that granted the FARC access to core-like profits and facilitated the incorporation local cocaleros into their larger revolutionary project.[48]

To be sure, the FARC's involvement in coca production in the Caguán led to the establishment of tactical market-based alliances between themselves and the urban narco-trafficking elites that continued to monopolize local purchases of coca leaves and paste, the processing of powdered cocaine, and export routes to the United States and other consumer countries. However, it is incorrect to assert that the FARC's participation in the cocaine market is itself an indication of their

---

[47] In 1981–82, drug-traffickers associated with the powerful Medellín drug cartel in coordination with cattle ranchers, members of the Colombian army, and others formed a paramilitary organization called Death to Kidnappers (*Muerte a Secuestradores*, MAS), in response to the M-19 guerrilla group's high-profile kidnapping of Martha Neives Ochoa, the daughter of trafficking boss Fabio Ochoa. By the end of the decade, the MAS had a regional paramilitary presence in eight departments of the country, including Caquetá (Hristov 2009:65–68).

[48] Molano Bravo (1994); Richani (2002).

political involution, as some scholars have suggested.[49] Many scholars, for example, note that the FARC's greatest successes come from their social origins in the peasant economy, and specifically from their ability to protect rural producers, squatters, and frontier migrants from encroachment from landed elites. Wherever they went, the FARC's *modus operandi* was to enter a rural region and use their arms and insurgent military expertise against state forces, juridical powers, or private militias that would otherwise force local peasant communities from their lands. And to build up their military and organizational capacity, they would invariably tax production or extract resources and revenues from the local host population, no matter what that population produced.[50] In this sense, their decision to protect Caquetá's cocaleros was not significantly different from their protection of rural communities that specialized in other agricultural commodities.

But more importantly, the FARC has not been simply an armed revolutionary group that specialized in rural guerrilla insurgency. Unlike most other twentieth-century guerrilla groups that engaged in what Immanuel Wallerstein (2000:255) called the "two-step strategy" of first conquering state power and then changing society, the FARC's power has come from their ability to *effectively replace* the state with their own "alternative state-like" institutions and actions. Specifically, the FARC have historically operated as a low-level state-like organization that has grown in territorial strength in ways that mirrored the state formation processes that have given rise to modern nation-states.[51] As Charles Tilly (1985:118) points out, nation-states and other violence-wielding organizations (gangs, mafias, guerrillas, etc.) engage in four interrelated types of activities:

1. War making: eliminating or neutralizing their own rivals outside the territories in which they have clear and continuous priority as wielders of force
2. State making: eliminating or neutralizing their rivals inside those territories
3. Protection: eliminating or neutralizing the enemies of their clients
4. Extraction: acquiring the means of carrying out the first three activities – war making, state making, and protection.

In Caquetá's agrarian frontier, the FARC engaged in "war-making activities" in which they engaged in combat against the Colombian armed forces and other rival

---

[49] La Rotta (1996); Rangel Suárez (2000); Pécaut (1999, 2001); Sánchez (2001).

[50] Chernick (2005).

[51] The FARC's alternative state formation activities are well established in the scholarly literature (González et al. 2003; Hough 2011; Richani 2002).

armed groups over control of the region. They engaged in "state-making activities" in which they used coercive measures to neutralize or eliminate threats to their territorial authority from local political elites, state security forces, cattle ranchers, drug traffickers, or other individuals that resided or worked in the regions under their territorial control. They engaged in "protection activities" in which they defended the local population of cocaleros, frontier settlers, and their communities from threats to their livelihood from state forces, drug-traffickers, or cattle ranchers. Finally, they engaged in "extraction activities" in which they financed these other activities by taxing local inhabitants, acquiring rents from the local economy, and extorting money from local elites living within areas under their control. In this sense, we see that the FARC's specific role within Caquetá's narcotics trade did not lead to any significant *qualitative* changes in their objectives, organizational structure, or *modus operandi*. Rather, it changed their operations *quantitatively* in ways that enhanced their revolutionary objectives. Introducing coca into this guerrilla state formation matrix granted the FARC extraordinarily high extractive incomes that helped them significantly build up their war-making, state-making, and protective capacities.

Specifically, the FARC's extraction of rents occurred at all levels of the coca political economy. First, they instituted a progressive income tax system for the region, wherein they levied a tax of 4%–10% on the incomes of coca producers, merchants, and narco-traffickers. Nationally, this revenue helped finance a major expansion in their number of "guerrilla fronts" (i.e., battalions consisting of 40–200 armed soldiers) from seven in 1978 to thirty-two by 1987.[52] On a local level, in addition to financing their organizational growth, it also provided them with the financial means to upgrade their military equipment and weaponry, including the purchase of Soviet-made AK-47s and antiaircraft rocket launchers, as well as to acquire speedboats to charter the region's waterways, radio technologies to monitor government surveillance efforts, and other equipment. which they used to further consolidate their territorial control over Caquetá's frontier region. By the early 1980s, for example, the FARC had gotten so strong militarily that it was able to effectively halt the regional encroachment of both land-hungry and state security forces and antinarcotics police units who targeted coca farmers.[53]

The FARC's ability to protect coca farmers and other colono settlers in the Caguán provided locals with a degree of social and economic stability that was essentially unattainable in most other regions of the country (with the exception of the coffee regions under Fedecafé's influence). The promise of this income and

---

[52] OPPDHDIH (2001:5).
[53] Valencia (1998); Richani (2002:70, 76); Carroll (2011:129).

protection became highly appealing to the large populations of rural surplus labor who were being displaced by agro-industrialization and economic growth elsewhere. Thus, beginning in the early 1980s the steady inflow of migrants to the region swelled into a veritable river. Perhaps ironically, Caquetá's population quickly met national standards and became a formal department in 1982. The department's population jumped from just over 180,000 inhabitants in 1973 to well over 218,000 inhabitants by 1985, and over 310,000 by 1993. By then, the municipalities under de facto FARC control in the Middle and Lower Caguán region, including Cartagena del Chairá, Solano, and San Vicente del Caguán jumped to over 84,000 formally recognized settler households.[54]

Under the protection of the FARC, Caquetá's frontier region quickly transformed into one of the country's leading sites of coca production. A veritable coca-enclave, the Caguán consolidated into a powerful hegemonic labor regime that incorporated cocalero labor and livelihoods into the FARC's larger revolutionary project. At the core of FARC hegemony was their institution of a protective social compact vis-à-vis cocalero farmers that was surprisingly comparable to Fedecafé's Pacto Cafetero vis-à-vis the country's coffee farmers. Like Fedecafé's social compact during the years of the International Coffee Agreements, the FARC was able to access core-like amounts of wealth that subsidized the costs of production and reproduction of the region's cocalero farmers. Like Fedecafé's activities through the National Coffee Fund, the FARC imposed a price floor system on the local sale of coca that stabilized prices above production costs (between US$500 and US$600 per kilo of coca paste).[55] They also taxed all purchases between cocalero farmers and merchant buyers, with merchants paying 4%–10% of the cost of each transaction. This regulatory oversight of the market did not only protect cocaleros from what had been their vulnerabilities vis-à-vis drug-traffickers, it also routinized transactions in the local market in ways that enhanced trust and economic cooperation, leading to greater productivity and sales. With prices fixed above production costs and access to market outlets secured, cocalero farmers were able to accumulate enough wealth to pay off any debts they had incurred and even expand their yields beyond the limits of the labor power of their families. Many cocalero farmers used this newfound income to expand their farms. As their labor needs during harvests grew to exceed what their family could provide, they employed new migrants and seasonal laborers, *raspachines* (scrapers) to pick coca leaves. The FARC regulated this local labor market by enforcing "living wages" for all hired laborers, which provided new migrants the

---

[54] SINCHI (2000:25, 30).
[55] OPPDHDIH (2001:6).

means to acquire the income needed to eventually establish a plot of their own on unoccupied lands further into the agricultural frontier. Some farmers also used this newfound income to establish their own primitive laboratories to process their coca leaves into the more lucrative coca paste. To encourage this local vertical integration, the FARC would sell cocalero farmers the equipment and inputs needed for these laboratories at subsidized rates.[56]

Also, like Fedecafé, the FARC invested heavily in broader development measures intended to stabilize and subsidize the social reproduction needs of local producers and their communities. For example, they invested heavily in the construction of social infrastructure for the region. They began to coordinate volunteer work assignments (*mingas*) that built small-scale public works, such as footpaths, bridges, schoolhouses, and even public health clinics, all of which helped solidify their backing from the local peasantry. In contrast to the public works initiatives of Fedecafé for the coffee sector that received backing from the central state and foreign investors, the FARC's involvement in such local development ventures was limited by their need to maintain a degree of concealment from the central state.[57]

Importantly, and unlike Fedecafé, however, the FARC did not institute measures to encourage the full marketization of local cocaleros. They were not involved in market's higher end and therefore had no interest in the overall quality of powdered cocaine as experienced by consumers. Instead, they had a vested interest in making sure that the regions under their territorial control were economically viable and socially livable. To this end, they encouraged crop diversification on coca farms and banned the use of coca as a method of local payment. This did not only protect cocalero farmer families from market pressures that might otherwise have facilitated their conversion into fully marketized coca producers. It also protected the local economy from becoming over-dependent upon a single cash crop.[58]

Also different from Fedecafé was the fact that the FARC themselves had to take on the functions of the state rather than externalize them onto the Colombian government. This was particularly important given the fact that the region's burgeoning coca economy did not only attract inflows of colonos and *raspachines*. It also brought a "floating population" of sex workers, street vendors, businessmen, adventurers, and low-level drug-traffickers that grew to an estimated 30%–40% of the total population of the region by the mid-1980s. As Leah Carroll

[56] Andreas and Youngers (1989:545–51); Vargas Meza (1999:89–91).
[57] Jaramillo et al. (1989:175–76); Carroll (2011:129).
[58] Richani (2002:5, 70).

(2011:128–29) notes, "given the large numbers of bars, the plentiful supply of beer and money, and the large floating population of migrant worker-adventurers, incidents of personal violence flared up easily." The FARC controlled this vice-prone "coca culture" with policing and juridical actions. For example, they established local laws that punished thieves and other criminal activity. They patrolled the discos on Saturday nights to prevent violent incidents. They also imposed a "beer tax" whose revenues were disbursed by a locally elected committee and used to finance schools and other projects. Finally, they acted as a juridical force by mediating property conflicts and wage-contract disputes.

As a local labor regime, the FARC's hegemonic social cocalero compact in the Caguán essentially aligned the interests of local producers and inhabitants in obtaining a stable social livelihood with their own interests in revolutionary war making and alternative state making. As the FARC's power in the Caguán increased, the entire region became popularly known as *FARClandia*, a spinoff of the infamous *Hacienda Larandia* that had been the symbol of the fading power of the region's cattle ranching elites. Rather than act as a motor of ongoing displacement and dispossession, the FARC's protection of the coca economy of the Caguán became a magnet that attracted the country's rural surplus population. Migrants to the region fostered the FARC's growth either directly as full-time rank-and-file soldiers or indirectly as economic producers or active social citizens of what had become a *de facto* guerrilla state.

The Social Contradictions of FARC Counter-Hegemony in the Caguán

FARClandia's successes as an alternative social, political, and economic formation and a counter-hegemonic labor regime, however, was limited by a number of inherent tensions and contradictions. First, and perhaps most obviously, the FARC remained an illegal political entity and their *de facto* jurisprudence and sovereignty was not recognized under the United Nations' state system. In practice, this meant that the FARC's attempts to build and consolidate its territorial control over the region regularly butted heads with the central state's sovereignty claims. Consequently, FARClandia was subject to frequent army attacks and aerial fumigations aimed at destroying its inhabitant's coca crops. And in turn, the guerrillas had to continually expand their war-making and state-making activities by reallocating a significant portion of their finances to maintain their soldiers and buy military technology and weapons. And, although the FARC had by the first years of the 1980s established three fronts in the region, it was not equipped for an open and direct confrontation with the Colombian military itself.

As a result, their military activities needed to remain "low-intensity" in nature and their whereabouts had to remain by and large concealed from the central state. The territorial scope of FARClandia was thus limited to the frontier region itself, which provided natural protection against invasions from the Colombian army.

Second, while FARC's territorial isolation helped conceal and protect them from military invasions, the social and political isolation of the frontier population living within FARClandia effectively marginalized them from access to various types of state services that were not adequately provided by the insurgents themselves. This was especially problematic for the health and education of local inhabitants, who lacked access to state-run healthcare facilities, public schools, and other public utilities. Thus, even during the height of FARC counter-hegemony in the mid-1980s, the Caguán region desperately needed more health and sanitation investments and services, as it ranked highest in the nation for malaria incidence, had high rates of infant mortality, anemia, hepatitis, and parasites. By 1984, with a population of roughly 33,000, the region had only 22 schools and no vocational training for adults.[59]

The FARC, however, were aware of this limitation of their territorial control. They responded by engaging in efforts to further "institutionalize" the region into Colombia's national body politic. Their first efforts began by encouraging locals to participate in the local politics through the *Juntas de Acción Comunal* (JACs). Though the JAC had previously been a tool of the Turbayistas, a veritable "extended state" apparatus meant to generate communal loyalties to the political establishment, FARC leaders believed that the JACs would provide the Caguán's inhabitants with a legal vehicle to voice local demands directly to the departmental government and demand services in return while circumventing the political monopoly held by the Turbayistas at the departmental level.[60]

More opportunities for regional institutionalization arose during the years of the Betancur Administration (1982–86), when the central government engaged in peace talks with the FARC and began the democratization reforms that opened up new spaces for political engagement. On the one hand, as had occurred in the banana region of Urabá, President Betancur's cease-fire agreement with the FARC (May 1984–June 1987) and guarantees of state protections from military repression created a window of opportunity for the FARC to engage in formal political activities. In Caquetá, the FARC used this "neutral stance" of the central government to attempt to expand their influence up from FARClandia and into regions of the Upper Caguán and urban Florencia, where the Turbayistas

---

[59] Carroll (2011:129).
[60] Jaramillo et al. (1989:168).

continued to monopolize the political sphere. Between May 1983 and January of 1984, for example, the FARC was able to organize massive demonstrations of 5,000–6,000 people in Florencia that won written agreements from the Turbayista government to ensure greater access to credit and technical assistance and to uphold the human rights of locals. Active campaigning efforts by the FARC on the electoral arena helped their *Frente Democrático* party win a number of departmental assembly positions in the 1984 elections, including 80% of those for the municipality of Cartagena del Chairá. And by 1986, the FARC's *Union Patriotica* party (UP) had won some twenty-eight of the sixty-eight county council member positions, five of the fifteen total departmental assembly members, and the first ever election of a Communist-UP Representative in the country's national Congress.[61]

The FARC also became involved in a series of formal discussions (communal forums) with the Betancur Administration in 1984 and 1985 that were meant to include locals in the formulation of alternative social and economic development opportunities for the region. These forums resulted in the formation of what became known as the "Caguán Colonization Committee" (CCC), a delegation of local JACs, representatives of the state's agrarian developmental agencies, and FARC leaders that developed plans to ensure farmer access to land titles, credit, and marketing access for agricultural produce in order to move the region's economy away from its dependence upon coca production, fortify the agricultural economy, and protect the region's wildlife and tropical ecology. The CCC's actions resulted in a number of developments that helped integrate the region into the national economy and polity. For example, as early as 1984, a store-boat agricultural marketing system run by the IDEMA began cruising the region's dense waterways, buying agricultural produce from local farmers and selling needed supplies back at subsidized prices. To promote the peace process, the CCC was able to use state funds to commission an artist collective, the *Jornada de Artistas por la Paz* (Artists Peace Action), that brought nationally known artists and performers to the Lower Caguán region in an effort to draw attention to the peace and reform measures. Finally, the CCC established what it called the "Committee for the Investigation and Transfer of Technology to Support the Colonization of the Middle and Lower Caguán and Sunciya" (i.e., "Transfer Committee"). The Transfer Committee arranged for the construction of a local vocational training center, a day care center, twenty-three rural schoolhouses, a weather station, the creation of a 200 ha farm to experiment with the cultivation of rubber plants, the establishment of thirteen family community agricultural

---

[61] Carroll (2011:136–38).

enterprises, and the solidification of plans to develop an aqueduct in the Caguán. It also cowrote two separate development plans for the region, coordinated and financed three major research projects on the region, and met with President Betancur and the regional military commander to advocate on behalf of their initiatives.[62]

Similar to the ways that the 1980s democratization opened up spaces for Urabá's working class to mobilize on the banana plantations and into local politics, the democratization and peace negotiations during the Betancur years represented a period of intense optimism for rural workers and communities. In Caguán, it seemed that the state was finally recognizing its role in creating the swaths of precarious rural surplus labor that gravitated to the coca economy and the protective umbrella of the FARC. As Leah Carroll (2011:137–38) points out, Betancur himself "expressed enthusiastic support for the efforts of the Committee, and scolded the Departmental administration for not supporting the Caguán experiment more actively."

However, also similar to what happened in Urabá during this same period, the strengthening of bonds between the FARC and the Betancur administration were matched by strengthening bonds between reactionary elements of the Colombian military that refused to recognize the political nature of the guerrillas and local elites that were threatened by the open political activity of the guerrillas. Caquetá's governor, a Turbayista through and through, had opposed the peace negotiations and the CCC's activities from the start. To demonstrate his defiance, he wrote an open letter to the Transfer Committee in August of 1984 stating that the new development institution was a ploy of the FARC. The subsequent governor himself only began to participate in the Transfer Committee at Betancur's insistence, though the Committee itself complained of the departmental government's "lack of co-ordination and even outright sabotage" of their measures.[63]

The Colombian military also opposed the actions of the CCC. As early as June of 1982, national military leaders had circulated a document rejecting Betancur's proposed policies toward the guerrillas, advocating instead for the need to step up counter-insurgent military actions. By January of 1984, the Minister of Defense came to openly reject the policies of Betancur. And though he was soon dismissed from his post, similar sentiments continued to be heard publicly from military leaders. In fact, despite the formal cease-fire, army personnel were found

---

[62] The Transfer Committee consisted of twenty state agencies, the JACs, CAC, CCC, and the FARC, which sought to bring state resources into the region to support the peace process. A representative from INCORA became its director and its headquarters was established in the departmental capital, Florencia (Carroll 2011:132–38).

[63] Jaramillo et al. (1989:209–13, 216–18).

responsible for the killing of three, the arbitrary detention of twenty-nine, and the torture of five peasants in the Caguán region over this period. And perhaps a harbinger of things to come, the military was also able to establish a new base in Cartagena del Chairá by 1984.[64]

The election of Virgilio Barco to the presidency in 1986 marked a fundamental setback for the unusual alliance between the FARC's Caquetá fronts and the central state. In his inaugural address President Barco himself announced that the central government would take a "harder line" toward the peace process, and upon his arrival into the presidency he appointed a new governor to Caquetá who was a friend of the regional army commanders and an outspoken critic of the FARC and the so-called Caguán experiment. His "Presidential Counselor for Peace" prohibited any further participation of state entities in the Transfer Committee and instead created a new set of institutions, or "Rehabilitation Councils," that excluded the participation of the FARC but included representatives of the traditional parties and the Catholic Church.[65]

Relations between the central state and the FARC were further soured when Congressman Rodrigo Turbay reported the assassination of fourteen Liberal Party members by the FARC. The President responded by refusing to follow through on his promise to appoint county executives from the Patriotic Union wherever the party had won a plurality from the March 1986 elections, as he had done in Urabá. The UP, who dominated the elections in the municipalities of Puerto Rico, Paujil, Cartagena del Chairá, and Montanita, responded by refusing to accept the authority of any elected county executive administrations in the whole department. By early 1987, not only were the political opportunities granted to the FARC rapidly closing, but the cease-fire agreement had also begun to break down and skirmishes between the FARC and armed forces became more common. The FARC responded by denouncing the construction of a road from Paujil to Cartagena del Chairá by the army, which they considered to be a "clear violation of the spirit of the accords" and a sign of the government's push toward a more militarized strategy for the region. A last attempt to salvage the alliance came in April when the Caguán Committee invited the Presidential Counselor for Peace to the region, where he was met by 5,000 local participants who presented him with an elaborate new development proposal. Four months later, the Councilor had failed to appropriate the funds required for the project, and a mass peasant protest ensued. At the same time, the Commander of the XII Brigade of the Army announced that the military would begin to advance down to the Caguán.

---

[64] Delgado (1987:146); Carroll (2011:132, 140–41).

[65] Carroll (2011:140–41).

According to Leah Carroll (2011:141–43, 151), the FARC's decision to ambush an army convey in Puerto Rico in June, which left twenty-seven soldiers dead and forty-three wounded, "sent shock waves throughout the military and police establishment." President Barco responded by calling an immediate end to the cease-fire. The Turbayistas who had remained on the sideline throughout the period once again found themselves aligned with the central government, and were now lauded as "martyrs" in the national press. And they used this opportunity to begin once again to lobby for the exclusion of any governmental benefits for residents living in regions under the FARC's territorial control.

By 1988, the termination of the cease-fire and the Barco administration's "renewed policy of war" against the FARC in Caquetá indicated to the frontier population that the central state was once again renewing its policy favoring a coercive rather than consensual development policy for the region in favor of the interests of the local landed elites. The road constructed by the military to connect Paujil and Cartagena del Chairá had been completed, effectively destroying the FARC's previous monopolistic control over access routes to the frontier regions under their territorial control. With the road complete, the military embarked on a new mission to weed out the FARC from the Middle and Lower Caguán region once and for all. Operation *Alfa Justiciero*, the name of the military operation that followed, was a major project that included the use of eighty speedboats and established temporary military bases in six different frontier municipalities. And though the operation was not successful in uprooting the *de facto* state run by the FARC in Caquetá's frontier, it was successful in dramatically reducing the territorial boundaries of FARClandia, with Santafé de Caguán acting as the new "post-operation status quo" line of demarcation between regions controlled by the military and those controlled by the FARC.[66] During the implementation of Operation Alfa Justiciero, the number of incidents of state repression that occurred in the Upper Caguán region began to escalate. Throughout the operation, the Colombian military is cited as torturing nineteen people, including one UP county council member, arbitrarily detaining two others, and seriously wounding another. Two others were killed by unknown assassins, including another UP county executive and the treasurer of one of the community development projects associated with the peace process.[67]

The re-militarization policy of the central state through Operation *Alpha Justiciero* did not only help local elites reconsolidate their military control of the

---

[66] Author interview with Colombian military officer in Florencia, Caquetá on July 9, 2009.

[67] CIJP (1989).

Upper Caguán. It also helped them reconstruct the clientelistic Turbayista machine that monopolized local political positions. Large landowners living in FARC-controlled areas who had previously voted for the UP to "avoid ruffling feathers" returned their votes to the Turbayistas. Likewise, frontier settlers and rural and urban workers that began to vote for UP candidates during the previous administration began to think "think twice about voting their conscience" given the escalation of repression. Thus, in the 1988 elections, the UP only won one county executive position in Caquetá and their proportion of Departmental Assembly votes shrunk in half, falling from 35% to just 16%. This trend continued into the subsequent elections, as their share of the Departmental Assembly fell to 13% in 1990 and 11% for 1992.[68]

This waning of the political influence of the FARC-UP in the Upper Caguán was compounded by the strengthening of a political coalition of Turbayistas with other Liberals, who began a "departmental embargo" against any initiatives proposed by UP county executives for the department. Consequently, reformers and radicals began to believe that it would be more practical to run as Liberals so that they could at least obtain access to state resources.[69] Likewise, with the FARC's power once again relegated to the frontier regions of the Middle and Lower Caguán.[70]

Thus, by the closing years of the 1980s and 1990s, Caquetá's political-economy was once again divided geopolitically between a settled region that remained under the firm control of the Turbayista Liberals and cattle ranchers and a frontier region that remained a site of coca production under the counter-hegemonic control of FARC. However, in the ensuing years, the development policies of the Colombian state would radically transform in ways that would intensify the stakes of the conflict over which labor regime would prevail in rural Caquetá.

---

[68] Carroll (2011:143–44, 147–48).
[69] Carroll (2011:143, 147–48).
[70] Delgado (1987:174).

7

An Uncertain Future in the Caguán and Beyond

Caquetá produces coca base, not cocaine ... Coca leaf is only one of many crops that facilitates the subsistence of the peasantry ... When the issue of illicit cultivation came up during [the 2016 peace talks] in Havana, coca growers were considered to be growing a common and ordinary plant just like any other ... This opened the way for their legal participation in the government crop substitution program. And if the national government does not respect this, pitifully we are going to throw away this historic opportunity to really create a substitution process. The entire thing will be thrown right into the garbage."

Rigoberto Rodriguez, Caquetá Cocalero Social Movement
Leader (October 2019)

In Chapter 6, we examined the inverse relation between the failure of Colombia's state-directed agrarian developmentalist measures of the 1960s and the rise of the FARC's counter-hegemonic control of the coca regime in the Caguán. By the 1970s, these agrarian development measures contributed to the transformation of the region into a despotic cattle ranching regime under the aegis of the National Cattle Growers Association (Fedegán). Land-intensive but labor-expulsive, Caquetá's cattle regime expanded through ongoing cycles of displacement that came to a halt by the early 1980s when the region's migrants began to cultivate coca under the counter-hegemonic protection of the FARC guerrillas. As had occurred in Urabá during this period, the political democratization measures and peace talks between the FARC and the Betancur government of the 1980s opened up spaces for larger developmental opportunities to improve the lives of the rural population in the Caguán region. However, these spaces were closed by the late 1980s and early 1990s when relations between the FARC and the Barco and Gaviria administrations deteriorated. In Urabá, this closing of political opportunities coincided with the rise of paramilitarism, which had been essential to Augura's reconsolidation of control of the region's banana regime in the 1990s. However, as this chapter makes clear, state efforts to regain control of the region

Figure 7.1 State/paramilitary repression in Urabá and the Caguán, 1987–2017

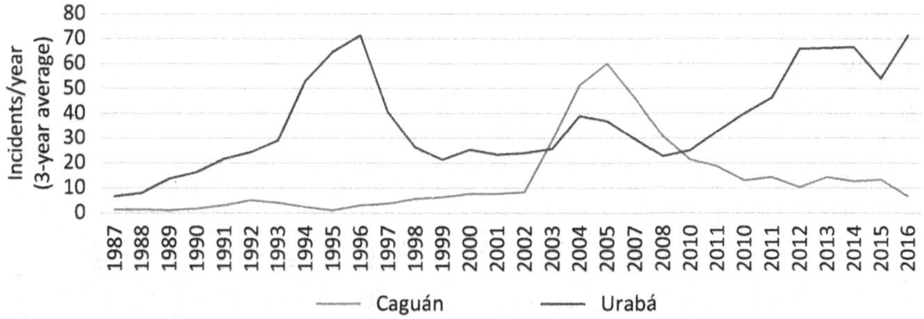

Source: Coercion Dataset

through a re-militarization strategy were effectively thwarted by the FARC, whose military and political presence was much harder to uproot as a consequence of their involvement in the coca economy.

Figure 7.1 compares the incidents of state and paramilitary repression in the greater Caguán region to that of Urabá, which had become emblematic of the growing power of Colombian paramilitarism during this period. We see that the number of incidents of state and paramilitary repression increased in Urabá steadily from the mid-1980s into the mid-1990s, and dropped to a floor-level of roughly twenty-five incidents per year into the early 2000s. During this same period, the incidents of state and paramilitary repression in the Caguán were virtually nonexistent, rising only slightly by the turn of the century. By the mid-2000s, however, the ability of the FARC to protect locals from repression unraveled, as the number of incidents jumped dramatically to levels similar to those experienced in Urabá during the peak years of paramilitary repression in the 1990s as well as more recently in the 2010s.

Not only did the FARC fall short on its role of protecting the region's cocaleros from state and paramilitary violence. During this period, the FARC also began to perpetuate acts of violence against locals. Figure 7.2 displays the number of incidents of FARC-perpetrated violence against civilian noncombatants living and working in the Caguán region from 1975 until 2017. Here we see that FARC repression remained virtually nonexistent from the mid-1970s when they had established a stronghold in the region and into the 1980s and mid-1990s when they consolidated their control over the region's burgeoning coca regime. However, by the late 1990s and into the mid-2000s, the FARC's ability to retain its control of the region by eliciting the active consent of the local population began to unravel. To be clear, the highpoint of FARC-perpetrated violence

Figure 7.2 FARC repression in the Caguán, 1975–2017

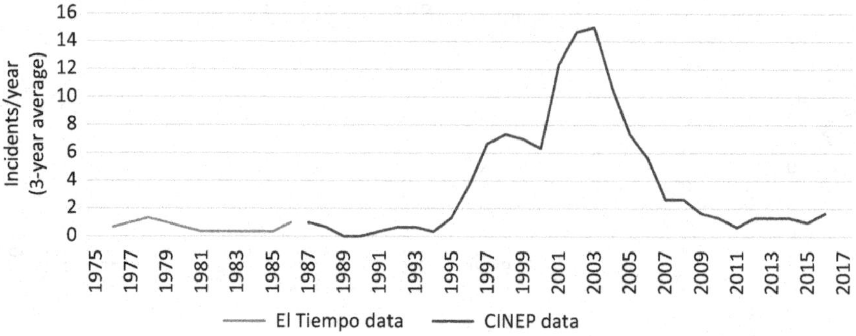

Source: Coercion Dataset

against local civilian noncombatants – roughly fifteen incidents in the early 2000s – paled in comparison to the average of fifty to sixty average incidents committed by state and paramilitary forces. Yet, as we shall see, this rise in FARC repression was emblematic of their loss of territorial control of the region and ultimately contributed to their demobilization by 2016.

Why did FARC counter-hegemony in the Caguán, which had been so resilient in the 1980s and 1990s, weaken to the point of collapse in the 2000s? And what livelihood strategies and development opportunities remain for the region's coca-lero farmers as the counter-hegemonic coca regime is dismantled? This final empirical chapter takes on these questions by situating the collapse of FARC counter-hegemony in comparative and world historical perspective.

In this chapter, I argue that the collapse of FARC counter-hegemony in the Caguán arose from the convergence of two major historical processes: the Colombian state's adoption of neoliberal policies seeking to open the countryside to foreign investment and the militarization of the region under the aegis of the US wars on drugs and terror. As we shall see, as long as the FARC remained in territorial control of large swaths of the countryside, efforts to transform Colombia's countryside into a new lucrative site of capital accumulation and a deregulated paradise for transnational corporations and foreign investors were effectively blocked. Because the Caguán was the FARC's most deeply entrenched territorial stronghold in the country, it became "ground zero" for a new military strategy meant to pave the way for a twenty-first-century development strategy rooted in the neoliberal transformation of the countryside.

To uproot the FARC, the Colombian government relied heavily on US support under the aegis of its global wars on drugs and terror. The United States, in turn, engaged in these military efforts to secure access to regional

Figure 7.3 Combat activity and FARC repression in the Caguán, 1975–2018

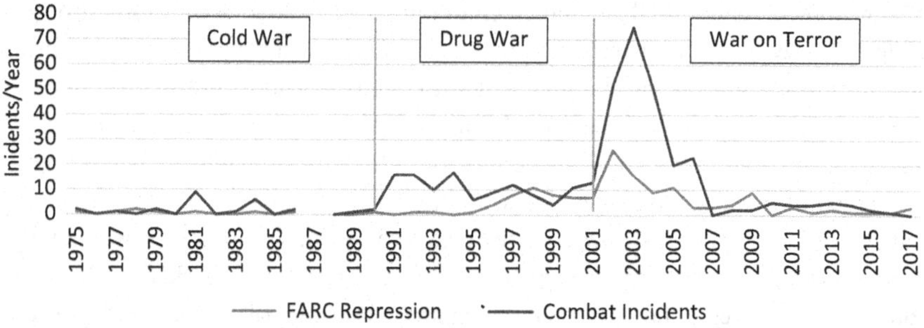

Source: Coercion Dataset

resources, labor, and raw materials while abandoning its support for developmentalist initiatives in the region. World historically, the militarization of rural Colombia was thus part and parcel of an emergent form of US geopolitical power that became heavily reliant on military aid and policing rather than developmental assistance as a mechanism of regional control. The growing impact of US militarization from the Cold War to the Drug War to the War on Terror on FARC counter-hegemony in the Caguán is evident in Figure 7.3. During the era of the Cold War, from 1975 until the close of the 1980s, both combat activity between Colombian state forces and the FARC as well as incidents of FARC repression against noncombatants remained low. This dynamic changed in the 1990s, when the Caguán region became a site of increased militarization under the auspices of combating illegal drug production. This first wave of heightened combat activity preceded an uptick in incidents of FARC repression by the close of the decade. Notably, a second wave of combat activity emerged in the region in the early 2000s, this time fostered by the War on Terror. It was the intensity of this second wave of militarization, I argue, that effectively dislodged FARC counter-hegemony in the region and ultimately paved the wave for both FARC demobilization in 2016 and the neoliberal transformation of the Caguán and rural Colombia more broadly. As the quote from Rigoberto above noted, the government peace talks with the FARC did provide new promises for future economic stability in the region. However, the government's willingness to deliver on the promises of an alternative future that meets the needs of cocalero farmers and other rural surplus populations has been all too uncertain.

I begin this chapter by analyzing how the adoption of neoliberal agrarian policies in the 1990s both accelerated nation-wide processes of rural dispossession that brought a massive new wave of migrants to the FARC's territorial stronghold in the Caguán region and increased the state's desire to occupy, control, and ultimately transform rural lands like the Caguán into new sites of neoliberal accumulation. As we shall see, neoliberal policies stimulated a transformation in Fedegán away from its early developmentalist origins as a supplier of cheap meat and hide for domestic production and into a global cattle industry producing exportable dairy products for the world market. This neoliberal transformation of Fedegán, in addition to the discovery of oil and other valuable rural resources, converged in the Caguán in the 1990s, making it the geographic focal point of the state's new development strategy. In the next two sections, I analyze how and why previous efforts to dislodge the guerrilla threat through US-backed Cold War containment strategies failed. I then demonstrate that the balance of power shifted to the Colombian military in the late 1990s and early 2000s, following a massive influx of US military aid that was appropriated under the banner of the US War on Drugs and War on Terror. I conclude this chapter with a discussion of the future economic prospects of the region's cocalero farmers and workers in the absence of FARC protection or a developmental alternative to capitalist accumulation through dispossession.

Neoliberalism and Its Limits in the Caguán

In August of 1990, Colombia's newly-elected president Cesar Gaviria announced the start of what he called a "Peaceful Revolution." In fact, this was the beginnings of the implementation of a package of orthodox neoliberal economic reforms, or *Apertura Económica*, that was intended to "shake the economy out of its slow-growth pattern" and "take advantage of the new opportunities offered by world trade."[1] Much in line with most neoliberal policy packages of the time, Gaviria's actions were meant to stimulate growth and productivity by exposing domestic industrial and agricultural producers directly to global market forces with minimal governmental regulatory interference. Since Gaviria, Colombian policymakers have increasingly liberalized trade and financial flows by phasing out trade restrictions such as tariffs and quotas and eliminating exchange rate controls, loosened labor and environmental safety laws to promote foreign investment and competitive domestic business practices, and privatized state-owned firms (telecommunications, banking, mining, oil) and domestic regulatory agencies.[2] Colombia has also entered numerous bilateral and regional free trade agreements, including the Andean Pact with Venezuela, Ecuador, and Bolivia (est. 1992), the G-3 trade

---

[1] Jaramillo (1998:38).
[2] Hristov (2014:82–85).

agreements with Venezuela and Mexico (est. 1995), the US-Colombia free trade agreement (est. 2012), the Canada-Colombia agreement (est. 2011), the Pacific Alliance with Peru, Chile, Mexico (est. 2011), and the European Union-Andes agreement with Peru and Ecuador (est. 2013).[3] In terms of its global commitments, Colombia became a signatory of the Uruguay Round of the General Agreement on Tariffs and Trade (1994) and a member of the World Trade Organization (est. 1999).

As a developmental model, neoliberalism's emphasis on market-led economic growth was an obvious reversal of the state's formal commitment to protecting rural livelihoods and domestic agricultural producers. In just one decade, each of the three hallmark agrarian development agencies created in the 1960s – IDEMA, INCORA, and the *Caja Agraria* – was liquidated or privatized. IDEMA's already meager staff of 3,378 employees in 1989 was cut to 1,516 in 1993, and was eventually fully liquidated by 1996. The *Caja Agraria* was transformed into the Entrepreneurial Development Bank (*Banco de Desarollo Empresarial*), becoming the *Banco Agrario de Colombia* in 1999. Finally, INCORA was liquidated and replaced with the more market-oriented *Instituto Colombiano de Desarollo Rural* (INCODER, est. 2003).[4] This said, the extent to which these neoliberal policies actually constituted a significant rupture from the *status quo ante* for local rural inhabitants in Colombia depended on whether or not they had been incorporated into a state-instituted protective social compact that neoliberal polices could in fact dismantle.[5] As we saw from the first case study, neoliberalism had very little

---

[3] The adoption of these neoliberal measures by the Gaviria Administration was by no means exceptional. Many governments across Latin America and the Caribbean, as well as throughout the former "Third World" were adopting neoliberal practices. What made Colombia's adoption of neoliberalism somewhat different from many other countries during this time was that it was not pressured to accept neoliberal policies as "conditionalities" imposed by the World Bank or IMF in order to access loans and continued development aid (McMichael 2008). Colombia had largely avoided the debt crisis of the 1980s, which suggests that Gaviria's efforts were driven primarily by domestic concerns aimed at stimulating rural economic growth (Jaramillo 1998).

[4] The number of land grants overseen by INCORA/INCODER, for example, dropped precipitously from nearly 14,000 titles of some 500,000 ha in 1990 to just over 2,000 titles of under 100,000 ha by 2001 (Faguet et al. 2015:18–19). For analyses of how Land Law 160 of 1994 impacted land titling, see Faguet et al. (2016); Peña-Huertas et al. (2017); and McKay (2017).

[5] See Bair and Hough (2012) for a distinction between neoliberalism as a logic of development and neoliberalism as a lived experience of workers and commodity producers.

direct impact on Colombia's cafeteros, whose protective social compact was instituted by Fedecafé rather than directly from the state. It was therefore the liberalization of the global coffee market, rather than the implementation of domestic neoliberal reforms, that undermined Fedecafé's Pacto Cafetero and destabilized cafetero livelihoods since 1989. Moreover, as we saw from the second case study, neoliberalism also had very little direct impact on Urabá's banana workers. This was because Urabá's workers had never been effectively incorporated into a hegemonic social compact but were instead forced to adapt to what has been essentially a liberalized and highly peripheralized global market niche since its emergence as an export enclave in the 1960s.[6] Finally, we have seen thus far from the case study of the Caguán, the state's agrarian development policies had done far more to stimulate the concentration of land in the hands of large-scale cattle ranchers than provide state protections for the country's frontier migrants.

Since the 1990s, Colombia's neoliberal policies have accelerated the dispossessing tendencies that were already built into the country's capitalist development trajectory. For example, large-scale commercial farmers that had historically been integrated into global markets, such as bananas and sugar cane exporters, actually increased their production by 34.5% and 53.5% respectively from 1990 to 2005. And African Palm producers, perhaps the most successful agricultural product under the neoliberal order, also increased production by a whopping 199% over this same period.[7] However, overall the neoliberal turn in Colombia has largely undermined the country's agricultural productivity. Notably, the national agricultural balance of imports and exports has favored domestic consumers seeking cheap products rather than domestic farmers. As Aurelio Suárez Montoya (2007:117) indicates, overall agricultural imports in Colombia grew by 424% while agricultural exports only grew by a mere 66% between 1991 and 2005. The influx of cheap agricultural imports – from just over 1.2 million tons (worth roughly US$404 million) in 1990 to nearly 9 million (US$4.2 billion) by 2010 – hit many domestic producers hard. Agriculture's contribution to Colombia's GDP, for example, shriveled from 17% in 1990 to a mere 7% by 2010. Likewise, the overall size of agricultural lands shrunk from 4.9 million hectares to 3.4 million while agricultural employment dropped from 31% to 19% between 1990 and 2010.[8] But more to the point, the hardest hit by the neoliberal turn in the rural economy were the small-scale farmers and subsistence peasants who had previously supplied local and regional markets with basic fruits, vegetables, and

---

[6] The brief exception was the passage of the short-lived Pacto Bananero in 1991–92.
[7] Suárez Montoya (2008:192).
[8] Fajardo (2014:72, 129, 101).

other agricultural commodities.[9] Producing agricultural goods for local markets has been an important means of campesino livelihoods, as it has shielded these producers from the risks of commodity production for the global market. Increasingly unable to compete with the influx of cheap imports and unable to access the provisions of subsidized credit and other state services, many have been forced to sell their land and migrated to the cities or other agricultural sectors looking for employment as landless wage workers.[10]

Given the destructive tendencies of Colombia's neoliberal agricultural policies, it is not surprising then that many of the rural landless and downwardly mobile have flocked to coca-producing regions, where they found a more stable livelihood as coca producers under the protection of the FARC. Nowhere was this more evident than in rural Caquetá. A massive wave of rural surplus migrants flocked to the region in the 1990s and early 2000s. Caquetá's population shot up from 218,485 inhabitants in 1985 to 311,464 in 1993 and 446,084 inhabitants by 2003, over 70% of which migrated to the rural coca-producing municipalities of the Middle and Lower Caguán.[11] This influx did not simply expand coca production southwards into the agricultural frontier. Rather, the total area dedicated to coca cultivation in Caquetá expanded to an estimated 30,000 ha that were scattered across twelve of Caquetá's sixteen municipalities.[12]

Like prior waves of mass migration to the region, this new wave of migrants in the 1990s created the potential for increased social conflict and disorder in the region. FARC leaders were indeed keenly aware of the social anomie and violence that could arise in frontier boom towns that lacked social oversight and policing. And they were also aware of the problems that could arise from a regional overdependence on cash crops like coca, which did not only subject producers to a volatile pricing market but also subjected them to antinarcotics interdiction

---

[9] The production of key staple produce, such as *cereales* (wheat, rice, potatoes, and beans) and *oleaginosas* (oil seed and nut products such as soybeans, maize, peanuts, almonds, sunflowers) dropped by 33% and 54%, respectively, between 1990 and 2005 (Suárez Montoya 2008:192).

[10] The number of land grants overseen by INCORA/INCODER, for example, dropped precipitously from nearly 14,000 titles of some 500,000 ha in 1990 to just over 2,000 titles of under 100,000 ha by 2001 (Faguet et al. 2015:18–19).

[11] DANE (2004).

[12] Coca production expanded into the municipalities of Albania, Cartagena del Chairá, Curillo, El Doncello, El Paujil, Milán, Puerto Rico, San José del Fragua, San Vicente del Caguán, Solano, Solita, and Valparaíso. Cartagena del Chairá, Milán, and Solano registered over 90% of its lands as being used for activity other than licit agriculture (SINCHI 2000:25, 30, 45–47).

efforts. As the *de facto* territorial state in the Middle and Lower Caguán, the FARC responded to this influx of migrants in a few ways. First, they instituted what became known as their "social manuals" (*manuales sociales de convivencia*), a set of economic and social norms intended to minimize conflict and regulate the economy. Economically, the *manuales sociales* required coca farmers to produce at least 5 ha of subsistence crops for every 2 ha of coca fields. These limits on coca production served a double purpose. On the one hand, they diminished cocalero reliance on the market to meet their social reproduction needs and therefore made it possible to keep production costs of coca leaves and paste cheap while retaining the ability to keep sales prices to external merchants high. On the other hand, by stimulating local production of subsistence goods, the FARC were able to maintain the region's economic autonomy while keeping a safe distance from national police forces. In fact, the FARC regularly patrolled the main road coming into the region and destroyed other roads that the state built to integrate the region more fully into the national political economy.[13] In this way, the FARC were able to incorporate this new influx of migrants in a regulated manner that ultimately contributed to the growth of the coca regime and the expansion of their social compact vis-à-vis local cocaleros.

It was also during this time that the FARC began to foster the development of community-based forms of political organization that would both institutionalize their territorial governance and selectively access vital resources from the central state. Building from their prior experiences with the Juntas de Acción Comunal (JACs), or community action boards, in the 1980s, the FARC began to systematically incorporate JACs into their own governance structures as a core strategy of local governance. As semi-autonomous community centers (*núcleos comunales*), the JACs provided a way for locals to express their demands both to the FARC and the state in a way that was ultimately overseen by local FARC leaders.[14] Akin to Fedecafé's municipal *Comités Cafeteros*, the JACs ultimately formulated local development plans, set rules and limits on the exploitation of natural and communal resources, regulated land use, and resolved juridical disputes. As one cocalero leader noted,

> it was through the JACs that the *manuales sociales de convivencia* were agreed upon and enacted. So it was there that people regulated how much coca should be planted in the community, what types of social behaviors (*comportamiento de las personas*) would be permitted. Each JAC had its own mini-constitution, and in it you would see the rules on, for example, if you

---

[13] Author interview with former INCORA agent in Florencia, Caquetá on July, 2009.

[14] Author interview with community activist in Florencia, Caquetá on July 6, 2009.

could cut down one extra hectare of virgin forest, you would have a fine of between one and 10 million pesos and be forced to plant two additional hectares of trees. Or, they would regulate fishing, making it illegal to dynamite the rivers for fish or to engage in commercial fishing . . .[15]

In this way, the FARC were able to construct and foster the growth of local social and political infrastructure that would facilitate social and communal norms, control processes of development and settlement, and bolster their own counter-hegemonic territorial control.

Indirectly then, the implementation of neoliberal reforms in the 1990s actually bolstered the strength of the FARC. In 1989, for example, the FARC operated only two of its thirty+ military fronts (*frentes militares*) in Caquetá. By 1996, the FARC expanded to well over seventy military fronts organized into seven regional blocs (*bloques*). By 1998, the FARC's Southern Bloc (*Bloque Sur*) grew to ten fronts operating across the departments of Caquetá, Putumayo, Huila and Cauca, five of which were based in the coca-growing regions of Caquetá alone.[16] By 2008, the FARC had reached its apex of strength when it grew to nearly 120 fronts and 30,000 soldiers operating across the entirety of Colombia's national landscape.[17]

Colombian neoliberalism, however, was not altogether favorable for the FARC in the Caguán. It also strengthened the resolve of neoliberalism's advocates in Colombia's political establishment who recognized that the FARC's control of large swaths of the countryside was a threat to foreign investment and economic growth. This was especially true for those factions of Colombia's capitalist class that had been courting transnational mining and oil companies as part of a new extractivist-based national model of development and those who viewed the neoliberal transformation of the countryside as an opportunity to expand production into the global market.[18] In the Caguán, it was the latter which first began the neoliberal assault to eliminate the guerrillas. At the helm of this assault was Fedegán, which saw new opportunities for growth of the country's cattle industry under the neoliberal model. During the developmentalist period in the 1960s and 1970s, Colombia's cattle industry was largely disorganized and diffuse. Cattle production served local markets. Quality control standards were minimal and the state invested very little in its infrastructural needs (irrigation systems, refrigeration, storage facilities, improved grasses and seeds). Though Fedegán attempted

---

[15] Author interview with cocalero activist via WhatsApp on October 17, 2019.
[16] Echandía Castilla (1999:45–50).
[17] Brittain (2010:16–20).
[18] See Avilés (2006, 2012); Hristov (2014); Richani (2020) for an analysis of the growing hegemony of the neoliberal faction of Colombia's capitalist class since the 1990s.

to elicit state support and investments for the industry, the central state considered cattle ranching to be an economic activity that was primarily useful for providing relatively inexpensive meats and dairy products to local urban workers. It was not considered to be a mode in itself for generating revenues for the state. And though Fedegán itself was a national industry group (*gremio*) like Fedecafé and Augura, under the developmental model its role was limited to the provincial and individualistic interests of local producers rather than offering a model for national capitalist development.[19] Consequently, Fedegán's position within the nation's ruling class remained marginal relative to other industry groups such as Fedecafé or Augura. For example, Fedegán's demands for state support for the cattle industry, including the need to establish a National Cattle Fund with a quota system akin to Fedecafé's National Coffee Fund, fell on deaf ears. Into the 1980s, cattle production remained geared towards internal consumption, hovering at roughly 3 million cows slaughtered per year between 1982 and 1990.[20] And although milk consumption increased from 2.0 billion liters consumed in 1979 to 3.9 billion in 1990, the market for dairy products remained limited to the domestic market which was its priority under the developmental model.[21]

These constraints on Colombia's cattle industry began to change in 1991 when Fedegán began to argue that Article 150.12 of the new Colombian Constitution established the responsibility of the state to form "fiscal or para-fiscal entities" to assist with failing sectors. These efforts culminated two years later when Agrarian Reform Law 101 of 1993 established the legal basis for the creation of Agricultural and Fishing Parafiscal Funds (*Fondos Parafiscales Agropecuarios y Pesqueros*). Its passage therefore gave way to Law 89 of 1993 which established the Cattle and Milk Quota (*Cuota de Fomento Ganadero y Lechero*) and paved the way for the creation of the National Cattle Fund (*Fondo Ganadero Nacional*), a powerful new state regulatory agency that was signed by President Gaviria in April of 1994.[22] Modeled on its predecessor in the coffee sector, the National Coffee Fund (*Fondo Nacional Cafetero*), the National Cattle Fund was specifically designed to protect local producers against the ebbs and flows of domestic cattle prices by regulating the domestic cattle market and investing heavily in the economic stability of cattle ranchers to ensure steady growth of cattle-based products to meet global demand. Thus, like the *Fondo Cafetero*, the National Cattle Fund adopted sales taxes that siphoned a portion surpluses made from

---

[19] Fedegán (2003:208).
[20] Fedegán (2003:207).
[21] MINAGRO (2002).
[22] Fedegán (2003:208–9).

purchases of cattle in domestic and international markets which went into a national fund (administered by Fedegán and representatives of the Ministry of Agriculture) that would be available for disbursement to meet the technical, financial and market needs of local producers.[23]

Preparing Colombia's domestic cattle industry for the global marketplace, however, required some significant transformations to the cattle ranching labor process. Foremost in this regard was the need to certify Colombian cattle according to the taste preferences as well as sanitary requirements of international importers. Fedegán announced its *Collaria Columbienses* program to investigate ways to improve the grasses used by cattle ranchers in order to improve the quality of the meat and dairy products to meet global taste standards. Under Colombia's participation in the regional free trade zone of the Andes (the Andean Pact, 1992), domestic producers were required to ensure that all cattle were free of the *Fiebra Aftosa* virus. A new law was passed to mandate anti-aftosa vaccinations and National Cattle Funds were allocated through Fedegán's new *Colombia without Aftosa* campaign.[24]

As one of the country's leading sites of cattle ranching, Caquetá was impacted directly by these changes. As early as 1994, roughly $2.4 million pesos of credit – amounting to 86% of all agricultural credit granted in Caqueta – were disbursed to local cattle ranchers.[25] By 1997, 60% of Caquetá's grasses were converted from "traditional" to a *Brachiaria* form of "improved" species. Moreover, Fedegán used its Cattle Fund to purchase new cattle grazing lands. By 1997, cattle ranchers had acquired over 2 million hectares in Caquetá, totaling 97.1% of all of the land used for licit agricultural activity.[26] Some of this growth in Caquetá's cattle industry was rooted in the old developmentalist focus on meat and hide production for the regional and national market.[27] In 1997, Fedegán also increased its taxes on sales and used these revenues to expand its investments in sanitization and export promotion measures. Between 1994 and 2003, the total rents (*recaudo*) collected by Fedegán through the quota system expanded from $3.319 to $32.978 million pesos.[28]

---

[23] Author interview with Fedegán representatives in Florencia, Caquetá on July 9, 2009.

[24] A similar set of initiatives was also launched to address the problem of *Brucelosis* in 2001 (Fedegán 2002, 2003:212–17).

[25] Castro Contrera (1995:40).

[26] SINCHI (2000:44–50).

[27] In 1984, for example, roughly 50% of Caquetá's meats were consumed within the department. By 1997 that percentage had dropped to 13%, with most arriving in the consumer markets of Valle del Cauca, Huila, Cundinamarca, Cauca, and Tolima.

[28] Fedegán (2003:210, 215).

Interestingly, however, the adaptation of Caquetá's cattle economy to the neoliberal model was not predominantly based upon domestic meat and hide consumption. In fact, between 1984 and 1997 the number of heads of cattle destined for slaughter (*hato carne*) in Caquetá decreased by 64%, consisting of 94% of the total cattle in 1984 and dropping to slightly over 20% in 1997. The adaptation of the cattle industry to the neoliberal model was therefore not related to meat production and exports, but rather to the expansion of the dairy sector. Between 1984 and 1997, the department experienced an average growth of 40,000 heads of bovine cattle, a growth of 45%. Caquetá's dual-use meat/milk (*doble propósito*) cattle alone increased from close of 63,200 heads in 1984 to over 1 million heads by 1997, jumping from only 5.5% of the total to over 73% over that same time period.[29]

The reason dairy producing cattle have been central to the neoliberal project does not necessarily have to do with the production and consumption of *drinkable* milk. In fact, while milk production has increased nationally from under 3.9 million liters in 1990 to close to 5.9 million liters in 2002, the number of volumes of liquid and lactose derivatives (*derivados lácteos y líquidas*) exported from Colombia remained under 5,000 tons throughout the 1990s until 2002. The key to the expansion of dairy cattle production rests with the exportation of *milk powders* and other *dry milk products*. By 2000, the amount of dry milk produced and processed nationally in Colombia had increased to roughly 30,000 tons. The value of the exports of dry milk versus liquid milk products is significant. Between 1997 and 2002, the total value of dry milk exported from Colombia grew from US$1.581 million to US$58.824 million. In contrast, the total value of liquid milks (*lácteos y líquidas*) only grew from US$4.445 million in 1997 to US$7.863 million in 2002.[30]

Importantly, this increase in the size and productivity of dry milk production in Caquetá did not come from the National Cattle Fund alone. Rather, much of the transformation and growth of the sector was driven by transnational corporations that were attracted to the region by neoliberal incentives. For example, those municipalities that dedicated over 75% of their production to dairy received the bulk of Fedegán's investments in improved grasses. Simultaneously, these same municipalities (and to a lesser extent other dairy producing municipalities) have received significant investments of technical assistance and credit from the Nestlé Corporation, which has come to dominate Caquetá's cattle ranching landscape.[31]

---

[29] SINCHI (2000:49).

[30] Fedegán (2003:111).

[31] The municipalities include Belen de Andaquíes, Cartagena del Chairá, La Montanita, El Paujil, Puerto Rico (SINCHI 2000:48).

In fact, the Nestlé Corporation had invested in Colombia's economy in various ways throughout the twentieth century. It began processing milk products as far back as the 1930s, though over 90% of these products were consumed locally and 80% of their ingredients consisted of locally produced ingredients.[32]

However, Colombia's adoption of business-friendly neoliberal policies prompted the Swiss giant to begin investing much more heavily in the country's cattle industry. In the 1990s, for example, Nestlé purchased over 1 million hectares of land in Caquetá alone, primarily by acting as a guarantor for loans lent to local ranchers from Colombia's agrarian bank. Nestlé also helped finance Fedegán's construction of much needed cattle ranching infrastructure in the region. For example, Nestlé created a rotary fund that funded the creation of electrical circuit systems, water storage facilities (*jagueyes*) for use during period of drought, and refrigeration plants. In conjunction with Fedegán, Nestlé also began financing studies to improve grass quality, produce more disease-resistant cattle breeds, and develop a phosphate-rich soil. Nestlé also played a central role in the expansion of processing and refrigeration plants in Caquetá. They installed a chain of refrigerating tanks and seventeen milk chilling stations, invested in road improvements, and bought carrier trucks to help connect Florencia's precondensation plant to the outer reaches of Caquetá's agrarian frontier. With the help of Colombia's Agrarian Bank and FINAGRO, Nestlé built over 170 local dairy market facilities (*acopios*), amplified the capacity of their refrigeration plant in El Doncello in 1992 and 1994, and drew up plans to expand the capacity of its plant in Florencia by 2009.[33] Not surprisingly, Nestlé became the largest buyer of milk products in Caquetá (purchasing 51% of all dairy sold) and the third largest buyer nationally by the turn of the century. This is significant given the fact that the dairy sector in Caquetá grew by an average of 5.9% per year between 1990 and 2005.[34]

---

[32] In 1974 Nestlé's subsidiaries in Colombia began buying dairy products from Caquetá; and in 1978 Nestlé inaugurated the opening of its first precondensation plant in Florencia where it began converting liquid into dry milk products. In 1986, it established a refrigerating plant to complement the growth of its production in El Doncello. It subsequently began investing in a series of "chilling stations" scattered throughout the department to assist in the transport of dairy as the cattle grazing areas extended outward following the expansion of the frontier. The holding capacity of these stations grew from 1 million liters in 1974 to 16.8 million liters in 1984 (Nestlé 2005a:17, 2005b:38).

[33] Author interview with Nestlé technical adviser in Florencia, Caquetá on July 7, 2009.

[34] Nestlé (2005a:4–16, 38–39, 2005b:38).

By the close of the twentieth century, Caquetá's cattle industry had received significant injections of capital meant to fortify the industry in preparation for a new era of growth under the neoliberal model. However, this injection was primarily limited to the Upper Caguán and other parts of Caquetá that had never transformed into significant sites of coca production or FARC territorial control. To meet expected demands of the market, Fedegán's directors believed that a southward expansion into the frontier-coca zones was inevitable. And to make matters more complicated, this desire for expansion and growth in the cattle industry was occurring at the same time that the FARC was expanding its territorial and military power throughout the countryside. Not surprisingly then, these oppositional political economies began to clash once again by the late 1990s. Fedegán, for its part, reported that by 1998, 41,689 of Colombia's 300,000 cattle ranchers held land in areas of guerrilla influence and were therefore subject to the guerillas' "revolutionary taxes."[35] In 1998 alone, a total of 472 cattle ranchers reported to have paid kidnap ransoms of roughly US$150,000 each to the guerrillas in order to avoid persecution.[36] Such incidents of guerrilla activities in cattle regions did not only strike fear in foreign investors and domestic cattle ranchers, it was also proving to have a negative impact on domestic cattle prices, which were considered to be "highly responsive to security conditions."[37] Fedegán and its neoliberal allies were therefore poised for a new strategy meant to uproot the guerrillas altogether, who had become both a threat to the future expansion of the region's cattle industry and a fundamental obstacle to the further transformation of rural Colombia into a new site of neoliberal capitalist investment.[38]

But it was not only Fedegán that viewed the guerrillas' control of large swaths of Colombia's countryside as a threat to their further expansion. International oil companies had spent decades exploring Colombia's untapped oil reserves, finding massive deposits of crude oil throughout the country's southeastern Amazonian forests and grasslands, including in the southern piedmont region of Caquetá. The US-based Occidental Oil Company, for example, partnered with Colombia's state-oil giant Ecopetrol to develop plans to extract the oil from these deposits and construct oil refineries and new pipelines in Caquetá and other departments (Arauca, Northern Santander, and Putumayo). However,

---

[35] Fedegán (2003:112–15).

[36] Richani (2002:142).

[37] SINCHI (2000:49–50).

[38] The most lucrative industry to benefit from the neoliberal investment climate has been foreign mining companies and energy companies seeking to invest in large-scale megaprojects (Chomsky et al. 2007; Diamond 2019; Hristov 2014).

these plans were held up due to the presence of guerrillas in these regions.[39] Other companies waiting for the chance to invest in Colombia's untapped rural geographies included construction contractors ready to construct megaprojects like highways, dams, and telecommunications infrastructure connecting these sites to the country's urban centers as well as agribusinesses like African palm oil, sugarcane, timber and biofuel companies.[40] Rural Colombia, and rural south-eastern Colombia in particular, was becoming a desirable potential site of neoliberal expansion and the FARC, in turn, were becoming the primary obstacle to the realization of these desires.

Colombia across the Arc of US World Hegemony: Developmentalism and the Cold War

The question of how to fight the FARC was not new to Colombian elites. Since their emergence in the 1960s, the FARC and other guerrilla insurgency groups had been ensconced in an ongoing game of cat and mouse with Colombian armed forces that had only intensified over time. Scholars point out that Colombia's counter-insurgency operations in Colombia since the 1960s were primarily a "containment strategy" devised to ensure that rural insurgency remained outside of the country's key political and economic centers.[41] So long as revolutionary groups did not fundamentally threaten key sites of capitalist investment and national development, they were viewed more as a regional annoyance to be controlled rather than a critical threat to the political dominance of the national state.[42] Moreover, because Colombia's political party leaders have long been distrustful of the autonomy and growth of the country's armed forces, they have been typically unwilling to raise the taxes to finance the organizational growth of the Armed Forces.[43] Instead, Colombian elites have relied on two added strategies to contain historic bouts of local armed rebellion, banditry, and social unrest.[44] The first, as we saw from the

---

[39] Hylton and Tauss (2016); Volckhausen (2019); Anzuoni (2019).

[40] Volckhausen (2019).

[41] Richani (2002); Livingstone (2004); Tate (2015).

[42] The fact that US military aid was designed to be used as part of a "containment strategy" is well documented in the scholarly literature (Avilés 2012; McClintock 1992; Richani 2002).

[43] Unlike many other Latin American countries, the Colombian military has rarely engaged directly in party politics or taken political power via coup d'états. The exception, of course, was the Rojas Pinillas' coup in 1953, which occurred peacefully.

[44] Sánchez and Meertens (2001); Kline (2015:20–26).

case of Urabá, has been the use of private security forces, local armed militias, and paramilitaries to fill the void left by the institutional weaknesses of the Colombian army. Second, they have relied heavily upon access to US military assistance and training. Like so many governments across the so-called Third World during the years of the Cold War, Colombia received steady provisions of weapons, air power, counterinsurgency training and logistics, and financial support in exchange for its commitment to pro-capitalist policies that kept domestic land, labor and resources open to world trade.[45] By the 1960s and 1970s, Colombia was the fifth largest recipient of US military aid in Latin America and deemed a critical geopolitical ally to the United States in the region.[46]

Although US military aid was a significant tool in its world hegemonic tool kit, direct forms of US intervention proved risky and unpredictable as they could trigger political backlash.[47] For this reason, both Colombian and US leaders during this period preferred to rely on developmental aid and assistance to contain social unrest and promote capitalist growth. As we have seen from the previous case studies, the exact developmental instruments of US hegemony in Colombia varied significantly depending upon the commodities produced and other local labor regime dynamics. US involvement in the International Coffee Agreements was central to its hegemony over coffee-producer countries while its support for vertical disintegration and domestic banana production was critical to its hegemony in the banana market. In rural regions like the Caguán, the US supported state-directed agrarian development initiatives such as the Caquetá Colonization Project and Integrated Rural Development.

---

[45] During World War II, the United States built air and naval bases in Colombia and established a nation-wide counter-espionage system running out of the embassy in Bogotá. When the Korean War broke out, Colombia was the only Latin American country to send troops to fight alongside US soldiers. In doing so, Colombian military men were trained by US commanders in the latest counterinsurgency strategies, which laid the groundwork for the further "professionalization" of Colombia's Armed Forces for decades to come. Likewise, Colombia was one of the first countries to send military officers for training at the "School of the Americas," where an estimated 7,917 officers were taught counterinsurgency strategies between 1950 and 1979. As Cold War concerns stepped up in the aftermath of the Cuban Revolution, US military aid and training flowed into Colombia as part of "Plan LASO" (Latin American Security Operation), a comprehensive counterinsurgency plan to contain the "communist threat" perceived to be building across the greater Andean region (Gill 2004; Livingstone 2004).

[46] Livingstone (2004:153–56).

[47] For analyses of backlashes against US militarization, see Holmes (2014).

The effectiveness of these diverse world hegemonic strategies, as we have seen, varied significantly. The reconstruction of the world coffee market under the ICA agreements was clearly the most successful in generating a stable hegemonic regime that was conducive to both local economic growth and US hegemony. Neither guerrilla insurgency nor militarization gained much traction in Viejo Caldas throughout the developmentalist decades. In contrast, the other developmentalist initiatives – vertical disintegration in Urabá and state-directed agrarian development in Caquetá – failed to establish labor regimes marked by the effective and consensual control of their respective working classes. Thus, by the 1970s and 1980s, each region became susceptible to guerrilla insurgency groups that integrated into local class conflicts. The FARC and the EPL became important allies of Urabá's plantation workers and political party activities. The FARC, in turn, became the primary means of protection of the Caguán's frontier migrants confronted by land-hungry cattle ranchers. Not surprisingly, both regions became sites of militarization.

But even when these conflicts did become sites of heightened militarization, US military aid to Colombia during the Cold War was directed more to containment than elimination. For example, because banana production in Urabá had become critical to the success of Colombia's developmental model in the 1960s and 1970s, and because US corporations had a vested interest in accessing stable supplies of bananas in the market, the United States was keen to provide the assistance needed to construct a military base in the banana-producing municipality of Carepa and to train military officers in counterinsurgency techniques. Yet, even with this assistance from the United States, it was not militarization per se, but paramilitarism, that uprooted the FARC and EPL and helped return control of the plantations back to Augura by the mid-1990s. In Caquetá, militarization took a different path. During the 1960s and 1970s, the regional presence of Colombia's military remained fairly small. Even during the peak years of militarization during the mid-late 1970s, military actions were meant to repress urban political activities in and around the department capital of Florencia rather than engage in full-scale attacks on FARC strongholds in the remote frontier regions of the Lower and Middle Caguán.[48] Clearly, at least during this period and into the 1980s, the Caguán was neither a core site of development nor considered a key economic base. Thus, the FARC's presence in the region, while an obstacle to the further expansion of cattle ranchers, did not post any significant threat to the security of the state and the ongoing viability of its developmentalist practices.

---

[48] Author interview with Colombian army official in Florencia, Caquetá on July 9, 2009.

All of this changed, however, in the 1990s. On the ground in Colombia, the FARC's rural roots had not only deepened in its existing territorial strongholds in regions such as the Caguán. They had also significantly expanded into other rural regions of the country, leading many of Colombia's political leaders to express fears that the guerrillas were becoming an existential threat to the continued viability of the state.[49] This frustration with the guerrillas was confounded by the passage of national neoliberal reforms, which promised an economic way out of the crisis through new rounds of foreign investment and rural industrial development but which were blocked by the presence of the guerrillas. That is, the FARC's rural strongholds had grown to become the primary obstacle to this goal of making rural Colombia safe for foreign investment and capitalist production for the global market. No longer confined to remote areas of country deemed to be of little economic value to the country's overall developmental trajectory, the FARC were becoming holders of some of the country's prime real estate under the neoliberal model.

Yet, the world historical context had shifted in ways that undermined the US government's most effective tools of rural social containment during the past half century: developmental assistance backed by US military aid. Geopolitically, US militarism had lost it *raison d'être*. The existential communist threat was swept into the dustbins of history when the Soviet Union dissolved and Russian and its former satellite republics embraced a rapid shift toward Western democracy and neoliberal capitalism. This was further compounded by a global wave of political democratization between 1989 and 1991 that ended some of the world's most notorious authoritarian regimes from Brazil to South Africa to Poland and the Philippines, demobilized and politically reincorporated Marxist guerrilla groups.[50] With no ideological Marxist alternative to Western capitalism and liberal democracy, US military leaders and political hawks began to frantically search for new justifications to maintain their budgets, ranks, and purpose.[51] Colombia, for its part, had indeed participated in this wave of democratization. The M-19, Quintin Lame, and factions of the EPL guerrillas had demobilized and a new, more inclusive constitution was ratified under Gaviria in 1991. Yet, its strongest guerrilla groups – the FARC, ELN, and factions of EPL – continued to wage their revolutionary war. This put Colombian leaders in a geopolitical bind. To describe these groups as self-interested, depoliticized mafias or "narcoguerrillas" would undermine their ability to tap into the coffers of US military aid, which was

---

[49] DeShazo et al. (2007).

[50] Robinson (1996); Tate (2015).

[51] Tate (2015:1).

slated for military operations that threatened national security. To describe them as Marxist revolutionaries, in turn, also fell on deaf ears in the US congress, which would not agree to increase military aid to Colombia to fight groups that were believed to be politically marginal vis-à-vis Colombia's electorate as well as operating against the tides of history.[52]

But it was not only that world capitalism had apparently won its war against world socialism. Geo-economically, the United States and US-dominated multilateral institutions began actively promoting a form of neoliberal capitalism that was at odds with the developmentalist forms of capitalism that had been so central to its world hegemonic influence since the 1940s and 1950s. Since the global economic recession of the mid-1970s, US governmental leaders had been struggling to find a way to re-stimulate economic growth and corporate profits in a world economy that had become increasingly competitive. Under the Reagan Administration in the 1980s, the United States began launching a full-scale attack on the ideology of state-directed and politically regulated capitalism and on the New Deal and Fair Deal institutions that had been so central to the expansion of US world hegemony during the previous half-century. US developmentalist assistance was pulled back dramatically and replaced by advocacy of neoliberal strategies of market deregulation, privatization, and global economic integration in order to promote domestic economic growth. These neoliberal policies became imperatives of the US-dominated World Bank and International Monetary Fund, whose "structural adjustment loans" demanded market liberalization from countries desperate to refinance their debts and obtain funds for domestic growth initiatives. Into the 1990s, the United States also began engaging in "free trade agreements" such as the North Atlantic Free Trade Agreement with Canada and Mexico (NAFTA, est. 1994) that paved the road for other bilateral agreements in the coming decades. It also began laying the foundation for a complete neoliberal rewriting of the rules of international trade, which took form in the establishment of the World Trade Organization in 1999. Overall, US advocacy of neoliberalism in the 1980s and 1990s entailed a systematic abandonment of the developmental institutions that had been so critical to the reconstruction of world capitalism under US hegemonic control during the postwar decades. Like the world hegemonic decline of Great Britain at the turn of the twentieth century, the 1980s and 1990s were the United States' "Belle Époque," wherein the United States engaged in efforts to retain its control of the commanding heights of the world economy in a world of increasing global competition.

---

[52] Tate (2015:31–32, 47–55).

Making Neoliberalism in Colombia: From the Cold War to the War on Drugs

Given the demise of US support for both developmental aid and counterinsurgency, it was not at all clear to President Gaviria how the Colombian state would regain the territorial control it needed to open the countryside to global capital. As it turned out, however, Colombia's political establishment found an unlikely arsenal of support for their efforts to uproot the guerrillas from the countryside: the US War on Drugs. Over the course of the 1990s, Gaviria was able to muster US support for the Colombian military's offensive against the FARC by labeling them a drug-trafficking organization that constituted a threat to US national security. Fighting Colombian guerrillas, under this new policy nexus, was an antinarcotics issue that could tap funding made available through the US drug war.[53]

To be clear, the US drug war had already been in existence since president candidate Richard Nixon began to employ the rhetoric of the "War on Drugs" to cull conservative voters fears and anger at the liberal drug politics associated with the student, antiwar, civil rights, and other social movements of the 1960s.[54] While it arose predominantly as a domestic set of initiatives, the war on drugs provided the political rationale underlying a number of foreign policy interventions in Mexico, Bolivia, and Peru in the late 1960s and into the 1970s.[55] It was not until the administration of President Ronald Reagan (1980–88), however, that the importation of illegal narcotics became redefined as a national security concern that could involve military actions. Reagan began this process when he started adopting the term "narco-guerrilla" to bolster domestic support for his wars

---

[53] Tate (2015:47–53).

[54] Nixon signed off on the Controlled Substances Act of 1970, which created the Drug Scheduling System that drew a sharp line between legal, medical, and illegal substances believed to be a threat to national well-being. And by 1973, Nixon has signed off on the Drug Enforcement Agency (DEA, est. 1973), a federal agency operating under the US Department of Justice designed to deploy federal police, intelligence, and the criminal justice system to combat drug-trafficking and distribution. Despite the harsh drug war rhetoric, Nixon's actual policies prioritized drug treatment as the primary means of redressing problems of domestic illegal drug addiction rather than the policing efforts of the DEA. Moreover, during its first decade of existence, the DEA focused almost entirely on domestic drug-trafficking organizations. International trafficking was mostly considered to be the responsibility of domestic governments, and therefore a foreign policy matter that required diplomacy (Reinarman and Levine 1997; Tate 2015).

[55] Walker (1989).

against leftist groups in Central America. By 1986, he issued "National Security Directive No. 221," which identified imports of illegal narcotics as a threat to hemispheric security and opened the way for counter-narcotics military actions in Bolivia.[56] Two years later, President George H. W. Bush (1988–92) broadened these efforts to include military aid to Colombia, Peru, and Ecuador through a $24 million total package called "Operation Snowcap."[57] However, the first major uptick of US drug war involvement in Colombia occurred in 1990 when President Bush announced his "Andean Initiative" (AI) drug strategy. This initiative provided $2.2 billion of military assistance to Bolivia, Peru, Ecuador, and Colombia to eradicate drug production at its source and combat drug-trafficking through interdiction and internationally coordinated policing efforts. Under this initiative, Colombia received a four-year aid package totaling approximately $500 million (1989–93), of which $183.4 million went to military assistance, $153.9 million went to crop substitution and eradication programs, $122 million to Colombian law enforcement, and $23.9 million to DEA support.[58]

Although the Andean Initiative provided new funds to Colombia's Armed Forces, it was officially defined as a counter-narcotics rather than a counter-insurgency action, and therefore strictly prohibited the use of US military assistance to fight Colombia's guerrillas directly. Over the next four years, it was the Colombian National Police, rather than the Colombian military, that acted at the forefront of the US-backed drug war.[59] By 1991, for example, Colombia's National Police had imprisoned some 1,533 domestic drug-traffickers, confiscated 606,955 tons of cocaine, fumigated some 1,838 ha of coca fields, and destroyed 293 coca-processing labs.[60] By 1993, increasingly sophisticated and highly coordinated antinarcotics actions between US and Colombian forces led to the

---

[56] In July of 1986, Reagan began providing the Bolivian government with military personnel and Blackhawk helicopters under "Operation Blast Furnace" to find and destroy Bolivian coca-processing plants that were believed to be suppliers of cocaine to the US market (Walker 1989).

[57] Walker (1994:4, 2001:26); Livingstone (2004:149); Camacho Guizado (2005:81).

[58] To help drug producer countries transition to legal economic activities, the United States agreed to reduce tariffs for ten years for select products imported from the Andean countries into the United States as an additional incentive (Crandall 2002:29–34; Perl 1992:40; Tokatlian 1994:133).

[59] Tate (2015:42–46) points out that US policymakers during this period were confident in the activities of the Colombian National Policy, which they saw as strong allies in the drug war. Internal reporting of the Colombian military, however, described them as "inept, corrupt, and abusive."

[60] Tokatlian (1994:130–41).

imprisonment and subsequent killing of Colombia's most powerful drug-trafficker Pablo Escobar in 1993.[61] By 1995, the heads of Colombia's most powerful drug cartels – the Medellín and Cali Cartels – were either killed or imprisoned, thus effectively decapitating their organizational structures.[62] These formal successes of Bush's Andean Initiative helped transform Colombia into the United States' strongest and most trusted ally in its global war on drugs.[63]

However, in practice US counter-narcotics activities in Colombia during this time were not only *unsuccessful* in curtailing the production and exportation of cocaine to the United States. They were also producing unintended political and social consequences that actually weakened the legitimacy of the Colombian state and strengthened the territorial grip of the FARC. First, while the influx of US military aid was not directed to counterinsurgency efforts, it boosted President Gaviria's confidence in Colombia's Armed Forces. Thus, immediately following the allocation of aid, President Gaviria launched *Operación Centuario*, a series of military assaults on the FARC headquarters of its Eastern Bloc (*Bloque Oriental*) in and around the Caguán. These military assaults on the FARC ebbed and flowed over the entire four years of Gaviria's administration, as they granted the president a way to boost his domestic political base by publicly punishing the FARC for refusing to demobilize and therefore partici-pate in the Constitutional Assembly of 1990. Yet, this uptick in military combat against the FARC attacks did little to dislodge the guerrillas from their control of the Caguán and other coca-growing regions and in fact bolstered FARC leaders' belief that they had gained the upper hand on the battlefield. Over the next few years, the FARC actually won a number of high-profile battles against the Colombian military, including successful ambushes against military facilities in towns of El Billar and Miraflores in Caquetá and in Mitú in the neighboring department of Vaupés.[64]

Second, the drug war's supply-side emphasis of targeting leaders of Colombia's largest drug-trafficking mafias did little to stem the demand for illegal drugs or to generate alternative employment for cocaleros and others involved in the cocaine market. The collapse of the organizational structures of the Medellín and Cali cartels thus opened spaces for the emergence of smaller and less-centralized "cartelitos" that arose to fill the voids in the market. Among the most powerful groups to move into the market during this time were the AUC and the FARC,

---

[61] Bowden (2001).
[62] Camacho Guizado (2005:78–79).
[63] Crandall (2002:37).
[64] Kline (2015:37).

both of which seized the opportunity to vertically integrate the market in areas under their territorial control in order to capture more wealth from the market.[65]

Third, evidence on Colombian exports of cocaine to the United States showed that powdered cocaine was becoming both cheaper and more readily available.[66] Convinced that drug exports could be curtailed by cutting Colombian cartels from their supply lines, the Clinton Administration supplemented Bush's Andean Initiative with a so-called air-bridge strategy in 1994, which used US-run ground radar systems located in southern Colombia and US-made helicopters and planes to intercept traffickers carrying Bolivian and Peruvian coca paste to refineries in Colombia. Over the next few years, this strategy was proving more successful in curbing the transportation of Peruvian and Bolivian coca into Colombia. However, the closing of the air-bridge across the Andes led to a massive rise in coca production in the very regions of southern Colombia that had become territorial strongholds of the FARC.[67] Thus, between 1989 and 1998, coca production is estimated to have increased by 140%, from roughly 33,900 to 81,400 metric tons. Between 1996 and 1999, the number of hectares dedicated to coca production rose from 62,280 to 120,000 ha.[68] Not surprisingly then, this growth in the coca sector infused the FARC with new military recruits and new income streams. One study estimated the FARC's total earnings from the drug trade to be as high as US$400 million per year. In addition to another US$500 million the FARC garnered from other activities such revolutionary taxes, kidnapping, extortion, robbery, "commissions" collected from local governments and businesses, as well as its own business ventures, this influx of drug monies brought the FARC's estimated overall annual revenues roughly to US$1 billion, or roughly US$100 million per month.[69]

Finally, to curtail increases in coca production across southern Colombia, the Clinton Administration helped finance the initiation of aerial fumigations of coca farms in 1994. These aerial fumigations sprayed Monsanto Corporation's Round-Up, a highly toxic and controversial glyphosate ingredient, from low-flying US military planes that traversed the coca-producing regions of Caquetá and its neighboring departments, Putumayo and Guaviare. Between 1994 and 1999, some 65,000 ha of land were sprayed. Yet, these efforts failed to curtail production, as producers responded by expanding their farms into more remote regions and increasing the overall size of their farms. Thus, during this same period, coca

---

[65] Romero (2003); Hristov (2009, 2014); Ballvé (2012).

[66] Bagley and Walker (1994:26–27, 69).

[67] Tate (2015:114–15).

[68] Bagley (2005:21–23).

[69] Kline (2015:46).

production in southern Colombia actually increased from roughly 45,000 ha to 160,199 ha.[70] Making matters worse, the spraying of glyophosate killed staple food sources that were planted alongside the coca plants, poisoned the natural rivers and streams that provided them with fresh drinking water, and led to outbreaks of cancers and physical deformities in exposed local populations.[71] By 1996 and 1997, these aerial fumigations triggered a mass movement of cocaleros that began to protest the counter-narcotics efforts of the Colombian and US governments. By August of 1996, mass demonstrations by cocalero farmers that spread across the capital cities of Caquetá, Putumayo, and Guaviare clashed with Colombian security forces. The violence led to rioting in Caquetá's capital city, Florencia, as well as other demonstrations over the next year. When it became clear to authorities that the protests were supported, if not coordinated, by local FARC activists, the government responded with a heavy hand. Caquetá's new governor declared the department to be a "special zone for public order" in order to beef up the military and police presence in region. By the final months of 1997, the army initiated an offensive to wrest control of the Caguán from the FARC. The guerrillas responded with strong offensives of their own in the municipalities of Puerto Rico and El Doncello. In March of 1998, the FARC's Southern Bloc delivered a debilitating blow to the Army's Third Mobile Brigade in the munici- pality of Cartagena del Chairá, which effectively crippled the military's efforts. Angered by the onslaught by the armed forces and by Samper's US-backed counter-narcotics policies, the FARC began their own efforts to pressure local politicians into supporting a break with such national policies and organized a boycott of the upcoming presidential elections.[72]

As the drug war's military initiatives deteriorated in the Caguán, bilateral relations between the US and Colombian governments were taking a turn for the worse as well. In 1994, Colombia's newly elected President Ernesto Samper (1994–98) was found to have accepted millions of dollars in campaign financing from the Cali Cartel. The Clinton Administration responded immediately by revoking Samper's visa and "de-certifying" Colombia from eligibility to receive any US foreign aid other than counter-narcotics assistance. US financial assistance to Colombia was thus immediately suspended, voting privileges from multilateral development banks were rescinded, and all trade-preference statuses of Colombian products were dropped. Colombia's creditworthiness was thus

---

[70] Clemencia Ramírez (2011:59–60).

[71] For a discussion of the health impact of the aerial spraying of glyphosate in Colombia, see Livingstone (2004:112–14); Álvarez (2007); Clemencia Ramírez (2011); Tate (2015).

[72] OPPDHDIH (2001:10); Livingstone (2004:112–21); Clemencia Ramírez (2011:4).

obliterated in the eyes of foreign financial and commercial investors. And though the Clinton administration refused to impose trade sanctions as mandated by US law, aid to Colombia was cut in 1996 and 1997.[73] In order to regain the trust of the Clinton Administration and display his innocence before the eyes of the world community, Samper stepped up his rhetoric in support of the US' antinarcotics operations. In May of 1996, Samper also issued a presidential decree that established "special zones for public order" to assist in the criminalization of "subversives" and that permitted the establishment of government-sanctioned militia groups (*Cooperativas para la Vigilancia y Seguridad Privada*, CONVIVIR). Yet, rather than help regain control of the drug-producing regions of the country, Samper's actions actually poured greater fuel on the crisis. International and domestic human rights groups began to publish shocking reports that documented the mass atrocities committed by the AUC and other paramilitary groups. And mounting evidence was documenting compliance, if not participation, of segments of the Colombian military in those atrocities.[74]

By the closing years of the Samper Administration, Colombia's involvement in the US war on drugs was producing unintended and highly adverse consequences on the ground. Politically, Samper had lost political capital by revealing himself to be subject to pressures from both the US government as well as from the narco-traffickers who had displayed their economic might through their efforts to bribe national political figures. Militarily, the weaknesses of the armed forces were exposed through a series of humiliating losses to the FARC on the battlefield. And, the legitimacy of the government was waning as militarism and paramilitarism arose as the primary mechanisms intended to restore social control and capitalist order in regions marked by social unrest. Economically, Colombia's de-certification from foreign aid damaged Colombia's creditworthiness and led to massive capital flight. By 1997, the Colombian economy had entered its worst recession in seventy years, with the economy contracting by 6% and unemployment levels reaching 18%.[75] Like the closing years of the 1970s when the legitimacy of the National Front regime had begun to crumble, Colombia's neoliberal political establishment at the close of the 1990s was plunging into its own legitimacy crisis. And once again broad sectors of the population were calling for a reevaluation of the politics of the central government and a resumption of peace talks that would put an end to the country's political violence and chaos.

---

[73] Walker (2001:27–28); Crandall (2002:42–43); Thoumi (2002:145, 2003:173).

[74] Crandall (2002:109); Camacho Guizado (2005:81); Livingstone (2004:60, 199); OPPDHDIH (2001:8).

[75] Bagley (2005:39).

Plan Colombia: From Developmental Project to US-Backed Neoliberal War

Like Belisario Betancur some two decades earlier, Conservative Party candidate Andrés Pastrana was elected president in 1998 on a "Citizens Mandate for Peace" ticket that promised to address the socioeconomic underpinnings of the guerrilla war, expanding narcotics sector and bubbling social unrest. Before taking office, Pastrana met with FARC leader Manuel Marulanda to explore the possibilities for future peace. Once in office, Pastrana formally recognized the FARC's political character in order to pave the way for legal negotiations, ordered a complete withdrawal of security forces from a 42,000 square square kilometer-sized demilitarized zone (*Zona de Despeje*) in and around the Caguán, and called an end to all military operations and intelligence gathering in the region to facilitate peace talks.[76] Pastrana also met during this time with US president Clinton, who agreed to recertify Colombia and normalize bilateral relations between the countries. In a further gesture of support to Pastrana, Clinton also secretly sent emissaries to meet with the FARC in Costa Rica in December of 1998 to discuss their willingness to undertake drug eradication programs as part of the peace process.[77] With Pastrana's backing from Clinton, the geopolitical stage appeared to be set for a major new aid package to help Pastrana regain control of Colombia's chaotic countryside *consensually* by instituting social and economic reform measures.

Pastrana's original national development policy plan, *Change in Order to Build Peace, 1998–2002*, was a veritable Marshall Plan that sought external funding for economic development projects and institution-building measures.[78] The total price tag for the measures was estimated to be roughly US$7.5 billion to be spent over a three-year period beginning in 2000. Colombia, Pastrana announced, would contribute $4 billion toward the effort. The remainder, he hoped, would

---

[76] OPPDHDIH (2001:7–8).

[77] The discovery of this by the Republican-dominated congress, however, led to an onslaught of verbal attacks against Clinton for meeting with "terrorists." The fallout became so controversial over the subsequent weeks that Clinton publically disavowed the plan and pledged to refrain from further discussions (Bagley 2005:40; Tickner 2003).

[78] The Plan included the strengthening of such state institutions as the judiciary, human capital development through an expansion of educational programs, the promotion of "associative enterprises" to strengthen the social capital of poor neighborhoods, greater protection of the environment and human rights, and a mass illicit crop substitution program. See Tate (2015:141–45) for a detailed analysis of the original plan and its transformation.

come from foreign governments and multilateral institutions, including the United States, the European Union, International Monetary Fund, World Bank, and International Development Bank. As it turned out, the European Union and multilateral agencies each pledged support of roughly US$1 billion. And the initial reception of Pastrana's development plan in Washington seemed promising. Secretary of State Madeleine Albright, for example, singled out Colombia (along with Nigeria, Indonesia, and Ukraine) as needing "special attention" because it "can be a major force for stability and progress in its region" and because it is "at a critical point along the democratic path."[79]

However, the year was 1998, not 1958. And as Pastrana's plan cycled through the US policy establishment in 1998 and 1999, the majority of representatives in US Congress, the heads of US foreign policy think tanks, and military leaders all converged on their views that Colombia's social and political crisis at the time was an illegal narcotics problem that required militarization rather than an economic crisis requiring institution-building and developmental aid.[80] Making matters worse, the peace talks were rapidly deteriorating on the ground in the Caguán. Although the Colombian military indeed halted assaults on the FARC during the first year of the ceasefire agreement, paramilitary groups had entered the region in full force as they had done in Urabá and other contested regions in years prior. As evident from Figure 7.4, during the three years of the cease-fire from 1999 to 2001, paramilitarism became the primary form of repression in the region, jumping from four incidents in 1998 to twenty-four by 2001.

The FARC were also criticized for violating the "spirit of the accords" by continuing to carry out selective kidnappings and assassinations, threatening local mayors and judges, conducting illegal searches and seizures, and extorting money from governmental agencies and businesses. They were also accused of using their control of the demilitarized zone to begin a major rearmament program that included training new troops and purchasing new weaponry, in addition to continuing to participate in local drug-trafficking operations. The demilitarized zone was believed to hold some 35,000 ha of lands dedicated to coca cultivation and roughly 37 private land strips to transport coca paste to urban narcotics processers and exporters. Government distrust of the FARC also peaked in March of 1999, when the guerrillas were reported to have murdered three US citizens working as indigenous campaigners.[81]

---

[79] Bagley (2005:42).

[80] Tate (2015).

[81] Livingstone (2004:161); Bagley (2005:31).

Figure 7.4 State and paramilitary repression in the Caguán, 1987–2017

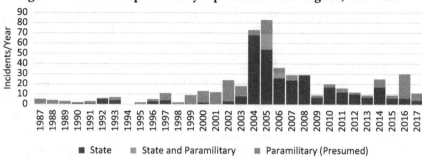

Source: Coercion Dataset

By August of 2000, the Clinton administration approved the initial release of a US$1.32 billion aid package for Colombia that grew to a total of US$2.44 billion by 2003. However, as it passed through the halls of Congress, the plan was fundamentally transformed into a predominantly military rather than development aid package. Roughly 80.5% of aid was slated to Colombian military and police forces with the remaining 19.5% to be used for judicial reform measures and other state institutions.[82] To be sure, like the Andean Initiative before it, *Plan Colombia* was intended to be an antinarcotics effort, so restrictions were put in place by US Congress to ensure that all operations carried out by Colombia's new US-financed antinarcotics units be directed toward "drug control missions" rather than counterinsurgency missions directed against the guerrillas. New to Plan Colombia, however, was its formal adherence to human rights norms established under the 1996 Leahy Amendment to the US international affairs budget that barred US assistance to any foreign military unit known to engage in human rights violations. To address evidence from human rights reports detailing Colombian military participation in various human rights atrocities, Pastrana removed four generals from active military service due to their open support for the activities carried out by the paramilitaries. He also disbanded Colombia's "Intelligence Brigade" (*Brigada XX*), known to have close connections to the AUC, and declared the CONVIVIR illegal under Colombian law. Finally, the US explicitly earmarked US$93 million of the budget for Plan Colombia to be used for strengthening human rights and the administration of justice and democracy.[83]

Despite its human rights-friendly antinarcotics rhetoric, in practice, Plan Colombia appears to have been primarily a counterinsurgency strategy meant to

---

[82] Camacho Guizado (2005:84–85); Isaacson (2003:15, 2005:245).

[83] Tickner (2003:24–27); Crandall (2002:106–7); Bagley (2005:32, 42–43).

dislodge Colombian guerrilla groups from their rural strongholds. Roughly two-thirds of the 80% of funds for security forces, for example, was directed to the Colombian military itself.[84] And perhaps more telling of its intent to defeat the FARC militarily, the antinarcotics operations and military actions carried out under Plan Colombia were conducted almost exclusively in FARC-controlled regions of southern Colombia despite evidence that coca production had spread throughout many parts of rural Colombia, including regions that had come under the effective control of the state or paramilitary groups. As Figure 7.3 depicted, combat activity in the Caguán skyrocketed upward from the onset of activities in 1999 into the closing year of Pastrana's term in 2002. And while this military drive was not yet effective in dislodging the FARC, it facilitated the expansion of paramilitarism into the region, as evidenced from Figure 7.4. Indeed, FARC Commander Raul Reyes responded publicly to the militarization that ensued, calling Plan Colombia "nothing more than a thinly disguised declaration of war against the FARC."[85]

As a counter-narcotics strategy, however, Plan Colombia was more mixed.[86] Aerial spraying diminished the overall acreage of Caquetá's coca production from 39,400 ha in 1998 to 14,516 ha by 2002. However, coca cultivation and processing still employed roughly 50% of Caquetá's total rural workforce and the number of coca farms in the region remained high, an estimated 6,638 by the close of 2002.[87] Moreover, efforts to eradicate coca fields in rural Caquetá helped spread coca cultivation to new regions of the country during this time.[88] Nationally, Colombia's illegal narcotics sector actually increased to an estimated US$3.5 billion, more than two and a half times greater than that generated by coffee

---

[84] This influx of military aid financed the creation of 3 new antinarcotics battalions within the Colombian military, the purchase of 22 UH-60 Blackhawk helicopters and other military and police aircraft, arms and munitions, personnel training for counter-narcotics measures, and payment to private contractors to help protect Colombia's oil pipelines from sabotage from the ELN guerrillas (Tate 2015).

[85] According to Bagley (2005:41–43), General Peter Pace, commander of the US Southern Command, echoed these words, stating that Colombia has had "real emigration because of the terrorism and the attacks and the Marxist guerrillas taking over substantial portions of their country. And we suggest that the only way we can help them is to help them fight drugs. And I think we need to be more realistic about that. And it will be a tragedy if we stand here and allow them to fall or to be undermined or have their economy destroyed as a result of this guerrilla effort."

[86] Díaz and Sánchez Torres (2004).

[87] SINCHI (n.d.).

[88] Clemencia Ramírez (2011:62–63).

exports, and making it the largest coca exporter in the world, supplying an estimated 80% of the US cocaine market.[89] Overall, by the closing years of the Pastrana Administration, Plan Colombia appeared to be pouring fuel on Colombia's domestic fires. Paramilitarism, drug-trafficking, and guerrilla insurgency activities had all multiplied across the vast rural regions of the country. Masses of internally displaced rural people running from escalating violence in the countryside flooded into Colombia's cities, only to find lack of access to adequate housing and job opportunities in the formal economy. As crimes such as kidnappings, extortion, and assassinations increased, the general sense of insecurity intensified and many Colombians became utterly fatigued with the promise of social reform through leftist guerrilla insurgency. The social and political context was shifting, but it was not clear in which direction it would go.

From the Drug War to the War on Terror: Álvaro Uribe and the Collapse of FARC Counter-Hegemony

US military involvement in rural Colombia changed decisively with the historical convergence of the election of dissident Liberal Álvaro Uribe Velez in May 2002 and the consolidation of US President George Bush II's "War on Terror" campaign in the aftermath of the Al-Qaeda attack on September 11, 2001. Uribe won the presidency on a hardline "democratic security" ticket that promised to defeat the country's guerrillas militarily rather than succumb to another failed peace negotiation strategy. This militaristic rhetoric resonated with large swaths of the Colombian electorate, who gave him 53% of the country's votes with a record high 47% electoral participation.[90] Once in office, Uribe openly refused to accept the political nature of the guerrillas, instead calling them "terrorists" and "dragons" and refusing to negotiate without a unilateral cease-fire.[91]

Aiming to further beef up Colombia's armed forces, Uribe looked to Washington for political and military support from the recently inaugurated administration of George W. Bush (2000–8). Uribe's hardline politics resonated with the hawkish members of George W. Bush's administration, but Bush himself was initially reluctant to invest more taxpayer dollars on Colombia's

---

[89] Isaacson (2003:13); Bagley (2005:21–22).

[90] Tokatlian (2005:71).

[91] In a 2003 speech, Uribe elaborated on the logic of democratic security, stating, "If we speak of peace without teeth the dragons will eat us, those dragons that we have in Colombia; we need to show our teeth to the violent ones." Quoted in Kline (2009:39).

antinarcotics efforts. This reluctance changed, however, following Al-Qaeda's attacks on New York's World Trade Center and the US Pentagon on September 11, 2001. The attacks gave Bush's hawks – Vice President Dick Cheney, Defense Secretary Donald Rumsfeld, and advisers Paul Wolfowitz and Richard Perle – the opportunity to redefine and expand the global presence of the US military and reassert US global power into the twenty-first century, carrying out plans they first developed in the immediate aftermath of the collapse of the Soviet Union.[92] Just one week later, Bush laid out this new global hegemonic plan with his new *National Security Strategy of the United States*, which claimed that the United States was locked in a global war against anti-democratic terrorists who did not operate according to the norms of interstate warfare. Thus, the US military must engage in pre-emptive strikes and military actions against terror groups and the countries that gave them safe harbor, as well as beef up its aid to governments willing to engage in warfare against their own domestic terrorists. To promote these efforts, Bush declared that this new "war on terror" was indeed "the decisive ideological struggle of the 21st century and the calling of our generation."[93]

As it turned out, Bush's war on terror provided a convenient rationale for Álvaro Uribe's domestic war against Colombia's guerrillas, as both administrations described the FARC as the Western Hemisphere's homegrown terrorist menace.[94] By September 2002, US congress passed a massive new military aid package under the Andean Regional Initiative (ARI) to Andes countries to help fight illegal armed groups involved in transnational drug trafficking and terrorist activities. Under the ARI, Colombia received US$1.67 billion to purchase weapons and surveillance equipment and finance the creation of new "counter terror" army commando battalions.[95] Like the AI and Plan Colombia before it, the ARI was meant to facilitate Colombia's antinarcotics efforts through military and policing activities. What was different about the ARI, however, was that it was broadly *antiterror* rather than singularly *antiillegal narcotics* in its focus. It, therefore, removed the legal barriers separating the two wars against armed

---

[92] Arrighi (2005a, 2005b).

[93] BBC News (2006).

[94] Former Secretary of State, Colin Powell, explicitly expressed the political logic connecting Bush's and Uribe's wars in a March 21, 2002 speech: "It's terrorism that threatens stability in Colombia. And if it threatens stability in Colombia, it threatens stability in our part of the world, in our neighborhood, in our backyard. And I think that's something that should be of concern to us" (Powell 2002).

[95] Center for International Policy (CIP) (n.d., accessed July 25, 2020 at http://ciponline .org/colombia/aidtable.htm).

insurgents and drug-trafficking mafias.[96] This made it legally possible for Uribe to launch a coordinated front consisting of Colombia's armed forces *and* national police directly against any illegal armed terrorist group operating in Colombia, be they guerrilla, paramilitary, or drug mafia. And importantly, it also granted US special military operatives leeway to facilitate and participate in these actions.[97]

This influx of unprecedented US military aid granted Uribe both the military resources and the political wherewithal to step up his fight against the FARC and other guerrilla groups and ultimately tilt the scales from decades of containment to a full-on elimination strategy. In practice, Uribe's war against the guerrillas was twofold. On the one hand, he *waged peace* with the country's largest paramilitary group, the United Self-Defenses of Colombia (AUC), and even stimulated the further penetration of paramilitarism into Colombian civil society. As early as 2002, Uribe began to lay the ground for "peace talks" with the AUC by meeting with paramilitary leaders Carlos Castaño Gil and Salvatore Mancuso and making promises of pardons for crimes committed against noncombatants and of humanitarian assistance to any paramilitary fighter willing to lay down their guns. By the close of his first year in office, Uribe had signed a formal "cease-fire" with the AUC despite any evidence of significant combat activity between government military forces and paramilitaries. And by June 2005, Uribe signed off on a controversial "Justice and Peace Law" (Law 975) that suspended traditional prison and provided lighter sentences for demobilized fighters who confessed to committing human rights violations.[98] The law was immediately criticized by human rights groups, which argued that Uribe was essentially letting right-wing death squads off the hook for their crimes, even allowing them to retain the estimated 10 million hectares of land and countless assets they had acquired through their

---

[96] In fact, the FARC, ELN and AUC had all been listed in the US State Department's list of Foreign Terrorist Organization since 2001.

[97] Like Plan Colombia, Andean Regional Initiative funds were contingent upon Colombia's record of human rights violations; and legal restrictions were set to ensure the separation of military from paramilitary activity. Yet, despite this legal formality, as late as 2003 a Human Rights Watch report had found evidence demonstrating that the link between the military and paramilitary groups remained as strong as ever (Díaz and Sánchez Torres 2004; Rojas and Meltzer 2005).

[98] The law allowed demobilized AUC fighters to serve time on farms instead of prisons, limited sentences to no more than eight years, and granted them the right to retain the assets they acquired during their time as paramilitary combatants. Victims of AUC terror, in turn, were not compensated financially for their losses and their lost assets were not returned.

use of terror against civilian noncombatants.[99] Moreover, evidence began mounting that Uribe and his family had worked closely with paramilitaries and drug-trafficking organizations since the mid-1990s.[100] Uribe's broad popularity, however, shielded him from these accusations and he went on the offensive accusing human rights activists and leftist critics of his policies as being "supporters" and "accomplices" of the FARC. By May 2004, Uribe granted the AUC its own 142 square-mile demilitarized zone in the town of Santa Fe de Ralito in the department of Córdoba, a paramilitary territorial stronghold located in Colombia's northern coast. By the close of 2006, some 30,000 AUC fighters had formally demobilized. Salvatore Mancuso, who became the AUC's leader following the death of Fidel Castaño in 2004, turned in his weapons along with thirteen other leaders who were extradited to the United States for drug-trafficking crimes by 2008.[101]

In terms of his war against the guerrillas, Uribe engaged in a two-pronged attack: undermining the guerrillas support from civilian noncombatants and directing a full-scale militarization campaign in guerrilla-controlled regions of the countryside. Regarding the former, Uribe created a vast network of citizen collaborators (*redes de cooperantes*) who were rewarded financially for providing information about illegal political and economic actors operating in their neighborhoods and communities.[102] He also established a practice called "Soldiers from My Town" (SMT), which provided quick training for local residents interested in becoming paid collaborators or new recruits to Colombian military and police forces. These low-level counter-intelligence actions were designed to legitimate the Colombian armed forces as advocates of peace and order while sowing distrust between guerrillas and the host populations living in their territorial strongholds.[103] Regarding the latter, Uribe used the influx of military aid under the ARI to create a slew of new counterinsurgency military brigades, urban antiterror forces, and "high mountain battalions" that were meant to be more mobile, organizationally flexible, and stealthy. He also expanded the overall size of

---

[99] Forero (2005); CJA (2010); Hristov (2014:134–35).

[100] This accusation that would come back to haunt him when a formal criminal investigation was launched against him and he was eventually forced into the courts by 2019 (Human Rights Watch 2020).

[101] As observers point out, the extradition of AUC leaders was a ploy used by Uribe to prevent them from testifying against him and therefore revealing his complicity in paramilitary activities (Human Rights Watch 2020).

[102] Ferrer (2002).

[103] Kline (2009:41, 2015:57); Evans (2011).

Colombia's police and armed forces by hiring some 96,000 new recruits.[104] Uribe then used this beefed-up military-policing apparatus to launch a multifaceted attack against the FARC, which he called "Plan Patriota." The first stage of the plan was meant to dislodge the guerrilla presence from inside and around the country's major cities, foremost among them the capital Bogotá. The second stage was directed to the south of the country, where some 18,000 national troops descended into the coca-growing territorial strongholds of the FARC with the goal of creating a permanent presence.[105]

The impact of Uribe's war on terror against the FARC in the Caguán is evident from the longitudinal coercion dataset. Figure 7.3, for example, shows that in the few short years from the close of the drug war in 2000–1 to the full-on onslaught under the war on terror in 2003–4, the number of incidents of combat activity between military forces and the FARC in the Caguán increased by 650%, from under ten to a high of seventy-five incidents per year. These intense battles caused significant FARC losses of personnel, soldiers, and resources and they also disrupted the boundaries of FARC territorial control in ways that undermined their legitimacy vis-à-vis local inhabitants. When forced to retreat under heavy fire, for example, the FARC ended up exposing communities that had long been FARC strongholds to military (and paramilitary) incursions and state efforts to consolidate their own forms of territorial control. Given the distrust of state forces in the politics of these communities, the territorial fluidity created by warfare undermined the FARC's ability to effectively protect local cocaleros and other civilian noncombatants from acts of state repression. Figure 7.4, in turn, high-lights how the militarization of the region diminished the FARC's ability to protect locals from state and paramilitary violence. The overall incidents of state-paramilitary repression in the region skyrocketed from a yearly average of well under ten incidents during the years of the drug war in the 1990s to forty-five incidents in 2002 and up to ninety-seven incidents by 2005 during the peak years

---

[104] Under Uribe, the Colombian military created seven new "high mountain battalions" designed to chase the FARC to its typical mountain jungle refuges upon direct attack from the army, fifteen mobile brigades that moved across broad regions of the country, fourteen urban antiterrorist forces to provide a continued state presence in the country's barrios de invasion (shantytowns), thirty-two anti-kidnapping police units (GAULAS), and fifty-four mobile, mounted antinarcotics police units. Citizen-soldiers trained under SMT spread to become a continual watchful presence in 754 of Colombia's 1,112 municipalities. Of the 96,000 new members of Colombia's police and armed forces, 4,335 were marines, 20,000 mounted police, 14,000 regular police aids, and 13,000 army soldiers (Kline 2015).

[105] Kline (2009:46, 57).

of the war on terror. Moreover, by distinguishing the perpetrator of these acts of repression, Figure 7.4 also shows how Uribe's war on terror essentially shifted the primary perpetrator of repression in the region from a predominance of paramilitary repression in the 1990s to an overwhelming predominance of acts of state repression that continued across the two terms of Uribe's presidency (2002–10) and later across the four years of the Santos Administration (2010–14). Overall all, this data suggests that the war on terror in the Caguán had effectively replaced paramilitarism with state terror as the primary means of subjugating and controlling the local population.

By defeating the FARC on the battlefield, Uribe's war on terror struck at the heart of FARC counter-hegemony. As discussed in Chapter 6, the FARC's ability to garner broad social legitimacy as the *de facto* state in regions under their control came both from their ability to effectively protect frontier migrants militarily from displacement and state violence as well as their ability to protect them economically by incorporating them into a regulated coca labor regime as junior partners. This heightened military assault on the FARC's historic strongholds in regions like the Caguán was highly effective precisely because it undermined the FARC's capacity to protect locals. And to build up their protective capabilities, they needed to extract even more from the very people whose trust was faltering. In their efforts to retain territorial control of the region, the FARC needed to expand their military power, which itself required new revenue streams. In the past, most of their revenues were collected through "revolutionary taxes" on coca and coca paste production and sales to merchants connected to drug-trafficking organizations operating out of Colombia's cities. This form of revenue created a mutual economic dependence between the FARC and cocaleros who benefitted from stable and relatively high prices for their crops.

To prepare for the onslaught of military incursions directed by the Uribe Administration, the FARC stepped up its engagement in extractive activities that brought them short-term revenues but which strained their relations with the local cocalero population. One such strategy adopted was the direct pillage of local banks and stores and the kidnapping of selected individuals who could provide lucrative ransom in exchange for their release. They also began engaging in kidnappings known as *pescas milagrosas* (miraculous catches) wherein the guerrillas installed random roadblocks along busy highways and roads, confiscated expensive personal belongings of individuals and detained those who appeared to offer the potential for lucrative ransoms. These pillages and kidnappings exposed the coercive side of the FARC's territorial control, which deteriorated their legitimacy and therefore raised the probability that further coercive measures would be required to extract resources from the local population. This uptick in the FARC's use of violence is evident in Figure 7.5. From late 1999 to 2001, the

Figure 7.5 FARC violent extraction activities in Caguán, 1992–2011

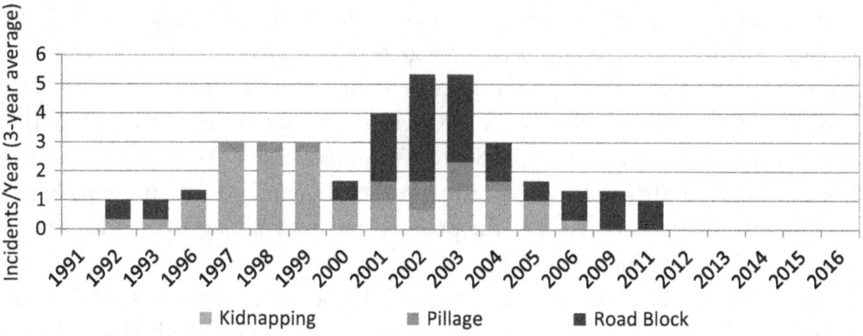

Source: Coercion Dataset

FARC stepped up its extractive activities, particularly kidnapping for ransom, to increase its revenues and ultimately counter the onslaught of state militarization brought on under Plan Colombia. These extractive activities bumped up even further into the years of Uribe's first term, when we can see a substantial increase in the number of FARC roadblocks that served the double purpose of controlling the movement of people and materials flowing into the region and potentially leading to a miraculous catch.

While these extractive actions brought the FARC new revenue streams intended to maintain their territorial strongholds, their efforts to combat military assaults and incursions by state forces brought heavy casualties and often mass displacements of locals who increasingly sought safe harbor and refuge in urban regions of the country that were strongholds of the Colombian state. When territorially displaced by combat, state forces (and sometimes paramilitary groups) moved in. When state forces retained their hold of a town or region, inhabitants with clear and close relations with the FARC became subject to intense repression. When the military forces receded or when the state failed to retain territorial control, the FARC typically moved back in, but with less trust in the fealty of the local population as some locals may have flipped sides.

This fluidity of local territorial rule undermined the FARC's capacity to protect locals from individual acts of state and paramilitary repression and often required a re-tightening of their grip over the flows of labor and commodities into and out of their former strongholds. In rural towns likes those scattered across the Caguán, this attempt to reassert their power locally often exposed new vulnerabilities and strains on their legitimacy, which could lead to distrust and even repressive violence between the FARC and locals. To be sure, FARC counter-hegemony had always been rooted first and foremost in its ability to engage in acts of alternative state-making violence to consolidate local forms of territorial control

Figure 7.6 Occupation of victims of FARC violence in Caguán, 1990–2017

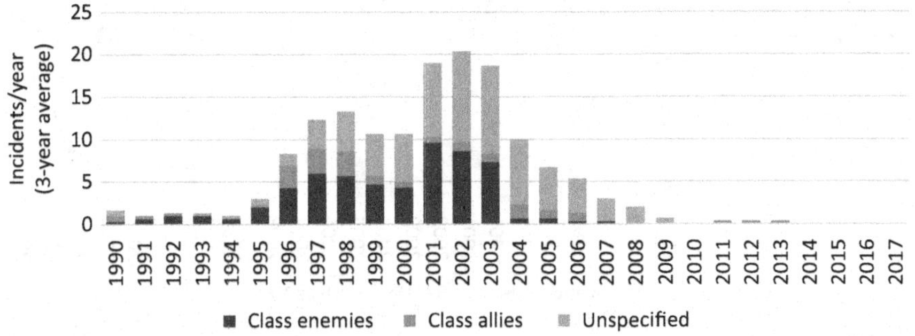

Source: Coercion Dataset

and facilitate processes of counter-insurgent state formation. As in so many revolutionary insurgency groups the world over, targeted assassinations, death threats, kidnapping, and acts of extortion and forced taxation were all part of the FARC's repertoire of violence.[106] However, these acts of violence were historically directed at their class enemies – Colombia's oligarchy, state and paramilitary forces – rather than workers, peasants, and other subaltern groups and classes. Under the pressure of heightened militarization in the early 2000s, the FARC's use of violence against noncombatants not only increased, but also became less discriminating in terms of the class backgrounds of their victims.

Figures 7.6 and 7.7 provide empirical evidence of the correlation between the militarization campaign under Uribe's US-backed war on terror and the uptick in indiscriminate acts of FARC violence in the region. Figure 7.6 analyzes the occupation of the victims of FARC violence against noncombatants in the Caguán, distinguishing between the FARC's historic class allies (campesino farmers, workers, village inhabitants, and community members) and their class adversaries (state security forces, political officials, industrialists, and landed elites). The number of incidents of FARC violence against their noncombatant class enemies hovered below five per year until 1996, when they increased to under fifteen per year by 2000. As Plan Colombia and the war on terror heated up, the number of acts of FARC repression against everyone including unspecified non-combatants jumped significantly to a high of over twenty incidents in 2002. During Uribe's first term in office, these incidents began to drop steadily, and particularly so for the FARC's class enemies. By the close of Uribe's second term,

---

[106] Hough (2011).

Figure 7.7 Size of victim group of FARC violence in Caguán, 1990–2017

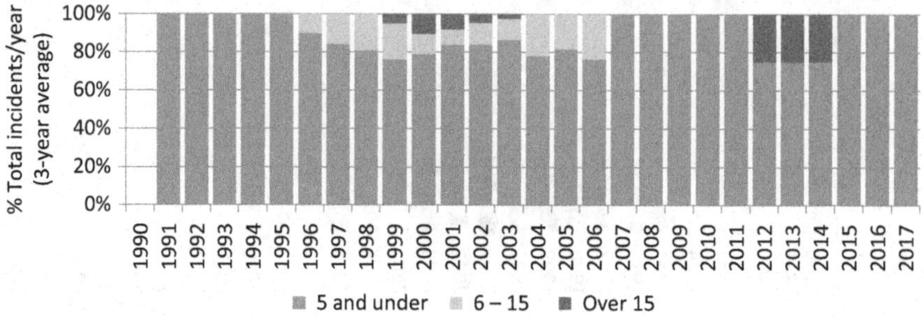

■ 5 and under ▓ 6 – 15 ■ Over 15

Source: Coercion Dataset

FARC repression in the Caguán had been essentially eliminated for all noncombatants, regardless of their position in the class structure.

Figure 7.7 also substantiates the point that FARC counter-hegemony was collapsing under the weight of Uribe's all-out militarization campaign. As distrust between the FARC and locals deteriorated, so did their ability to selectively use coercive means to maintain control of the local population and sustain their alternative state-making activities. The size of the victim group of FARC violence, a powerful measure of their ability to engage in discriminating acts of selective violence rather than indiscriminating acts of terror,[107] increased significantly in the Caguán during the peak years of warfare in the early 2000s. Again, while these actions paled in comparison to those of the Colombian state and to the actions of paramilitaries during this time, such acts of FARC violence contributed to their delegitimation vis-à-vis locals, which in turn made it more difficult for them to sustain their counter-hegemonic control of the region's coca regime.

The FARC's engagement in these acts of violence in the Caguán and other rural strongholds did not only expose the coercive side of their territorial rule to locals. Their actions sparked broader criticism of their actions from significant portions of Colombia's national population, human rights organizations, and international observers. In July of 2004, for example, the United Nations High Commission for Human Rights publically condemned the FARC for its involvement in human rights violations against unarmed civilians and contributing to ongoing processes of internal displacement.[108] Moreover, more and more Colombians were drawn to Uribe's politics of democratic security as a step up from the chaos of the 1990s. Between 2002 and 2009, for example, the number of

---

[107] Weinstein (2006); Metelits (2009); Hough (2011).
[108] UNHCHR (2004).

homicides fell from 28,837 to 15,817, kidnappings dropped from 1,708 to 181, and terrorist attacks against noncombatants plunged from 1,645 to 486.[109] And perhaps just as importantly, the defeats of guerrilla groups across large swaths of the countryside pushed them into even more marginal spaces along Colombia's external frontiers, allowing greater local and regional travel for urban and rural dwellers alike.[110] Predictably then, Uribe's popularity continued to wax into his second term as the FARC's support base waned.[111]

Making matters worse for the FARC, in early March 2008, one of the FARC's key leaders, Raul Reyes, was killed in a controversial aerial bombing in an Ecuadorian border town with Colombia. A week later, another FARC leader, Iván Ríos, was killed by one of his own bodyguards, which precipitated a raid that resulted in the military's appropriation of a number of FARC laptop computers that had invaluable information on their organizational workings and plans. Finally, on March 28, the FARC's leader since their founding forty-four years earlier, Manuel Marulanda Vélez (alias *Tirofijo*) died of a heart attack. With half of their key leaders dead and their number of regular soldiers rapidly dwindling, the FARC began to retreat from all but their steadiest territorial strongholds. Forced to flee and remain mobile, they also began a series of prisoner releases, whose public statements about their treatment during captivity only further soured public support for the guerrillas. By June, massive national as well as international protests against the FARC poured onto the streets calling for their demobilization and a lasting end to the conflict.[112]

Indeed, by the 2010 presidential election, Uribe's popularity remained high despite a series of scandals that he was complicit in paramilitarism and mounting evidence that his administration was complicit in grave human rights violations, both of which chipped away at his support.[113] Facing these scandals and unwilling

---

[109] Kline (2015:67).

[110] Averill (2019).

[111] Opinion polls, while clearly biased to favor the politics of urban and relatively well-off populations using telephone land lines, echoed these sentiments. Two 2008 polls, for example, showed massive support for military actions against the guerrillas and record-high approval ratings for Uribe and his *Partido Social de Unidad Nacional* political party. For a critique of the biases of polls conducted by Gallop and El Tiempo, see Brittain (2010:40–42).

[112] BBC News (2008); Forero and Brulliard (2008).

[113] One scandal, known generally as the "parapolitics" scandal, identified personal and professional links between paramilitary groups and nearly a third of Colombian senators and representatives, including Uribe. A second scandal, known as the "false positives" scandal, broke out in mid-2008 when human rights groups discovered that

to engage in another political-constitutional fight to allow indefinite executive terms, Uribe promoted his trusted Defense Minister, Juan Manuel Santos, to run in the 2010 presidential elections as his hand-picked successor. Santos was a good choice for Uribe, as he had proved to be a tough and committed opponent to the FARC. He was also a political insider, a journalist by trade and conservative economist by training, and a member of the influential Santos family, which essentially controlled Colombia's news cycle through their ownership and editorial management of the national paper, *El Tiempo*. Yet, shortly after his election, Santos (2010–18) openly acknowledged the FARC's political nature and expressed a desire to pull the FARC back into peace talks by promising a peace process that would put social and political reforms at the center of its agenda. Although this symbolic legitimation of the FARC's political nature angered Uribe, who founded a new oppositional party (*Centro Democrático*) to challenge it, Santos' dual-pronged strategy of continuing to fight the FARC while promising the possibility of social reforms through peace talks ultimately proved effective. During his first term in office, Colombian military forces managed to kill two other key FARC leaders, Víctor Julio Suárez Rojas (alias Mono Jojoy) in September 2010 and Guillermo León Sáenz Vargas (alias Alfonso Cano) in November 2011, while also bringing the group's overall numbers down to an estimated 7,000 soldiers.

Meanwhile, Santos had established a backchannel contact with FARC leaders early on that resulted in ongoing secret preliminary talks with FARC leaders in Havana, Cuba in February 2012. By August, Santos and the FARC signed onto a formal document outlining the conditions of a formal peace process, the rules by which the negotiations would operate, and the five thematic issues that would be negotiated. Two months later, the talks were formally launched in Oslo, Norway and then moved back to Havana where they remained until their closure.[114] By December 2014, the FARC declared a universal cease-fire and the Colombian military followed suit with a declaration that it would end all bombings and raids on FARC forces by March 2015. By September, government negotiators and the FARC signed off on the "Special Jurisdiction for Peace" (*Jurisdicción Especial para la Paz*), which set the legal parameters for the FARC's return to civilian life in a highly publicized meeting of President Santos and his delegation with FARC

---

the Colombian military had been luring poor and mentally impaired civilians to remote parts of country with offers of work, killing them, and ultimately presenting them to authorities as guerrillas killed in combat in order to inflate their total body count and promote their accomplishments under Uribe's policies of Democratic Security.

[114] Nylander et al. (2018).

negotiators, including Rodrigo Londoño Echeverri (alias Timochenko). In June 2016, in a ceremony attended by an international crowd of supporters that included guarantor countries (Cuba and Norway), UN Secretary Ban Ki-moon, Cuban President Raúl Castro, various Latin American presidents, as well as representatives of the European Union and the United States, Santos and Timochenko signed what became the formal peace agreement to "end the conflict" through a permanent bilateral ceasefire, the cessation of hostilities and the FARC's surrender of all of their weapons. The agreement passed Colombian congress on November 29–30, 2016, marking the official end to the conflict. Formally, the FARC insurgency movement had ended.

Clearly, Santos' ability to negotiate an end to the conflicts had stood on the shoulders of over a decade of intense militarization that undermined the FARC's counter-hegemonic presence in historic strongholds like the Caguán and dislodged them from the most economically cherished regions of the countryside. Unlike their high point in the late 1990s and early 2000s, the FARC agreed to disarm once they had been thoroughly beaten on the battle-field. While the peace process brought with it renewed hopes for a democratization of Colombian political life and greater security from violence, as we have seen from this chapter, the removal of the FARC from rural strongholds like the Caguán was essentially the last salvo of a struggle by Colombian elites to regain control of the countryside and transform it into a neoliberal capitalist paradise.

This inflow of capital is evidenced in Figure 7.8. During Uribe's time in office, net flows of foreign direct investment skyrocketed upward from just under US$200 million in 2002 to over $1 billion by 2008. Under Santos, these flows

Figure 7.8 Net inflows of foreign direct investment in Colombia, 1970–2018

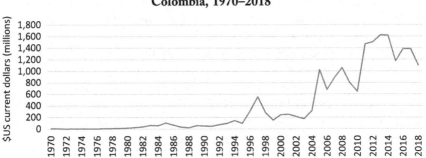

Source: World Bank (n.d.), accessed on July 28, 2020 at https://datacatalog.worldbank.org/dataset/world-development-indicators

reached heights of over $1.6 billion.[115] The question remained, however, what would become of the populations like the cocaleros of the Caguán that had become dependent upon FARC protection precisely because the developmental and neoliberal practices of the Colombian state had closed off opportunities for alternative livelihoods.

Uncertain Futures in the Caguán and Beyond, 2016–Present

The peace process initially held promise for both demobilized FARC militants and the communities that had received their protection from state and paramilitary terror over the previous decades. The final revised peace agreement, ratified unanimously by both houses of Colombia's congress, set out an ambitious six-point plan that included a veritable alphabet soup of subdirectives, policy goals, and new institutions, including: (1) comprehensive rural development; (2) promotion of political participation and democratic pluralism; (3) ending the armed conflict and reincorporating FARC militants back into civilian life; (4) solving the problem of illegal drug cultivation, use, and commercialization; (5) promotion of victim's rights; and (6) rules regarding the implementation and verification of the process. In response to the conditions that led to the FARC's original formation, the peace accords promised to address two of their most valued political concerns: campesino demands for land and agrarian reform as well as a democratization of the political system to ensure rural political voices be heard. In terms of agrarian reform, the Comprehensive Rural Reform (*Reforma Rural Integral*, RRI) agency was created to promote agricultural productivity and integrate marginalized and war-torn rural regions of the country into the national economy through the creation of a rural road network, social development investments, infrastructural investments, and an asset forfeiture system designed to recover state lands acquired illegally. It also created a Land Fund (*Fondo de Tierras*) that would distribute 3 million hectares of unused and untitled land to landless rural families and formalize 7 million additional hectares of land whose owners lacked formal titles. To promote greater democratic participation, the peace accords established state guarantees for social movements and organizations engaged in social protests, created grants to fund community radio projects and alternative media sources, created Territorial Councils (*Consejos Territoriales*) providing citizenship oversight of government planning and funding initiatives, and initiated a set of measures to more easily identify alternative political party and social movement

---

[115] World Bank (n.d.).

actors, modernize the electoral system, and give special recognition to political actors living in marginalized rural communities affected by violence.

Especially relevant to demobilized FARC members were the government's promises of security and protection from targeted assassinations once they laid down their weapons, their recognition of the legality of the FARC's new political party (the Common Alternative Revolutionary Force, same acronym: FARC), and their guarantee of at least five seats in each chamber of congress for the proceeding ten years. In the months following its signature, over 7,000 FARC fighters handed over their weapons and received their "one-off financial support package" that would grant them a monthly basic wage (equivalent to 90% of the minimum salary for the next two years), and access to social security and other social services and jobs training. The FARC's arsenal of weapons, more than 37,000 tons of rifles, pistols, ammunition, and grenade launchers, were melted down and converted by Colombian artists into national sculptures and monuments dedicated to future peace and justice.[116]

Most relevant to the country's cocaleros was "Item 4: Solution to the Problem of Illicit Drugs." Here, the government committed to finding a definitive solution to agrarian origins of the problem of illicit drugs and to a "historical clarification" of the relationship between the illicit narcotics economy and the armed conflict. At the heart of the former was the creation of the National Comprehensive Program for the Substitution of Crops Used for Illicit Purposes (*Programa Nacional Integral de Substitución de Cultivos de Uso Ilícito*, or PNIS). Under the agreement, the country's coca-growing farmers, workers, and communities were formally recognized as campesino farmers who engaged in the illicit narcotics economy as a mechanism of economic survival rather than stigmatized as drug-traffickers subject to criminal laws. The PNIS program was thus developed to deliberately encourage cocalero participation in the crop substitution process and the formulation of state-directed alternatives. Specifically, cocalero farmer families who voluntarily uprooted their coca plants and coca workers who agreed not to participate in the coca economy would receive immediate food assistance and bimonthly salary payments to subsidize their transition to legal crops and livelihoods.[117] Santos' goal was to eradicate up to 100,000 ha of land used for coca

---

[116] Casey and Daniels (2017); Daniels (2018, 2019).

[117] Overall, families enrolled in the PNIS program would receive $36 million pesos (roughly US$11,250) over the course of two years. This would include two million pesos (US$3,750) every two months for a year for immediate economic needs, 19 million pesos (US$6,000) to finance alternative economic projects, 1.8 million pesos (US$562) to promote food sovereignty, and 3.2 million pesos (US$950) in technical assistance toward alternative economic projects (King and Wherry 2018).

cultivation, 50% of which would be done through the PNIS program and the remaining 50% through the forced eradication practices of the past. In the two years following its inception, 132,000 cocalero families living across 14 of Colombia's departments had signed up for the PNIS program and thousands of others were still waiting for approval.[118] Indeed, many cocaleros were initially cautiously optimistic that the Colombian state would indeed provide a roadmap of assistance toward an economic livelihood in the formal economy.

Yet, since 2016, residents of the Caguán have become increasingly frustrated with the peace process and its promises of a secure livelihood to former FARC members and cocalero communities. One source of frustration has been with the PNIS program itself. To be sure, there are still some 100,000 cocalero families with links to the PNIS program in Caquetá. Some are taking advantage of the opening of access to new markets as fish farmers or even small cattle ranchers.[119] However, much like its historical predecessors in the Caquetá Colonization Project and the Integrated Rural Development initiatives of INCORA, the rural development initiatives created out of the peace process have suffered from problems of institutional support and inefficacy that have done little to redress the problems of land titling and marketing of agricultural produce. The payment delivery system of the PNIS program has been particularly weak. Almost as soon as it was implemented, signatories of the payment system complained that the PNIS payments were delivered late, far less than the amount promised, or not at all.[120] The RRI and Land Fund, in turn, have also done little to redistribute rural land acquired forcibly by paramilitaries, landed elites, and drug-traffickers or reverse the decades-long process of rural land concentration through land title provisions.[121]

These problems with the government's delivery of meaningful land titling and rural assistance have been confounded by the dispossessing tendencies of the extractivist and agro-capitalist investments that poured into the rural regions

---

[118] Puerta and Chaparro (2019); UNODC (2019b); FIP (2020).

[119] Graser et al. (2020).

[120] One study found that only 51% of the 62,182 families that had completed their registration with the PNIS program had received at least a first payment by March 2018 and only 11% had received technical assistance to facilitate their conversion to alternative legal crops (FIP 2018).

[121] In terms of land titling, by the closing months of 2018, however, only 22% of municipalities and 15.2% of villages with PNIS registrants had received formal land titles (FIP 2018). In terms of land concentration, at the time of the agreement's signing, Colombia's Agrarian Census documented that only 0.4% of Colombia's population owned 46.4% of total productive land whereas 70% owned a mere 5%.

abandoned by the FARC. Large-scale mega-projects, oil refineries and pipelines, mining and new transportation infrastructure popped up in ecologically fragile zones while agro-industrial biofuel production, cattle ranching, and timber production plowed into former coca-growing lands and untouched tropical forest lands.[122] In the few short years since the peace accords, the rate of deforestation of virgin forest hinterlands in Colombia nearly doubled from roughly 120,000 ha in 2015 to over 220,000 ha by the close of 2017, with Caquetá fairing the poorest. For example, former FARC stronghold San Vicente del Caguán ranked worst of Colombia's 644 municipalities, losing 19,652 ha (10% of all of the country's deforested lands) in 2018, while Cartagena del Chairá ranked third with 17,740 ha and Solano 9th with 6,508.[123]

In part, this deforestation was driven by specific industrial groups who saw the lands abandoned by the FARC as opportunities for capitalization and financial predation. Land values in Caquetá, for example, rose by as much as 300% in some rural municipalities of the department, which sparked a land grab by wealthy investors and corporations.[124] Some seven hydroelectric plants cropped up across the river ways leading southward from the slopes of Caquetá's cordilleras in the Amazon river basin. Concessions to begin tapping forty-four new sites of petroleum extraction were granted to Colombia's state oil industry Ecopetrol and its international affiliates, with one major oil well constructed in San Vicente del Caguán and another in the municipality of Valparaiso. New licenses to extract gold along the alluvial channels of southern Caquetá were also granted, sparking a mini gold rush of desperate landless families dredging the streams and dynamiting mountains in search for gold and other precious metals, while leaving the region's water sources polluted with the cyanide, mercury, and other noxious chemicals used to separate alluvial gold from ore and sediment.[125] Finally, and perhaps not surprisingly, the largest contributor to deforestation in Colombia has been the cattle industry, which is responsible for some 80% of deforestation in the southern Amazonian basin regions of Colombia that had been under FARC control. The overall size of cattle herds took its biggest jump in decades following the peace accords, rising from roughly 22.5 million to close to 26 million cows from 2014 to the close of 2017. In Caquetá alone, the herd of bovine cattle jumped from 1,304,403 million in 2014 to 2,379,898 by the close of 2019, with the highest

---

[122] Mendez Garzón and Valánszki (2019) estimated that the armed conflict itself has contributed to an estimated 6.2 million hectares of deforested land over the past two decades.

[123] IDEAM (n.d.).

[124] Volckhausen (2019).

[125] DuPée (2018).

increases in the Caguán regions of San Vicente del Caguán, Cartagena del Chairá, and Puerto Rico.[126]

With the rural development initiatives on shaky grounds and the influx of land-intensive capital contributing to heightened forms of rural economic instability, many of the region's cocaleros have turned once again to replanting coca to make a living. According to the UN Office of Drug Control (UNODC 2019b), Colombia's coca cultivation actually grew significantly in the years following the peace accords, from a decade-long low of 96,000 ha in 2015 to a record high of 171,000 ha and 169,000 ha by 2017 and 2018, respectively. This increase occurred despite the roughly 32,000 ha that were voluntarily uprooted by cocalero families registered under the PNIS program and the 143,000 that were forcibly eradicated under existing antinarcotics practices.[127] Caquetá, which had always ranked high among coca-cultivating departments, increased its production from 7,712 ha of coca fields to 11,762 ha by the close of 2018.[128]

Unlike the previous period of coca cultivation, when the FARC engaged in regulatory market initiatives and protected cocaleros from state and paramilitary repression, today's cocaleros must operate in a market that is controlled by drug-trafficking mafias, paramilitary BACRIM, and in addition to numerous dissident FARC groups that have arisen since the peace accords were signed in 2016.[129] This movement of various armed groups *en masse* into the lower, rural rungs of Colombia's illegal narcotics market has brought with it a resurgence of drug-related violence and anomic terror that has affected the very regions most willing to undergo coca eradication practices.[130] A study conducted by the Bogota-based think tank, *Fundación Ideas para la Paz* (FIP 2018:5–6), for example, found that

---

[126] Torrijos Rivera (2019).

[127] Puerta and Chaparro (2019).

[128] UNODC (2019a, 2019b).

[129] A dissident group from the FARC's 1st and 43rd Fronts that operated along the southwestern border of Colombia refused to demobilize as part of the peace process. This group is believed to be led by Miguel Botache Santillana (who goes by various aliases, including Gentil Duarte, Euclides Mora, Jhon 40, Giovanny Chuspas, and Julián Choll) (Insight Crime 2019). The estimated number of these dissidents is between 1,200 and 3,000 combatants, making them between 10% and 20% of the 13,000 FARC members who disarmed (Charles 2019).

[130] Many of the first targets of these armed groups were former FARC fighters or cocalero community leaders who had trusted that the government would follow through on its promises of protection and security from these acts. In fact, the UN Verification Commission overseeing the peace process reported "deep concern" that as of July 2019, 123 demobilized FARC fighters had been killed, 10 disappeared, and

after a decade of steady decrease, Colombia's homicide rate increased during the two years following the peace accord. The average homicide rate was significantly higher for municipalities with populations registered for the PNIS program than municipalities that continued to grow coca uninterrupted and for municipalities that did not grow coca (54.7% vs. 39.5% and 21.7%, respectively). Many of those killed were social activists and community leaders that challenged the entrance of illegal armed groups seeking local control of the cocaine market and were promised protection from government security forces. A study conducted by Colombia's Attorneys General Office (Fiscalía General 2019), for example, found that the 2018 homicide rate was highest in the 161 municipalities that had previously been sites of FARC territorial presence: 2,957 homicides were registered in 2018, a 30% increase from 2016. Similarly, a report conducted by the UN High Commission for Peace (UNHCHR 2017) found over 105 human rights activists, including 73 local community leaders, 18 social movement activists, and 14 demonstrators were killed in 2017 in regions that had formerly been FARC strongholds. A more recent UN report (UNVMC 2019b) found that this rate has climbed since then to total number of 173 killings, 14 disappearances, and 29 attempted homicides of former FARC members by the close of 2019. These startling numbers even prompted the UN's Secretary General, Antonio Guterres, to call on the Duque Administration to use more effective measures to protect former combatants and to adopt specific measures to protect their family members, including children, who have been subject to this backlash of repression.

Perhaps throwing even more fuel onto the fire, President Duque has also been critically opposed to the peace process and has thrown monkey wrenches into the alternative crop production programs and other political reforms created by the accords of 2016. Upon taking office, Duque slashed the budget of the PNIS program and other peace process initiatives by US$140 million while increasing defense spending by 53%. He also began to publicly challenge the legitimacy of farmer claims that they have not received full reimbursement or timely payments through the PNIS system. Finally, he supported the reversal of Colombia's Constitutional Court's 2017 ban on the aerial spraying of glyphosate as one of the government's strategies of forced narcotics eradication.[131] Critics of Duque's decision to return to aerial spraying have pointed out that it constitutes a violation

---

17 subject to attempted homicides since 2016 (UNVMC 2019a, 2019b,). See Diamond (2018) for an analysis of FARC dissidents' return to the drug trade.

[131] Aerial spraying of glyphosate was the primary strategy of illegal crop destruction under Plan Colombia, but observers from the World Health Organization found that it was "probably carcinogenic," convincing former President Santos to ban its use in 2015 (King and Wherry 2018).

of the core assumptions of the peace agreement, which framed coca cultivation as an economic survival strategy of rural campesino families that could not otherwise make a living from the formal or legal economy. And because aerial fumigations destroy coca fields as well as the legal subsistence crops that are planted alongside coca and the air, land, and water that cocalero communities depend upon for their survival, it represents a direct attack on campesino livelihoods and an indication of the state's lack of concern for their well-being.[132]

On the ground in places like the Caguán, the situation is increasingly tense and uncertain. The evidence suggests that the Colombian military has done little to ameliorate violence and may have even helped fuel it. For example, after the FARC's demobilization the Colombian army expanded its regular presence deep into the southern agricultural frontier regions that had previously been inaccessible in years prior. As Figure 7.4 illustrated, this militarization of the region contributed to an escalation of incidents of paramilitary-perpetrated violence against civilian noncombatants. By 2016 and 2017, not only had paramilitarism once again eclipsed state violence. The number of incidents of paramilitary repression jumped to heights that had not been experienced since the first wave of paramilitarism under Plan Colombia. Additionally, the movement of state forces into the region has helped, unintentionally or not, transform Caquetá into a pipeline of cocaine trafficked southward from the country's urban processing zones into Brazil through Amazonian river routes. As one local journalist informed me,

> Caquetá has been converted into a cocaine trading route to Brazil. Coca produced in Valle de Cauca enters Caquetá, goes south on the Caguán River through Cartagena del Chairá, or through Putumayo or Guaviare to Brazil. There are like 6 military checkpoints along this path, from Cartagena down to the hamlet of Montserrat. Caquetá doesn't produce cocaine. How is that cocaine passing into Brazil through us?[133]

Overall, the peace process appears to have subjected cocalero families and communities to the full weight of Colombian neoliberalism. Duque's government continues to view the Caguán as just a potential sight for capitalization and extractive predation. It has thus far fallen far short in its promises to protect the livelihoods of rural communities from both the armed violence of drug-trafficking groups and from the dispossessing tendencies of capital accumulation in the countryside. With few choice, many cocalero communities have decided to build upon the social infrastructure that had originally been developed under the FARC

---

[132] Romero Sala (2019).

[133] Author interview with local journalist via Skype on July 21, 2018.

to retain their social solidarity networks and local forms of community representation to force the Colombian government to deliver on its promises to bolster rural livelihoods. Most evident in this regard has been the rise of the social movement organization, *Coordinadora Nacional de Cultivadores de Coca, Amapola y Marijuana* (COCCAM, est. 2017). COCCAM grew as a network of coca, opium, and marijuana farmers and farm workers that acted as presence during the peace negotiations to pressure the FARC and the government to recognize their demands for a sustainable, alternative livelihood as rural farming communities. When the peace deal was signed in November 2016, they planned a national meeting in Popayán, Cauca in January 2017 that would bring together producers from all over the country to act as a watchdog to the implementation of the peace agreement, ensure the government's commitment to crop substitution, and engage in social movement actions and political communication to draw attention to the process as it unfolded on the ground. Since then, the COCCAM has developed into an important and sustained presence in the regions abandoned by the FARC. They have organized protests against government proposals to reinstate aerial fumigations, the targeted assassination of cocalero activists and community leaders, and the processes of ecological destruction and land displacement arising from megaprojects and extractivist industries. As a former FARC stronghold, the Caquetá has one of the most vibrant COCCAM chapters in the country. As Rigoberto Rodriguez, the COCCAM-Caquetá's Technical Secretary, pointed out to me, "[because] the cocaleros of Caquetá have been so well-organized . . ., they have been able to pressure the government to deliver on roughly 95% its promises for PNIS payments, which is well above the average for other regions."

While the COCCAM movement is emerging as an important counterweight to the politics of the state, alternatives to coca continue to be few and far. Not only has the peace process opened the doors to the dispossessing and marginalizing consequences of the region's neoliberal transformation. The reemergence of coca production has occurred in a market that has itself become a violent neoliberal dystopia that has further deteriorated campesino livelihoods. Market actors with little desire or need to incorporate the social needs of producers or workers into the coca labor regime have opened the way for its full commodification and its potential for despotism. This said, there have been some important parallels between the cocalero struggles of present-day Caguán and those of the cafeteros of Viejo Caldas. Like the cafeteros, who had historically been afforded a social compact that included promises of Fedecafé (and governmental) protection of their livelihoods and who have since used these promises as a moral economy of rights that the cafetero movement of today continues to mobilize upon, today's cocaleros are equally emboldened by the FARC's historic social compact and the peace processes' promises of future protection and stable economic livelihoods.

Of course, unlike the cafetero struggle, which has claimed that coffee – a legal and highly esteemed commodity – has brought modernization and development to Colombia, the cocaleros have been unable to make a similar claim about the national significance of cocaine. While certainly a lucrative commodity that has granted hundreds of thousands of Colombian farmers and rural workers the ability to survive the failures of developmentalism and neoliberalism, coca remains a highly stigmatized commodity that is associated with violence and corruption rather than social and economic modernization. And despite the peace process' formal acknowledgment of the underlying social realities of the coca market and the political character of the FARC, the COCCAM movement and the cocaleros more generally continue to struggle with their claims that they are neither drug-trafficking criminals nor radical revolutionaries, but instead people simply making a living at the margins of the market.

Conclusion

Toward Labor-Friendly Development in an Era of World-Systemic Crisis

Now over two decades into the twenty-first century, historical capitalism has proven to be just as unstable as it was a century ago. The world economic stability and market expansion associated with US world hegemony have long been swept into the dustbins of history. The postwar Fordism-Keynesian practices in the global north and state-directed developmentalism in the global south that were advocated by the US foreign policy establishment did not only fail to universalize the goals of high mass consumption and capitalist peace. The industrialization and marketization of large segments of the South produced serious social problems, including mass unemployment, over-urbanization, and despotic labor regimes that neither statist-developmentalism nor US world hegemonic interventions were equipped to resolve. Neoliberal policies that heralded the global self-regulating market arose in this historical juncture, with the US jumping ship from its prior hegemonic commitments to support development and instead pushing forcefully for global austerity practices and economic liberalization. It was during this time of world historical transition in the 1980s and 1990s that economists discussed the death of the field of development economics, policymakers proclaimed that there was no alternative to neoliberalism, and labor scholars theorized a race to the bottom in wages and work conditions that would result in market despotism as the predominant labor regime across the globe.

Far from universalizing market despotism, the past two decades have experienced another worldwide wave of social protests and labor militancy that has destabilized political regimes throughout the globe. The Arab Spring protests that spread across the Middle East and North Africa, the anti-austerity and occupy movements of Europe and the Americas, and massive waves of labor unrest in China and Southeast Asia, have all exposed the precaritization of social life that has surfaced under neoliberalism and global market's destructive impulse. This crisis of neoliberalism has exacerbated the decline of the architecture of US hegemony. As national populations polarize between supporting increasingly authoritarian leaders who promise order through ethnonationalism and left populists promising radical democratic alternatives, both critics of the right and left appear to be jumping off the globalization bandwagon and experimenting with new forms of statist populisms. Indeed, well before the 2020 COVID-19 pandemic plunged the world economy into a global depression, the legitimacy of the US-led hegemonic order had already been eroding as the retrenchment of protective social compacts via neoliberal practices exacerbated the social problems associated with the waged and unwaged livelihoods of the world's population. By pulling back the protective covers of the state, neoliberalism has left exposed a population of precarious and unemployed workers who have been both dispossessed of the means of production and stripped of their capacities to engage in viable social reproduction. Indeed, the time is ripe for developmental alternatives.

This global social and economic turbulence of the twenty-first century has indeed given new gravitas to what I have called *Gramsci's questions*; that is, under what conditions do workers and commodity producers acquiesce to capitalist labor processes and market imperatives and under what conditions must labor control be obtained through overt expressions of coercion? This was a particularly interesting question during Antonio Gramsci's own lifetime (1891–1937), when an upsurge in working-class militancy via labor unions and socialist parties throughout Europe and North America was incorporated into liberal capitalist national societies rather than fundamentally transforming them. And I believe it is an especially crucial question in the present era of twenty-first-century capitalism, when the world's workers have experienced decades of neoliberal policies that have largely dismantled the state-directed social welfarist and developmentalist compacts that were established in response to the wave of social unrest, labor militancy, and despotism witnessed by Gramsci. Now well into the twenty-first century, the neoliberal experiment with unregulated global markets and fully commodified livelihoods is proving highly unstable, if not outright destructive, as a lived experience for workers, as a means of promoting national development, as a strategy of political legitimation for elected officials and state policymakers, and as a weapon of world hegemonic power.

This book's analysis of the varied trajectories of labor regime dynamics in three commodity-export producing regions of rural Colombia over the *longue durée* was an attempt to better identify the social conditions under which consensual rather than coercive labor regimes prevailed across space and over time. Empirically, the book was framed around two distinct sets of questions. First, why did we see such stark variation across rural Colombia during the postwar developmental decades, with hegemony predominating in the coffee regime of Viejo Caldas and despotism in the banana and cattle regimes of Urabá and Caquetá, respectively? And second, why did these divergent, albeit stable, rural labor regimes converge toward crises of labor control as we entered the era of neoliberal globalization in the 1980s and 1990s, with mass social unrest predominating in Viejo Caldas and Urabá and counter-hegemony arising in rural Caquetá with the consolidation of a coca regime under the protection of the FARC? Let us take each question in turn.

Spatial Variation: Hegemony in Viejo Caldas and Despotism in Urabá and the Caguán?

The empirical findings of this book point to the central importance of *peripheral proletarianization* in shaping local labor regime outcomes in rural Colombia. Neither experiences of peripheralization nor processes of proletarianization alone were significantly determining of whether a regime swung toward hegemony, despotism, or crisis. Yet the convergence of these two processes within one local regime made hegemonic forms of labor control structurally unlikely. The combination of fully marketized livelihoods and a highly competitive and volatile market did not only make commodity production a precarious and risky venture for the farmers, plantation owners, capitalist investors, or developmentalist organizations that hoped to profit from the market. It produced a form of social and economic instability for commodity producers and workers, which necessitated overt expressions of labor control and repression. Simply put, the cases of Colombia's coffee, bananas and frontier regions demonstrated how processes of peripheral proletarianization have forced labor regime actors to adjust to global market dictates that polarize the interests of labor and capital and push regimes toward either crises of legitimacy or crises of profitability. In turn, hegemonic and counter-hegemonic regimes only arose when peripheralization was not associated with the full-marketization of producer livelihoods, or when fully marketized livelihoods were not forced to adapt to the whims of peripheralized markets. Given the causal importance of peripheral proletarianization in setting the structural bounds of local labor regime dynamics across rural Colombia, the guiding aims of this book were therefore to identify and explain exactly when, how, and why these processes diverged or converged onto a single site.

As Chapter 2 highlighted, the first experience of a hegemonic labor regime arose in Viejo Caldas well before the heyday of Fedecafé hegemony in the postwar decades. Indeed, the frontier settlers of the region interspersed coffee trees alongside subsistence products on their smallholdings, producing more coffee when prices were higher in the market and retaining their "exit option" when prices invariably dropped. The profits they obtained through coffee production were far from the core-like profits that would flow into Fedecafé's National Coffee Fund in the decades to come. The British-led world market was centered on liberalized market practices that placed severe obstacles in the path of coffee-producing governments and domestic elites, who entered what was essentially a peripheralized market niche. Yet the coffee-producing farmers of Viejo Caldas were not subject to capitalist violence or state repression to encourage their production of this global commodity. They engaged in what was a highly peripheralized market niche on their own terms precisely because they retained control of their land and labor and thus averted efforts that would fully proletarianize their livelihoods. In contrast, it was on the large coffee estates that peripheral proletarianization took hold by the 1920s. And it was on these plantations that we saw the rise of powerful labor struggles when prices dropped, the appearance of acts of capitalist repression, and ultimately the victory of coffee workers as the estates were subdivided among the workers through the enactment of Land Law 200 of 1936.

The years from the Great Depression into World War II proved critical to the proletarianization of Colombia's coffee sector. As we also saw in Chapter 2, because the world's largest coffee-exporting country, Brazil, had developed a proletarianized structure of production akin to Colombia's large estates, the collapse of prices in the 1930s wreaked havoc on their sector. This provided Colombia with an opportunity to use its largely unaffected smallholder structure of production to fill the export niche that arose in the temporary absence of Brazilian exports. Liberal Colombian reformers granted Fedecafé, then a group of elite financiers that pumped money and credit to Viejo Caldas' frontier small-holders, parastatal status and a mandate to reorganize the sector using a small-holder structure of production. Fedecafé thus invested heavily in the marketization of smallholding producers in an effort to transform them from subsistence campesinos into fully marketized cafetero farmers. By the 1940s and into the 1950s, Fedecafé had successfully established a highly rationalized, Fordist system of coffee production across Viejo Caldas and beyond.

Given this history, the key questions become how and why this market-dependent labor regime consolidated with the active participation of cafeteros. Why did hegemony coexist with full proletarianization? Chapter 2 demonstrated that Fedecafé engaged in a set of regulatory practices that protected Colombia's cafeteros from the volatility of prices in the world coffee market and bolstered their productive capacities through loan provisions, extension services, and other developmentalist initiatives. This protective social compact, the Pacto Cafetero, invested heavily in the material conditions of the country's cafeteros while also promoting the status and social identity of cafeteros by marketing coffee production as a nationalist endeavor responsible for the modernization of the country. By incorporating cafeteros into this developmentalist social compact, Fedecafé was able to obtain control of the labor process, deciding exactly what would be produced (which coffee seeds varieties), how they would be produced (what technologies were used to cultivate, harvest, and process), and how much would be produced without directly controlling the means of production (land, labor).

If Chapter 2 explained how Fedecafé engaged in actions that fully proletarianized Viejo Caldas' coffee labor regime, Chapter 3 explains how and why this succeeded hegemonically rather than eliciting a more despotic system of labor control. Here we saw that the Pacto Cafetero was made economically viable because Fedecafé was able to take advantage of geopolitical opportunities arising from an aspirant US world hegemon to access core-like profits and therefore avoid the pitfalls of peripheral proletarianization. Fedecafé's movement up to a core-like nodal location in the global coffee commodity chain first arose during World War II, when the US government participated in the Inter-American Coffee Agreement to combat the spreading influence of the Axis powers into the Americas, which the US foreign policy establishment had long considered to be part of its hemispheric backyard. The IACA was supplanted by the International Coffee Agreements as the United States entered its Cold War against Soviet Communism and engaged in developmentalist measures meant to contain the spread of the Cuban Revolution to other parts of Latin America and the Caribbean. By politically regulating the world coffee market, the ICAs stabilized prices and created the institutional stability needed for the long-term expansion of the market, thus opening opportunities for upgrading that had otherwise been closed-off to coffee producer-exporters.

By providing Fedecafé with predictable and relatively high coffee prices as well as a guaranteed world market niche for their exports, the ICAs granted Fedecafé an opportunity to use coffee production as a strategy of domestic economic growth and development. During the decades of the ICAs, core-like profits poured into the FNC, which was then used to reinvest in further growth in the sector as well as redistributed back down to cafetero producers as part of the promises of the moral economy of the Pacto Cafetero. In short, hegemony arose in Viejo Caldas because Fedecafé was able to exploit the world historical context of rising US world hegemony to move out of its peripheral market niche and institute the type of redistributive social compact that was typically limited to workers in core regions of world capitalism. Thus, the Fordism of the Fedecafé's Pacto Cafetero was not only Fordist in terms of its marked rationalization of production on Colombia's coffee fields. It was also Fordist in the sense that, while rural and agricultural in nature, it facilitated the growth of a robust middle class in Colombia that resembled the experiences of United Auto Workers and other unionized industrial workers in the United States during the postwar decades.

If the first case study explains how hegemony arose in Viejo Caldas, the second case study explains how and why despotism prevailed in the banana regime of Urabá during the same historical period. Like its counterpart in Viejo Caldas, the labor regime dynamics that took hold in Urabá by the 1960s were indeed shaped by prior experiences of banana export production in Colombia's Santa Marta region in the early decades of the twentieth century. Chapter 4 showed how transnational banana corporations protected their investments from the competitive dictates of the *laissez faire* world market by vertically integrating and controlling all the nodes of the commodity chain from production to sales and marketing. Despotic labor regimes came to predominate across the production end of these markets, where the demands of fully proletarianized labor forces living in isolated and disease-prone banana enclaves were repressed by Latin American and Caribbean governments that sought foreign investment as a means of buttressing their domestic power. As the analysis of Santa Marta's labor regime pointed out, this situation of peripheral proletarianization produced a despotic regime that erupted into a wave of labor unrest that was violently put down by Colombian security forces during the massacre of 1928.

But if Santa Marta's despotism could be explained by the contradictions of peripheral proletarianization that existed during the 1920s and 1930s, decades of declining British world hegemony, why did despotism come to characterize Urabá's banana regime during the heyday of US world hegemony? If US world hegemony provided the world market opportunities Fedecafé needed to establish its developmentalist and solidly hegemonic Pacto Cafetero, why didn't we see a similarly hegemonic Pacto Bananero arise in Urabá? As we saw from the second case study, the rise of US world hegemony during the postwar decades did indeed provide new market opportunities to promote domestic development in both Viejo Caldas and Urabá. However, whereas US hegemony provided Fedecafé the opportunity to *move up* the coffee commodity chain to obtain core-like profits through the geopolitically regulated IACA and ICA quota agreements, US hegemony in the world banana market manifested in the vertical-disintegration of the transnational banana corporations. Vertical disintegration provided domestic banana-producing states like Colombia the ability to *move into* the production niches of the world banana market as a way of promoting national development and economic growth. By helping to foster domestic banana production through aid provisions and the like, the United States was able to pacify the wave of labor radicalism and economic nationalism that had arisen across the banana-enclaves of Latin America and retain its hegemonic influence within the global banana trade. Domestic producer-exporters and their governments were incorporated as junior partners into the vertically integrated structures of an expanding world banana market. The problem with vertical-disintegration, however, was that it did not permit Augura the ability to move up the banana chain to obtain the core-like profits that could have otherwise been reinvested as a redistributive social compact. And because the collective action efforts of the Union of Banana Producing Countries failed to geopolitically restructure the market akin to its counterpart in the coffee market, Augura's banana regime became incorporated into a highly peripheralized market niche that exacerbated the contradictions of peripheral proletarianization on the ground in Urabá.

This difference between *moving into* rather than *moving up* the global banana commodity chain was a critical factor that explains why the economic opportunities provided to Augura were vastly different from those provided to Fedecafé. However, in itself, it does not explain why Urabá's banana regime consolidated into a largely stable, albeit highly despotic, regime in the 1960s and 1970s rather than unravelling into periodic crises of labor control. To explain why despotism predominated rather than crisis, this study had to dig down into national, local and interregional dynamics. As we saw from Chapter 5, the most critical factor that explains the rise of despotism in Urabá was Augura's heavy reliance upon state repression and political exclusion to avert banana worker demands for a greater redistribution of wealth. The leaders of the National Front regime that came to power in Colombia in 1958 were avowedly developmentalist in their orientation to the national economy. They viewed the successes of Fedecafé's actions in the coffee market as evidence of the social progress and economic growth that could arise from systems of global commodity production in the countryside. It is not surprising, then, that they had high hopes for Augura's efforts to develop a robust banana export sector in Urabá that would become an equally powerful engine of growth.

However, because the growth of Urabá's banana regime rested upon the need to keep wages low and regulations on working conditions minimal, a dynamic arose in which economic growth produced local poverty. When Urabá's banana workers began to organize unions and engage in local politics, Augura's ability to persist in the market became threatened, and this in turn threatened to sabotage the state's developmental goals. Two state-directed actions became critically important as mechanisms of labor control in Urabá. First was the direct use of state security forces, backed in part by US military assistance to Colombia, to repress labor militancy and social unrest. Second was the exclusionary tendencies of the National Front regime itself, which erected institutional obstacles that helped the region's political elites, the Guerrista Liberals, monopolize power. For at least two decades, this combination of repression and political marginalization were indeed effective in containing banana worker demands for a greater redistribution of the wealth created by the export sector.

Here, it is also critical to point out that the ugliness of this form of brute despotic power in Urabá did not lead to a significant political delegitimation of the National Front regime during the 1960s and the bulk of the 1970s. As we saw from Chapter 4, a similar form of brutal despotism in Santa Marta eventually tarnished the reputation of the Colombia's Conservative Republic and led to the rise of at least sixteen years of Liberal Party hegemony. Why didn't the despotism of Urabá in the 1960s and 1970s lead to a similar shift in the political establishment during this time? Or put differently, why was the political regime essentially stable during this time? The answer, as we saw from Chapter 5, was due in large part to the viability of the coffee regime in Viejo Caldas. That is, Fedecafé's Pacto Cafetero was not only effective as a way of incorporating massive numbers of rural farmers and their families into a hegemonic social compact that expanded the country's coffee sector. It also turned large swaths of the Colombian countryside into ardent political supporters of the National Front regime. It is unlikely that the elitist Liberal and Conservative parties would have retained such political buoyancy in the 1960s and 1970s had the coffee regime of Viejo Caldas and beyond been experiencing similarly despotic conditions as that of Urabá. In short, while global dynamics of US world hegemony help provide the structural context of peripheral proletarianization in Urabá, it was national, local and inter-regional factors that explain why it tended toward despotism rather than crisis.

Finally, if the importance of banana production to the developmentalist goals of the National Front helps explain why despotism consolidated in Urabá, why did a similarly despotic regime arise in rural Caquetá, where the production of cheap hides and meats for domestic consumption appeared to be a less likely engine of regional economic growth and development than banana production to the global market? Here again we see the importance of national, local, and interregional factors. First, as Chapter 6 demonstrated, frontier colonization in rural Caquetá played a critical, and indeed changing, role in Colombia's political economy under the National Front regime. The settlement of the region first arose as a safety valve for rural populations that had been displaced from the land by capitalist development projects or rural sectarian violence during the years of *La Violencia*. The ability of these rural surplus migrants to settle the frontier by establishing subsistence smallholdings along its external borders provided an opportunity for National Front leaders to showcase its newly established agrarian development agencies and therefore expand the territorial presence of the state into Caquetá's rural hinterlands.

However, as the years passed, a despotic regime driven by the cattle rancher association, Fedegán, took root. Under Fedegan, the region transformed into a producer of low-cost meats and hides for a national market that was itself becoming increasingly proletarianized. So while these meats and hides were not global commodities that could directly generate economic growth as was occurring with coffee in Viejo Caldas and bananas in Urabá, Fedegán's cattle regime facilitated the expansion of the developmentalist model indirectly by providing cheap and needed consumer goods to a national population that was becoming urban and income-dependent. In other words, Colombia's political elites had a reason to prioritize the expansion of the cattle grazing areas into the frontier hinterlands of Caquetá and elsewhere over the demands for land by frontier settlers that were being forcibly evicted by local cattle ranching elites. Consequently, it is not surprising that these political party bosses turned the other way when their own developmentalist agrarian agencies became corrupted by local landed elites and local juridical and security forces operated as tools of dispossession in the region.

As had occurred in Urabá, the exclusionary politics of the National Front also helped buttress Fedegán despotism in the region. Like their Guerrista Liberal counterparts, the Turbayista Liberals of Caquetá maintained a solid monopoly over local political offices, which proved critical to the continued marginalization of the local population of settlers. Finally, it is important to point out that the mere existence of the frontier itself played a role in the consolidation of despotism in the region during this period. The fact that evicted settlers could move their families deeper into the frontier rather than succumb to a proletarian livelihood had they moved to another region meant that Fedegán was able to incorporate cycles of dispossession into its strategy of capitalist expansion. That is, because cattle production is land-intensive and labor-expulsive, Fedegán was able to externalize the costs of cutting down virgin forests onto frontier colonos, then reap the economic benefits of transforming them into cattle grazing lands once these colonos were displaced. This cycle of dispossession itself helped keep the costs of cattle production significantly cheaper than it would have been had cattle ranchers been forced to pay workers to clear forests or to pay settlers for their land. In other words, what made this despotic regime relatively stable during this period was the stability of the National Front regime itself and the labor processes that facilitated the further marginalization of the frontier population.

To summarize, the causes of spatial variation across rural Colombia during the postwar developmental decades were diverse, locally contingent, and yet structured by world historical forces. The geopolitics of US world hegemony shaped the broader contours of each by imbuing Colombian political elites with the notion that profits could be made, economic growth and development stimulated, and national modernization impelled through systems of commodity production for the market. However, the opportunities that opened with the rise of US hegemony manifested differently across these different commodity markets, with important ramifications on whether these regimes would become hegemonic, despotic, or crisis-prone. US world hegemony played a key role in restructuring the coffee commodity chain in ways that facilitated Colombia's movement up the chain from a peripheral to a core-like niche. Access to core-like profits became essential to Fedecafé's hegemony on the ground in Viejo Caldas. In turn, the impact on US world hegemony in Colombia's banana and cattle market only facilitated Augura and Fedegan's movement into a peripheral location in their respective chains. Consequently, it was despotism rather than crisis that prevailed in the bananas and cattle regimes, though the precise causes of this despotism were due to a combination of factors operating at the national, local, and interregional scales.

Temporal Variation: The Loss of Labor Control in Viejo Caldas, Urabá, and the Caguán?

The heart of the temporal puzzle is the question of why rural Colombia's diverse local labor regimes converged toward crises of labor control as the postwar developmental decades passed and became replaced by neoliberal globalization. Since the 1990s, the hegemony of Viejo Caldas unraveled, giving way to endemic and powerful waves of cafetero protests that continue to paralyze Fedecafé's control of the sector. The despotism that had been so effective in quelling labor unrest in Urabá gave way to unprecedented labor militancy and political mobilization that undermined Augura's control of the region's plantations in the mid-1980s and early 1990s. Likewise, Fedegán's tight grip over processes of frontier expansion and cattle production in the Caguán was replaced by a burgeoning coca regime under the control of the FARC that operated outside of the effective control of the Colombian state and in opposition to the region's cattle ranching industry. If the temporal theories of neoliberal globalization fall short of explaining this broad convergence to crises of control in the 1980s and 1990s, what were the causes of crisis during this period?

Like the spatial puzzle, this book's comparative-historical case studies point to an equally complex set of causes operating across distinct scales of analysis. As Chapter 3 made clear, the shift from hegemony to crisis in Viejo Caldas was driven primarily by *global forces* related to the decline of US world hegemony. Indeed, the US-backed ICA agreements were successful in their efforts to promote national development and economic growth across the world's coffee-producing regions during the postwar decades. And although the expansion of the developmentalist coffee market at first served the interests of the United States by helping reconstruct the world market following its near destruction from the Great Depression and World War II and by extending the geopolitical influence of the United States into radicalized regions of the Third World, the ICA's success backfired on the United States by the 1980s. In the 1960s and 1970s, large coffee producers like Colombia and Brazil used the opportunities provided by the ICAs to upgrade up the coffee chain to access core-like profits while new coffee-producing countries moved into the market in order to promote their own domestic developmentalist initiatives. However, by the 1980s, fissures emerged within the International Coffee Organization between larger and smaller, older and newer coffee-producing countries, with the former trying to hold onto their fixed market niches granted to them under the ICA and newer countries frustrated by the ICA's restrictions on their market access.

This geopolitical rift was exacerbated by the United States, whose transnational coffee corporations began reinvesting in speculative ventures in coffee financial markets and ultimately undermined the structural power of coffee producers in general by decoupling production from profits. By the late 1980s, the United States successfully created an alliance with the smaller producer countries to withdraw from the ICA and take advantage of the world market's deregulation. Thus, it was the abrogation of the ICA in 1989 and the liberalization of the world market that re-peripheralized Colombia's market niche and ultimately undermined Fedecafé's ability to easily reinvest in both further accumulation processes and the redistributive measures at the core of its Pacto Cafetero.

Yet, we also saw from the first case study that peripheralization in itself does not necessarily create the structural conditions that prompt crises of labor control. Indeed, peripheralization predominated during the first decades of the twentieth century, but it coexisted with a hegemonic form of production because the smallholders of Viejo Caldas at the time were not fully marketized in terms of their class reproduction. Neither fully capitalized in terms of how they produced coffee, nor fully dependent upon the production of coffee to meet their family's reproduction needs, peripheralization did not in itself constitute a threat to their livelihoods. Yet, by the time Colombia's location in the coffee chain was re-peripheralized in the closing decades of the twentieth century, the coffee-producing farmers of Viejo Caldas had become fully marketized cafetero producers whose livelihoods depended upon a highly capitalized and rationalized use of their labor and land. With coffee as their essential income and coffee production as their primary social identity, the cafeteros of Viejo Caldas have drawn upon the promises of the moral economy of the Pacto Cafetero as their survival strategy. For Fedecafé, the endemic nature of cafetero unrest and crisis brought on by market peripheralization has forced them to address questions of how to maintain its Fordist production system and sustain fully capitalized cafetero farms without the favorable global market conditions that had made this possible during the postwar decades of the twentieth century. Over the past two decades, this crisis has only deepened, as cafetero protests have become stronger and Fedecafé has struggled to meet the demands of cafeteros from below and global market imperatives from above with even more highly capitalized production techniques.

If the causes of the shift from hegemony to crisis in Viejo Caldas were ultimately global in nature, the shift from despotism to crisis in the banana regime of Urabá stemmed from processes occurring at the *national scale*. That is, Urabá's niche in the global banana market was from its beginnings peripheral in nature.

The US-centered dollar market was both highly competitive for producers and deregulated in terms of its pricing and volumes of bananas traded. Clearly then, the shift to a crisis of labor control was not prompted by any changes to the global market. Rather, as we saw from Chapter 4, it was the democratization of Colombia's political system in the 1980s – including the peace processes and political reforms instituted under the Betancur and Barco Administrations – that undermined the mechanisms of labor control Augura had depended upon to maintain their peripheral niche in the banana commodity chain during the previous decades. Permitting the unionization of banana workers, legalizing strikes, allowing guerrillas to openly organize on the plantations and participate in local elections, all opened spaces for Urabá's fully proletarianized banana workers to mobilize for redistributive and protective measures to better their lives. Yet, precisely because their niche was peripheral, worker successes on the plantations and in local political offices threatened the continued viability of Augura in the market. It was only through the paramilitarization of the region in the 1990s that Augura's crisis of labor control was reversed. Put differently, paramilitarism became the solution to the social contradictions of peripheral proletarianization that existed in the context of political democratization.

Thus, while the shift from despotism to crisis in Urabá was prompted by national factors associated with the democratization of the region, the regime's return to despotism through paramilitarization in the mid-1990s was prompted by a complex interplay of *global and local factors*. As we saw from Chapter 5, the AUC paramilitaries were indeed financed in part by Colombian drug-trafficking mafias that wanted to control the greater Urabá region in order to both open a transit route from its urban cocaine-processing centers in the central highlands to the Caribbean coast and to obtain land that they could use to launder the profits they made in the illegal market. Moreover, the AUC was also financed by US fruit corporations like Chiquita Brands, which paid the AUC to protect its assets and suppliers from threats from guerrillas, and, in doing so, ultimately gave a green-light to paramilitaries to systematically kill off workers and leftist politicians that threatened to upend Augura's control of the labor process. In short, the rise of paramilitarism was indeed a local solution to a national problem – the fact that political democratization undermined Augura's existing strategies of labor control. Yet, the AUC was fueled by cocaine traffickers and banana conglomerates whose profits accrued through global market activities.

Finally, if crisis in Viejo Caldas was prompted by global factors, and crisis in Urabá came from national factors, the third case study of the shift in labor regime dynamics in the Caguán arose from a complex mix of *local and national factors*. As was true in Urabá, Fedegán control of Caquetá's cattle regime in the 1960s and 1970s rested heavily on the despotism of Colombia's political system. However, it was not the democratization of the political regime that caused the shift from despotism to counter-hegemony by the early 1980s. Nor was the shift caused by the mere entrance of the FARC into the region or the rise of coca production alone. As we saw from Chapter 6, the FARC entered the frontier regions of Caquetá in the early 1970s, but they lacked the military capacity needed to significantly push back against the expanding cattle frontier, let alone subvert Fedegán's control of the region.

Likewise, coca production first popped up in remote regions of the Caguán in the mid-1970s. Yet, because the FARC refused to participate in the illegal narcotics economy at that time, those frontier settlers that produced coca leaf were forced to accept the despotic market conditions offered by urban drug-trafficking mafias. Because these drug traffickers lacked either a vested interest in the overall well-being of cocaleros or a desire for taking on the social and political responsibilities of establishing a state-like presence in the region, the local coca market during this period was largely a competitive buyers' market that tended to worsen cocalero social and economic instability. It was not until FARC leaders decided to incorporate cocalero production into their revolutionary war making and local state making activities that their military powers grew strong enough to push back against state and cattle ranching violence. For two decades, the FARC controlled the region, acting as a *de facto* state and overseeing a counter-hegemonic coca labor regime that absorbed rural surplus labor that had been repelled by Colombia's developmentalist agrarian policies and that were being increasingly expelled as neoliberal policies took hold at the close of the century.

As we saw from Chapter 7, neither neoliberalism nor globalization undermined FARC counter-hegemony in the Caguán. The adoption of neoliberal agrarian policies in the 1990s actually strengthened the FARC by pushing rural surplus migrants into the region, where they were welcomed as farmers, workers and soldiers. The rise of the global cocaine market, in turn, poured monopolistic wealth into the FARC's war making and alternative state making machine. Instead, the collapse of FARC counter-hegemony resulted from the convergence of global and national processes. Globally, the United States replaced developmentalist aid as its key mechanism of maintaining hegemonic influence in the region with a crude form of neoliberal militarism. Of course, militarism was part and parcel of US world hegemony during its peak years and Colombia's National Front regimes received ample amounts of US military aid and support to fight the country's Marxist guerrillas. However, this aid was used primarily as a containment strategy seeking to push rural insurgents into marginalized regions of the country. This strategy changed to an all-out elimination strategy when the US globalized its War on Drugs in the 1980s and 1990s and later expanded its military interventions under the US War on Terror at the turn of the twenty-first century. By then, US military aid under *Plan Colombia* and *Plan Patriota* had become essential components of the "Democratic Security" practices of the Uribe Administration, which viewed the guerrillas as an existential threat to the Colombian state and the key obstacle to the full implementation of neoliberal policies across the countryside.

In summary, the causes of the temporal convergence toward crises of labor control, as well as the causes of a return to forms of labor control, were equally diverse, locally contingent, and yet structured by world historical forces. Colombia's adoption of the neoliberal turn, as we saw, was most destructive to the extent that it ruptured the *status quo ante* of specific sets of fully proletarianized workers and global commodity producing farmers. In none of the cases examined in this book did neoliberalism directly and negatively impact workers. To be sure, it is worth noting that it has had indirect consequences for Colombian cafeteros, bananeros, and cocaleros. By opening up the countryside to global economic competition, neoliberal agrarian reforms pulled the rug from the few remaining developmentalist agencies that rural inhabitants could use to access land and local markets for their produce. And in the absence of protective covering from developmental organizations, be they Fedecafé or the FARC, rural farmers are less able to meet their subsistence needs by producing agricultural goods for the local market. However, the dispossessing tendencies of capitalist development in Colombia has been a long-standing historical reality rather than a mere manifestation of the contemporary era.

Globalization, in turn, is even less useful as concept to understand these labor regime trajectories because capitalism's forays into rural Colombia, at least in terms of the major developmental commodities analyzed here, were always global in nature. The most pressing temporal issue at stake for rural Colombians was neither neoliberalism nor globalization, but the rise and fall of US world hegemony. During the postwar decades, the US played a key role in reconstructing the world market by providing global security and order to investors, expanding consumer markets for global commodities through its advocacy of Fordist-welfarist policies, and using its influence over multilateral regulatory institutions to stabilize financial flows and currency markets. The United States also became an ardent supporter of developmentalist initiatives that encouraged state leaders across the global south to invest in global commodity production and invite foreign investment as a safe and promising means of stimulating domestic economic growth and stability. The push and pull of restructured and expanding global markets under US world hegemony thus opened new possibilities for local regime actors who could shake up and challenge what had otherwise been structurally determined core-periphery positions within the global coffee and banana chains. Yet, as we have seen, the capacity for local regime actors to successfully exploit the opportunities opened by US world hegemony differed starkly across the three commodities analyzed. Fedecafé was successful in exploiting these opportunities, which allowed them to upgrade to a core-like position in the global commodity chain. However, because their upgrading depended upon the persistence of the US-backed ICA quota system, Fedecafé was also the only labor regime organization to experience firsthand the negative consequences of US world hegemonic decline. Indeed, the US government's abandonment of the ICA quota system and support for market liberalization resulted in the downgrading of Colombia's niche in the coffee chain in ways that undermined Fedecafé's hegemony in Viejo Caldas.

In sharp contrast to the de-peripheralization and re-peripheralization of Colombia's coffee regime, the country's banana regime remained stuck in a peripheralized niche of the global banana chain despite the sweeping economic restructuring that occurred under US world hegemony in the postwar decades. Under the vertically integrated market system, Colombia's banana regime of Santa Marta experienced the labor repression and authoritarianism that had become typical of Latin America's banana export zones. And while a hemispheric wave of labor militancy and economic nationalism ultimately challenged this market system, the formation of a vertically integrated banana market in the 1960s and 1970s did not significantly improve the lot of Colombian banana workers in the country's new enclave of Urabá. Instead, as efforts to upgrade through the UPBC failed and new producer-exporters moved into the market, Urabá's peripheral niche in the market became unavoidable.. Thus, by the 1990s, the decline of US hegemony indeed closed off opportunities for upgrading in both the coffee and banana markets.

Overall then, the US' abandonment of the International Coffee Agreement's quota system, its continued support for the deregulated US dollar market, and its efforts to dismantle the protected European APC banana market have only intensified competition among coffee- and banana-producing countries over the past few decades. For these legal agricultural commodity markets, US hegemonic decline has brought with it a sharp peripheralization of economic activities that has exacerbated the social contradictions of Colombia's labor regimes on the ground. The only exception to this historical twist has been the international cocaine market, which through its illegality has offered locals access to the types of upgrading possibilities and core-like profits that have always been difficult to obtain in "legitimate" commodity chains, but which have become an even more distant reality for producers in rural Colombia.

Toward a New Politics of Labor and Development in an Era of World-Systemic Chaos

What then does this study tell us about the prospects for rural social stability and labor-friendly forms of development in Colombia and other regions at the margins of the global market, as we witness the demise of US world hegemony and a new form of twenty-first-century capitalism characterized by systemic chaos?

Regarding prospects for future stability and justice for rural Colombians, this study highlights at least two major implications. First, this book contradicts analysts and observers who argue that Colombia's protracted social crisis and endemic violence result from the inability of the Colombian state to effectively control the region and its population. As the case studies demonstrated, the Colombian state has played a central role in the historical trajectories of each local labor regime. Moreover, the emergence of despotism and social crisis did not come as the result of state weakness, but instead from political intransigence. With few exceptions, the Colombian state has consistently prioritized a form of rural development that has evicted farmers from their land, concentrated wealth, and sold off the most fertile regions to investors. This dispossessing tendency of Colombian development has not only produced heightened rural instability, local forms of political corruption, and masses of landless rural surplus migrants that have contributed to the overpopulation and institutional crises of Colombian cities. It has been the primary reason for the growth of illegal market, state, and class formations. Put simply, far from playing a "destabilizing role" in Colombian society, as Gonzalo Sánchez (2001:4) argued, the illegal narcotics economy and the presence of illegal armed groups are better understood as symptoms of a deep-rooted crisis of Colombian development. This historical shortsightedness has undoubtedly contributed to the popularity of *Uribismo* as well as to the Hobbesian politics of Colombian society at large. Any effort to realistically move toward a lasting peace must first recognize and implicate the politics of the state in the creation of today's crises.

Second, it is not only that the politics of the state have consistently favored the interests of capital over labor, and landed elite over subsistence farmer. When presented with demands from workers and farmers from below, Colombian economic policymakers of both the developmentalist and neoliberal variants continue to view the way forward as one that deepens the country's dependence on the world market rather than diminishes it. As we saw from the case studies, this developmentalist lure of global commodity production for export to the world market was indeed strong during the postwar decades, and perhaps for good reasons. The world's most powerful capitalist superpower, the United States, had emerged from the World War II with its economic engine intact and its global military strength at its apex. Over the next quarter century, US hegemonic actions cultivated the expansion of the global market and made it ever more alluring, as Colombian policymakers were offered provisions of developmental aid, support for the geopolitical restructuring of markets, and ample doses of militarization to ease their fears of rural radicalism and unrest. However, the ability to translate global commodity production into an actual engine of local economic growth, social welfare, and working-class stability shrank as the United States reversed its foreign economic policy away from supporting developmentalist initiatives in favor of neoliberal state policies, free trade agreements, and unregulated flows of financial capital. Yet, despite the closing of opportunities to avoid peripheralization in the world market, Colombian policymakers continue down the marketization track. And this trend toward a deepening marketization of agrarian lives through policies that roll back state protections for workers to lure capital only exacerbates the social contradictions that have given rise to crisis and despotism in the first place.

To be sure, there are ample signs that the current trends of deepening social contradictions brought on by neoliberalism are indeed unraveling. And in the interstices, new political imaginations are emerging that challenge the continued penetration of the market into Colombian society and the violence-prone neoliberal politics of the state. As we saw from Chapter 3, the cafetero movement's transformation into a broad coalition of agrarian producers under the umbrella group *Dignidad Agropecuaria* is one sign of the broad frustrations of the population with neoliberal policies that have exposed the countryside to global market imperatives. The massive wave of protests in 2013, and more recently the national *cacerolazo* protests of November–December 2019 sent shockwaves across Colombia's political establishment and alerted leftist candidates that anti-neoliberal and anti-Uribismo platforms can gain widespread electoral support from the population. Indeed, candidates from Colombia's leftist *Polo-Democrático, Colombia Humana,* and *Partido Verde* parties have gained broad support among voters and won a surprising number of upset victories in major mayoral, gubernatorial, and senate races. These are promising signs that the Colombian electorate is becoming increasingly critical of the ability of neoliberal policies to deliver on their promises of generating forms of economic growth that deliver social stability and social well-being.

If indeed the antimarket politics of Colombia's left continue to grow, the major question of course thus becomes, once in power, what realistic alternative policies exist? What types of development are capable of producing social and economic stability in an era of twenty-first-century global market turbulence? While this study cannot provide a concrete roadmap toward the future, its adoption of a world historical perspective is informative and suggests at least three possible developmental options.

The first would require a fundamental and critical rethinking of the role that Colombia has played in supporting US geopolitical influence in the broader Latin American and Caribbean region. During the postwar decades, the Colombian government's support of US policies brought with it clear domestic social and economic rewards. Colombian advocacy of developmentalist policies, whether through Fedecafé and the ICO, Augura and the UBPC, or the Caquetá Colonization Plan and INCORA, was intended to not only stimulate local production for the market but also to thwart radical alternatives that might subvert both the further expansions of the global market and challenge US power in the broader region. For this, the Colombian government was rewarded with doses of development and military aid that in some instances undermined the monopolistic hold of US corporations over global markets.

When the US government began to advocate for neoliberalism rather than protective and geopolitically regulated markets in the 1980s, the viability of the market as a mechanism of sustaining protective social compacts, hegemonic labor regimes, and stable forms of domestic development diminished. Importantly, we saw that the Colombian government continued to receive military aid to stabilize extant systems of commodity production and retain political control of the country in the face of threats from drug-traffickers and guerrilla groups despite the shrinking of developmental opportunities. Whereas military repression of workers could have been justified by Colombian elites as a temporary and necessary (albeit sinister) measure to allow future development, nowadays it is not clear what the Colombian government gets in return for being the United States' best ally in the region.

This is not to say that Colombia should cut ties with the United States, or even antagonize relations. Rather, it simply means that future Colombian leaders need not worry about pulling out of or radically transforming the conditions of their existing trade and policy agreements with the United States, or about adopting domestic policies that do not automatically prioritize the interests of foreign investors and transnational corporations over domestic producers and workers. The most obvious example in this regard is Colombia's continued support for the US Wars on Drugs and Terror. Decriminalization of Colombia's cocaine market would certainly diminish the role of illegal armed groups and mafias as regulators of the market and reduce drug-related violence and the harm caused by it. Legalization, in turn, could open opportunities for the Colombian government to hegemonically expand its influence into drug-trafficking and drug-producing regions of the country and generate much needed tax revenues to extend social services to these regions. One can imagine a Colombian National Cocalero Fund that functions similarly to the National Coffee Fund that had been so important to the economic vitality and social stability of Viejo Caldas during the previous century. Such actions would certainly put Colombian policymakers at odds with their North American counterparts. However, this might be a better developmental bet than the militarized neoliberalism demanded by the United States.

Second is the need to confront the problem of market peripheralization. As we saw from the historical case studies, peripheralization was challenged in Colombia's coffee and banana regimes through transnational collective action strategies among producer-exporter countries that geopolitically restructured the world coffee and banana markets. Not surprisingly, this unrest erupted across the producer ends of Latin America's coffee and bananas markets, and it did so during a similarly tumultuous period of world-systemic contraction and market chaos. Moreover, these waves were critical to the rise of economically nationalist governments and transnational producer alliances that viewed unregulated world markets and *laissez faire* capitalism as antithetical to their goals of promoting domestic economic growth.

To be sure, while the institutional restructuring of these markets was eventually facilitated by an aspiring US world hegemon who feared more radical threats from below, there is no reason to believe that similar geopolitical alliances need to wait for another rising world hegemon before a reconstructed and politically regulated market can emerge. Indeed, as today's neoliberal world market fails to deliver on its promises to generate ample profits across the entirety of the world market, the global conditions appear more favorable to a realignment of South–South geopolitical actions that can re-embed the market to serve domestic social and political interests. Indeed, there have been signs of growing demands for a new international coffee agreement within the ICO.[1] Frustrated with the volatility of coffee prices in the market, Fedecafé has also engaged in efforts to pull Colombian Milds from trade in the speculative financial derivatives markets on the New York and London Stock exchange.[2] Cocoa producer-exporters have likewise begun to experiment with market schemes that artificially hold their commodities off the global market to raise prices, just as coffee producers had done a century before.[3] These efforts reflect growing frustrations with the broken promises of liberal markets to tropical commodity-producing regions of the world whose governments have been lured to neoliberalism over the past four decades.

Finally, it must be pointed out that these efforts to re-embed the world market through geopolitical alliance-building or the definancialization of capital are only the most conservative of future development options. Perhaps more likely is the shift to a politics that does not attempt to avoid problems caused by peripheralization but instead challenges the problem of proletarianization itself. Indeed,

---

[1] El Tiempo (2019).
[2] Brown (2019).
[3] Wexler (2020).

there is much that the Colombian state can do to diminish its citizens' dependence on the world market to meet their social reproduction needs. This book points to at least two paths forward. First is the need to redistribute productive and fertile land to agrarian producer families and bolster state marketing and extensions services with the goal of promoting national food sovereignty and domestic agricultural production. Rather than stimulate the types of agricultural hyper-productivity required by global markets, requiring vast economies of scale, labor-replacing productive technologies, and expensive fertilizers and petrochemicals that destroy local ecologies and worsen rural health, investing in the welfare and well-being of rural farmers who produce for local and national markets provides a structural set of imperatives to protect local ecologies and campesino livelihoods. And stabilizing conditions in the countryside would in fact reverse trends of over-urbanization and all of the problems now associated with it, including heightened criminal activities, traffic and transportation overflow, rising costs of city services, and the like.

Second, the state can reduce the population's costs of living by investing in the expansion of public education, health and social services, promoting social insurance protections, and otherwise expand the welfare state. Key in this regard would be to invest in universal basic income payments or other actions that would provide multiple income sources. This would not only provide more income to families that need it most. By reducing the relevance of income generated from workplaces, such interventions would greatly strengthen the structural power of labor vis-à-vis employers. Currently, the Colombian government does provide targeted income payments to low-income families with children. Expanding these efforts to the national population would diminish the problems created by their market dependence and increase the likelihood of unionization and agrarian collective action.

Critics of these state-directed welfarist policies meant to de-commodify liveli-hoods would no doubt criticize their costs, and perhaps even argue that they would increase inflationary pressures and living costs. Such arguments, however, fall flat in places like Colombia, where employers have regularly drawn upon the use of violence to quell demands for a greater redistribution of wealth. Since the 1990s, and perhaps even before then, the politics of the state have centered on keeping production costs as low as possible in order to draw foreign investment and facilitate domestic capital's articulation into world markets. This gamble has not only failed in its efforts to generate the types of growth needed to pull the country's workers out of poverty. It has generated industries that have become dependent upon systemic human rights violations in order to adapt to the dictates of world capitalism. A much better developmental gamble would be to invest directly in the well-being of the Colombian population, through the types of welfarist policies described above. An educated, healthy, and stable rural and urban working class in Colombia might be attractive to foreign investors seeking productive returns on their investments. However, even if capital does not come, Colombia would be left with an educated and healthy population.[4]

Looking forward, whether Colombian development continues its downward neoliberal spiral or veers off this track depends upon the political imaginary and political actions of the population. This study provides some insight into how Colombian workers and rural producers adapted to, fostered the expansion of, and indeed challenged the primacy of the market in their lives. Future research can take up where this book left off by providing important insights into how the social contradictions of the present are likely to play out in the years to come. First, much more can be learned about the factionalism and internal politics that have arisen within the developmental organizations analyzed in this book. The future developmental directions of Fedecafé, Fedegán, Augura, and even the internal politics of the Colombian government can provide insight into the opportunities and obstacles to social transformation within these organizations. This study was limited by its broad brushstrokes approach to the role these organizations played in their developmental trajectories. Future research can unpack the internal struggles that have made these trajectories possible and that inform how actors within these organizations themselves determine the politics of what is possible in the future.

Second, any future developmental politics must grapple with the ways that protective social compacts drew boundaries around who would be included and excluded, who merited protection and who did not, and why. As we saw from this book, the class struggles over accessing a viable livelihood through production for the market was indeed constituted by what Immanuel Wallerstein described as "the systems-level problem." The wealth generated by labor in capitalist markets cannot be universally redistributed without fundamentally undermining the market's ability to make profits. This means that even the coveted protective social compacts that generated hegemony on the ground in Colombia were exercises in boundary-drawing that excluded certain market actors from the privileges of inclusion. The prime example of this is apparent in today's *Dignidad Cafetera* movement. While the producer-based identity that has become so central to the

---

[4] This is precisely the point Giovanni Arrighi made regarding the contradictions of proletarianized forms of development, both during his early work analyzing migratory labor supplies in Rhodesia, during his research in rural Calabrian, and at the close of his life when he took interest in China's economic ascendency as the rest of the world turned to neoliberal policies rooted in labor despotism and dispossession (Bair et al. 2019).

movement's moral economy has been useful in forging alliances across those agrarian producer groups that have been hurt by market liberalization, it does not present any experiential grounds for a class politics that is not rooted in downward economic mobility or the experience of expulsion from state protections. Clearly, this is a political-ideological obstacle for any movement that would seek broader, if not class-wide, alliances with social groups that were never included in such protective compacts, privileged with state protections, or considered to be legitimate farmers or workers. Any future politics that seeks broad and inclusionary coalitions must grapple with how to limit the presence of their market in their lives as well as in their political imaginations and identities.

Appendix

The coercion dataset used in this book indicates broad increases and decreases in the number of incidents of labor repression that occurred within each micro-region over time, its measurements are ordinal (0,1,2,3 ... incidents/year) rather than nominal in nature (high/low), making it difficult to clearly demarcate the analytical boundaries between "silent compulsions" and "extra-economic force." Of course, designating what is a high and low number of incidents of labor repression for any given place at any given time is a necessarily arbitrary and normative venture. For example, in comparison to other countries Colombia has extraordinarily high levels of political violence. So what may appear to be an extremely high level of labor repression in one region at a given time may in fact be equal to or below the national average. As a consequence, rather than use the coercion data to compare local levels of labor repression to national or international averages, high/low levels of violence were only considered to be relative indicators. They were used to either compare the number of incidents of labor repression occurring within one region at a given period of time to earlier and later period of time within that same region (comparisons over time) or to compare the number of incidents of repression occurring within one region at a given time to the number of incidents occurring in other regions at the same period in time (comparisons over space).

This coercion dataset was particularly useful in distinguishing situations of "counter-hegemony" from "crises of control." The latter is characterized by high levels of labor repression while the former describes a situation in which the central state (and capital) exercises little influence, therefore resulting in low levels of labor repression. The violence that predominates under "counter-hegemonic" regimes therefore tends to occur as acts of warfare rather than as acts of labor repression. This was evident, for example, in the low levels of labor repression that occurred during the period of FARC "counter-hegemony" in the Caguán in the 1980s and 1990s. This contrasts sharply with the "crisis of control" situation in Urabá during this same time period, in which local banana plantation owners exercised high levels of repression despite the presence of the FARC. In other words, their use of violence as a mechanism of labor repression was not effective in suppressing banana worker militancy, nor of ridding the region of the guerrillas.

Though useful for distinguishing "counter-hegemony" from "crises of control," I was cautious to use this data by itself as the only indicator distinguishing situations of "hegemony" from "despotism." As James Scott (1985) so eloquently points out in his critique of theories of hegemony and false consciousness, low levels of labor repression can be an indicator of the acquiescence of subaltern groups and class to the authority of capitalist elites or it can instead indicate the effective domination of these groups and classes through prior acts of violence or through the threat of violence. That is, open forms of class conflict are not necessarily the "norm" of class relations under historical capitalism. Collective mobilization efforts by subaltern groups and classes may be avoided precisely because they tend to trigger open forms of labor repression. Thus, if one looks only to levels of labor repression as an indicator of "hegemony" or "despotism," one may overlook the everyday forms of resistance and everyday forms of domination that class conflicts can take on at the micro-level.[1]

For this reason, the coercion dataset was used in conjunction with secondary sources that were able to more deeply examine the exact nature of labor–capital conflict and class struggle at each given time and place. For example, the levels of labor repression in Urabá since the demobilization of the AUC paramilitaries in 2006 have been relatively low, comparable to the levels now found in the coffee region of Viejo Caldas. Understanding the prehistory of this period of diminished labor repression, in addition to a careful analysis of the secondary texts showing the resurgence of short-lived incidents repression during momentary periods of labor militancy since then, is therefore essential in helping to distinguish the perpetuation of "despotism" from, say, the "hegemony" of Viejo Caldas during the 1980s.

---

[1] See Scott (1985); Joseph and Nugent (1994).

References

Abbott, Roderick. 2009. *A Socio-Economic History of the International Banana Trade, 1870–1930*. Fiesole, Italy: European Union University.

Adams, Franklin. 1911. *The Banana and Its Relatives*, vol. 32. Washington, DC: Pan American Union.

Akiyama, Takamasa, John Baffes, Donald Larson, Panos Varangis, and John Baffes. 2001. *Commodity Market Reforms: Lessons of Two Decades*. Washington, DC: The World Bank.

Alexander, Michelle. 2010. *The New Jim Crow: Mass Incarceration in the Age of Colorblindness*. New York: The New Press.

Allen, Larry. 2001. *The Global Financial System, 1750–2000*. London: Reaktion Books.

Álvarez, María D. 2007. "Forests under Fire." *NACLA*, September 25. https://nacla.org/article/forests-under-fire

America's Watch. 1990. *The Drug War in Colombia: The Neglected Tragedy of Political Violence*. New York: Human Rights Watch.

Andreas, Peter, and Coletta Youngers. 1989. "U. S. Drug Policy and the Andean Cocaine Industry." *World Policy Journal* 6(3):529–62.

Anner, Mark. 2015. "Labor Control Regimes and Worker Resistance in Global Supply Chains." *Labor History* 56(3):292–307.

Anzuoni, Mario. 2019. "Occidental Enters Four Oil Blocks in Southern Colombia: ANH." *Reuters*, June 11. www.reuters.com/article/us-colombia-oil/occidental-enters-four-oil-blocks-in-southern-colombia-anh-idUSKCN1TC2JI

Araghi, Farshad. 1995. "Global Depeasantization, 1945–1990." *The Sociological Quarterly* 36(2):337–68.

———. 2000. "The Great Global Enclosure of Our Times: Peasants and the Agrarian Question at the End of the Twentieth Century." Pp. 145–60 in *Hungry for Profit: The Agribusiness Threat to Farmers, Food, and the Environment*, edited by Fred Magdoff, John Bellamy Foster, and Frederick H. Buttel. New York: Monthly Review Press.

Archila Neira, Mauricio. 1995. *Donde esta la Clase Obrera?: Huelgas en Colombia, 1946–1990*. Bogotá, Colombia: CINEP (Centro de Investigación y Educación Popular).

Archila Neira, Mauricio, Alvaro Delgado Guzmán, Martha Cecilia García Velandia, and Esmeralda Prada Mantilla. 2002. *25 Años de Luchas Sociales en Colombia: 1975–2000*. Bogotá, Colombia: CINEP.

Archila Neira, Mauricio, and Mauricio Pardo, eds. 2001. *Movimientos Sociales, Estado y Democracia en Colombia*. Bogotá, Colombia: Universidad Nacional de Colombia, Centro de Estudios Sociales, Instituto Colombiano de Antropología e Historia.

Ariza, Eduardo, María Clemencia Ramírez, and Leonardo Vega. 1998. *Atlas Cultural de la Amazonia Colombiana: La Construcción del Territorio en el Siglo XX*. Bogotá, Colombia: Ministerio de Cultura-Instituto Colombiano de Antropología, Corpes Orinoquia, Corpes Amazonia.

Arlacchi, Pino. 1986. *Mafia Business: The Mafia Ethic and the Spirit of Capitalism*. London and New York: Verso.

Arley Bolaños, Edinson. 2017. "Tranquilandia y las Tierras de la Familia Lara." *El Espectador*, December 14. www.elespectador.com/colombia-20/conflicto/i-tranquilandia-y-las-tierras-de-la-familia-lara-article/

Arrighi, Giovanni. 1970. "Labour Supplies in Historical Perspective: A Study of the Proletarianization of the African Peasantry in Rhodesia." *The Journal of Development Studies* 6(3):197–234.

———. 1994. *The Long Twentieth Century: Money, Power, and the Origins of Our Times*. London and New York: Verso.

———. 2002. "The African Crisis: World Systemic and Regional Aspects." *New Left Review* 15(May/June):5–36.

———. 2005a. "Hegemony Unravelling – 1." *New Left Review* 32:23–80.

———. 2005b. "Hegemony Unravelling – 2." *New Left Review* 33:83–116.

———. 2009. *Adam Smith in Beijing: Lineages of the 21st Century*. London and New York: Verso.

Arrighi, Giovanni, Nicole Aschoff, and Ben Scully. 2010. "Accumulation by Dispossession and Its Limits: The Southern Africa Paradigm Revisited." *Studies in Comparative International Development* 45(4):410–38.

Arrighi, Giovanni, and Jessica Drangel. 1986. "The Stratification of the World-Economy: An Exploration of the Semiperipheral Zone." *Review (Fernand Braudel Center)* 10(1):9–74.

Arrighi, Giovanni, and Fortunata Piselli. 1987. "Capitalist Development in Hostile Environments: Feuds, Class Struggles, and Migrations in a Peripheral Region of Southern Italy." *Review (Fernand Braudel Center)* 10(4):649–751.

Arrighi, Giovanni, and Beverly J. Silver. 1999. *Chaos and Governance in the Modern World System*. Minneapolis: University of Minnesota Press.

Arrighi, Giovanni, Beverly J. Silver, and Benjamin D. Brewer. 2003. "Industrial Convergence, Globalization, and the Persistence of the North-South Divide." *Studies in Comparative International Development* 38(1):3.

Arthur, Henry B., James P. Houck, and George L. Beckford. 1986. *Tropical Agribusiness Structures and Adjustments-Bananas*. Boston: Division of Research, Graduate School of Business Administration, Harvard University.

Averill, Graham. 2019. "The Colombian Comeback." *Outside Online*, July 16. www.outsideonline.com/2399499/colombia-travel-safety-2019

Avilés, William. 2006. "Paramilitarism and Colombia's Low-Intensity Democracy." *Journal of Latin American Studies* 38(2):379–408.

———. 2012. *Global Capitalism, Democracy, and Civil-Military Relations in Colombia.* Albany: State University of New York Press.

Bacon, Christopher M., V. Ernesto Mendez, Stephen R. Gliessman, Jonathan A. Fox, and David Goodman, eds. 2008. *Confronting the Coffee Crisis: Fair Trade, Sustainable Livelihoods and Ecosystems in Mexico and Central America.* Cambridge, MA: MIT Press.

Baer, Werner. 1972. "Import Substitution and Industrialization in Latin America: Experiences and Interpretations." *Latin American Research Review* 7(1):95–122.

Bagley, Bruce Michael. 2005. "Drug Trafficking, Political Violence, and U.S. Policy in Colombia under the Clinton Administration." Pp. 21–52 in *Elusive Peace: International, National, and Local Dimensions of Conflict in Colombia,* edited by Cristina Rojas and Judy Meltzer. New York: Palgrave Macmillan.

Bagley, Bruce Michael, and William Walker. 1994. *Drug Trafficking in the Americas.* Miami, FL: University of Miami.

Baglioni, Elena. 2018. "Labour Control and the Labour Question in Global Production Networks: Exploitation and Disciplining in Senegalese Export Horticulture." *Journal of Economic Geography* 18(1):111–37.

Bair, Jennifer. 2009. *Frontiers of Commodity Chain Research.* Stanford, CA: Stanford University Press.

Bair, Jennifer, Kevan Harris, and Phillip A. Hough. 2019. "Roads from Calabria: The Arrighian Approach to Agrarian Political Economy." *Journal of Agrarian Change* 19(3):391–406.

Bair, Jennifer, and Phillip A. Hough. 2012. "The Legacies of Partial Possession: From Agrarian Struggle to Neoliberal Restructuring in Mexico and Colombia." *International Journal of Comparative Sociology* 53(5–6):345–66.

Bair, Jennifer, and Marion Werner. 2011. "Commodity Chains and the Uneven Geographies of Global Capitalism: A Disarticulations Perspective." *Environment and Planning A: Economy and Space* 43(5):988–97.

Bales, Kevin, Zoe Trodd, and Alex Kent Williamson. 2009. *Modern Slavery: The Secret World of 27 Million People,* 1 ed. New York: Oneworld Publications.

Ballvé, Teo. 2012. "Everyday State Formation: Territory, Decentralization, and the Narco Landgrab in Colombia." *Environment and Planning D: Society and Space* 30(4): 603–22.

———. 2019. "Narco-Frontiers: A Spatial Framework for Drug-Fuelled Accumulation." *Journal of Agrarian Change* 19(2):211–24.

Banco de la República. n.d. "Estadísticas BANREP." *Estadísticas BANREP.* www.banrep .gov.co/es/-estadisticas (December 28, 2020).

Barker, Howard, William Camp, and Clare Hasler. 2009. *Report of the Special Litigation Committee: Chiquita Brands, Inc. – Executive Summary.* Vol. 792. District Court, Southern District of Florida.

Barrientos, Stephanie, Gary Gereffi, and Arianna Rossi. 2011. "Economic and Social Upgrading in Global Production Networks: A New Paradigm for a Changing World." *International Labour Review* 150(3–4):319–40.

Bates, Robert H. 1997. *Open-Economy Politics: The Political Economy of the World Coffee Trade*. Princeton, NJ: Princeton University Press.

BBC News. 2006. "Bush Urges Americans to Back War." *BBC News*, September 12. http://news.bbc.co.uk/2/hi/americas/5337080.stm

———. 2008. "Colombians in Huge Farc Protest." *BBC News*, February 4. http://news.bbc.co.uk/2/hi/americas/7225824.stm

Bejarano, Ana María. 2001. "Conflicto y Paz En Colombia: Cuatro Tesis Con Implicaciones Para La Negociación En Curso." Presented at the Berkeley Center for Latin American Studies, Colombia in Context Working Papers, Berkeley, CA.

Beltrán, Harvey. 1996. *Urabá: La Verdad de Cada Cual*. Bogotá, Colombia: Castillo Editorial.

Benanav, Aaron. 2019a. "Automation and the Future of Work – I." *New Left Review* 119 (Sept./Oct.):5–38.

———. 2019b. "Automation and the Future of Work – 2." *New Left Review* 120(Nov./Dec.):117–46.

Bergquist, Charles. 1986. *Labor in Latin America*. Stanford, CA: Stanford University Press.

———. 2001. "Waging War and Negotiating Peace: The Contemporary Crisis in Historical Perspective." Pp. 195–212 in *Violence in Colombia, 1990–2000: Waging War and Negotiating Peace*, edited by Charles Bergquist, Ricardo Peñaranda, and Gonzalo Sánchez. Wilmington, DE: Scholarly Resources, Inc.

Bergquist, Charles, Ricardo Peñaranda, and Gonzalo Sánchez, eds. 1992. *Violence in Colombia: The Contemporary Crisis in Historical Perspective*. Wilmington, DE: Scholarly Resources, Inc.

———, eds. 2001. *Violence in Colombia, 1990–2000: Waging War and Negotiating Peace*. Wilmington, DE: Scholarly Resources, Inc.

Beyer, Robert Carlyle. 1949. "The Marketing History of Colombian Coffee." *Agricultural History* 8:279–85.

Boletín de los inmarcesibles. 2007. *Boletín de Los Inmarcesibles*. Latin American Studies Association, Sección Colombia.

Bonacich, Edna, and Richard Appelbaum. 2000. *Behind the Label: Inequality in the Los Angeles Apparel Industry*. Berkeley: University of California Press.

Botero Herrera, Fernando. 1990. *Urabá: Colonización, Violencia y Crisis Del Estado*. Medellín, Colombia: Universidad de Antioquia.

Botero Herrera, Fernando, and Diego Sierra Botero. 1981. *El Mercado de Fuerza de Trabajo en la Zona Bananera de Urabá*. Medellín, Colombia: Universidad de Antioquia, Facultad de Ciencias Económicas, Centro de Investigaciones Económicas.

Bourgois, Philippe 1989. *Ethnicity at Work: Divided Labor on a Central American Banana Plantation*. Baltimore: Johns Hopkins University Press.

———. 1995. *In Search of Respect: Selling Crack in El Barrio*. Cambridge and New York: Cambridge University Press.

———. 2003. "One Hundred Years of United Fruit Company Letters." Pp. 103–44 in *Banana Wars: Power, Production, and History in the Americas*, edited by Steve Striffler and Mark Moberg. Durham, NC: Duke University Press.

Bowden, Mark. 2001. *Killing Pablo: The Hunt for the World's Greatest Outlaw*. New York: Atlantic Monthly.

Brittain, James J. 2005. "The FARC-EP in Colombia: A Revolutionary Exception in an Age of Imperialist Expansion." *Monthly Review* 57(4):20.

———. 2010. *Revolutionary Social Change in Colombia: The Origin and Direction of the FARC-EP*. London and New York: Pluto Press.

Brown, Nick. 2019. "Colombian Coffee Leaders Explore Alternatives to C Market as Prices Sag." *Daily Coffee News by Roast Magazine*, February 28. https://dailycoffeenews.com/2019/02/28/colombian-coffee-leaders-explore-alternatives-to-c-market-as-prices-sag/

Brücher, Wolfgang. 1974. *La Colonización de La Selva Pluvial En El Piedemonte Amazónico de Colombia: El Territorio Comprendido Entre El Río Ariari y El Ecuador*. Bogotá, Colombia: Agustín Codazzi.

Bucheli, Marcelo. 2003. "United Fruit Company in Latin America." Pp. 80–100 in *Banana Wars: Power, Production, and History in the Americas*, edited by Steve Striffler and Mark Moberg. Durham, NC: Duke University Press.

———. 2005. *Bananas and Business: The United Fruit Company in Columbia, 1899–2000*. New York: New York University Press.

———. 2008. "Multinational Corporations, Totalitarian Regimes and Economic Nationalism: United Fruit Company in Central America, 1899–1975." *Business History* 50(4):433–54.

Burawoy, Michael. 1979. *Manufacturing Consent: Changes in the Labor Process under Monopoly Capitalism*. Chicago: University of Chicago Press.

———. 1983. "Between the Labor Process and the State: The Changing Face of Factory Regimes under Advanced Capitalism." *American Sociological Review* 48(5):587–605.

———. 1985. *The Politics of Production: Factory Regimes under Capitalism and Socialism*. London and New York: Verso.

———. 2003. "For a Sociological Marxism: The Complementary Convergence of Antonio Gramsci and Karl Polanyi." *Politics & Society* 31(2):193–261.

———. 2013. "Ethnographic Fallacies: Reflections on Labour Studies in the Era of Market Fundamentalism." *Work, Employment and Society* 27(3):526–36.

———. 2015. "Facing an Unequal World." *Current Sociology* 63(1):5–34.

Burawoy, Michael, Joseph Blum, Sheba George, Zsuzsa Gille, Teresa Gowan, Lynne Haney, Maren Klawiter, Steven Lopez, Sean O. Riain, and Millie Thayer, eds. 2000. *Global Ethngraphy: Forces, Connections, and Imaginations in a Postmodern World*. Berkeley: University of California Press.

Bushnell, David. 1992. "Politics and Violence in Nineteenth-Century Colombia." Pp. 11–30 in *Violence in Colombia: The Contemporary Crisis in Historical Perspective*, edited by Charles Bergquist, Ricardo Peñaranda, and Gonzalo Sánchez. Wilmington, DE: Scholarly Resources, Inc.

CAJSC. 1994. *Urabá: Informes Regionales de Derechos Humanos*. Bogotá, Colombia: La Comisión Colombiana de Juristas Seccional Colombiana.

Calhoun, Craig, and Georgi Derluguian, eds. 2011. *Aftermath: A New Global Economic Order?* New York: New York University Press.

Camacho Guizado, Álvaro. 2005. "Plan Colombia and the Andean Regional Initiative: The Ups and Downs of a Policy." Pp. 77–95 in *Elusive Peace: International, National, and Local Dimensions of Conflict in Colombia*, edited by C. Rojas and J. Meltzer. Durham, NC: Palgrave Macmillan.

Campling, Liam, and Elizabeth Havice. 2019. "Bringing the Environment into GVC Analysis: Antecedents and Advances." Pp. 214–27 in *Handbook on Global Value Chains*. Cheltenham and Northampton, MA: Edward Elgar Publishing.

Caracol Radio. 2007. "A 600 Mil Hectáreas Se Amplió El Programa de Renovación Cafetera." *Caracol Radio*, January 12. https://caracol.com.co/radio/2007/11/30/econo mia/1196437260_514062.html

Cardoso, Fernando Henrique, and Enzo Faletto. 1979. *Dependency and Development in Latin America*. Berkeley: University of California Press.

Carpenter, Ted Galen. 2003. *Bad Neighbor Policy: Washington's Futile War on Drugs in Latin America*. Hampshire, England: Palgrave Macmillan and Houndsmills.

Carroll, Leah Anne. 2000. "Violent Democratization: The Effect of Political Reform on Rural Social Conflict in Colombia." University of California, Berkeley, Berkeley.

———. 2011. *Violent Democratization: Social Movements, Elites, and Politics in Colombia's Rural War Zones, 1984–2008*. Notre Dame, IN: University of Notre Dame Press.

Casey, Nicholas. 2017. "After Decades of War, Colombian Farmers Face a New Test: Peace." *New York Times*, July 18. www.nytimes.com/2017/07/18/world/americas/colombia-cocaine-farc-peace-drugs.html

Casey, Nicholas, and Joe Parkin Daniels. 2017. "'Goodbye, Weapons!' FARC Disarmament in Colombia Signals New Era." *The New York Times*, June 27. www.nytimes.com/2017/06/27/world/americas/colombia-farc-rebels-disarmament.html#:~:text='%20FARC%20Disarmament%20in%20Colombia%20Signals%20New%20Era,-President%20Juan%20Manuel&text=MESETAS%2C%20Colombia%20%E2%80%94%20As%20United%20Nations,52%20years%20of%20guerrilla%20war

Castro Contrera, Sandra. 1995. "Caquetá: Entre Las Dos Economias." *Sintesis Economica Ano* 20:35–43.

Cenicafé. 1999. *Cenicafé*. Chinchiná, Caldas: Centro Nacional de Investigaciones de Café, Federación Nacional de Cafeteros de Colombia.

Chapman, Peter. 2007. *Bananas: How the United Fruit Company Shaped the World*. New York: Canongate Books.

Charles, Mathew. 2019. "Why Colombia's Dissident FARC Rebels Are Taking Up Arms Again." *World Politics Review*, September 4. www.worldpoliticsreview.com/articles/28163/why-colombia-s-dissident-farc-rebels-are-taking-up-arms-again

Chernick, Marc. 1991. *Colombia's "War on Drugs" vs The United States' "War on Drugs"*. Washington, DC: Washington Office on Latin America.

———. 1999. "Negotiating Peace amid Multiple Forms of Violence: The Protracted Search for a Settlement to the Armed Conflicts in Colombia." Pp. 159–96 in *Comparative Peace Processes in Latin America*, edited by Cynthia J. Arnson. Stanford, CA: Stanford University Press.

———. 2003. "Colombia: International Involvement in Protracted Peacemaking." Pp. 233–66 in *From Promise to Practice: Strengthening UN Capacities for the Prevention of Violent Conflict*, edited by C. L. Sriram and K. Wermester. Boulder, CO: Lynne Rienner Publishers.

———. 1988. "Negotiated Settlement to Armed Conflict: Lessons from the Colombian Peace Process." *Journal of Interamerican Studies and World Affairs* 30(4):53–88.

———. 2005. "Economic Resources and Internal Armed Conflicts: Lessons from the Colombian Case." Pp. 178–205 in *Rethinking the Economics of War: The Intersection of Need, Creed, and Greed*, edited by Cynthia J. Arnson and I. William Zartman. Washington, DC: Woodrow Wilson Center Press.

Chomsky, Aviva. 2008. *Linked Labor Histories: New England, Colombia, and the Making of a Global Working Class*. Durham, NC: Duke University Press Books.

Chomsky, Aviva, Garry Leech, and Steve Striffler. 2007. *The People Behind Colombian Coal*, 1st ed. Bogotá, Colombia: Casa Editorial Pisando Callos.

Christie, Keith H. 1978. "Antioqueño Colonization in Western Colombia: A Reappraisal." *The Hispanic American Historical Review* 58(2):260–83.

———. 1986. *Oligarcas, Campesinos y Política En Colombia: Aspectos de La Historia Socio-Política de La Frontera Antioqueña*. Bogotá, Colombia: Universidad Nacional de Colombia.

Ciccantell, Paul, and David Smith. 2009. "Rethinking Global Commodity Chains: Integrating Extraction, Transport, and Manufacturing." *International Journal of Comparative Sociology* 50(3–4):361–84.

CIJP. 1989. *Justicia y Paz, Volume 3*. Bogotá, Colombia: Comisión Intercongregacional de Justicia y Paz.

CIP. n.d. "Center for International Policy's Colombia Program." *Center for International Policy's Colombia Program*. http://ciponline.org/colombia/aidtable.htm (accessed on July 25, 2020).

Ciro, Estefanía. 2018. "Las Tierras de La Coca En El Caquetá: Más Allá de La Erradicación y La Sustitución." *AlaOrilladelRío*, July 6. http://alaorilladelrio.com/2018/07/06/las-tierras-de-la-coca-en-el-caqueta-mas-alla-de-la-erradicacion-y-la-sustitucion/

CJA. 2010. *Colombia: The Justice and Peace Law*. San Francisco, CA: Center for Justice and Accountability.

Clarence-Smith, William Gervase, and Steven Topik, eds. 2003. *The Global Coffee Economy in Africa, Asia, and Latin America, 1500–1989*. Cambridge and New York: Cambridge University Press.

Clarno, Andy. 2017. *Neoliberal Apartheid: Palestine/Israel and South Africa after 1994*. Chicago: University of Chicago Press.

Clemencia Ramírez, María. 2011. *Between the Guerrillas and the State: The Cocalero Movement, Citizenship, and Identity in the Colombian Amazon*. Durham, NC: Duke University Press.

CNMH. 2017. *La Tierra No Basta: Colonización, Baldíos, Conflicto y Organizaciones Sociales En El Caquetá*. Bogotá, Colombia: Centro Nacional de Memoria Histórica.

Cohen, Steven. 2014. "How Chiquita Bananas Undermined the Global War on Terror." *Think Progress*, August 2. https://archive.thinkprogress.org/how-chiquita-bananas-undermined-the-global-war-on-terror-8b4642268ac3/

Collins, Jane L. 2003. *Threads: Gender, Labor, and Power in the Global Apparel Industry*. Chicago: University of Chicago Press.

CONPES. 2004. *Lineamientos Para Optimizar La Política De Desarrollo Urbano*. 3305. Bogotá, Colombia: Consejo Nacional de Política Económica y Social.

Correa Montoya, Guillermo, Lina Paola Malagón Díaz, Ana María Díaz, Leidy Sanjuán, José Luciano Sanín Vásquez, and Élver Fernando Herrera. 2009. *Death Isn't Mute*. Medellín, Colombia: Escuela Nacional Sindical.

Cowie, Jefferson. 1999. *Capital Moves: RCA's Seventy-Year Quest for Cheap Labor*. Ithica, NY: Cornell University Press.

Crandall, Russell. 2002. *Driven by Drugs: U.S. Policy toward Colombia*. Boulder, CO: Lynne Rienner Publishers.

La Crónica del Quindío. 2018. "'Situación de La Caficultura Es Crítica y No Tiene Cambio a Corto Plazo': Federación de Cafeteros." *La Crónica Del Quindío*. www.cronicadelquindio.com/noticias/economia/situacin-de-la-caficultura-es-crtica-y-no-tiene-cambio-a-corto-plazo-federacin-de-cafeteros

Cubides, Fernando. 2001. "From Private to Public Violence: The Paramilitaries." Pp. 127–49 in *Violence in Colombia: Waging War and Negotiating Peace*. Wilmington, DE: Scholarly Resources, Inc.

DANE. 2004. *Statistical Yearbook*. Bogotá, Colombia: Departamento Administrativo Nacional de Estadística.

Daniels, Joe Parkin. 2018. "Colombian Artist Melts Guns into Tiles to Make 'anti-Monument' to Conflict." *The Guardian*, December 10. www.theguardian.com/world/2018/dec/10/doris-salcedo-colombian-artist-melts-guns-tiles-peace-monument

———. 2019. "'Journalist Finally Brings Attackers to Justice but Warns: 'Colombia's Sliding Backwards.'" *The Guardian*, June 16. www.theguardian.com/world/2019/jun/16/colombia-journalist-threats-violence

Davies, Peter. 1990. *Fyffes and the Banana: Musa Sapientum. A Centenary History, 1888–1988*. Atlantic Highlands, NJ: Athlone Press.

Daviron, Benoit, and Stefano Ponte. 2005. *The Coffee Paradox: Global Markets, Commodity Trade and the Elusive Promise of Development*. London and New York: Zed Books Ltd.

Davis, Mike. 2006. *Planet of Slums*. London and New York: Verso.

DeAngelis, Massimo. 2001. "Marx and Primitive Accumulation: The Continuous Character of Capital's 'Enclosures.'" *The Commoner* N2(September):1–22.

———. 2004. "Separating the Doing and the Deed: Capital and the Continuous Character of Enclosures." *Historical Materialism* 12(2):57–87.

Delgado, Álvaro. 1987. *Luchas Sociales En El Caquetá*. Bogotá, Colombia: Ediciones Ceis.

Delgado, Giancarlos. 2020. "Violencia Antisindical En La Agroindustria de La Palma de Aceite En El Magdalena Medio (1971–2018)." Medellín, Colombia: Escuela Nacional Sindical – Agencia de Informacion Laboral.

Derlugian, Georgi. 2005. *Bourdieu's Secret Admirer in the Caucasus: A World-System Biography*. Chicago: University of Chicago Press.

DeShazo, Peter, Tanya Primiani, and Phillip McLean. 2007. *Back from the Brink: Evaluating Progress in Colombia, 1999–2007*. Washington, DC: Center for Strategic and International Studies.

Diamond, Alex. 2018. "Murder in Colombia's Peace Laboratory/Homicidio En El Laboratorio de Paz Colombiano." *NACLA*, July 19. https://nacla.org/news/2018/07/24/murder-colombia%E2%80%99s-peace-laboratory-homicidio-en-el-laboratorio-de-paz-colombiano

———. 2019. "Will Megaprojects Destroy Colombia's Peace Process?" *NACLA*, August 5. https://nacla.org/news/2020/03/03/will-megaprojects-destroy-colombia%E2%80%99s-peace-process

Díaz, Ana María, and Fabio José Sánchez Torres. 2004. *Geografía de los Cultivos Ilícitos y Conflicto Armado en Colombia*. Bogotá, Colombia: Universidad de los Andes, Facultad de Economía, CEDE.

Dicken, Peter. 2015. *Global Shift, Seventh Edition: Mapping the Changing Contours of the World Economy*. New York: Guilford Publications.

Dicum, Gregory. 2006. "Fair to the Last Drop?" *Boston Globe*, October 26. http://archive.boston.com/news/globe/ideas/articles/2006/10/22/headline_fair_to_the_last_drop/

DNP. n.d. "Información Cafetera: Tabla 89 - Ventas de Fertilizantes Realizadas Por La Federación Nacional de Cafeteros, 1985–2008." *Estadísticas Sectoriales*. www.dnp.gov.co/programas/agricultura/estadisticas-del-sector-agropecuario/Paginas/informacion-cafetera.aspx (accessed on March 2, 2019).

Dudley, Steven. 2004. *Walking Ghosts: Murder and Guerrilla Politics in Colombia*. New York: Routledge.

Dunaway, Wilma, ed. 2014. *Gendered Commodity Chains: Seeing Women's Work and Households in Global Production*. Stanford, CA: Stanford University Press.

DuPée, Matthew. 2018. "Already a Scourge, Illegal Gold Mining in Colombia Is Getting Worse." *World Politics Review*, July 27.

Echandía Castilla, Camilo. 1999. *El Conflicto Armado y las Manifestaciones de Violencia en las Regiones de Colombia*. Bogotá, Colombia: Presidencia de la Rep'ublica de Colombia, Oficina del Alto Comisionado para la Paz, Oberservatorio de Violencia; Imprenta Nacional.

Echavarría, Juan José, Pilar Esguerra, Daniela McAllister, and Carlos Felipe Robayo. 2014. *Report Written by the Commission on Coffee Competitiveness in Colombia*. Bogotá, Colombia: Commission on Coffee Competitiveness in Colombia.

El Tiempo. 2004. "Fuimos Otras Víctimas de Guerra." *El Tiempo*, November 24. www.eltiempo.com/archivo/documento/MAM-1587591

———. 2019. "Cafeteros piden parte justa en negocio de US$ 200.000 millones." *El Tiempo*, July 11. www.eltiempo.com/economia/sectores/conclusiones-del-foro-mundial-del-cafe-2019-en-brasil-387390

Escobar, Arturo. 1995. *Encountering Development: The Making and Unmaking of the Third World*. Princeton, NJ: Princeton University Press.

Escobar Moreno, José David. 2019. "La disidencia de 'Iván Márquez' es "anacrónica" y 'destinada al fracaso.'" *El Espectador*, August 30. www.elespectador.com/noticias/judicial/la-disidencia-de-ivan-marquez-es-anacronica-y-destinada-al-fracaso-articulo-878726

Euraque, Dario. 2003. "The Threat of Blackness to the Mestizo Nation: Race and Ethnicity in the Honduran Banana Economy, 1920s and 1930s." Pp. 229–49 in *Banana Wars: Power, Production, and History in the Americas*, edited by Steve Striffler and Mark Moberg. Durham, NC: Duke University Press.

Evans, Michael. 2011. "WikiLeaks on Colombia – Uribe's Informants Network Employed Ex-Paramilitaries; More Trouble for Former Army Commanders." *Unredacted*, March 7. https://unredacted.com/2011/03/07/wikileaks-on-colombia-%e2%80%93-uribe%e2%80%99s-informants-network-employed-ex-paramilitaries-more-trouble-for-former-army-commanders/

Faguet, Jean-Paul, Fábio Sanchez, and Marta-Juanita Villavecses. 2015. *Land Reform, Latifundia and Social Development at Local Level in Colombia, 1961–2010*. SSRN Scholarly Paper. ID 2568641. Rochester, NY: Social Science Research Network.

———. 2016. "The Paradox of Land Reform, Inequality and Local Development in Colombia." LSE Research Online. https://core.ac.uk/reader/42486930

Fairtrade International. 2015. *Scope and Benefits of Fairtrade*. Vol. 7. Bonn, Germany: Fairtrade International.

Fajardo, Darío. 2014. *Las Guerras de la Agricultura Colombiana, 1980–2010*. Bogotá, Colombia: Instituto Latinoamericano para una Sociedad y un Derecho Alternativos (ILSA).

FAO. 1986. *The World Banana Economy, 1970–1984: Structure, Performance, and Prospects*. Rome: Food & Agriculture Organization of the United Nations.

———. 2003. *The World Banana Economy, 1985–2002*. Rome: Food & Agriculture Organization of the United Nations.

———. 2018. *Banana Statistical Compendium 2017*. Rome: Food & Agriculture Organization of the United Nations.

FAOSTAT. n.d. "Food and Agriculture Data." *FAOSTAT Food and Agriculture Data*. www.fao.org/faostat/en/#home (accessed on February 9, 2020).

Fedecafé. n.d.-a. "Federación Nacional de Cafeteros de Colombia, Coffee Statistics Database." *Federación Nacional de Cafeteros de Colombia, Coffee Statistics Database*. https://federaciondecafeteros.org/wp/coffee-statistics/?lang=en (accessed on February 20, 2019).

———. n.d.-b. "Federación Nacional de Cafeteros de Colombia, Homepage." *Federación Nacional de Cafeteros de Colombia*. https://federaciondecafeteros.org/wp/?lang=en (accessed on December 28, 2020).

Fedegán. 2002. *Normas Fundamentales*. Bogotá, Colombia: Fedegán.

———. 2003. *40 Años al Servicio de La Ganaderia Colombiana*. Bogotá, Colombia: Fedegán.

Federici, Silvia. 2004. *Caliban and the Witch: Women, the Body and Primitive Accumulation*. New York: Autonomedia.

Fellner, Kim. 2008. *Wrestling with Starbucks: Conscience, Capital, Cappuccino*. New Brunswick, NJ: Rutgers University Press.

Ferguson, James. 2015. *Give a Man a Fish: Reflections on the New Politics of Distribution.* Durham, NC: Duke University Press.

Ferreira, Francisco, Julian Messina, Jamele Rigolina, Luis-Felipe López-Calva, Maria Ana Lugo, and Renos Vakis. 2013. *Economic Mobility and the Rise of the Latin American Middle Class.* 73823. Washington, DC: World Bank.

Ferrer, Yadira. 2002. "Colombia: Uribe Launches Controversial Network of Informers." *Inter Press Service,* August 9. www.ipsnews.net/2002/08/colombia-uribe-launches-con troversial-network-of-informers/

FIP. 2018. *¿En Qué Va La Sustitución de Cultivos Ilícitos? Balance Del 2017 y Lo Que Viene En 2018.* 03. Bogotá, Colombia: Fundación Ideas para la Paz.

———. 2020. *Informe de Gestión 2019.* Bogotá, Colombia: Fundación Ideas para la Paz.

Fiscalía General. 2019. *Fiscalía Logra Histórico Esclarecimiento de Homicidios.* Bogotá, Colombia: Fiscalía General de la Nación.

FLIP. n.d. "Fundación Para La Libertad de Prensa, Cartografías de La Información." *Cartografías de La Información.* https://flip.org.co/cartografias-informacion/ (accessed on June 24, 2019).

Forero, Juan. 2005. "New Colombia Law Grants Concessions to Paramilitaries." *The New York Times,* June 23. www.nytimes.com/2005/06/23/world/americas/new-colombia-law-grants-concessions-to-paramilitaries.html

Forero, Juan, and Karin Brulliard. 2008. "Anti-FARC Rallies Held Worldwide." *The Washington Post Company,* February 5. www.washingtonpost.com/wp-dyn/content/article/2008/02/04/AR2008020403019.html

Fornos, Carolina, Timothy Power, and James Garand. 2004. "Explaining Voter Turnout in Latin America, 1980 to 2000." *Comparative Political Studies* 37(8):909–40.

Forster, Cindy. 2003. "'The Macondo of Guatemala': Banana Workers and National Revolution in Tiquisate, 1944–1954." Pp. 191–228 in *Banana Wars: Power, Production, and History in the Americas,* edited by Steve Striffler and Mark Moberg. Durham, NC: Duke University Press.

Frank, Andre Gunder. 1966. *The Development of Underdevelopment.* Boston, MA: New England Free Press.

———. 1967. *Capitalism and Underdevelopment in Latin America.* New York: New York University Press.

Frank, Dana. 2005. *Bananeras: Women Transforming the Banana Unions of Latin America.* Cambridge, MA: South End Press.

Fridell, Gavin. 2014. *Coffee.* Malden, MA: Polity Press.

Frundt, Henry J. 2009. *Fair Bananas: Farmers, Workers, and Consumers Strive to Change an Industry.* Tucson: University of Arizona Press.

Furtado, Celso. 1964. *Desenvolvimento e Subdesenvolvimento.* Berkeley: University of California Press.

———. 1970. *Economic Development of Latin America: A Survey from Colonial Times to the Cuban Revolution.* Cambridge and New York: Cambridge University Press.

Galeano, Eduardo. 1973. *Open Veins of Latin America: Five Centuries of the Pillage of a Continent.* New York: Monthly Review Press.

Gallant, Thomas. 1999. "Brigandage, Piracy, Capitalism and State-Formation: Transnational Crime in an Historical World-Systems Perspective." Pp. 23–61 in *States and Illegal Networks*, edited by J. Heyman and A. Smart. London: Berg Press.

Gambetta, Diego. 1993. *The Sicilian Mafia: The Business of Private Protection*. Cambridge, MA and London: Harvard University Press.

García, Clara Inés. 1996. *Urabá: Región, Actores y Conflicto, 1960–1990*. Medellín, Colombia: Inter-Universidad de Antioquia.

García Márquez, Gabriel. 1982. "The Solitude of Latin America, Nobel Lecture, 8 December 1982." Stockholm, Sweden: The Nobel Foundation.

Gereffi, Gary. 2005. "The Global Economy: Organization, Governance, and Development." Pp. 160–82 in *The Handbook of Economic Sociology*, 2nd ed., edited by N. Smelser and R. Swedberg. Princeton, NJ: Princeton University Press.

———. 2018. *Global Value Chains and Development: Redefining the Contours of 21st Century Capitalism*. Cambridge and New York: Cambridge University Press.

———. 2019. "Economic Upgrading in Global Value Chains." Pp. 240–54 in *Handbook on Global Value Chains*, edited by S. Ponte, G. Gereffi, and G. Raj-Reichert. Cheltenham and Northampton, MA: Edward Elgar Publishing.

Gereffi, Gary, and Miguel Korzeniewicz. 1994. *Commodity Chains and Global Capitalism*. Westport, CT: Praeger.

Gilhodes, Pierre. 1972. *Las Luchas Agrarias En Colombia*. Bogotá, Colombia: Editorial Tigre de Papel.

Gill, Lesley. 2004. *The School of the Americas: Military Training and Political Violence in the Americas*. Durham, NC: Duke University Press.

———. 2016. *A Century of Violence in a Red City: Popular Struggle, Counterinsurgency, and Human Rights in Colombia*. Durham, NC: Duke University Press.

Giovannucci, Daniele, and Freek Jan Koekoek. 2003. *The State of Sustainable Coffee: A Study of Twelve Major Markets*. SSRN Scholarly Paper. ID 996763. Rochester, NY: Social Science Research Network.

Giovannucci, Daniele, José Leibovich, Diego Pizano, Gonzalo Paredes, Santiago Montenegro, Hector Arévalo, and Panos Varangis. 2002. *Colombia Coffee Sector Study*. SSRN Scholarly Paper. SSRN 996138. Washington, DC: World Bank.

Golash-Boza, Tanya Maria. 2015. *Deported*. New York: New York University Press.

González, Ángel. 2014. "Single-Serve Coffee Revolution Brews Industry Change." *The Seattle Times*, February 15. www.seattletimes.com/business/single-serve-coffee-revolu tion-brews-industry-change/

González, Fernán E., Ingrid J. Bolívar, and Teófilo Vázquez. 2003. *Violencia Política en Colombia: De la Nación Fragmentada a la Construcción del Estado*. Bogotá, Colombia: Centro de Investigación y Educación Popular.

González Trujillo, Héctor Eduvin, José Francisco Ramón Mahe, and Rafael Torrijos Rivera. 2003. *Caquetá: Tradición y Vocación Ganadera*. Florencia, Caquetá: Comité Department de Ganaderos del Caquetá.

Goodman, David. 2008. "The International Coffee Crisis: A Review of the Issues." Pp. 3–25 in *Confronting the Coffee Crisis: Fair Trade, Sustainable Livelihoods and*

Ecosystems in Mexico and Central America, edited by C. Bacon, E. Méndez, S. Gliessman, D. Goodman, and J. Fox. Cambridge, MA: The MIT Press.

Goodwin, Jeff. 2001. *No Other Way Out: States and Revolutionary Movements, 1945–1991.* Cambridge and New York: Cambridge University Press.

Gowan, Teresa. 2010. *Hobos, Hustlers, and Backsliders: Homeless in San Francisco.* Minneapolis: University of Minnesota Press.

Graser, Maximilian, Michelle Bonatti, Luca Eufemia, Héctor Morales, Marcos Lana, Katharina Löhr, and Stefan Sieber. 2020. "Peacebuilding in Rural Colombia – A Collective Perception of the Integrated Rural Reform (IRR) in the Department of Caquetá (Amazon)." *Land* 9(36):1–17.

Green, W. John. 2003. *Gaitanismo, Left Liberalism, and Popular Mobilization in Colombia.* Gainesville: University Press of Florida.

Gresser, Charis, and Sophia Tickell. 2002. *Mugged: Poverty in Your Coffee Cup.* Oxford: Oxfam International.

Grossman, Lawrence S. 1998. *The Political Ecology of Bananas: Contract Farming, Peasants, and Agrarian Change in the Eastern Caribbean.* Chapel Hill: University of North Carolina Press.

Guhl, Andrés. 2008. *Café y Cambio de Paisaje en Colombia, 1970–2005.* Medellín, Colombia: Fondo Editorial Universidad Eafit.

Gusfield, Joseph R. 1996. *Contested Meanings: The Construction of Alcohol Problems.* Madison: University of Wisconsin Press.

Gutiérrez Sanín, Francisco. 2008. "Telling the Difference: Guerrillas and Paramilitaries in the Colombian War." *Politics & Society* 36(1):3–34.

Harris, Kevan. 2017. *A Social Revolution: Politics and the Welfare State in Iran.* Berkeley: University of California Press.

Harris, Kevan, and Phillip A. Hough. 2021. "Labor Regimes, Social Reproduction, and Boundary-Drawing Strategies across the Arc of U.S. World Hegemony." in *Labour Regimes and Global Production, Series on Economic Transformations*, edited by Elena Baglioni, Liam Campling, Neil M. Coe, and Adrian Smith. Newcastle upon Tyne: Agenda Publishing.

Hart, Gillian Patricia. 2002. *Disabling Globalization: Places of Power in Post-Apartheid South Africa.* Berkeley: University of California Press.

Harvey, David. 1989. *The Condition of Postmodernity: An Enquiry into the Origins of Cultural Change.* New York: Basil Blackwell.

———. 2003. *The New Imperialism.* Oxford and New York: Oxford University Press.

Hatton, Erin. 2011. *The Temp Economy: From Kelly Girls to Permatemps in Postwar America.* Philadelphia: Temple University Press.

Haye, Bethany. 2018. "Colombia Committed to Sustainability." *STiR Coffee and Tea*, June 4. https://stir-tea-coffee.com/api/content/45a406f8-6847-11c8-a9b2-12408cbff2b0/

Hershberg, Eric, and Fred Rosen, eds. 2006. *Latin America after Neoliberalism: Turning the Tide in the 21st Century?* New York: New Press.

Hirschman, Albert. 1963. *Journeys towards Progress: Studies of Economy Policy-Making in Latin America.* New York: Twentieth Century Fund.

Hobsbawm, Eric. 1975. *The Age of Capital: 1848–1875. First.* London: Weidenfeld & Nicolson Ltd.

Holmes, Amy Austin. 2014. *Social Unrest and American Military Bases in Turkey and Germany since 1945.* Cambridge and New York: Cambridge University Press.

Hopkins, Terence K., and Immanuel Wallerstein. 1977. "Patterns of Development of the Modern World-System." *Review (Fernand Braudel Center)* 1(2):111–45.

———. 1986. "Commodity Chains in the World-Economy Prior to 1800." *Review (Fernand Braudel Center)* 10(1):157–70.

Hough, Phillip A. 2007. "Trajectories of Hegemony and Domination in Colombia: A Comparative Analysis of the Coffee, Banana and Coca Regions from the Rise of Developmentalism to the Era of Neoliberalism." The Johns Hopkins University, Baltimore.

———. 2011. "Guerrilla Insurgency as Organized Crime: Explaining the So-Called 'Political Involution' of the Revolutionary Armed Forces of Colombia." *Politics & Society* 39(3):379–414.

———. 2015. "'It's Our Turn Now': Colombia's Agricultural Movement Is the Biggest in the Country's History." *NACLA*, February 18. https://nacla.org/news/2015/02/18/% E2%80%9Cit%E2%80%99s-our-turn-now%E2%80%9D-colombia%E2%80%99s-agricultural-movement-biggest-country%27s-history

Hristov, Jasmin. 2009. *Blood and Capital: The Paramilitarization of Colombia.* Athens: Ohio University Press.

———. 2014. *Paramilitarism and Neoliberalism: Violent Systems of Capital Accumulation in Colombia and Beyond.* London and New York: Pluto Press.

Human Rights Watch. 2010. *World Report 2010.* New York: Human Rights Watch.

———. 2019. *World Report 2019.* New York: Human Rights Watch.

———. 2020. "Colombia: Seek Ex-Paramilitary Commander's Extradition." *Human Rights Watch*, August 15. www.hrw.org/news/2020/08/15/colombia-seek-ex-paramili tary-commanders-extradition#

Humphrey, John, and Hubert Schmitz. 2002. "How Does Insertion in Global Value Chains Affect Upgrading in Industrial Clusters?" *Regional Studies* 36(9):1017–27.

Hylton, Forrest. 2006. *Evil Hour in Colombia.* London and New York: Verso.

Hylton, Forrest, and Aaron Tauss. 2016. "Peace in Colombia: A New Growth Strategy." *NACLA Report on the Americas* 48(3):253–59.

Ibáñez Londoño, Ana María, Juan Carlos Muñoz Mora, and Philip Verwimp. 2013. *Abandoning Coffee under the Threat of Violence and the Presence of Illicit Crops. Evidence from Colombia.* Bogotá, Colombia: Universidad de los Andes – CEDE.

ICO. n.d. "International Coffee Organization, Historical Data on the Global Coffee Trade." *International Coffee Organization, Historical Data on the Global Coffee Trade.* www.ico.org/new_historical.asp?section=Statistics (accessed on July 25, 2020).

IDEA. n.d. "International Institute for Democracy and Electoral Assistance, Voter Turnout Database." *Voter Turnout Database.* www.idea.int/data-tools/question-coun tries-view/521/82/ctr (accessed on December 12, 2020).

IDEAM. n.d. "Instituto de Hidrología, Meteorología y Estudios Ambientales, Sistema de Monitoreo de Bosques y Carbono." *Instituto de Hidrología, Meteorología y Estudios Ambientales, Sistema de Monitoreo de Bosques y Carbono.* http://smbyc.ideam.gov.co/MonitoreoBC-WEB/reg/indexLogOn.jsp (accessed on July 28, 2020).

IDMC. n.d. "Internal Displacement Monitoring Centre, Displacement Data." *Internal Displacement Monitoring Centre, Displacement Data.* www.internal-displacement.org/ (accessed on Retrieved June 4, 2019).

ILO. 2009. *The Cost of Coercion: Global Report on Forced Labour.* Geneva: International Labour Office, Geneva.

———. 2017. *Global Estimates of Modern Slavery: Forced Labour and Forced Marriage – Executive Summary.* Geneva: Alliance 8.7 – ILO.

———. 2018. *Women and Men in the Informal Economy: A Statistical Picture*, 3rd ed. Geneva: International Labour Office.

Insight Crime. 2019. "Miguel Botache Santillana, Alias 'Gentil Duarte.'" *Insight Crime*, October 27. https://insightcrime.org/colombia-organized-crime-news/miguel-botache-santillana-alias-gentil-duarte/

Isaacson, Adam. 2003. "Washington's 'New War' in Colombia." *NACLA Report on the Americas* 36(5):13–18.

———. 2005. "Appendix." Pp. 239–45 in *Elusive Peace: International, National, and Local Dimensions of Conflict in Colombia*, edited by C. Rojas and J. Meltzer. New York: Palgrave Macmillan.

ITUC. 2016. *2016 ITUC Global Rights Index – The World's Worst Countries for Workers.* Bogotá, Colombia: International Trade Union Confederation.

———. 2018. *2018 ITUC Global Rights Index – The World's Worst Countries for Workers.* Brussels, Belgium: International Trade Union Confederation.

Jaffee, Daniel. 2007. *Brewing Justice: Fair Trade Coffee, Sustainability, and Survival.* 1st ed. Berkeley: University of California Press.

Jaramillo, Carlos Felipe. 1998. *Liberalization, Crisis, and Change in Colombian Agriculture.* Boulder, CO: Westview Press.

Jaramillo, Jaime, Leonidas Mora, and Fernando Cubides. 1989. *Colonización, Coca y Guerrilla.* Bogotá, Colombia: Universidad Nacional de Colombia.

Jeffries, Stuart. 2016. *Grand Hotel Abyss: The Lives of the Frankfurt School.* London and New York: Verso.

Jiménez, Michael F. 1995b. "At the Banquet of Civilization: The Limits of Planter Hegemony in Early-Twentieth-Century Colombia." Pp. 262–94 in *Coffee, Society, and Power in Latin America*, edited by William Roseberry, Lowell Gudmundson, and Mario Samper Kutschbach. Baltimore: Johns Hopkins University Press.

Jonas, Andrew E. G. 1996. "Local Labour Control Regimes: Uneven Development and the Social Regulation of Production." *Regional Studies* 30(4):323–38.

Joseph, Gilbert M., and Daniel Nugent, eds. 1994. *Everyday Forms of State Formation: Revolution and the Negotiation of Rule in Modern Mexico.* Durham, NC: Duke University Press Books.

Junguito, Roberto, and Diego Pizano. 1991. *Producción de Café En Colombia*. Vol. 1. Bogotá, Colombia: Fedesarrollo-Fondo Cultural Cafetera.

———. 1993. *El Comercio Exterior y la Política Internacional del Café*. Bogotá, Colombia: Fedesarrollo-Fondo Cultural Cafetera.

———. 1997. *Instituciones e Instrumentos de La Política Cafetera En Colombia*. Bogotá, Colombia: Fedesarrollo-Fondo Cultural Cafetera.

Karataşlı, Şahan Savaş, Sefika Kumral, Ben Scully, and Smriti Upadhyay. 2015. "Class, Crisis, and the 2011 Protest Wave: Cyclical and Secular Trends in Global Labor Unrest." Pp. 194–210 in *Overcoming Global Inequalities*, edited by I. Wallerstein, C. Chase-Dunn, and C. Suter. New York: Routledge.

Karnes, Thomas L. 1978. *Tropical Enterprise: The Standard Fruit and Steamship Company in Latin America*. Baton Rouge: Louisiana State University Press.

Kepner, Charles D. 1936. *Social Aspects of the Banana Empire: A Case Study of Economic Imperialism*. New York: Columbia University Press.

Kepner, Charles D., and Jay Henry Soothill. 1967. *The Banana Empire: A Case Study of Economic Imperialism*. New York: The Vanguard Press.

King, Evan, and Samantha Wherry. 2018. "Eradicating Peace in Colombia." *NACLA*, December 6. https://nacla.org/news/2018/12/07/eradicating-peace-colombia

Kline, Harvey F. 2009. *Showing Teeth to the Dragons: State-Building by Colombian President Alvaro Uribe Velez 2002–2006*. Tuscaloosa: University of Alabama Press.

Kline, Harvey F. 2015. *Fighting Monsters in the Abyss: The Second Administration of Colombian President Álvaro Uribe Vélez, 2006–2010*. Tuscaloosa: University of Alabama Press.

Koeppel, Dan. 2008. *Banana: The Fate of the Fruit That Changed the World*. New York: Penguin Group.

Krasner, Stephen D. 1973. "Business Government Relations: The Case of the International Coffee Agreement." *International Organization* 27(4):495–516.

Krauthausen, Ciro, and Luis Fernando Sarmiento. 1991. *Cocaína & Co: Un Mercado Ilegal Por Dentro*. Bogotá, Colombia: Universidad Nacional de Colombia, Instituto de Estudios Políticos y Relaciones Internacionales.

Krippner, Greta R. 2011. *Capitalizing on Crisis: The Political Origins of the Rise of Finance*. Cambridge, MA and London: Harvard University Press.

La Rotta, Jesús Enrique. 1996. *Finanzas de la Subversión Colombiana: Una Forma de Explotar una Nación*. Bogotá, Colombia: Editorial Los Ultimos Patriotas.

Lane, Frederic Chapin. 1979. *Profits from Power: Readings in Protection Rent and Violence-Controlling Enterprises*. Albany, NY: State University of New York Press.

Langley, Lester D., and Thomas D. Schoonover. 1995. *The Banana Men: American Mercenaries and Entrepreneurs in Central America, 1880–1930*. Lexington: University Press of Kentucky.

Leal Buitrago, Francisco. 2004. "Armed Actors in the Colombian Conflict." Pp. 87–105 in *Armed Actors: Organised Violence and State Failure in Latin America*, edited by Kees Koonings and Dirk Kruijt. London and New York: Zed Books Ltd.

Lee, Ching Kwan. 2007. *Against the Law: Labor Protests in China's Rustbelt and Sunbelt*. Berkeley: University of California Press.

Leech, Garry. 2011. *The FARC: The Longest Insurgency*. London and New York: Zed Books Ltd.

LeGrand, Catherine. 1986. *Frontier Expansion and Peasant Protest in Colombia, 1850–1936*. Albuquerque: University of New Mexico Press.

———. 1994. *El Agro y La Cuestión Social*. Bogotá, Colombia: Tercer Mundo Editores.

———. 1998. "Living in Macondo: Economy and Culture in a United Fruit Company Banana Enclave in Colombia." Pp. 333–68 in *Close Encounters of Empire: Writing the Cultural History of US-Latin American Relations*, edited by Gilbert M. Joseph, Catherine C. LeGrand, and Ricardo D. Salvatore. Durham, NC: Duke University Press.

———. 2003. "The Colombian Crisis in Historical Perspective." *Canadian Journal of Latin American and Caribbean Studies/Revue Canadienne Des Études Latino-Américaines et Caraïbes* 28(55–56):165–209.

Lerche, Jens. 2007. "A Global Alliance against Forced Labour? Unfree Labour, Neo-Liberal Globalization and the International Labour Organization." *Journal of Agrarian Change* 7(4):425–52.

Levien, Michael. 2017. "From Primitive Accumulation to Regimes of Dispossession." Pp. 49–75 in *The Land Question in India: State, Dispossession, and Capitalist Transition*, edited by Anthony P. D'Costa and Achin Chakraborty. Oxford and New York: Oxford University Press.

———. 2018. *Dispossession without Development: Land Grabs in Neoliberal India*. Oxford and New York: Oxford University Press.

Lichtenstein, Nelson, ed. 2006. *Wal-Mart: The Face of Twenty-First-Century Capitalism*. New York: New Press.

Linton, Magnus. 2014. *Cocaina: A Book on Those Who Make It*. Berkeley, CA: Soft Skull Press.

Livingstone, Grace. 2004. *Inside Colombia: Drugs, Democracy and War*. New Brunswick, NJ: Rutgers University Press.

London, Christopher. 1995. "From Coffee Consciousness to the Coffee Family: Reformation and Hegemony in Colombia's Coffee Fields." Paper presented at the 1995 Meeting of the Latin American Studies Association, Washington, DC, September 28–30, 1995.

———. 1997. "Class Relations and Capitalist Development: Subsumption in the Colombian Coffee Industry, 1928–92." *The Journal of Peasant Studies* 24(4):269–95.

———. 1999. "Desarrollismo, Democracia y La Crisis Cafetera: Una Interpretación Cultural." Pp. 95–149 in *Conflictos Regionales: La Crisis del Eje Cafetero*, edited by Gonzalo Sánchez. Santafé de Bogotá: Fundación Friedrich Ebert de Colombia.

Luttinger, Nina, and Gregory Dicum. 2006. *The Coffee Book: Anatomy of an Industry from Crop to the Last Drop*. London and New York: The New Press.

Macias, Amanda. 2015. "10 Facts Reveal the Absurdity of Pablo Escobar's Wealth." *Business Insider*, September 21. www.businessinsider.in/defense/10-facts-that-reveal-the-absurdity-of-pablo-escobars-wealth/slidelist/49050689.cms

Markoff, John. 1996. *Waves of Democracy: Social Movements and Political Change*. Thousand Oaks, CA: Pine Forge Press.

Marsh, Robin Ruth. 1983. *Development Strategies in Rural Colombia: The Case of Caquetá.* Berkeley: University of California Press.

Martz, John. 1997. *The Politics of Clientelism: Democracy and the State in Colombia.* New Brunswick, NJ: Transaction Publishers.

Marx, Karl. 1976. *Capital: A Critique of Political Economy.* New York: Penguin Books Limited.

May, Stacy, and Galo Plaza Lasso. 1958. *The United Fruit Company in Latin America.* Washington, DC: National Planning Association.

McClintock, Michael. 1992. *Instruments of Statecraft: U.S. Guerrilla Warfare, Counterinsurgency, and Counter-Terrorism, 1940–1990.* New York: Pantheon Books.

McKay, Ben M. 2017. "Democratising Land Control: Towards Rights, Reform and Restitution in Post-Conflict Colombia." *Canadian Journal of Development Studies / Revue Canadienne d'études Du Développement* 39(2):163–81.

McMichael, Philip. 1990. "Incorporating Comparison within a World-Historical Perspective: An Alternative Comparative Method." *American Sociological Review* 55:385–97.

———. 2008. *Development and Social Change: A Global Perspective*, 4th ed. Thousand Oaks, CA: Pine Forge Press.

McSweeney, Kendra, Nazih Richani, Zoe Pearson, Jennifer Devine, and David J. Wrathall. 2017. "Why Do Narcos Invest in Rural Land?" *Journal of Latin American Geography* 16(2):3–29.

Medina Gallego, Carlos. 1990. *Autodefensas, Paramilitares y Narcotráfico en Colombia: Origen, Desarrollo y Consolidación: El Caso "Puerto Boyacá."* Bogotá, Colombia: Editorial Documentos Periodísticos.

Melo, Diego. 2013. "2013: The Year of Social Protest and Repression in Colombia (Pt 1)." *Colombia Reports*, November 14. https://colombiareports.com/2013-year-social-pro test-repression-colombia-pt-1/

Mendez Garzón, Fernando, and István Valánszki. 2019. "Repercussions in the Landscape of Colombian Amazonas (Caquetá and Putumayo Region) Caused by Deforestation and Illicit Crops during the Internal Armed Conflict; a Review." *Proceedings of the Fábos Conference on Landscape and Greenway Planning* 6(1):1–14.

Metelits, Claire. 2009. *Inside Insurgency: Violence, Civilians, and Revolutionary Group Behavior.* New York: New York University Press.

Milkman, Ruth. 1997. *Farewell to the Factory: Auto Workers in the Late Twentieth Century.* Berkeley: University of California Press.

Milkman, Ruth, and Ed Ott. 2014. *New Labor in New York: Precarious Workers and the Future of the Labor Movement.* Ithaca, NY: Cornell University Press.

MINAGRO. 2002. *Anuario 2002: Estadístico Del Sector Agropecuario y Pesquero.* Bogotá, Colombia: Ministerio de Agricultura y Desarollo Rural.

Moberg, Mark. 1996. "Myths That Divide: Immigrant Labor and Class Segmentation in the Belizean Banana Industry." *American Ethnologist* 23(2):311–30.

———. 2003. "Responsible Men and Sharp Yankees: The United Fruit Company, Resident Elites, and Colonial State in British Honduras." Pp. 145–70 in *Banana*

Wars: Power, Production, and History in the Americas, edited by Steve Striffler and Mark Moberg. Durham, NC: Duke University Press.

———. 2008. *Slipping Away: Banana Politics and Fair Trade in the Eastern Caribbean.* New York: Berghahn Books.

Mohan, Rakesh. 1994. *Understanding the Developing Metropolis: Lessons from the City Study of Bogota and Cali, Colombia.* New York: Oxford University Press.

Molano Bravo, Alfredo. 1994. "Algunas Consideraciones sobre Colonización y Violencia." in *El agro y la cuestión social.* Bogotá, Colombia: Banco Ganadero.

———. 2004. "Coca, Land and Corruption." Pp. 63–76 in *Colombia from the Inside: Perspectives on Drugs, War and Peace*, edited by M. Baud and D. Meertens. Amsterdam: Centre for Latin American Research and Documentation.

Morales-de la Cruz, Fernando. 2017. "The Unacceptable Human Cost of Coffee." *Huffington Post*, July 27. www.huffpost.com/entry/the-unacceptable-human-cost-of-coffee_b_597a40c1e4b09982b7376304#:~:text=The%20business%20model%20of%20the,cost%20in%20coffee%20producing%20nations

Murphy, Helen, and Carlos Vargas. 2019. "Colombian Duque's Bid to Change Peace Deal Rattles Sabers, but War. . ." *Reuters*, March 17. www.reuters.com/article/us-colombia-peace-analysis/colombian-duques-bid-to-change-peace-deal-rattles-sabers-but-war-unlikely-idUSKCN1QY0MO

Myers, Gordon. 2004. *Banana Wars – The Price of Free Trade: A Caribbean Perspective.* London and New York: Zed Books Ltd.

Ness, Immanuel. 2015. *Southern Insurgency: The Coming of the Global Working Class.* London and New York: Pluto Press.

Nestlé. 2005a. *Nestlé En Caguán.* Bogotá, Colombia: Nestlé.

———. 2005b. *Nestlé En Caquetá.* Bogotá, Colombia: Nestlé.

Nielson, Kirk. 2012. "Chiquita in the Dock." *The Progressive*, January 25. https://progressive.org/latest/chiquita-dock/

Niño, Oscar Arcila, Gloria González León, Franz Gutiérrez Rey, Adriana Rodríguez Salazar, and Carlos Ariel Salazar. 2000. *Caquetá: Construcción de un Territorio Amazónico en el Siglo XX.* Bogotá, Colombia: Instituto Amazónico de Investigaciones Científicas (SINCHI).

Nylander, Dag, Rita Sandberg, and Idun Tvedt. 2018. *Designing Peace: The Colombian Peace Process.* NOREF Norwegian Centre for Conflict Resolution.

Olaya, Ana Cecilia. 1998. "Caguán." Pp. 96–98 in *La Violencia y el Municipio Colombiano, 1980–1997*, edited by F. Cubides. Bogotá, Colombia: Universidad Nacional de Colombia, Centro de Estudios Sociales.

OPPDHDIH. 2001. *Panorama Actual Del Suroriente Colombiana.* Bogotá, Colombia: Observatorio del Programa Presidencial de Derechos Humanos y Derecho Internacional Humanitario.

Oquendo, Catalina. 2004a. "Bloque Bananero: Adios a Las Armas." *El Tiempo*, November 26. www.eltiempo.com/archivo/documento/MAM-1504566

———. 2004b. "Le Llego La Hora al 'Bloque Bananero.'" *El Tiempo*, November 22. www.eltiempo.com/archivo/documento/MAM-1582026

———. 2004c. "Rompen Filas En Urabá." *El Tiempo*, November 25. www.eltiempo.com/archivo/documento/MAM-1501955

Oquist, Paul H. 1978. *Violencia, Conflicto y Política en Colombia*. Bogotá, Colombia: Banco Popular.

Ortiz Sarmiento, Carlos Miguel. 1992. "The 'Business of the Violence': The Quindío in the 1950s and 1960s." Pp. 125–54 in *Violence in Colombia: The Contemporary Crisis in Historical Perspective*, edited by C. Bergquist, R. Peñaranda, and G. Sánchez. Wilmington, DE: Scholarly Resources, Inc.

———. 1999. *Urabá: Tras las Huellas de los Inmigrantes, 1955–1990*. Santafé de Bogotá: Icfes.

———. 2007. *Urabá: Pulsiones de Vida y Desafíos de Muerte*. Medellín, Colombia: La Carreta Editores.

Ortiz, Sutti. 1999. *Harvesting Coffee, Bargaining Wages: Rural Labor Markets in Colombia, 1975–1990*. Ann Arbor: University of Michigan Press.

Ostertag, Carlos F., Oscar A. Sandoval, Juan F. Barona, and Carolina Mancilla. 2014. *An Evaluation of Fairtrade Impact on Smallholders and Workers in the Banana Sector in Northern Colombia*. Ulrecht, Netherlands: Corporation for Rural Business Development.

Oxfam. 2017. *A Snapshot of Inequality: What the Latest Agricultural Census Reveals about Land Distribution in Colombia*. Oxford: Oxfam International.

Palacios, Marco. 1980. *Coffee in Colombia, 1850–1970*. Cambridge and New York: Cambridge University Press.

———. 2006. *Between Legitimacy and Violence: A History of Colombia, 1875–2002*. Durham, NC: Duke University Press.

Parsons, James J. 1967. *Antioquia's Corridor to the Sea: An Historical Geography of the Settlement of Urabá*. Berkeley: University of California Press.

Pattenden, Jonathan. 2016. "Working at the Margins of Global Production Networks: Local Labour Control Regimes and Rural-Based Labourers in South India." *Third World Quarterly* 37(10):1809–33.

Pécaut, Daniel. 1999. "From the Banality of Violence to Real Terror: The Case of Colombia." Pp. 141–67 in *Societies of Fear: The Legacy of Civil War, Violence and Terror in Latin America*, edited by Kees Koonings and Dirk Kruijt. London and New York: Zed Books Ltd.

———. 2001. *Guerra Contra la Sociedad*. Bogotá, Colombia: Espasa Hoy.

Peña-Huertas, Rocío del Pilar, Luis Enrique Ruiz, María Mónica Parada, Santiago Zuleta, and Ricardo Álvarez. 2017. "Legal Dispossession and Civil War in Colombia." *Journal of Agrarian Change* 17(4):759–69.

Perelman, Michael. 2000. *The Invention of Capitalism: Classical Political Economy and the Secret History of Primitive Accumulation*. Durham, NC: Duke University Press.

Pérez-Liñán, Aníbal. 2001. "Neoinstitutional Accounts of Voter Turnout: Moving beyond Industrial Democracies." *Electoral Studies* 20:281–97.

Perl, Raphael. 1992. "United States Andean Drug Policy: Background and Issues for Decisionmakers." *Journal of Interamerican Studies and World Affairs* 34(3):13–35.

Petrovic, Misha, and Gary G. Hamilton. 2006. "Making Global Markets: Wal-Mart and Its Suppliers." Pp. 107–41 in *Wal-Mart: The Face of Twenty-First-Century Capitalism*, edited by Nelson Lichtenstein. New York: New Press.

Ploetz, Randy C. 2005. "Panama Disease: An Old Nemesis Rears Its Ugly Head." *Plant Health Progress* 6(1):18.

Polanyi, Karl. 2001. *The Great Transformation: The Political and Economic Origins of Our Time*. Boston: Beacon Press.

Ponte, Stefano, Gary Gereffi, and Gale Raj-Reichert. 2019. *Handbook on Global Value Chains*. Cheltenham and Northampton, MA: Edward Elgar Publishing.

della Porta, Donatella. 2015. *Social Movements in Times of Austerity: Bringing Capitalism Back into Protest Analysis*. Malden, MA: Polity Press.

Powell, Colin. 2002. *Secretary of State Colin Powell before the Foreign Operations Subcommittee*. Washington, DC www.govinfo.gov/content/pkg/CHRG-106hhrg65738/html/CHRG-106hhrg65738.htm

Prashad, Vijay, and Teo Ballvé, eds. 2006. *Dispatches from Latin America: On the Frontlines Against Neoliberalism*. Cambridge, MA: South End Press.

Puerta, Felipe, and Maria Paula Chaparro. 2019. "A Death Foretold: Colombia's Crop Substitution Program." *InSight Crime*, April 1. https://insightcrime.org/news/analysis/a-death-foretold-colombias-crop-substitution-program/

Ramírez, Luis Fernando, Gabriel Silva, Luis Carlos Valenzuela, Alvaro Villegas, and Luis Carlos Villegas. 2002. *El Café, Capital Social Estratégico*. Bogotá, Colombia: Comision de Ajuste de la Institucionalidad Cafetera.

Ramírez Tobón, William. 1997. *Urabá: Los Inciertos Confines de Una Crisis*. Bogotá, Colombia: Planeta.

Rangel Suárez, Alfredo. 2000. "Parasites and Predators: Guerrillas and the Insurrection Economy of Colombia." *Journal of International Affairs* 53(2):577.

Raynolds, Laura. 2003. "The Global Banana Trade." Pp. 23–47 in *Banana Wars: Power, Production, and History in the Americas*, edited by Steve Striffler and Mark Moberg. Durham, NC: Duke University Press.

Reinarman, Craig, and Harry Levine, eds. 1997. *Crack in America: Demon Drugs and Social Justice*. Berkeley: University of California Press.

Reno, William. 1999. *Warlord Politics and African States*. Boulder, CO: Lynne Rienner Publishers.

Restrepo, Luis Alberto. 2004. "Violence and Fear in Colombia: Fragmentation of Space, Contraction of Time and Forms of Evasion." Pp. 172–85 in *Armed Actors: Organised Violence and State Failure in Latin America*, edited by Kees Koonings and Dirk Kruijt. London and New York: Zed Books Ltd.

Rettberg, Angelika. 2010. "Global Markets, Local Conflict: Violence in the Colombian Coffee Region after the Breakdown of the International Coffee Agreement." *Latin American Perspectives* 37(2):111–32.

Rey de Marulanda, Nora, and Juan Pablo Córdoba Garcés. 1990. "El Sector Bananero de Urabá: Perspectivas Económicas Actuales y de Mediano Plazo." *CO-BAC, Santafé de Bogotá* No. Doc. 11289.

Reyes Posada, Alejandro. 2009. *Guerreros y Campesinos: Despojo de La Tierra En Colombia*. Bogotá, Colombia: Grupo Editorial Norma.

Richani, Nazih. 2002. *Systems of Violence: The Political Economy of War and Peace in Colombia*. Albany: State University of New York Press.

———. 2020. "Fragmented Hegemony and the Dismantling of the War System in Colombia." *Studies in Conflict & Terrorism* 43(4):325–50.

Rivera Zapata, Guillermo. 2004. "El Modelo de Concertación En Urabá Visto Por SINTRAINAGRO." *Revista Augura* 1:27–30.

RNEC. n.d. "Registraduría Nacional Del Estado Civil, Histórico de Resultados, Electoral." *Registraduría Nacional Del Estado Civil, Histórico de Resultados, Electoral*. www .registraduria.gov.co/-Historico-de-Resultados-3635- (accessed on July 25, 2019).

Robinson, William I. 1996. *Promoting Polyarchy: Globalization, US Intervention, and Hegemony*. Cambridge and New York: Cambridge University Press.

Robledo, Jorge Enrique. 1998. *El Café en Colombia: Un Análisis Independiente*. Bogotá, Colombia: El Áncora Editores.

———. 1999. "Crisis Cafetera y Conflicto Social: La Federación de Cafeteros y Sus Institucionales." *Conflictos Regionales: La Crisis Del Eje Cafetero*. Bogotá, Colombia: Instituto de Estudios Políticos y Relaciones Inter-Nacionales de La Univ. Nacional (IEPRI), pp. 19–46.

Roche, Julian. 1998. *International Banana Trade*. Cambridge: Woodhead Publishing Ltd.

Roediger, David. 1991. *The Wages of Whiteness: Race and the Making of the American Working Class*. London and New York: Verso.

Rojas, Cristina, and Judy Meltzer. 2005. *Elusive Peace: International, National, and Local Dimensions of Conflict in Colombia*. Durham, NC: Palgrave Macmillan.

Roldán, Mary. 2002. *Blood and Fire: La Violencia in Antioquia, Colombia, 1946–1953*. Durham, NC: Duke University Press.

Romero, Mauricio. 2003. "Reform and Reaction: Paramilitary Groups in Contemporary Colombia." Pp. 178–208 in *Irregular Armed Forces and Their Role in Politics and State Formation*, edited by D. Davis and A. Pereira. Cambridge and New York: Cambridge University Press.

Romero Sala, Mar. 2019. "Drug Trafficking and Colombian 'Peace.'" *Global Americans*, May 18. https://theglobalamericans.org/2019/05/drug-trafficking-and-colombian-peace/

Rose, Sonya O. 1997. "Class Formation and the Quintessential Worker." Pp. 133–66 in *Reworking Class*, edited by John R. Hall. Ithaca, NY: Cornell University Press.

Roseberry, William. 1995. "Latin American Peasant Studies in a 'Postcolonial' Era." *Journal of Latin American Anthropology* 1(1):150–77.

Ross, Robert J. S. 2004. *Slaves to Fashion: Poverty and Abuse in the New Sweatshops*. Ann Arbor: University of Michigan Press.

Rothstein, Jeffrey S. 2016. *When Good Jobs Go Bad: Globalization, De-Unionization, and Declining Job Quality in the North American Auto Industry*. New Brunswick, NJ: Rutgers University Press.

Safford, Frank. 1965. "Foreign and National Enterprise in Nineteenth-Century Colombia." *Business History Review* 39(4):503–26.

Safford, Frank, and Marco Palacios. 2001. *Colombia: Fragmented Land, Divided Society*, 1 ed. New York: Oxford University Press.

Salvación Agropecuaria. 2015. "Por La Salvación De La Producción Agropecuaria Nacional, Promoveremos Referendo De Iniciativa Popular." https://dignidadagropecuaria .org/por-la-salvacion-de-la-produccion-agropecuaria-nacional-promoveremos-referendo-de-iniciativa-popular/#.X-n7HthKiUk (accessed on December 28, 2020).

Samper Kutschbach, Mario. 1995. "In Difficult Times: Colombian and Costa Rican Coffee Growers from Prosperity to Crisis, 1920–1936." Pp. 151–80 in *Coffee, Society, and Power in Latin America*, edited by William Roseberry, Lowell Gudmundson, and Mario Samper Kutschbach. Baltimore: Johns Hopkins University Press.

Samper, Mario, and Radin Fernando. 2003. "Historical Statistics of Coffee Production and Trade from 1700 to 1960." Pp. 411–62 in *The Global Coffee Economy in Africa, Asia, and Latin América*, edited by W. G. Clarence-Smith and S. Topik. Cambridge and New York: Cambridge University Press.

Sánchez, Gonzalo. 2001. "Introduction: Problems for Violence, Prospects for Peace." in Pp. 1–38 *Violence in Colombia, 1990–2000: Waging War and Negotiating Peace*, edited by Charles Bergquist, Ricardo Peñaranda, and Gonzalo Sánchez. Wilmington, DE: Scholarly Resources, Inc.

Sánchez, Gonzalo, and Donny Meertens. 2001. *Bandits, Peasants, and Politics: The Case of "La Violencia" in Colombia*. Austin: University of Texas Press.

Sandilands, Roger. 2017. *Albert Hirschman, Lauchlin Currie, "Linkages" Theory, and Paul Rosenstein Rodan's "Big Push."* 1717. Glasgow: University of Strathclyde Business School, Department of Economics.

Sassen, Saskia. 2014. *Expulsions: Brutality and Complexity in the Global Economy*. Cambridge and London: Harvard University Press.

Scott, James C. 1985. *Weapons of the Weak: Everyday Forms of Peasant Resistance*. New Haven, CT and London: Yale University Press.

Selwyn, Ben. 2013. "Social Upgrading and Labour in Global Production Networks: A Critique and an Alternative Conception." *Competition and Change* 17(1):75–90.

Sheridan, Michael. 2013. "After the Colombian Coffee Strike: What Is $444 Million Really Worth?" *Daily Coffee News by Roast Magazine*, March 20. https://dailycoffeenews.com/2013/03/20/after-the-colombian-coffee-strike-what-is-444-million-really-worth/

———. 2015. "Q&A on Colombian Institutional Reform with the FNC's Luis Fernando Samper." *Daily Coffee News by Roast Magazine*, May 19. https://dailycoffeenews.com/2015/05/19/qa-on-colombian-institutional-reform-with-the-fncs-luis-fernando-samper/

Silva, Eduardo. 2009. *Challenging Neoliberalism in Latin America*. Cambridge and New York: Cambridge University Press.

Silver, Beverly J. 2003. *Forces of Labor: Workers' Movements and Globalization since 1870*. Cambridge and New York: Cambridge University Press.

Silver, Beverly J., and Eric Slater. 1999. "The Social Origins of World Hegemonies." Pp. 151–216 in *Chaos and Governance in the Modern World System*, edited by Giovanni Arrighi and Beverly J. Silver. Minneapolis: University of Minnesota Press.

SINCHI. 2000. *Caquetá: Dinamica de un Proceso.* Edited by L. M. Mantilla Cardenas. Bogotá, Colombia: Instituto Amazónico de Investigaciones Científicas (SINCHI).

SINCHI. n.d. "Socio-Environmental Dynamic Research Program, INÍRIDA Database." *Socio-Environmental Dynamic Research Program, INÍRIDA Database.* https://en.sinchi .org.co/inirida (accessed on July 25, 2020).

Smith, Joan, and Immanuel Wallerstein. 1992. *Creating and Transforming Households: The Constraints of the World-Economy.* Cambridge, and New York: Cambridge University Press.

Soluri, John. 2003. "Banana Cultures: Linking the Production and Consumption of Export Bananas, 1800–1980." Pp. 48–79 in *Banana Wars: Power, Production, and History in the Americas*, edited by Steve Striffler and Mark Moberg. Durham, NC: Duke University Press.

Starbucks. n.d. "Starbucks Company Timeline." *Starbucks Coffee Company.* www.starbucks .com/about-us/company-information/starbucks-company-timeline (accessed on March 14, 2019).

Steiner, Claudia. 2000. *Imaginación y Poder: El Encuentro del Interior con la Costa en Urabá, 1900–1960.* Medellín, Colombia: Universidad de Antioquia.

Stern, Steve. 1988. "Feudalism, Capitalism, and the World-System in the Perspective of Latin America and the Caribbean." *American Historical Review* 93(4):829–72.

Stewart, R. G. 1992. *Coffee: The Political Economy of an Export Industry in Papua New Guinea.* Boulder, CO: Westview Press.

Stolcke, Verena. 1995. "The Labors of Coffee in Latin America: The Hidden Charm of Family Labor and Self-Provisioning." Pp. 65–93 in *Coffee, Society, and Power in Latin America*, edited by William Roseberry, Lowell Gudmundson, and Mario Samper Kutschbach. Baltimore: Johns Hopkins University Press.

Striffler, Steve. 2002. *In the Shadows of State and Capital: The United Fruit Company, Popular Struggle, and Agrarian Restructuring in Ecuador, 1900–1995.* Durham, NC: Duke University Press.

———. 2003. "The Logic of the Enclave: United Fruit, Popular Struggle, and Capitalist Transformation in Ecuador." Pp. 171–90 in *Banana Wars: Power, Production, and History in the Americas*, edited by Steve Striffler and Mark Moberg. Durham, NC: Duke University Press.

Striffler, Steve, and Mark Moberg, eds. 2003. *Banana Wars: Power, Production, and History in the Americas.* Durham, NC: Duke University Press.

Suárez Montoya, Aurelio. 2007. *El Modelo Agrícola Colombiano y los Alimentos en la Globalización.* Bogotá, Colombia: Ediciones Aurora.

———. 2008. "Agricultura y Libre Comercio En Colombia." Pp. 181–212 in *La Cuestión Agraria Hoy: Colombia, Tierra Sin Campesinos*, edited by Héctor León Moncayo. Bogotá, Colombia: Publicaciones ILSA.

Sutton, Paul. 1997. "The Banana Regime of the European Union, the Caribbean, and Latin America." *Journal of Interamerican Studies and World Affairs* 39(2):5–36.

Suwandi, Intan. 2019. *Value Chains: The New Economic Imperialism.* New York: Monthly Review Press.

Talbot, John M. 2004. *Grounds for Agreement: The Political Economy of the Coffee Commodity Chain*. Oxford: Rowman & Littlefield Publishers.

———. 2009. "The Comparative Advantages of Tropical Commodity Chain Analysis." Pp. 93–109 in *Frontiers of Commodity Chain Research*, edited by Jennifer Bair. Stanford, CA: Stanford University Press.

Tate, Winifred. 2015. *Drugs, Thugs, and Diplomats: U.S. Policymaking in Colombia*. Stanford, CA: Stanford University Press.

Taylor, Phil, Kirsty Newsome, and Al Rainnie. 2013. "'Putting Labor in Its Place': Global Value Chains and Labour Process Analysis." *Competition and Change* 17(1):1–5.

Thoumi, Francisco. 2002. "Illegal Drugs in Colombia: From Illegal Economic Boom to Social Crisis." *The ANNALS of the American Academy of Political and Social Science* 582(1):102–16.

———. 2003. *Illegal Drugs, Economy, and Society in the Andes*. New York: Woodrow Wilson Center Press.

Tickner, Arlene. 2003. "Colombia and the United States: From Counternarcotics to Counterterrorism." *Current History* 102(661):77.

Tilly, Charles. 1985. "War-Making and State-Making as Organized Crime." Pp. 169–91 in *Bringing the State Back In*, edited by Peter Evans, Dietrich Rueschemeyer, and Theda Skocpol. Cambridge and New York: Cambridge University Press.

———. 1990. *Coercion, Capital, and European States, AD 990–1992*. Cambridge, MA: Basil Blackwell.

———. 1995. "Globalization Threatens Labor's Rights." *International Labor and Working-Class History* 47:1–23.

———. 2002. "Violent Organizations." Paper presented at the Annual Meeting of the American Sociological Association, Chicago, August 18, 2002.

Tokatlian, Juan Gabriel. 1994. "Drug Summitry: A Colombian Perspective." Pp. 138–50 in *Drug Trafficking in the Americas*, edited by B. Bagley and W. Walker. New Brunswick, NJ: Transaction Publishers.

———. 2005. "Colombia: Internal War, Regional Insecurity, and Foreign Intervention." Pp. 53–74 in *Elusive Peace: International, National, and Local Dimensions of Conflict in Colombia*, edited by C. Rojas and J. Meltzer. New York: Palgrave Macmillan.

Tomich, Dale. 2016. *Slavery in the Circuit of Sugar*, 2nd ed. Albany: State University of New York Press.

———. 2017. "The 'Second Slavery': Bonded Labor and the Transformation of the Nineteenth-Century World Economy." Pp. 1326–49 in *Critical Readings on Global Slavery*, edited by Damian Alan Pargas and Felicia Roşu. Leide, the Netherlands and Boston: Brill.

Topik, Steven. 2003. "The Integration of the World Coffee Market." Pp. 21–49 in *The Global Coffee Economy in Africa, Asia and Latin America, 1500–1989*, edited by W. G. Clarence-Smith and S. Topik. Cambridge and New York: Cambridge University Press.

Torrijos Rivera, Rafael. 2019. *Cifras de Contexto Ganadero Caquetá 2019*. Florencia, Caquetá, Colombia: Comité Departamental de Ganadero del Caquetá.

UNDP. 2008. *Capacity Development: Empowering People and Institutions. Annual Report.* New York: United Nations Development Programme.

UNHCHR. 2004. "FARC-EP Violan El DIH En San Carlos, Antioquia." Press release of the UN Office of the High Commissioner for Human Rights on July 13, 2004, Bogotá, Colombia. www.hchr.org.co/publico/comunicados/2004/cp0423.pdf

———. 2017. "ONU Derechos Humanos Expresa Preocupación Por Homicidios, Estigmatización y Hostigamientos a Defensores y Defensoras de Derechos Humanos En Colombia." Press release of the UN Office of the High Commissioner for Human Rights on December 20, 2017, Bogotá, Colombia. www.hchr.org.co/files/comunica dos/2017/ONU-DDHH-preocupada-homicidios-estigmatizacion-y-hostigamientos-a-defensores.pdf

———. 2018. *Global Report 2018.* Geneva: UNHCR – The UN Refugee Agency.

UNODC. 2019a. *Colombia: Monitoreo de Territorios Afectados Por Cultivos Ilícitos, 2018.* Vienna: United Nations Office on Drugs and Crime.

———. 2019b. *Programa Nacional Integral de Sustitución de Cultivos Ilícitos – PNIS. Informe No. 19.* Vienna: United Nations Office on Drugs and Crime.

———. 2011. *World Drug Report 2011.* Vienna: United Nations Office on Drugs and Crime.

UNVMC. 2019a. *Press Release Report of the Secretary-General to the Security Council on the UN Verification Mission in Colombia.* Bogotá, Colombia: United Nations Verification Mission in Colombia.

———. 2019b. *UN Verification Mission in Colombia Condemns Assassination of Former FARC Combatant in Reintegration Area.* Bogotá, Colombia: United Nations Verification Mission in Colombia.

Urrutia, Miguel. 1991. "On the Absence of Economic Populism in Colombia." Pp. 369–91 in *The Macroeconomics of Populism in Latin America*, edited by R. Dornbusch and S. Edwards. Chicago: University of Chicago Press.

USAID. n.d. "USAID: Foreign Aid Explorer Database." *USAID: Foreign Aid Explorer Database.* https://explorer.usaid.gov/aid-trends.html (accessed on April 9, 2019).

USDA. 1965. *U.S. Food Consumption: Sources and Trends, 1909–1963.* No. 364. Washington, DC: United States Department of Agriculture.

———. 2016. *Agricultural Statistics 2016.* Washington, DC: National Agricultural Statistics Service.

USDA-GAIN. 2018. *Colombian Coffee Production Decreases after Five Years of Growth. Global Agricultural Information Network.* Washington, DC: United States Department of Agriculture.

Valencia, Alberto. 1998. "Caquetá: Violencia y Conflicto Social." Pp. 131–54 in *Conflictos Regionales: Amazonia y Orinoquia*, edited by J. J. Gonzales Arias. Bogotá, Colombia: IEPRI y FESCOL.

Vallecilla Gordillo, Jaime. 2001. *Café y Crecimiento Económico Regional: El Antiguo Caldas, 1870–1970.* Manizales, Colombia: Universidad de Caldas.

Vallecilla Gordillo, Jaime, Sergio PRADA, Gustavo OCHOA, Paola VANEGAS, and Cristina GOMÉZ. 2005. "Cien Años Del Café En Caldas." Estudios Regionales, CRECE, Manizales, Colombia, 16.

Vargas Meza, Ricardo. 1999. *Fumigación y Conflicto: Políticas Antidrogas y Deslegitimación Del Estado En Colombia.* Bogotá, Colombia: Tercer Mundo Editores.

Verdad Abierta. 2008. "Banana 'para-republic.'" *Verdad Abierta,* October 21. https://verdadabierta.com/banana-para-republic/

Volckhausen, Taran. 2019. "Land Grabbing, Cattle Ranching Ravage Colombian Amazon after FARC Demobilization." *Mongabay,* May 5. https://news.mongabay.com/2019/05/land-grabbing-cattle-ranching-ravage-colombian-amazon-after-farc-demobiliza tion/#:~:text=Land%20grabbing%2C%20cattle%20ranching%20ravage%20Colombian%20Amazon%20after%20FARC%20demobilization,-by%20Taran%20Volckhausen& text=Colonizers%20are%20also%20displacing%20indigenous,yet%20to%20face%20ser ious%20consequences

Volkov, Vadim. 2002. *Violent Entrepreneurs: The Use of Force in the Making of Russian Capitalism.* Ithaca, NY: Cornell University Press.

Wacquant, Loïc. 2009. *Punishing the Poor: The Neoliberal Government of Social Insecurity.* Durham, NC: Duke University Press.

Walker, William. 1989. *Drug Control in the Americas.* Albuquerque: University of New Mexico Press.

———. 1994. "The Foreign Narcotics Policy of the United States since 1980: An End to the War on Drugs?" *International Journal* 49(1):37–65.

———. 2001. "A Reprise for 'Nation Building' Low Intensity Conflict Spreads in the Andes." *NACLA Report on the Americas* 35(1):23–28.

Wallerstein, Immanuel. 1995. "Response: Declining States, Declining Rights?" *International Labor and Working-Class History* 47:24–27.

———. 2000. "Globalization or the Age of Transition?: A Long-Term View of the Trajectory of the World-System." *International Sociology* 15(2):249–65.

———. 1974. *The Modern World-System I: Capitalist Agriculture and the Origins of the European World-Economy in the Sixteenth Century.* New York: Academic Press.

———. 2004. *World-Systems Analysis: An Introduction.* Durham, NC: Duke University Press.

Webster, Eddie, Edward Webster, Robert Lambert, and Andries Bezuidenhout. 2008. *Grounding Globalization: Labour in the Age of Insecurity.* Malden, MA: Blackwell Publishing.

Weeks, Kathi. 2011. *The Problem with Work: Feminism, Marxism, Antiwork Politics, and Postwork Imaginaries.* Durham, NC: Duke University Press.

Weinstein, Jeremy M. 2006. *Inside Rebellion: The Politics of Insurgent Violence.* Cambridge and New York: Cambridge University Press.

Wells, Allan. 2003. "Conclusions: Dialectical Bananas." Pp. 316–34 in *Banana Wars: Power, Production, and History in the Americas,* edited by Steve Striffler and Mark Moberg. Durham, NC: Duke University Press.

Wexler, Alexandra. 2020. "Cocoa Cartel Stirs Up Global Chocolate Market." *Wall Street Journal,* January 5. www.wsj.com/articles/new-cocoa-cartel-could-overhaul-global-chocolate-industry-11578261601

Wickham-Crowley, Timothy P. 1992. *Guerrillas and Revolution in Latin America: A Comparative Study of Insurgents and Regimes Since 1956*. Princeton, NJ: Princeton University Press.

Woodcock, Jamie. 2017. *Working the Phones: Control and Resistance in Call Centres*. London and New York: Pluto Press.

Woody, Christopher. 2017. "Colombia Produces Most of the World's Cocaine – and Output Is at a Record-High." *Business Insider*, March 8. www.businessinsider.com/colombia-top-cocaine-producing-countries-record-production-2017-3

World Bank. 2012. "Colombian Middle Class Grows over Past Decade." *World Bank News*, November 13. www.worldbank.org/en/news/feature/2012/11/13/colombia-middle-class-grows-over-past-decade

———. n.d. "World Bank Development Indicators Database." *World Bank Development Indicators Database*. https://datacatalog.worldbank.org/dataset/world-development-indicators (accessed on July 28, 2020).

Wright, Erik Olin. 2000. "Working-Class Power, Capitalist-Class Interest, and Class Compromise." *American Journal of Sociology* 105(4):957–1002.

Zamosc, Leon. 1986. *The Agrarian Question and the Peasant Movement in Colombia by Leon Zamosc*. Cambridge and New York: Cambridge University Press.

Zolberg, Aristide R. 1995. "Response: Working-Class Dissolution." *International Labor and Working-Class History* 47:28–38.

Index

Printed in the United States
by Baker & Taylor Publisher Services